"十二五"国家重点出版物出版规划项目
地域建筑文化遗产及城市与建筑可持续发展研究丛书
国家自然科学基金资助项目
中俄政府间科技合作项目
黑龙江省科技计划项目

# 中东铁路建筑文化遗产

Architectural Cultural Heritage of
Chinese Eastern Railway

刘大平　卞秉利　李琦　著

哈尔滨工业大学出版社

# 前　言

中东铁路建筑作为20世纪最重要的建筑文化遗产之一，在中国近代建筑史中占有非常重要的地位。复杂的建造历史背景与特殊的地域自然环境，以及不断发展完善中的政治与文化演化进程，孕育出中东铁路建筑独具地域性与多样性的建筑文化特质。

至今，中东铁路沿途仍然分布着众多的城镇以及大量中东铁路时期的建筑1 000余座，其类型涉及站舍、机车库、水塔、工区、厂房、仓库、浴池、兵营、马厩、医院、俱乐部、办公楼、学校、教堂以及各式住宅、公寓等，此外还有大量的桥梁、涵洞、隧道等。从已掌握的历史资料和实际现场调研结果可以看出，这些中东铁路历史建筑大多经过精心的设计和建造，其建筑形态不但具有丰富的多样性，同时也明显地呈现出跨文化传播的特征。因此，这些建筑文化遗产对我们今天深入研究中国近代建筑史、研究20世纪初中国铁路工业发展史、揭示我国近代建筑技术发展的水平、正确解读近代建筑文化传播现象以及对东北地域建筑文化影响等一系列问题，都是非常有必要、有价值的。

正是这些吸引众多的国内外近代历史学与建筑史学的学者加入相关课题的研究，国家相关部门也对此给予了极大的关注和支持。我们申请的国家自然科学基金资助项目《文化线路视野下的中东铁路建筑文化特质与保护研究》（2013—2016）以及中俄政府间科技合作项目《中国中东铁路与俄罗斯西伯利亚铁路（远东段）沿线建筑文化遗产特色及保护策略研究》（2016—2017）有幸先后获得批准。通过这些研究课题的支持，我们对中东铁路建筑文化遗产进行了多年的持续研究，并结合研究成果先后撰写并出版了《文化线路视野下的中东铁路建筑文化解读》《中东铁路沿线近代城镇规划与建筑形态研究》《中东铁路历史建筑构筑形态与技术》等几部著作。目前，后续的专题研究还在进行当中。

中东铁路建筑文化遗产所具有的多样性是其最重要的特征之一，其中建筑功能类型的多样性在我国近代铁路工业遗产中表现得比较突出。这一点在我们对中东铁路沿线的历史城镇与建筑进行了大量的田野调查，同时也通过各种渠道收集了较多中东铁路时期的设计图纸和历史图片之后，随着课题研究的进展而不断得到印证。应该说，这一多样性在整条铁路的设计之初就已经形成了，并在其建造和发展的过程中又不断得以充实和丰富。直至百余年后的今天，在面对中东铁路沿线城镇现存的建筑遗产时，我们仍能感受到这一点的存在。

本书按照中东铁路建筑文化遗产的功能类型进行分析解读，希望这样可以更加清晰地认识和了解这份建筑遗产的多样性，并让更多对中东铁路建筑文化遗产感兴趣的学者和同仁一起来认识和共享这份宝贵遗产的技术成就和艺术魅力，同时对深化这份遗产的研究与保护工作提供更多有益的帮助。这也是本书撰写的初衷和愿望。

刘大平

2019.8.30

# Introduction

The Chinese Eastern Railway (CER) buildings, as one of the most important architectural cultural heritage, play a great important role in Chinese modern architectural history. Because of the complicated construction background and particularly natural-regional environment, as well as gradually developing and improving course of the political and cultural evolution, an uniquely regional and multifarious architectural cultural property is come into being.

Until now, there are still many towns distributed along the line and more than 1,000 buildings remained from the CER construction period, such as stations in different grade and size, engine houses, water towers, factory buildings, work areas, storages, bathrooms, military camps, stables, hospitals, clubs, offices, schools, churches, a lot of residences and apartments, also as well as a large number of bridges, culverts and tunnels etc. It can be seen from the existing historical document and actual field survey that the historical buildings along the CER line are designed and built carefully, whose style not only fully expresses rich diversity, but also clearly presents an intercultural diffusion feature. Therefore, these cultural heritages are all important and valuable for us to make deep study of Chinese modern architectural history, to learn Chinese railway industry phylogeny, to reveal the development level of Chinese modern architectural technology, to correct interpret of modern architectural cultural spreading phenomenon and their influence to the Chinese northeast region culture.

That is why numerous researchers in modern and architectural history at home and abroad are attracted to study the related projects which are paid great attention and supported by the National Related Departments, such as the National Natural Science Funds "A study on the architectural culture characteristics and protection of the Chinese Eastern Railway from the cultural perspective", the project of scientific and technological cooperation between China and Russia Government "A study on the property and protection strategy of the architectural cultural heritage along Chinese Eastern Railway and Russian Siberia Railway (Far East Section)". On the basis of financial support of these research projects and multi-year continuous study, several scholarly books have been written and published, including *An Interpretation of the Architectural Culture of the Chinese Eastern Railway from the Cultural Perspective, A Research on Modern Urban Planning and Architecture along Chinese Eastern Railway and The Construction and Technology of Heritage Buildings along Chinese Easter Railway*. At present, The reseaches are still in progress.

The variety of the CER architectural cultural heritage is one of the most important characteristics. It is conformed at this point by large field survey of the historical towns and buildings along the line, as well as a great number of design drawings and old photos collected during the deep study. It is fair to say that these diversity has formed in the beginning of the CER design, and gradually substantiated and enriched in its construction and development.

In this book, the architectural heritage are analyzed and interpreted according to the functional types, which is possible for us to better understand the diversity of these heritage, and to share these valuable technological achievement and its artistic charm with the scholars and colleagues who are interested in the CER architectural cultural heritage. Finally, it will provide useful reference to study and protect these architectural heritage, which is our original intention and desire of writing this book.

LIU Daping
30th August, 2019

# 目 录
## Contents

**导言 中东铁路建筑文化遗产多样性解析 / 1**
    0.1 中东铁路建筑文化遗产多样性生成的时代动因 / 1
    0.2 中东铁路建筑文化遗产多样性形成的文化机制 / 7
    0.3 中东铁路建筑功能的多样性成因 / 11
    0.4 地域性的多样化建筑技术与材料表达 / 17
    0.5 总结 / 22

**Preface   The Diversity of Architectural Heritage along the Chinese Eastern Railway / 23**
    0.1 Historical development / 23
    0.2 Cultural diversity in architectural heritage along the Chinese Eastern Railway / 31
    0.3 Origin of diverse functions of the CER architecture / 38
    0.4 Regional and diversified architectural technology and material expression / 45
    0.5 Conclusion / 52

**1 站舍 / 55**
    1.1 站舍的选址及平面布局 / 55
    1.2 站舍的标准化设计 / 55
    1.3 站舍风格的多样化 / 56
    Train Stations / 56

**2 机车库 / 105**
    2.1 机车库的分布特点 / 105
    2.2 机车库的平面布局 / 105
    2.3 机车库的建造技术特点 / 106
    Train Garage / 106

**3 水塔 / 125**
    3.1 水塔的空间与结构特点 / 125
    3.2 建造技术与艺术的高度统一 / 125
    Water Towers / 126

## 4 工区 / 135
4.1 普通工区 / 135
4.2 防御性工区 / 135
Work Areas / 136

## 5 厂房 / 155
5.1 铁路机械厂 / 155
5.2 电力工厂 / 155
5.3 煤矿与船舶工厂 / 156
Plants / 156

## 6 仓库、厕所及其他辅助用房 / 167
6.1 厕所 / 167
6.2 仓库 / 167
Storehouse, Lavatory and Other Assistant Room / 168

## 7 浴池 / 179
7.1 中东铁路浴池的规模和分布 / 179
7.2 中东铁路浴池的平面布局与形态特点 / 179
7.3 中东铁路浴池的建造技术 / 179
Common Bathing Room / 180

## 8 兵营 / 189
8.1 兵营的类型与布局方式 / 189
8.2 营房建筑的空间形式与建造特点 / 189
8.3 马厩 / 190
8.4 马匹医院 / 191
Military Camp / 191

## 9 碉堡及其他军事设施 / 225
9.1 碉堡 / 225
9.2 弹药库及瞭望台 / 225
Fortified Tower and Other Military Facilities / 226

**10 警察署及监狱 / 235**
  10.1 警察署 / 235
  10.2 监狱 / 235
  Police Stations and Prisons / 236

**11 医疗建筑 / 245**
  11.1 医疗建筑的分布方式与规划选址 / 245
  11.2 医疗建筑的平面布局 / 245
  11.3 先进的医疗方式及理念 / 246
  Medical Buildings / 246

**12 休闲建筑 / 263**
  12.1 俱乐部 / 263
  12.2 度假旅馆 / 263
  12.3 休闲公园 / 264
  Leisure Architectures / 264

**13 办公建筑 / 281**
  13.1 中东铁路管理局大楼 / 281
  13.2 铁路下属机构的办公用房 / 281
  Office Buildings / 282

**14 校舍 / 299**
  14.1 俄侨子弟学校 / 299
  14.2 中东铁路职业教育学校 / 299
  Schools / 300

**15 教堂 / 315**
  15.1 中东铁路教堂的分布及选址 / 315
  15.2 中东铁路教堂的类型及特点 / 315
  15.3 中东铁路教堂的建筑特点 / 315
  Churches / 316

## 16 居住建筑 / 333
16.1 住宅建筑的类型 / 333
16.2 住宅建筑的平面布局 / 333
16.3 住宅的标准化设计 / 333
16.4 住宅的防寒保温措施 / 334
Residences / 334

## 17 道桥设施 / 379
17.1 桥梁类型与特点 / 379
17.2 隧道、涵洞及铁路展线 / 379
17.3 道桥设施的分布 / 380
Bridges, Tunnels and Other Infrastructures / 380

## 18 铁路机车 / 411
Traction Locomotives / 411

## 附录 1 车站、会让站分布简图 / 418
Appendix 1 A Diagram of Stations and Passing Loops of the CER

## 附录 2 铁路供水站点分布图 / 422
Appendix 2 A Diagram of Water Supply Stations of the CER

## 参考文献 / 426
References

## 图片来源 / 427
Picture Credits

## 后记 / 430
Postscript / 431

# 导言
# 中东铁路建筑文化遗产多样性解析

中东铁路位于中国东北地区，是一条由沙皇俄国主导，修建于 19 世纪末至 20 世纪初的跨国铁路。中东铁路主线由满洲里至绥芬河，南部支线从哈尔滨直通旅顺口，全长 2 489.2 千米，跨越中国四省，途经山地、丘陵、湿地、平原、海岸等丰富多样的地貌环境。在几十年跌宕起伏的历史进程中，沿中东铁路展开的附属地内孕育了数以千计的交通、工业、军事、公共、居住建筑、各类工程构筑物及城市市政设施。历经百年沧桑，中东铁路沿线保留下来的建筑无疑是一份意义重大、影响深远、面貌独特瑰丽的宝贵文化遗产。

中东铁路建筑文化遗产数量庞大，在功能类型、艺术形式以及技术材料的应用方面有着强烈的多样性表征和浓郁的地域性特色。究其原因，是不同民族的建筑传统、日趋成熟的摩登潮流以及现代探索中新技术与新材料的转型实验等多种因素，在特定时局的动力驱使以及多种形式的文化扩散模式作用下，依托广袤丰富的自然环境互相交织作用而成。建筑具有自然与社会的双重属性，是记录人类文明的坚实载体。中东铁路建筑文化遗产书写的是时代节点上纷繁复杂的社会变迁历程，是近代中国东北波澜壮阔的文化演化经历。因此，对建筑的解读要全面地推演其所属时代的技术发展水平与社会文化环境。

## 0.1 中东铁路建筑文化遗产多样性生成的时代动因

中东铁路是特殊时代下政治需求所催生的跨文化产物，它忠实地记录了当时世界格局的变迁过程。作为中东铁路建筑，一方面，沙皇俄国的地缘政治宏观策略奠定了其主导风格与基本格局；另一方面，风云变幻的时局、动荡不定的权属在很大程度上强化了其建筑文化遗产的多样性特征。同时，在工业文明的冲击下，全世界都进入了一个技术与文化的转型探索期：或实践新知，或固守传统；或渐进改良，或另辟蹊径——在文明演进的十字路口上，呈现一派纷繁杂乱却又生机勃勃的景象。这些探索，像一股激荡的电流通过中东铁路的钢轨注入中国东北的土地上，将这个尚且荒芜的边缘文化区卷入世界发展的洪潮之中。

### 0.1.1 近代世界格局下地缘政治变迁的现实表现

中东铁路作为一条跨国铁路线，肇始于沙皇俄国西伯利亚大铁路的修建。19 世纪 30 年代，由于资本主义向纵深发展，俄国迫切需要打开本国市场，同时获取更多生产原料，因此，有了修建一条贯穿工商业发展落后但矿产资源丰富的东部地区的西伯利亚大铁路的刍议。19 世纪 40 年代，伴随着铁路工业技术的逐渐成熟，世界各国开始进行大规模的铁路建设，并在五六十年代进入高潮，吸引了大量资本的投入，也加快了城市的发展与财富的积累。与此同时，国际中心转向太平洋沿岸，建立中心地区与远东地区的交通运输联系对俄国来说具有了国家发展层面上的战略意义。19 世纪六七十年代，列强掀起了瓜分世界的狂潮，争相涌入亚洲市场，俄国面临着前所未有的竞争压力。

19世纪80年代，俄国与欧美各国在太平洋沿岸和中亚地区的竞争愈演愈烈，矛盾日益尖锐。为了应对可能出现的冲突，强化对边疆地区的控制，俄国亟须一条便捷的铁路运输线路作为强有力的军事保障。

19世纪80年代之前，西伯利亚大铁路方案出自大地主与资产阶级，强调经济效益；80年代中期，伴随国际形势的变化，铁路转为国家的军事战略需求，成为军队补给的运输线路，向沙俄国防工业提供原材料。在近代沙俄国内发展需求与国际形势的双重影响下，西伯利亚大铁路变成了应对世界局势变化的国家级战略工具。沙俄政府希望凭该铁路增强其贸易优势，为在欧洲与亚洲可能出现的政治、经济、军事对抗上掌握主动权，加强其在太平洋地区的竞争力。这使西伯利亚大铁路的建设与运营成为一个国家项目，铁路与经济计划和政治战略结合起来。在此背景下，由国家整合资金，西伯利亚大铁路于1891年从符拉迪沃斯托克（海参崴）与车里雅宾斯克东西两端同时破土动工，1904年西伯利亚大铁路全线通车，收尾工作持续到1916年。

西伯利亚大铁路的最东部线路走向有三种方案：一是沿阿穆尔河北岸至符拉迪沃斯托克，二是由乌兰乌德向南经恰克图过中国张家口直到北京，三是由赤塔穿过中国东北北部地区到达符拉迪沃斯托克。在铁路修建工程的实际操作中，本为首选的方案一的线路勘测工作并未完成，且距离过远，收益周期较长，而方案三更经济，同时也能加强对中国东北地区的影响，沙俄政府遂决定向中国政府"借地筑路"。尽管这个方案最终成功实施并通车，但随着时局变化，沙俄政府意识到在本国境内修建铁路仍有必要，因此从1908年开始按照方案一进行西伯利亚大铁路东段国内部分的建设，即阿穆尔铁路。

19世纪中叶沙俄推翻《尼布楚条约》，与清政府签订《瑷珲条约》与《中俄北京条约》，将黑龙江以北、乌苏里江以东地区划归俄国，使得俄国东部与中国东北地区联系更加紧密，极大地破坏了中国的领土完整。1896年，清政府与俄国签订期冀于实现"御敌互助"的《中俄密约》，条约允许俄国军舰在战争状态时进入中国任何港口；允许沙俄政府修筑一条穿越中国东北通向符拉迪沃斯托克的铁路线；允许俄国利用中东铁路运送士兵和给养等。《中俄密约》的签订确保了这条跨国铁路的"合法性"，在政策与舆论上做好了准备。1897年德国占领胶州湾，同年俄国即以"兑现御敌互助约定"为由，强租旅顺大连湾，并于1898年签订《中俄旅大租地条约》，获准修筑从哈尔滨通往大连的中东铁路支线。沙俄政府根据风云变幻的国际形势不断调整着国家战略方向与对华政策，这在很大程度上决定了中东铁路的空间格局，影响了其线路的最终走向。

1898年6月9日，中东铁路工程局进驻哈尔滨香坊区的"田家烧锅"并开始办公，宣布中东铁路全线正式开工；以哈尔滨为中心分为东、西、南三段，从六处开始对向施工。1903年7月14日，中东铁路全线通车。

1904年2月，日俄战争爆发。1905年9月，日俄双方在朴次茅斯签订《朴次茅斯和约》，约定俄国把对旅大的租借地及宽城子（今长春）至旅顺口的中东铁路南部支线所有权转让给日本，俄国则继续掌控宽城子以北的小段支线以及主干线。至此，中东铁路开始了南北分治的局面，由满洲里至绥芬河的干线部分由俄国主导；南部支线则由日本控制，称作"南满铁路"。两段线路所在地区的建设与发展过程步入了完全不同的轨道，形成了各自的特征。干线上的建筑文化以铁路建筑风格为主，古典主义与折中主义等西方样式为辅，缀以新艺术运动与装饰艺术等新风尚，同时部分融合中国传统建筑样式。南部支线的建筑发展则有着明显的现代主义探索倾向，同时夹杂着中国与日本传统木构架建筑营造。

俄方设立的中东铁路管理局掌握着中东铁路附属地内部的行政管理、司法管理和驻军的权利。中东铁路附属地内依托火车站点形成了众多规模不等的城镇，形成了面积广大、远超普通租借地权利边界的"国中之国"。日俄战争结束的谈判中，美国提出"门户开放政策"，要求中东铁路附属地向西方国家开放。不久，来自世界各地的货物汇集哈尔滨，使哈尔滨成为中国东北地区最大的贸易城市、远东最负盛名的文化中心，吸纳了来自多国的先进技术、艺术风格与文化传统，极大地扩充了整个地域内的文化基因库。

1917年，俄国的"二月革命"与"十月革命"导致了大规模的移民潮，俄国贵族、地主、富商、艺术家和工程师们逃离本国，沿着中东铁路来到哈尔滨、大连。这些移民的进驻带来大量资金与技术，也带来了俄国上流社会的生活模式与文化理念。哈尔滨铁路城市的建筑文化与城市风貌发生转变，趋向结构清晰、华丽丰富的中心城市特征。沿线其他城镇的移民人口也大量增加，中东铁路附属地城镇的发展空前繁荣。

俄国沙皇政权垮台使得中东铁路管理局失去对中东铁路的控制权。1920年9月23日，北洋政府以大总统命令，停止对驻华沙俄公使、领事所施行的待遇。1920年10月31日，北洋政府公布《东省特别区法院编制条例》13条规定原中东铁路附属地改称东省特别区。1921年2月5日，北洋政府令，设置东省特别区市政管理局，接管哈尔滨及铁路沿线各地的市政权。铁路沿线地区开始建立各级政府和司法机关，居住在这里的俄罗斯人也不再享有治外法权。1924年5月31日，北洋政府和苏联在北京签订《中俄解决悬案大纲协定》与《暂行管理中东铁路协定》，中苏两国随即恢复外交关系。然而，出于国家利益，苏联并没有兑现在协定中就中国主权利益等方面的承诺，协定成为一纸空文。

1925年1月，苏联违反《中俄解决悬案大纲协定》，私下与日本进行交易，单方面宣布继续承认《朴次茅斯和约》。1929年7月发生中国为收回苏联在中国东北铁路特权的"中东铁路事件"，但最终以失败告终。1935年3月23日，苏联以1.4亿日元的价格将中东铁路及支线卖给了由日本人操控的伪满洲国。至此，存在了40余年的"铁路附属地"这一特殊地理区划形式也一并退出了中国近代历史舞台。中东铁路沿线地区的城镇经济也由繁盛转向衰落，建设活动趋于停滞。日本移民与中东铁路工作人员对原有俄式建筑进行适应性利用与改造，以满足自身的生活习惯。因此，中东铁路干线附属地内的城镇结构与建筑形态基本保持了俄治时期的特征与风貌，建筑文化被较为完整地保留了下来。

1937年11月5日，日本与伪满洲国签订《关于撤销在满洲国的治外法权和转让南满铁路附属地行政权条约》，表面上是日本将在伪满洲国的所有治外法权予以撤销，移交南满铁路附属地行政权，实则是为了掩盖日本帝国主义的侵华罪行。

1945年2月11日，美国、英国和苏联在苏联雅尔塔签署了严重损害中国主权的《苏、美、英三国关于日本的协定》，其中有关中东铁路的内容有：中东铁路由中苏合办，共同经营。同年8月，中国与苏联签订《关于中国长春铁路的协定》，合并中东铁路和原有的南满铁路为"中国长春铁路"（简称中长铁路），由中苏共同所有、共同经营。1952年，苏联将中东铁路完全交还中国。

近代跌宕起伏的世界局势与中国本土的政治环境催生了中东铁路，也塑造了中东铁路附属地内的实际面貌与文化内涵，是形成中东铁路建筑文化遗产以铁路建筑文化为主体，多民族建筑传统共存的深层动因。这些建筑文化随着时代不断发展、变异、融合、交织而形成显著的多样性特征。

**0.1.2　文明转型期建筑技术探索的必然特征**

18世纪后半叶，起自英国的工业革命与源于法国的民主革命引发了西方文明转型，随后从发源中心扩展到整个西方世界，并随着西方文明的扩张传播到世界其他地区。工业革命为社会生产带来了史无前例的技术支持，各种机械的发明与应用极大地提高了生产能力与工作效率，工业化时代就此拉开帷幕。煤炭与钢铁工业为大规模机械化生产提供原料，以铁路与轮船为支撑的运输业满足了工业生产在深度与广度上规模扩张的运输与通信需求。

伴随着手工业制品让位于机械化大生产制造的标准化工业产品，社会经济关系也开始转变，农业、建筑业转向商品化，生产资料占有者的注意力转向资本的积累与运作。资产阶级进一步发展，需要建立利于自身发展的政权与话语体系来适应工业经济的社会组织和生活方式。民主革命将陈旧而不合时宜的社会、文化、政治模式彻底改变。这是西方文明自我转变中最重要的一次，自此西方甚至全世界都进入了一个全新的时代。

在整个文明转型的过程中，科学技术与文化艺术发展进入了一个探索期。在建筑方面体现为：一方面，新的功能需要匹配新的空间形式，新的空间形式则要寻求新的技术支持；另一方面，在新技术尚未成型的情况下也不得不以传统的材料与结构形式予以维持。在同一个时间与空间内，对已有技术传统的维护和改良与在新兴科学支持下的锐意创新同时并存。所有的发展方向上都存在着无限可能，这是一个无法用某种风格或者样式标签化的时代。

中东铁路的修建正值工业革命后全面的文明转型期，此时适应新时代发展需求的技术已经有一定的成果，但尚未完全成熟，在有限的经验下进行着尝试与探索。与此同时，传统技术也尚未完全被抛弃。在快速建设的需求下，体系完备、经验纯熟的传统建筑结构形式与构造做法有着更实际的操作能力与现实意义。

从数量上来看，中东铁路沿线建筑的结构与材料类型以传统形式为主，包括砖（石）砌体结构、木结构、拱形结构等。这些传统结构类型在标准化建造的设计及施工理念的指导下，保证了中东铁路工程的迅速完成。这类建筑也最能体现中东铁路建筑风格特征与俄罗斯的民族建筑文化传统。在沿线的建筑中也能见到传统的结构形式在工业技术的支持下得到改良与完善的实例。如一般应用于建筑地下室或多层建筑一层的波形拱板结构。这类结构一般以钢轨为梁，两条钢梁之间砌筑弧度较小的砖拱，以此为一个结构单元，多个单元连续排列成为一个波浪状的连续曲面。这种结构的原型是欧洲较为古老的一种传统结构形式，但传统方法中均以木材为梁，拱顶材料也相对随意。经过改良后，结构的逻辑更加清晰，形态更为完整，性能也更强，是中东铁路沿线建筑中一种较为独特的构筑方式。

在中东铁路沿线各类建筑与工程设施中，新的结构形式包括金属框架结构、金属桁架结构、钢筋混凝土结构及悬索结构等；新的材料包含金属、混凝土、玻璃等。这些新技术、新材料的应用形式多种多样，既有比较成熟的现代技术的直接应用，也有对材料与结构不很成熟的实验性引入。前者数量较少，多应用于桥梁、隧道等工程难度较高的铁路工程设施，如中东铁路沿线大量的金属铁路桥，其材料选择、结构形式以及节点构造方式均为标准化处理，对材料特性的利用以及其具体的受力方式也较为合理，已经是相当成熟的技术体系。大部分的桥梁主体结构保存良好，至今仍在发挥功效，可见其极高的技术水平。而中东铁路沿线一些矩形机车库以及其他工业建筑，由于建筑跨度大，传统的木结构屋架无法应对，因此多采用钢结构屋架，屋架的结构形式没有统一样式，如在中东铁路哈尔滨总工厂的不同厂房中就有豪式屋架、芬克式屋架、复合屋架及直角三角屋架等类型。在碉堡的构筑上体现的是一种对全新建筑材料的实验。由于这类军事设施的防御性特质对结构性能要求很高而功能性不强，因此均采用未配筋或配筋很少的混凝土建造，墙体极厚，空间利用率很低，材料的利用效率相对较低。

体现在中东铁路沿线建筑中另一种较为普遍的技术探索是新材料、新技术与传统的结构、材料及构造方式的混合应用。这类建筑一般是以传统构筑为主体，新的技术与材料在局部运用。如扇形机车库建筑，其带有扶壁的外墙为砖石砌筑，是结构的主体，屋顶为钢筋混凝土浇筑成的筒形结构单元连续排列，上覆金属屋面，内部空间以钢柱支撑，形成钢框架结构。这类机车库建筑的外部形象是传统的砖石建筑样式，然而其内部结构类型与材料应用，甚至空间的形式都具有强烈的工业化特征。其他新材料、新技术的局部应用范围更小，也更不明显。如在建筑的局部空间以钢梁（多为钢轨）代替木梁，或在多层建筑的楼梯、阳台等悬挑部位使用钢梁承重，也有部分建筑楼板以钢筋混凝土浇筑。

无论是传统建筑技术的熟练应用还是现代化的新式探索，都需要放置在东北地区丰富多样的自然环境中，都需要根据气候与地质条件进行地域性的表达，技术上适应性的细微调整也使得其多样性特征更明显。对当时封闭落后的东北地区来说，新旧技术都是具有示范效应的文明成果，当地居民在各类建造活动中自主地进行着借鉴与学习，并形成了更多的技术与材料的表现形式。

**0.1.3 时代转折中建筑艺术多元化的发展记录**

文明转型期技术传统的转变与进化相较而言是迅速而剧烈的，社会组织形式与意识形态次之，而艺术则有着相当的滞后性，需要比前两者有更长的适应周期。因此，艺术表达的探索很难与技术的发展同步。在建筑上，新的材料与结构往往仍以经典的风格或传统的样式相匹配，以此来适应社会的主流审美需求。但是新的材料与结构又不可避免地表现出其特有的艺术特征，进而有了各种局部或整体的新的艺术表达尝试。

中东铁路修建时期，前现代主义的探索已经积累了相当的成果。金属材料在工业化大生产的支持下被大量应用于建筑上，针对其材料特性与标准化生产特征的美学表达已有实例，突破了原有经典风格的美学框架。新艺术运动与装饰艺术运动也成为当时的前沿风尚，为后来现代建筑的横空出世开辟了道路。铁路修建完成、附属地城镇快速发展的20世纪20年代，正是西方世界现代建筑的萌芽期。然而，这股风潮却未能经由铁路进入沿线地区，当时城镇建设中主要的建筑风格仍是西方的各类传统样式。在此背景下，中东铁路沿线建筑风格则非常多元，包括铁路特有的风格、俄国传统的乡村田园式建筑、以古典主义与折中主义为代表的经典风格、新艺术与装饰艺术风格以及近代工业建筑风格。

铁路建筑风格构成了中东铁路的整体形象。这类建筑以砖石砌体结构为主，形体简单，坡屋顶以砖、石、木为主要材料，以砖石材料本身的砌筑方式构成墙面装饰，搭配以木构件的雕饰。其主要是居住建筑和小型公共建筑，数量最大，分布最广，是中东铁路建筑文化遗产的主体。值得一提的是，这种建筑风格虽然受到俄罗斯砖石建筑传统的影响，但不能归于俄罗斯传统风格，是在中东铁路建设中形成的一种带有标准化倾向的特殊样式。

俄国传统的田园风格建筑以木材为主要材料，最能代表其特点的是数量众多的木刻楞和板式木住宅以及木结构的东正教教堂。由于东正教在俄国世俗与精神生活中占有重要地位，教堂建筑在任何聚居点都是必不可少的，所以沿线具有一定规模的站点均会配套建设。在二等及以下站点形成的中小城镇内，教堂按照对应城镇等级规模的标准化建筑图纸建造，如满洲里的谢拉菲姆教堂、横道河子的圣母进堂教堂以及一面坡的谢尔盖教堂等。这类教堂建筑装饰细腻繁复，形体错落有致，俄罗斯民族风味浓郁，一般是城镇中最为华丽的建筑。位于哈尔滨的圣·尼古拉教堂也是木结构，但形式独特华美，符合其位于枢纽城市的中心地位。东正教砖石教堂建筑的砌筑精巧，结合洋葱头穹顶，数量相对较少，大多集中在哈尔滨等大城市中，仅个别散落在中小城镇内，也是典型的俄罗斯民族传统建筑。

西方经典建筑风格主要集中在中东铁路干线的哈尔滨、南部支线的大连等大城市中，其他城镇中则仅个别存在，数量很少。其风格类型包括古典主义风格、哥特风格、文艺复兴风格、巴洛克风格等，同时也有少量的其他民族建筑风格。这些风格的建筑数量有限，少有呈现为独立的风格样式，多以一种风格为主，与其他风格混搭的折中方式表现。这类风格的建筑一般为公共与商业功能建筑，是城市的重要组成部分，虽然是中东铁路刺激下经济发展的产物，是中东铁路建筑文化遗产的一部分，但并不与中东铁路直接相关。如各种洋行、银行、剧院以及领事馆、办公楼等。

中东铁路附属地内新兴的建筑风格包括近代工业建筑风格、新艺术风格、装饰主义风格等。近代工业建筑风格主要表现在沿线的大型工业建筑上，这些建筑中应用新的建筑材料与技术，体现着工业化的技术理念与建造逻辑，但在建筑形象上还维持着传统的砖石建筑表情。这种特征比较明显地体现在沿线不同规模的机车库建筑上，虽然其内部空间与结构形式都以工业化需求为出发点，但外部却是传统的砖石样式。机车库建筑与沿线其他砖石建筑在外部形态上最大的区别是其巨大的建筑尺度：无论是整体体量还是局部构件都体现出铁路工业的超常规规模。铁路机车库具有单元式空间特征，外部形象与内部空间相统一，正立面屋顶轮廓多呈折线形，这些成为其较为典型的形式符号。另一类最能体现工业化特征的建筑是铁路工厂车间，其中最典型的是中东铁路哈尔滨总工厂。这些铁路工业建筑的立面形象有较高的统一性，但在细节装饰上又千差万别，辨识度很高。

中东铁路附属地内建筑艺术成就最为突出的是新艺术运动风格。这种风格以浪漫洒脱的曲线装饰元素为典型特点，多表现在建筑的门窗洞口造型或者扶手栏杆等金属构件上。虽然新艺术运动持续时间较短，并未能形成一种真正意义上的全新建筑潮流，但中东铁路沿线仍然出现了一批质量上乘、艺术品质极高的新艺术建筑。这种风格的建筑包括体量较小的高级官员住宅，也包括各类大型公共建筑，如中东铁路管理局、哈尔滨火车站、满洲里火车站以及绥芬河火车站等。现存于哈尔滨南岗区的几处中东铁路高级官员住宅，无论从整体轮廓还是局部细节都体现出强烈的新艺术特征，而风格表现最为完整、形式语言运用最典型的则当属哈尔滨火车站。以新艺术运动风格图案为装饰元素的金属构件则大量应用于各类建筑中，与其他风格相结合，形成了极具地方特色的建筑形象。新艺术运动风格建筑主要集中于哈尔滨等沿线较发达城市，在其他相对等级较低的站点中较少发现，一般仅作为一种点缀式的装饰符号出现，如一面坡的小住宅墙面和富拉尔基疗养建筑入口处应用的同心圆组合三条竖线的图案就是典型新艺术语言，兴安岭隧道的出口处也有新艺术风格的装饰。另外，装饰艺术风格建筑也出现在哈尔滨，但出现得较晚且数量极少。

中东铁路沿线建筑文化遗产艺术方面的另一个特征是地域性，在俄式建筑中具体表现为吸收中国传统建筑语言，是寻求平衡恰当的地域建筑艺术表达的实践。同时，中国本土工匠也积极学习近代技术，融合本民族传统于西式风格之中，创造了独具一格的艺术形式。

## 0.2 中东铁路建筑文化遗产多样性形成的文化机制

中东铁路的建设与运营是一段典型的跨文化传播过程，是在特定的世界局势中、特定的社会发展水平下、特定的地理环境里，不同民族文化传统、不同文明形式的一次碰撞与交融。中东铁路建筑文化遗产是文化传播与扩散现象的客观证据，体现了在文化迁移机制下，两种传统里多种类型的文化主体的多样文化选择与接受模式。包容的文化生态环境保证了文化基因库的丰富性，为文化融合和变异提供了基本的素材，是形成多样性文化表型与地域性风格的深层原因。

### 0.2.1 边缘荒地上的文化迁移扩散

1840年鸦片战争的失败标志着近代中国对西方的防御崩溃，在先进科技的震动与屡次失败的彷徨中，中国本土的传统文化几乎丧失了竞争力。洋务运动掀起了以强国为目标的主动性探索，倾向于技术的引入与制度的学习，带有技术崇拜情结，形成了一种对"西技"的全盘接受态势。传统的技术与文化被搁置一旁，甚至被盲目否定与摒弃。这种伴随着文化流失与变革阵痛的现代化探索，几乎是近代中国文化演化的缩影。

中东铁路所在的中国东北地区一直是华夏文明的边缘区，该区域的本土文化本身是中原正统文化的一个文化亚种，其文化环境也相对简单，传统文化根基薄弱，甚至没有能与外来文化抗衡的主体文化，整体上处于文化荒地状态。具体来看，这种荒地特征以中东铁路干线地区最为典型。例如，在中东铁路修筑前，干线上部分后来依附中东铁路发展起来的附属地城镇仍处于以农耕渔猎为主要生产方式的原始村落状态，有些地区甚至荒无人烟。因此干线地区原有人口基数小，本土的原始建设量少，后期发展中聚集的人口构成主要为俄方技术人员与工人，从中原地区引入的工匠与劳工以及其他移民。相较而言，南部支线地区与外界联系稍强，个别城镇聚落有一定的人口规模与建设基础，本土的传统特征也更强。

一般情况下，文化交汇地区生存压力大、文化不稳定，加之边缘的隔离作用，使其比核心地区文化可塑性更强，更易发生变化。在这种地域环境中，外来文化的竞争压力小，更易被接受而得到广泛传播，这为中东铁路建筑文化的扩散与多样性形成提供了有利的土壤。在中东铁路的影响下，这一边缘地区内本应迟滞的现代化转型反而走在了前面。

中东铁路建筑文化的传播是一种典型的迁移扩散形式的传播。由于特定的工期需求与建设模式，中东铁路在极短时间内即完成基础工程并全线通车。惊人的建设速度背后是精密的前期计划、功能优先的设计与施工理念以及调动起来的一切可用资源。在快速建设的实际操作中，现代工程手段是最主要的技术支持，标准化的设计理念则是最有效的应对策略。中东铁路沿线建筑的部分构件，如门窗节点、木梁、木柱以及桥梁设施的金属杆件等，都具有标准化产品特征，其规格尺寸、图案样式都有一定的规矩，方便运输与安装。建筑的体量规模、空间形式、功能布局、结构做法以及外部形态也有标准图纸作为参照，如各站点按照等级不同有着相对应的站舍形式，不同户型组合的住宅根据实际需求成组布置，城镇的功能布局也根据站点职能与等级需求有标准的规划模式。这种快速建设的方式奠定了干线大部分城镇的结构与风貌，很大程度上影响了其最终的发展形态。

由于东北地区地形复杂，标准化的城镇布局模式只能作为一个参考，面对不同的自然环境需要进行调整和修改以灵活应对。如在一面坡与扎兰屯，由于地势平坦、风景优美，城镇结构基本能够按照标准图纸建设，同时依附自然山水景观开辟城镇公园，供本地市民及临近站点的职工与官员休闲度假。而在横道河子，由于地处山地中，建筑无法呈棋盘式布局，因此顺应山势，将教堂布置在城镇高处，机车库安排在平坦的铁路线旁，军事医疗等建筑居于外围，住宅或依山，或傍水，布局相对自由。同时，由于不同地区资源类型不同，在就地取材的大原则下，每个地区都有其自身的材料特征，或石，或木，或砖，各有所侧重。因此，虽然以标准化设计的理念作为基础，但实际环境的复杂多样使得城镇与建筑呈现多种风貌，统一中有着多样化。

在以此为特征的迅速建设过程中，正是因为反应时间短暂且本土文化弱势，中东铁路建设的工程与设计人员作为文化的直接载体，将来自文化源地的建筑文化近乎完美地移植到中国东北地区这一文化荒地之上。

在中东铁路建设初期，外来文化受到的最严重的文化抵抗是发自民间的义和团运动。在该运动中，中东铁路线路及各类设施遭到破坏，工程人员也受到攻击，工程进度一度停滞，俄方不得不加派护路队兵力进行驱逐与护卫工作。这种本土文化对外来文化冲击的强势回应给工程主导者敲响了警钟，使其不得不制定相应对策。最直接的影响是军事部署加强，中东铁路沿线建筑类型与宏观的功能布局发生了一定的改变。这种文化冲突也是后续发展中文化渗透与融合的一个前奏。

中东铁路通车后，后续的建设并未停止，铁路管理局进一步完善着沿线的各类附属设施。这个过程逐渐转变成在铁路经济效益促动下的地区发展，站点的建设活动、运输及贸易等相关产业吸引了越来越多的中外移民。一些站点逐渐人口充盈，成为规模可观的重要城镇。在这个过程中，俄方建设与经营的中东铁路成为一个坚固的骨架，大量移民如同血肉般将铁路附属地充实起来，使得中东铁路附属地充溢着人气与生机。在中东铁路的繁荣期，文化由异地迁移转为融合与涵化，不同民族与不同形式的文化在相互影响之下进入了新的演化过程，并最终形成了具有强烈地域特征的中东铁路建筑文化。

### 0.2.2 多种主体参与的文化选择模式

作为参与文化传播过程的载体，人口是文化基因的表达主体与核心容器。对中东铁路来说，人口构成主要有两类。第一类是俄国移民，其中包括参与铁路早期建设的技术、工程人员及其家属，铁路运营阶段的职工、官员及其家属以及后期发展过程中的普通移民和商人。第二类是国内居民，其中包括在工程期间从山东、河北各地招募来的工匠与劳工，本地原生居民以及后期陆续迁移而来的移民。不同文化主体携带着不同的文化基因，也有着不同的文化选择与接受标准。

中东铁路沿线建筑的技术类型与形态表现主要是由前期的工程设计人员所确定的。这些技术人员与设计师携带着正宗的文化基因，又有着优秀的专业素养，能够在建筑上将自身的建筑传统较为精确地表达出来。在沿线的教堂建筑上可以看到，其外部形态风格较为纯正，构造技术也极其纯熟，是传统建筑文化完整而精准的移植。在城镇快速发展的繁荣期，大量的贵族资本家在城市中进行投资建设活动，也聘请专业建筑师与工程师进行设计，这些建筑则通常表现为西方各类传统建筑风格，其形式与风格的表达也相对纯正。

在直接移植本民族传统的过程中，一方面，这些设计师与工程师也有着强烈的创作欲望，尝试着学习与运用新的形式语言，实践当时流行的时代前沿艺术风潮与技术形式，如新艺术运动风格、装饰艺术风格以及工业建筑中的各种技术思考与形态探索。另一方面，当时的设计师也已经意识到建筑的地域性表达问题，并有意识地进行了实验性的尝试。在早期的设计图纸中可以看到，各种功能类型的建筑都有俄式建筑主体结合中国传统建筑符号的设计方案，这是俄国建筑师在设计中有意识地选择与借鉴中国传统建筑文化元素的典型实例。这种对于建筑文化融合的主动性探索一般仅能由受到过专业建筑设计训练、具有职业素养的设计师完成，是比较宝贵的设计思考。中东铁路早期建筑建设速度快，标准化程度高，样式比较统一。通车后沿线城镇的普通俄国移民进行的建设活动通常是住宅建设，相对具有个性化的特征，更多受个人趣味的主导，但在整体上仍统一于原有的城镇建筑风貌。在这一类建筑中，则很少见到对中国建筑元素的提取与借鉴，一般均是俄罗斯本民族的传统风味。

在中东铁路的建设中，主要的劳动力是中国人，包括大量从中原地区招募的工匠。这些工匠本身掌握着中国传统建筑的工艺与做法，熟悉建筑施工的流程，有着丰富的营造经验。与本地居民及工匠相比，中原工匠掌握着更加正统的建筑技术与艺术形式。在施工活动中，这些工匠很自然地会将自己掌握的建筑传统表达在全新的建筑体系中。如在红砖构筑的墙面上穿插砌筑灰砖，形成双喜字图案；在梁头、封檐板等木构件上雕刻中国传统纹样等。这是中国工匠对于本民族文化的一种无意识表达，是文化自觉性的具体表现。由于中国工匠在铁路建设工程中并不掌握话语权，因此，这种表现仅体现在建筑的细节之处，是一种浅层次的平面化陈述。

在俄国建筑师进行的融合实验方案中，也多是一种符号的抽取与生硬的拼合，较少体现深层次的传统对话。但在实际工程中，由于有中国工匠的参与，或许能将简单的元素抽取深化到结构与构造做法的深度上。如传统瓦屋面与砖石结构结合的具体做法，在历史照片中可以看到部分站舍外廊与建筑屋面结合成一个整体，屋面形成了反宇曲线，这种形式的建造应该有中国工匠参与才能完成。在整个中东铁路建设过程中，中国工匠一直是文化传播的对象，是技术与形式学习的被动接受者。全新的建筑体系与前所未见的建筑样式、现代化的施工方法及组织管理模式极大地冲击着他们原有的知识体系，为其后续进行的其他一般建造工作提供了新的思路。

在城市发展的繁盛期，中国居民逐渐汇聚，形成具有强烈的中国本土特征的城镇街市，最典型的如哈尔滨道外区。在这些地区的建设活动中，中国工匠们大展身手，将西式的建筑结构、材料用法、空间形式以及艺术符号等运用在各类建筑的设计与建设中，同时也将自身已经掌握圆熟的传统技巧自如地表达出来，形成了一种杂糅中西建筑文化、极具个性的建筑风格。或许设计与建造这类建筑仍是参与中东铁路建设的同一批工匠，但由于服务对象改变，建设活动的氛围更加自由，最终的表达形式也完全不同了。在这里，中国工匠掌握选择的主动权，他们提取所需的技术与艺术元素，具有一种吸取先进技术与实现自身文化价值的双重自觉性。

在商业因素成为主导城镇建设发展因素的时期，具有各种职业身份或不同国家、民族背景的业主的个人喜好与品味对建筑风格影响较大，也在一定程度上体现其个人的民族文化传统，是一个间接影响建筑文化表达结果的主体。这类建筑也多为市街商业与公共建筑，与中东铁路并不直接相关。另外，信息传播媒介的进步，如建筑图纸、画册、照片甚至电影影像等的出现，都改变了文化传播的形式，也在较大程度上推动了不同文化基因的流动，使得文化的选择与接受能够在更多环境下、更长的时间里、更广的空间范围内发生。中东铁路沿线地区文化传播中的信息载体、进行被动接受与主动选择的主体的多种类型，以及多样的反应机制是中东铁路建筑文化遗产多样的内在动力。

### 0.2.3 包容与创新并重的文化表达方式

中东铁路沿线的建筑风格体现出多元文化并置与自由合成的特点，中东铁路附属地内文化的对话过程最直接地体现在建筑的整体风格与局部的艺术表现上。中东铁路建筑文化的艺术特色表现出包容和创新两个特点。包容是通过建筑文化的多元性传达出来的，主要体现在前文所述的多元的艺术风格与样式上。创新则是文化交流的结果，是经过不同文化主体参与，通过多种文化融合途径而生成的独特风格。其中最能体现中俄文化对话与创新特征的是综合了俄国和中国的传统建筑样式的"俄中合璧"式建筑，是独属于中东铁路附属地的原创性建筑风格。这种"合璧"表现，从简单的形式模仿到空间、结构、技术的深度整合，生动地体现出了两种文化由浅入深的融合过程。

早期融合式建筑是直接将中国传统建筑符号和标志性语言移植在俄式砖石建筑主体上，取得形象上的"合璧"效果。建筑的内部空间结构主要满足现代功能或俄国生活与工作习惯，在材料选择上多为就地取材。在具体形式要素方面，这类建筑大部分借鉴中国传统大屋顶做法，多采用悬山式屋顶，屋面与屋脊平直，两端收头的做法则千差万别。比较重要的建筑屋面有反宇做法，正脊有龙纹等图案，两端设鸱尾，有似是而非的垂脊，垂脊上的装饰只是示意性地使用了数目不定的类似仙人走兽的装饰性构件。这些做法没有固定的模式和章法，呈现出自由组合的状态，形成多种多样的形象效果。这种直接拼合两种建筑传统中的典型元素——中国大屋顶与俄式砖石结构主体——的做法是最为常见的一种融合方式，在工程设计图纸与历史照片的记录中均可见不少实例，但实际留存的例子寥寥无几，推测是由于这种融合方式在建造技术与实际应用中并不成熟，功能上或有缺陷，没能经受住时间的检验。中国传统的装饰母题也出现在檐下装饰里，如屋顶两端木质十字垂带以及雨棚上出现的象征多子多寿的石榴形与桃形收头；雕刻的莲花、寿桃等中国传统吉祥图案等。个别建筑上还将墙面石材雕刻成桃形，或用不同颜色的砖砌筑双喜字图案等。这些做法既有俄国设计师设计阶段的本土化实践，也有本地工匠根据自身的经验与喜好在施工过程中的创造。

另一种融合方式是单元空间的整体镶嵌，即把中国传统风格的小体量单元空间直接贴合到俄式建筑主体上去。如俄式砖石建筑的阳光房，是虽不纯正但味道十足的中国木构形式，这种形式的建筑留存的实例极少，多见于设计图纸与历史照片。相较于提取节点元素，这种完整的空间单元更能表现出俄国建筑师对中国木构架建筑体系的初步理解水平，是一种对空间形式需求与艺术元素的借鉴，实际的构架处理仍然是运用俄式阳光房的建造方式。尽管如此，这也是俄国建筑师与工程师在建筑文化上更进一步的融合探索。还有一种镶嵌方式是在附属地内典型西式建筑风格的建筑前面加装一个中式门斗、亭子或牌楼。从历史资料中可以见到，这类组合中的中国元素相对独立而风格纯正，也并未出现在其所依附的建筑图纸中，推测应为中国工匠完成，是两种传统的简单并置。这些做法通常会与前述方法混合使用，如带有中式亭、廊的建筑，主体屋顶的形式也通常带有中国元素。

中东铁路附属地建筑文化较为深入的融合方式包括中俄建筑结构与构造技术的组合使用，以及空间层次上的借鉴与丰富等。技术上，俄国设计师吸收中国屋架、檐下构造以及大屋顶的屋面做法，了解烧制瓦的材料特性与使用方式等。随着建筑师对这些做法与技术的掌握，中国传统元素更加有机、自然地融合到了俄式建筑中。如在一些俄式建筑屋顶构造中，可以见到中国抬梁式屋架的影子。这种吸收应该发生在实际施工过程中，是俄国建筑师与本土工匠互动的结果。空间上，一些站舍建筑的屋面与候车雨棚连接起来，以反宇的做法使屋面形成舒展的弧线，雨棚下则形成了建筑室内过渡的灰空间，与中国传统建筑的檐廊空间非常相似。但是这种做法使得屋面过长，结构不够合理，无法承受东北地区冬天的雪荷载，因此没有实物保留下来。

以上述方式融合而成的建筑，风格还是以俄式为主。随着对中国传统建筑的深入理解与技术的基本掌握，俄国建筑师甚至开始尝试完全用中国传统建筑形式来设计建筑。如哈尔滨普育中学（现哈三中），在 20 世纪 20 年代重建的双城堡和阿什河车站。这些建筑没有拘泥于规矩的轴线布局模式，采用由功能出发的现代平面形式，外观上则是比较纯粹的中国建筑样式，基本上没有外来文化的痕迹了。这是俄国建筑师融入自己的设计原则，采用中国传统建筑语言进行设计的建筑，是不同文化的建筑思维深度融合的见证。普育中学建成后影响较大，报纸评述是"前所未有的建筑风格……是将中国传统建筑风格与欧洲建筑风格融合到一起的第一次成功尝试"。

与此同时，中国本土工匠也在快速地吸收着外来文化，进行着自觉的融合尝试。他们不受其原有的结构与装饰逻辑框架束缚，积极利用先进的建筑技术，根据自己的理解与喜好对各类建筑风格与艺术形式进行选取与重构，同时加入已经烂熟于心的传统文化元素，糅合成一种独具特色、生机勃勃的新的建筑样式。这类建筑一般均为砖混结构，砖砌墙面上自如地加入各种西式元素，而每种元素的样式又均经过了重新设计，添入了中国的民俗符号。多层建筑的沿街立面背后是院落式的布局空间，多进深的空间也能见到中国传统院落空间组织方式的影子。整体看上去给人一种熟悉又独特、纷杂而充满生机的感受。

中东铁路附属地内的文化传播，是一个不同主体双向选择的过程。在文化表达上，包容性保证了文化元素的原料充足，是后续发展融合的基础。而创新性则是经由模仿、学习及深层交流的互动过程，通过拼贴、并置、重构等不同的操作方法，生成具有地域特征的艺术风格，展现独特的文化面貌。

## 0.3 中东铁路建筑功能的多样性成因

铁路工业是一个庞大复杂的现代化技术体系，地理空间跨度大，建设与运营都需要多个部门、多种职业之间的协同合作。虽然技术性与专业性强，但是同时又与普通生活及经济活动息息相关。中东铁路建筑的功能类型完整丰富，共同勾画出了中东铁路附属地的社会环境和人工场景，其中不同的建筑类型分别强调中东铁路建筑文化的不同侧面：铁路交通站舍及其附属建筑、铁路工业建筑及工程设施这两个大类表现出近代交通工业的特点及工业技术水平；护路军事及警署建筑再现了当时文化传播过程中动荡不安的国际政治环境和文化激烈碰撞的场面；铁路社区居住建筑体现了中东铁路附属地作为租借地和移民聚居区的移民文化的构成特点；市街公共与综合服务建筑则勾画出中东铁路附属地城市化发展的速度与水平。

**0.3.1 中东铁路工业的综合性功能需求**

中东铁路沿线为满足运营需求建造的配套设施主要包括铁路工业建筑、铁路交通站舍及其附属建筑和道路、桥梁等各类工程设施。这类建筑的建设时期最早，是保证中东铁路通车的基础元素。其中一些建筑，如低等级站舍、机车库等，在建设初期以形式简单、快速建造的临时建筑替代，在铁路通车后才逐步重建与完善，形成今天的面貌。另一些建筑与设施则是在当时技术水平限制下为满足特殊配给与运营需求而建设，如为蒸汽机车补水的水塔和更换车头、添加燃料的补给点等。虽然在现代技术条件下这类建筑已经失去了功能上的意义，但是它们却最能体现中东铁路的时代特色与技术特点。

中东铁路交通站舍及其附属建筑主要包括火车站舍、机车库、机务段管埋建筑、货运站场、水塔、工区以及其他附属设施等。这些建筑是中东铁路运营管理与维护检修的功能主体，是构成中东铁路遗产的基础元素。其他各种类型的建筑或是旨在服务于铁路主体的功能补充，或是围绕这些基本功能衍生、发展而来。其中，火车站舍是铁路站点的标志性建筑，也是中东铁路建筑风格的最佳载体，是展现中东铁路建筑文化的直接窗口。中东铁路建设中将站点由高至低分为五个等级，并根据重要程度与职能特点确定站点规模与形制，按照标准化图纸建设。后来，随着中东铁路交通的发展，一些新的站点陆续增补建设，原有站点也出现了级别变化，中东铁路建设初期的许多临时站点纷纷新建了规模更大、建筑空间质量及艺术水平更高的新站舍，使得中东铁路沿线建筑形式更加丰富。重要站点，如哈尔滨、绥芬河、满洲里的站舍，均为典型的新艺术建筑风格，形态完整精美，结构上也应用先进的形式，是能为城市形象增辉的艺术佳品。现存历史图纸中有未建成的南部支线大连站舍设计图纸，从中可见其建筑规模庞大，外部细节丰富华丽，不逊于哈尔滨火车站。

铁路是工业文明的象征，中东铁路沿线建筑中最能够体现工业化特征的建筑类型是机车库。这类建筑是存放和维修火车机车的大型库房，主要由库房、放射状的轨道、圆形调车池台三部分组成。机车库建筑大量使用金属与水泥等现代材料，以现代化的结构支撑体系建造高耸、深远的大跨度空间单元，再根据规模需求将多个空间单元组合，形成扇形的平面形制，具有强烈的机械化大生产特征，在设计建造中也体现出明显的标准化倾向。机车检修库房也是一种特殊的机车库，专门用于车辆检修，库位数量通常并不多，无须借用圆形调车池台，因此建筑被简化成普通矩形平面。

水塔是中东铁路车站附属建筑中一个极富特色的类型，其作用是给牵引车头补充用水或给铁路工厂、住宅区提供工业及生活用水。中东铁路的俄式水塔基本是按照两套定型图纸建造起来的标准化设计产物。水塔基座上开有窄长采光窗，同时具有瞭望和射击的功能，因此水塔也具有一定程度的军事防御功能。水塔轮廓简洁、装饰丰富，是中东铁路附属地建筑文化遗产的一种标志性符号。

其他的辅助建筑，如工区建筑，是线路检修与防护的站点，建筑成组出现，一般呈院落式布局，可分为有围墙式与无围墙式两种。其他如货运站场仓库及管理用房、机务段办公室等建筑多分布在规模较大的站点，满足存储与办公功能，建筑形式与当地其他类型建筑相统一。水泵房、检修养护用房等建筑大多体量小，形制简单而坚固耐用，紧挨铁路线，并不一定分布在站点附近。

铁路工业建筑主要是在修筑铁路过程中应运而生的，如与建材加工、机械制造及设备维修有关的工厂。这些大型工业厂房不仅推动了工业技术的发展，也是当时建筑技术水平的最佳体现。中东铁路沿线最早的工业建筑是加工铁路材料和组装、维修机械设备的大型厂房。由于近代的工业生产方式强调机械操作流程的连续性和空间的灵活性，因此高大、宽阔、深远成为空间的基本要求。中东铁路哈尔滨总工厂以其庞大的规模、先进的空间技术成为当时现代化水平较高的工业建筑群。其建厂的投资、选址、技术标准都很高，有十一个分厂，是"集蒸汽机车、客车、货车维修、加工"为一体的综合性工厂。

铁路工程设施则主要包括沿线数量巨大的桥梁、涵洞以及隧道，其数量、规模、分布特点是由中东铁路途经地区的地理环境决定的，是以人类智慧克服自然阻力的最佳表现。高超的技术与工艺水平在中东铁路建筑文化遗产中具有重要的价值。中东铁路沿线桥梁的类型很丰富，既有传统的石质拱桥，也有代表现代技术的钢结构桥梁。石拱桥根据跨度不同有单拱与多跨连续拱结构，桥身两端的引桥都会根据落差设计一到两个较小的拱形洞口，减小桥身结构自重的同时缓解洪水压力，增加大桥的抗冲击能力。跨度较小的金属桥梁为平板铁桥，中间一般不设承重柱，直接搭在两侧基础上。大型和特大型金属桥梁多采用钢桁梁结构，以混凝土或石材砌筑桥墩。这些桥梁大都建成于1899年至1903年间，使用当时最先进的结构形式，选用最新的建筑材料，是中东铁路沿线建筑技术的最高成就之一。涵洞是保护铁路基础的工程设施，多为石材砌筑，中东铁路沿线数量极多。部分尺度较大、净空较高的涵洞还起到联系铁路两边民众的交通作用。东北地区山体较多，中东铁路沿线开凿了多条隧道，其中大兴安岭隧道口修建有为在有限距离内提升铁轨标高的螺旋展线。部分隧道口以新艺术风格图案装饰，在地理位置重要的隧道口修建有碉堡。这些建筑及工程设施是中东铁路建筑遗产的本体，体现的是铁路工业本身的复杂性与综合性。

**0.3.2 中东铁路附属地的城镇生活与管理需要**

中东铁路沿线大部分地区是荒野之地，因此在铁路本体基本建设需求之外，还需要满足各类参与人员的日常生活需求，其中最基本也最迫切的是创造舒适的居住条件，大规模的铁路社区居住建筑应运而生。

中东铁路建筑中占有最大比例的建筑类型即是住宅。每一个铁路站点的居住建筑都是伴随着交通设施一同出现的，后来大批移民涌入，居住建筑的增长速度就更快了。中东铁路附属地内的住宅种类繁多、标准不一，已经成为一种独特的人居文化现象。中东铁路的居住建筑大致有三种基本类型：独户住宅、联户住宅和集合住宅。

独户住宅是比较高级的住宅形式，一般为中东铁路高级官员建设。这些住宅多位于城市中的优越地段，设计精良，样式多采用当时最流行的新艺术风格，一般为两层，功能丰富，部分住宅兼有办公功能。这一类住宅主要位于哈尔滨，体现着中心城市的潮流特点。其他城镇也有少量的独户式住宅，但等级相对不高，规模较小，样式以与城镇内其他住宅建筑统一为主。

联户住宅是中东铁路住宅中数量最多、标准化程度最高的一种类型。这类住宅的建筑密度普遍较低，布局方式灵活，对环境有很强的适应能力：既可组团布置，搭配院落构成"花园洋房"式的田园景观，也可以沿街线性排列，形成街道空间；在规模较小的火车站点也有散点状的自由分布。联户住宅的典型户数组合是：双户型、三户型、四户型、多户型。其平面布局非常紧凑，通常是所有住户的单元空间紧密组合成一个简洁的矩形，只在门斗或阳光间的位置出现凸出矩形轮廓的小体量空间。这种平面构成使得建筑的外墙面积较小，热耗与造价较低，也利于建造，根据规模和标准也能分成不同的模式。联户住宅外部形态设计往往通过带有不同装饰图案的阳光房、门斗、隅石、线脚等进行组合，同时利用不同材料的搭配，使得联户住宅建筑的整体形象一致，但在细节上却千差万别、各具特色。

中东铁路沿线集合住宅数量相对较少，但样式较多、特色鲜明。最简单的集合住宅是公寓或集体宿舍，这种建筑的空间构成比较单一，除了公用卫生间和管理用房外，主要是重复的居住单元，多设在铁路站区，如一面坡铁路职工宿舍。另外一种集合式住宅具有典型现代单元住宅的特点，可分为一梯两户或者一梯四户，户内的空间与功能划分更为合理，如横道河子工程师集合住宅。这类住宅提供了一种现代化的居住模式，也为当时东北地区的居民展现了一种全新的生活方式与理念。

伴随着中东铁路的进一步建设与运营，更多的工程师、技术人员与劳动工人携家属进驻到附属地中，逐渐发展成具有一定规模的移民聚落点。为满足日常的工作与世俗生活需求、完善城市配套建设，中东铁路沿线出现了功能丰富的公共建筑，包括与铁路相关的管理与办公建筑；满足日常生活需求的各类市政服务设施，如医院、学校、俱乐部、教堂、浴池、公厕、公园等。这些建筑直接或间接地服务于铁路建设与运营，由铁路发育衍生而来，总量不大，但极大地扩充了建筑功能类型，也体现了沿线重要站点的城镇化过程。

在中东铁路修建早期，施工事故、与中国居民冲突以及疾病频发，因此医院建筑是最早出现的公共建筑类型。中东铁路的医院具有不同规模，根据不同等级站点人口规模设计相应容纳能力的医疗建筑标准图纸。重要站点设规模大、功能全的集中式综合医院，如哈尔滨中东铁路中央医院；二、三等站设一定规模的医疗建筑群，采用单体建筑与群体布局，均经过标准设计，如横道河子医疗建筑群；小站一般设简单的医务室。自然环境优越的城镇中，医院建筑也带有休闲疗养功能，如一面坡医院。

文化休闲建筑类型较为多样，如俱乐部、休闲度假宾馆及疗养院所等。这类建筑多位于具有一定规模的城镇或临近山川、河流等环境优美的风景区，建筑形象丰富、活跃，风格多样，也是重要的人工景观。其中，俱乐部功能复合性最高，也最为普遍，给中东铁路沿线城镇带来了西洋生活方式和先进的文化设施，传播了现代化的休闲理念。为美化城镇环境、丰富居民休闲生活内容，中东铁路沿线一些站点内结合当地自然条件建设有公园，包含了亭台、水榭、吊桥、雕塑等设施。

中东铁路沿线教育类建筑主要分为培养铁路技术工人或工程人员的专业技术学校和服务于职工子女的铁路职工子弟学校。专业技术学校多位于重要城市，如哈尔滨、大连、满洲里等。铁路职工子弟学校在一些规模不大的城镇是与教堂建筑复合在一起的，类似于教会学校的模式。而在更大规模的城镇，学校则专门选址单独建设，并有了小学、中学的具体分类，如扎兰屯沙俄子弟小学等。

浴池是中东铁路管理局为铁路员工专门设置的服务性建筑。不同规模的车站具有相应规模的浴室标准设计图。

在一些远离城镇的站点，如会让站与工区等，浴池是一种标准配置的铁路附属建筑，面积很小；城镇内的浴池则规模较大，能容纳多人。其他的公共设施一般规模较小，但却能为居民日常生活提供极大的便利，如公厕、开水房、冷库、地窖等。其中，公厕虽然体量小、功能简单，但有采暖与通风排气设施。

附属地内与铁路相关的行政办公建筑主要是中东铁路管理局大楼和铁路下属机构的办公用房，如各地铁路交涉局、事务所、官署等。这类建筑多位于哈尔滨、满洲里、绥芬河等重要城市，建筑规模较大，形式也趋近中心城市的建筑风格。如哈尔滨中东铁路管理局，是沿线可见的体量最大的新艺术运动风格建筑。次级城镇内的普通办公建筑则通常与城镇内的其他建筑风貌相统一。

东正教堂是中东铁路沿线主要的宗教建筑，也是最能体现俄罗斯民族文化的建筑类型，多在城镇中心或最高点。虽然与铁路修建及营运没有直接关联，但却是俄国移民最重要的精神生活场所，即便在铁路建设初期条件有限的情况下，工地附近仍设有临时教堂。除为普通居民服务的社区教堂外，大规模驻军的站点还设有随军教堂。

另外，在门户开放政策实施后，一些重要城市中又增建了领事馆建筑。同时，随着商业活动的增加，金融、百货、旅馆等商业建筑也纷纷出现，这些建筑个性化强，建筑形式受到所在城市的影响较大，与中东铁路关系并不密切。这些为满足一般的日常生活与市镇管理需求而建设的建筑极大充实了中东铁路建筑的功能类型，这些建筑作为历史载体勾画出了当时中东铁路附属地内的居民生活方式与社会发展水平，也是东北地区在中东铁路的文明示范效应下进行现代转型的有力证据。

**0.3.3 特定时代环境下的多样化军事职能**

由于在政治、军事、经济和地方管理上具有的特殊地位，中东铁路沿线一直有俄国派驻的特殊军队——护路队驻扎，目的是保护铁路安全。在战争或局部冲突多发的时期，中东铁路驻留有大量的军队。中东铁路护路队组建于1897年，由于在中俄《合办东省铁路公司合同》中并未赋予沙俄在中东铁路沿线的驻军权和护路权，因此护路队名义上并不是正规军，且第一批护路队人数不多，并不能满足全线的护卫需求。在第一批护路队的进驻得到清政府的默许后，俄方开始进行护路队的扩编，并分批将其派入铁路附属地。1898年，南部支线开工修建，对军事力量的需求增大，至1900年，护路队人数达到4 500多人。为了应对1900年爆发的义和团运动，沙俄不断向中东铁路增派军队，扩充至11 000人，并增添了炮兵，这也意味着护路队职能由原来的防御性转向进攻性，这种转变在随之建造的建筑中也有所体现。

由于护路队人数较多，因此在第一次扩编后，中东铁路管理局根据各驻点的战略地位，搭配不同兵种，派驻相应规模的护路队。军事人员与护路设施被编配成不同的等级梯队，在哈尔滨设立总司令部，在富拉尔基、一面坡、铁岭等地设立分司令部，逐步建立起层级有序的军事战力布局体系，并随着局势变化进行适当的调整。与此同时，为保障安全运送修筑铁路所需的各种物资，护路队分出一部分兵力到铁路线外的要害地区设立据点，建造了一批满足士兵居住及储存物资需求的建筑。

日俄战争期间，中东铁路承担着主要的物资与军队的运输补给任务，是俄方军队的生命线。为加强对线路的保护，外阿穆尔军区增建了防护设施与防御工事，同时增添急救站及仓库等辅助建筑，这一时期是沿线军事建筑的建设高潮，规模与形态基本成型。日俄战争结束，俄国战败，失去了大部分南部支线的控制权，开始强化铁路干线附属地的军事部署，最多时外阿穆尔军区军队数量一度达到 7 万人。此后俄国本国动荡的局势也冲击和削弱了其在中东铁路附属地内的军事实力，"十月革命"后，中东铁路护路队人数急剧减少，至 1920 年时中东铁路护路队已经基本瓦解了。军事建筑与工事的建设基本停滞，虽然残余的沙俄势力也曾试图重组护路队，但并没有形成规模。可见，中东铁路沿线军事建筑的建设规模与布局方式在很大程度上受到当时国际形势及地区政治环境的影响，反映着近代中国东北错综复杂的历史格局。同时，中东铁路管理局在铁路附属地内具有司法自治权，中东铁路沿线多地设有警察机构。在此背景下，司令部、兵营、碉堡等军事建筑及设施和警察署、监狱等建筑大量出现，成为中东铁路附属建筑中独特的类型。

司令部是中东铁路沿线级别最高的军事建筑。1901 年 2 月 1 日，俄国将中东铁路护路队改编为"外阿穆尔军区"，总司令部设在哈尔滨。护路队在其他重要驻兵点，如博克图、横道河子等地，也都设有司令部。司令部为军官及士兵提供办公或集会场所，因此有综合服务性质。同兵营不同，司令部建筑一般坐落于城镇内部，如外阿穆尔军区司令部位于哈尔滨的市中心，博克图司令部也布置在镇中心。司令部建筑一般为多层建筑，其形象也趋向于与城市公共建筑相统一。

兵营是军事建筑组团，一般位于城镇外围，包括营房、马厩、军官住宅、食堂、禁闭室及仓库等附属建筑。营房是护路队士兵的住宅，属于带有军事性质的居住类建筑。中东铁路的营房有标准的设计图纸，建筑规模与形象也趋于一致。也有较大的兵营采用非标准化设计，建筑层数也不仅限于单层，如满洲里东大营。营房建筑体量大，根据兵员需求可以进行规模上的调整，一般是在面宽方向上进行缩减或增加。规模最小的营房与普通住宅相近，大体量的兵营面宽则近 90 米，如昂昂溪兵营等。马厩是护路队骑兵兵营的附属建筑，是一种独具特色的建筑类型。从形式上看，马厩接近于简化的兵营，但墙面一般设高窗，屋面常有用于换气的排风窗。室内空间简单，标准的马厩布置两排拴马柱。在规模较小的骑兵兵营中，马厩建筑更简单，与仓库近似，必要时一些普通的民用建筑也会被临时充作马厩之用。另一类个性强烈的军事建筑则是弹药库。根据规划图纸可以发现，弹药库建筑的布局方位与兵营有一定距离，既要方便存取、护卫与管理，又要防止爆炸带来不必要的人员伤亡与附带损失。其建筑形式较独特，为半圆形轮廓，内部空间呈桶状。其他存放军事物资与器械的库房空间形式简单，外部形态也没什么特点。军官住宅与普通的铁路住宅区别不大。

沿铁路线一定距离内会设有工区与小型驻扎营地。距离城镇较远的工区一般与小型营地形式相同，设有防御性的围墙，围合而成的院落空间内排列功能性建筑。在具有重要战略意义的大桥的桥头或隧道口多建有高大坚固的碉堡，如兴安岭碉堡、富拉尔基桥头堡等。这些碉堡以混凝土浇筑，墙体厚重，素混凝土表面不着装饰。另外，沿线还有瞭望塔及哨所，水塔也具有瞭望与射击功能，在一定程度上属于军事建筑。

警署与监狱建筑多位于城镇内部。警署建筑同兵营形式相近，但有更强的民用建筑气息，与城镇建筑风格相和谐，如博克图警察署、扎兰屯森林警察大队等。监狱建筑多位于城镇内部，通常以一个封闭的院落围合一组建筑，监舍全部用砖石砌筑而成，坚固厚实的墙体装饰较少，气氛紧张严肃，如满洲里监狱、旅顺监狱等。

## 0.4 地域性的多样化建筑技术与材料表达

人类学家普遍认为技术进步导致社会变迁，并随之影响意识形态，重大的技术发明与科学发现会自行扩散与传播，这是文化扩张的直接动力。中东铁路沿线建筑体现了多样化的建筑技术与材料表达方式，其中既有传统建造活动中世代累积的建构巧思，也有现代化材料与结构形式的试探性运用，这两种形式的导入都是中国东北地区的建筑，甚至是社会现代化转型重要的一环。本土自然环境与社会文化环境在承载这种多样化技术与材料表现的同时，也在一定程度上将其予以重塑，形成了强烈的地域性特征。

### 0.4.1 应对复杂环境的建造技术需求

中东铁路建筑遗产中多种技术形式的应用，体现的是当时社会背景与科技水平下面对实际建造活动中的具体需求而建立的应对策略。首先，为满足大量建设的时限要求，需要运用已有且相当完备的成熟技术体系，即传统的木结构与砖石砌筑结构及其各种变体。以标准图纸在形式上予以规范化，保证在操作中得心应手而又不必陷入费时的具体形式设计中去。其次，为了解决铁路工业对建筑的大跨度空间需求，引入钢框架式的支撑结构与多种钢结构屋架形式，同时结合传统砖石做法，形成一种混合的技术表达方式。最后，东北地区的特定地理环境与气候条件也影响了技术的具体应用形式，如墙体厚度、基础埋深、屋架做法等。

传统结构形式主要是砖、石、木混合结构和以木材为主要材料的木刻楞及传统木框架结构。砖、石、木混合结构是以砖石墙体承重，支撑木屋架的结构体系。在一些室内空间跨度较大或带有凉廊式半开敞空间的建筑中，也以砖、石立柱或者实木立柱配合作为承重结构。如兵营与马厩建筑中，室内以两排木柱与屋架形成了一个整体的内框架，搭配承重的外墙形成了一种复合的结构体系。在内部空间分隔较多且跨度需求不大的低层建筑中，一般以木梁承托楼板或者屋架，木梁暴露在外，边角做切割修饰。个别建筑中也有使用钢轨替代木梁的，钢轨间砌筑平拱，这种形式多应用于地下室、楼梯等局部，没有大尺度、大范围的应用。砌筑类墙体的实际做法也比较灵活，有实心砌筑、空心砌筑、外筑内填等做法。其中，实心砌筑类墙体结构性能最好，外筑内填式墙体则简便且节省材料，应用也较广泛，而空心砌筑的墙体一般不用于承重。砖石砌筑的墙体厚重坚实，因此几乎被所有的军事建筑所采用。这一类结构的施工工艺简单，空间分隔容易，材料比较单一，取材方便且费用不高，适用的建筑面积较小，层数较低，被中东铁路沿线大部分民用建筑所采用。另外砖（石）拱结构作为一种历史悠久的传统结构类型多应用于桥梁与涵洞，在建筑中一般应用于门窗、洞口等局部。

木结构主要有木刻楞与木框架两种，其中木刻楞做法是俄罗斯民族的传统民居结构形式，具有原生态、施工简易、冬暖夏凉、结实耐用等优点。木刻楞建筑一般建在石头垒起的地基上，墙面都是由经过简单去皮之后的原木（或半圆木、方木）通过榫卯的方式垒叠起来的，是比较典型的井干式做法。这类结构形式大部分用于住宅与教堂建筑。木框架结构与木梁柱结构相似，在建筑入口门斗、仓房与厕所中应用较多，以单层的木板做其维护结构。由于这种结构类型能够形成通透轻盈的建筑形象，具有装饰效果，因此常用于凉廊、阳光房、景观亭、教堂的钟塔等建筑局部。木结构墙体本身质量较轻，而且大多木构建筑高度较小，因此木结构承担的荷载较小，比较稳定。木构墙体大多采用榫卯交接，同时墙体和基础间的联系是相对柔性的，遇外力作用可以产生一定的形变和移动，能够较好地消解外力影响。现存的很多砖石砌筑墙体都出现不同程度的开裂、损坏甚至变形,但木构建筑保存相对完好,这直接地反映了木构体系的优点。

新的结构形式一般应用在特殊类型的建筑上。如扇形机车库室内的支撑结构就是典型的钢框架结构,具体做法是以镂空的钢柱支撑波浪形的连续拱顶,拱顶内置钢筋龙骨,以现浇混凝土浇筑,属于钢筋混凝土结构的一种特殊类型。这种结构的拱弧度大,呈半圆形,特征鲜明。金属桁架结构是一种更先进的结构形式,应用也更广泛。钢桁架结构首先应用在铁路工厂和一些大型车站候车大厅等大跨度建筑的屋面构筑中。屋架结构类型包括豪式屋架、芬克式屋架、复合屋架、直角三角形屋架等;从跨度上分为单跨、双跨、三跨及多跨等。钢桁架结构在大型铁路桥梁中也有着典型的应用,其桁梁包括上弦桁梁、下弦桁梁、常规直桁梁等多种形式;早期上弦桁梁又分为曲上弦桁梁和直上弦桁梁两种,主要用于大跨度、多跨数的大型铁路桥。金属桁梁铁路桥的整体结构形式通常具有组合特征:石材砌筑桥墩、钢桁梁承载铁道线的基础台面,桥基通常用深沉箱基础。大型的钢结构铁路桥是中东铁路沿线最壮观、最典型的工业景观之一。小型钢桁架还出现在竖向结构构件中,如水塔水箱外部的支撑结构。混凝土结构分为有配筋和无配筋两种,其中有配筋的混凝土结构包括钢混承重墙结构、钢混框架结构。混凝土结构在当时应用并不广泛,只在对强度要求特别高的建筑和工程设施中大量采用,如无配筋的混凝土结构多用于建造铁路桥梁和隧道边的大型碉堡、掩体等;钢筋混凝土结构则多应用于建筑的楼板及屋顶等局部,与其他的结构混合使用。另外,钢悬索结构多应用在沿线城镇的景观桥上,现存实例仅见于扎兰屯公园吊桥。现代结构与传统建筑技术综合应用的典型实例是中东铁路哈尔滨总工厂,在其十一个分厂中,结构形式包括墙体与屋架承重和墙体、柱与屋架混合承重两种方式;屋架有木屋架和钢屋架;墙体包括砖墙和混凝土墙;柱则有木、钢筋混凝土、钢柱等不同类型。厂房的跨度有单跨、双跨、三跨以及多跨,屋架的形式也很多样。在同一座厂房中,不同跨度的空间会采用不同的屋架形式来满足结构需求。这类工业建筑有良好的自然采光和通风设计,充满技术理性。

**0.4.2 丰富资源支撑下的适宜材料选择**

中东铁路途经之地是物产最为富饶的地区。森林、煤矿等资源丰富,不仅为中东铁路的运营提供了充足的保障,也为中东铁路附属地建筑及设施的兴建提供了丰富的材料来源。建筑中大量地使用天然材料:木、砖、石等,这也成为中东铁路建筑的一大特色。本地材料与俄罗斯传统建筑技术相结合,使得中东铁路沿线建筑富有浓郁的异域风情和鲜明的地域色彩,影响了中东铁路沿线城镇的风貌基调,也成为东北地域建筑文化中举足轻重的部分。除了这些天然建筑材料外,代表了当时先进建筑材料技术的钢铁和混凝土也有不同程度的应用。

由于中东铁路途经东北森林资源最丰富的地区,因此木材是中东铁路最经典的建筑材料。应用方式主要包括作为枕木、墙体、桩、柱、梁、屋架等结构材料,作为墙板、地板、保温层等围护系统材料,以及作为雕花装饰板、雕花构件等内外装饰材料,其中木材作为门窗的应用最为普遍,包括各式木板门、拼花木门以及各式窗。另外木材还广泛用于大型铁路工程设施的施工模件和脚手架。大部分的木材构筑形成丰富的拼接肌理与细腻的纹饰图案,极大地美化了建筑形象。如木刻楞建筑以原木累叠成结构主体后,外侧一般覆盖一层企口拼接的木板,板条规则排列形成优美的韵律,部分板条端部还被加工成尖形、半圆形或其他重复图案,置于墙体中部偏上的部位或是山墙等处,于统一中形成富于变化的效果。在建筑室内铺设地板是将木材用作围护材料的较典型的做法，地板形式大致有两种类型，一种为条木地板，另一种为拼花木地板。在中东铁路沿线建筑中，条木地板比较大众化，常见于普通铁路职工住宅的卧室地面，条板的宽度不等，板材一般较长。其板材单元一般使用平口相接，使得地板的拼合不是很紧密。另外一种拼花木地板是相对较高级的室内地面装修，常出现在中东铁路长官的府邸中。其板材尺寸较小，板材单元一般带有企口，拼接更为紧密。

木材轻便易加工的特性又促使它成为最具装饰性的一种材料。不管是室内的木墙裙还是室外的门窗贴脸、雨棚，檐下的挂檐板、楼梯栏杆、栏板，抑或是其他附加的装饰构件，木材不仅可以做成优美的轮廓线脚，而且经常做成俄罗斯民间建筑中常见的装饰纹样，采用镂空雕刻，活泼轻巧而具有童话般的色彩。无论是在纯木构建筑中还是砖（石）木混合的建筑中，木饰构件都是最具吸引力的部分。木建筑或是木构件在使用过程中还经常被漆成各种鲜艳的色彩，既可以保护木构件，又赋予木建筑浓郁的俄罗斯民间建筑特色。

中东铁路途经大范围的山地环境，天然石材资源丰富，尤其是大兴安岭、张广才岭以及老爷岭，盛产花岗岩和石灰岩。因此，石材是中东铁路建筑的另一种最重要的天然材料。中东铁路沿线开设了大量的采石场和碎石加工厂，就地取材成为中东铁路筑路和房屋建筑工程中石材的主要获取办法。石材的使用方式包括：路基碎石、桥墩、建筑基础、墙体、地面铺装材料等，尤其在桥梁、隧道等铁路工程中用量很大，是重要的结构材料。在建筑上，石材除了用作基础材料外，还用作承重墙砌块材料。用作外墙材料的石材根据不同的石质、形状和色彩会拼装出丰富的立面效果。在级别较高的公共建筑中，经过精细化处理的石材也作为装饰面材。从石材砌筑方式上看，有规则式砌筑和不规则式砌筑两种。规则式砌筑的石材与砖材的砌筑形式相类似，以水平卧砌结合错缝和楔形立砌发券这两种形式为主；不规则式砌筑则可形成类似蜂窝纹、冰裂纹以及其他随机纹理，最典型的如虎皮石墙。一般由经过较精细加工的石材砌筑的外墙表面较为平整，墙体内部却常用碎石填砌，再灌以石膏、石灰砂浆，使之结合为一个整体。

中东铁路建筑最常用的人工材料是黏土砖，使用方式包括：建造建筑基础、承重或分隔空间的墙体以及室内外铺装材料等。中东铁路建筑中使用的砖分为红砖与青砖两种，中东铁路干线建筑大多采用俄制红砖，有的只在落影花饰和转角隅石等处采用地方产青砖，形成了以红砖为主、青砖为辅的状况。大面积的红砖墙面局部点缀青砖，形成了一种奇特的色彩与图案装饰效果。中东铁路南部支线，尤其是哈尔滨至长春段，建筑多以青砖为主，红砖为辅。砖结构建筑在中东铁路建筑文化遗产中占有最大比重，多为刷有涂料的清水墙面，根据砖的尺寸与模数特点通过简单的重复性砌筑和复杂多变的砌法组合来获得多样化的图案与光影效果。在具体的砌筑方式上，砖大部用于砌筑墙体，以平面满铺的顺面丁面结合的卧砖形式为主，如一皮顺一皮丁、三皮顺一皮丁等。这种形式同样用于砖砌的建筑基础、扶壁、勒脚等处。另外，砖石两种材料也常组合使用砌筑墙体，一般以石材砌筑主要墙体，在门窗洞口等需要形成规则形状等部位则使用红砖，既是对不同材料自身性质的利用，又形成了两种材质肌理与色彩的戏剧化对比，视觉效果极佳。另一种砖石复合墙体是在墙体外侧用石材砌筑，内侧砌砖，砖石之间以白灰黏结。

中东铁路沿线也有部分建筑采用中国瓦材，形成的建筑形象带有中国传统建筑意向，但俄式建筑中瓦的用量不多。其他人工材料，如陶片、釉片和琉璃片材是相对昂贵、用量较少的建材，是点缀性使用的特殊建筑材料，多出现在大型公共建筑内外檐装饰。

中东铁路建筑工程中最重要的现代材料是金属，除用来铺设铁路线路外，还广泛应用在铁路工程设施与建筑上。铁路桥、候车雨棚、跨线天桥、水塔等工程设施，都是以型钢为主要或局部主要结构材料；建筑中型钢的用途包括梁、柱、屋架及楼梯、平台梁；而女儿墙的装饰围栏、楼梯和阳台栏杆、屋面铺板、扶壁护面雨披、金属瓦、排水落水管、通风口，乃至合页、把手等连接件则大部分使用铸铁或铁皮。金属栏杆常常以新艺术运动风格的纹饰图案作为装饰，代表了全新的建筑艺术形式，而大量的铸铁构件以及钢柱、梁构成的钢框架结构则体现着工业化与产品化特征。混凝土作为一种高强度新材料在中东铁路沿线也有所应用，但并不广泛。混凝土在大型铁路工程设施以及碉堡等军事设施中用量较大，在早期的大型公共建筑和住宅及机车库等工业建筑中多与其他材料结合使用，常用于砌筑楼板，带有实验性色彩。玻璃在中东铁路建筑中大量应用，用于采光窗及屋面采光天窗、采光顶棚及住宅阳光房等。另外在砖、木建筑表面常刷有涂料或油漆，起装饰作用的同时保护材料免受腐蚀。

### 0.4.3 应对地域气候的多种措施

为应对东北地区特殊的气候条件，中东铁路沿线建筑中出现了多种技术手段与空间手法。这些尝试一方面塑造了中东铁路沿线建筑的个性特征，另一方面也增加了其空间与技术的多样性。

在城镇选址方面，考虑到高海拔、低温度等影响因素，中东铁路沿线的城镇绝大多数位于地势平坦、利于城市建设的平原地区，这些地区一般东、西、北三面环山，能够减弱气候的不利影响，冬季受寒冷季风的影响较小。建筑的布局一般有行列式与周边式两种，行列式建筑的东南－西北走向使其在与冬季主导季风平行的同时，获得最佳的朝向，减弱了西北季风对住宅的直接影响；周边式住宅的内向型布局形式形成了相对私密的内向空间，可以形成较为封闭的小气候环境，防风阻沙的效果很好。

在空间处理方面，中东铁路沿线建筑普遍设置砖石或木质门斗作为入口的缓冲空间，进入室内后，以玄关作为下一层缓冲。这种多重过渡空间的设计在最大程度上减弱了冬季低温和风雪侵袭生活空间的可能性。中东铁路一些大型公共建筑的入口处设计更独具匠心：室外不设踏步，在室内门厅中解决高差问题。这是一种非常人性化的设计细节，因为在冬季冰雪环境下室外台阶易结冰打滑，将台阶移入室内可避免人们因积雪结冰滑倒。同时室内高差可阻挡室外寒风的直接侵袭，使寒风在下沉空间内积聚，避免对其他空间的干扰。为了减少外墙面比例，避免过多的"冷山"墙，建筑的形体均较为简单，普通建筑平面多为规则的矩形。建筑功能排布紧凑，尤其是联排式住宅，这样能够在冬季充分利用住户之间的热量交换，减少热量的损失。

中东铁路沿线砖石建筑墙体厚度相对较大，最厚的可达1.5米，除基本的承重要求外，能够较好地满足防寒保温的需求。多种形式的复合材料墙体一般也是为加强抗寒能力而进行的构造改良。其中，砖与板夹墙体相结合的砖木复合墙体最具特点，墙体外侧为红砖砌筑，内侧为板夹墙体，板夹墙体填充锯末。一般情况下起到支撑结构作用的是板夹墙体部分，外侧砖墙只是作为"装饰"材料。从现存实例的状况来看，经过百余年的使用后，板夹墙体部分内填锯末依然完整干燥，保温能力不减。有时为了减少锯末用量和提高墙体承重能力，锯末中也会掺入一些碎砖块。砖墙和锯末复合墙体是一种"夹心"墙体：两侧为砖墙，中间填充锯末，在部分实例里也有锯末与泥土混合填充的做法。填充物比热小，黏结性好，加强了墙体的保温能力。由于该种墙体形式内外均呈现砖墙形式，因此外观完全看不出其"夹心"属性。同砖墙与板夹墙体的复合形式相比，该种墙体形式在具备较好的保温性能的同时还具备更优的结构性能。无论何种形式墙体，室内一侧墙面均覆盖倾斜细木条交成的菱形网格，其上抹灰增加密闭性，提高保温性能。在木刻楞墙体中，原木之间的缝隙被塞入毛毡、麻等纤维并以白灰泥抹缝，可防风防寒，保证了良好的保温效果。

中东铁路沿线大部分建筑的屋架为木质，形式有单坡、双坡、四坡、复斜式以及复折式等，其中双坡的桁架式木屋架最为多见。倾斜的坡屋面一方面适应东北地区冬季屋顶排雪的要求，另一方面可以在屋面和室内吊顶之间形成一个三角形断面的空气层，即"闷顶"。为保持闷顶空间的干燥通风，常在两侧山墙处设四季开敞的通风气窗，同时在吊顶上面铺满锯末、木屑等材料，以应对冬季寒风的侵入。

地下室也在防寒保温方面起到了积极作用，尽管地下室的出现有着各种目的，有的是出于储藏功能的考虑，有的是为了便于设备的安置，还有的是一种安全措施，但是作为建筑主体和大地之间的过渡媒介，地下室内冬暖夏凉，较大程度上弱化了地面对室温的直接影响。同时室内地板以木梁作为龙骨支撑，与地面之间留有一定厚度的空气夹层，既能防潮也能御寒。

在建筑的节点构造上，许多细节设计能够简单有效地达到减少能耗的目的，较为典型的为门窗构造。木门的门框与墙体的交接处都有毛毡嵌缝，接缝端口还有三角木条堵缝以防冷风侵入。子母门或对开门的母门边侧还有盖板，当门扇关闭后盖板会盖住门缝。通过这些细节的处理，减少门板构造的薄弱环节，减弱冷风在入口处的直接渗入。建筑窗户普遍尺度较小，且均为双层，以形成空气间层。为增加室内的采光面积，窗口均为向内的喇叭口。窗扇上部有一扇较小的换气窗，该换气窗可在避免室内热量大面积流失的同时达到快速换气的功能。窗户的中槛和下槛都设有横向木板，木板向外倾斜，可使雨雪、积水直接排向窗台，避免其进入窗户进而产生冻胀。同时窗扇外边框处理和门一样，也设盖板，使窗扇关闭后能够盖住窗缝，避免冷风直接进入室内。

建筑室内采暖方式主要有壁炉采暖、火墙采暖和集中采暖等。壁炉采暖是欧洲传统的采暖方式。壁炉是家庭空间中重要的组成部分，一般也是重要的装饰元素，中东铁路的修筑把这种建筑文化传播到了中东铁路沿线附属地内。由于这些建筑均与铁路相关，建成速度较快，居住者多为铁路职工，人员流动性很强，建筑经常更换主人，因此外表装饰华丽、场所归属感较强的开敞式壁炉出现较少，取而代之的是一种造型简单、装饰较少、能够兼顾多个房间取暖的封闭式壁炉。这类壁炉大致可以分为圆形、方形和转角形三种。火墙一般可以分为两种，即独立式与炉灶式。独立式火墙即火墙单独设置，表面积较大，散热较快，注重表面装饰，主要出现在公共建筑的走廊和一些中东铁路官员宅邸中。炉灶式火墙即火墙和炉灶毗连设计，炉灶满足做饭、烘烤、烧水等日常需求的同时为火墙加热，这种取暖方式仅用于住宅建筑中。集中采暖系统多应用在大型公共建筑中，一般将锅炉置于地下室，建筑室内墙体为暖气散热器留有凹槽，是相对现代化的采暖方式。

另外，建筑结合取暖系统设计换气系统，换气通道紧邻排烟通道而设，利用排烟通道内烟气的余温，将换气通道内的空气加热，通过热空气上升的原理来实现快速换气的目的。

## 0.5 总结

中东铁路历经清朝、中华民国至中华人民共和国成立，承载着近代中国一段风起云涌、跌宕起伏的历史进程，记录了沿线地区波澜壮阔的现代转型过程。文化上，中东铁路以铁路工业文明为依托，以移民文化为表现形式，富含俄、日等多种跨文化因素，对沿途地区社会结构、聚落形态、生活模式、建筑样式等产生深远影响，形成了有别于中国传统文化核心圈的边缘文化。中东铁路建筑文化遗产内在成因与外在形态的独特性促成了其浓烈的本土化特征，有着极高的历史与文化价值。

无论从内容上还是形态上，中东铁路建筑文化遗产都表现出异乎寻常的丰富性、完整性和独特性，构成了一个包含多样文化因素的复杂而缜密的系统。在功能类型上，中东铁路建筑群几乎囊括了当时人类生产、生活所涉及的所有建筑类型，每一种建筑类型都有着相应的空间形式及调度、组合手法：既有经典的轴线对称式平面布局，又有代表工业文明的大空间机械厂房。在建筑风格上，中东铁路建筑群以带有铁路工业特征的俄式建筑风格为主，兼有新艺术运动、古典主义等多种风格特征，它们有的呈现为独立的风格样式，有的则以折中或混搭的方式表现，而伴随文化交流衍生的中西混合样式则成为东北地区原生建筑文化的典型代表。整体上看，非中心站点城镇的建筑大部分呈现带有标准化设计痕迹的俄式风格，保证了该线路上的建筑群体风貌的一致性。在技术形态上，传统工艺延续与现代技术实践并行。中东铁路沿线建筑以砖、石、木混合承重以及木刳楞为主要结构形式，石（砖）拱结构多应用于桥梁。新的结构形式探索则包括金属框架结构、金属桁架结构、钢筋混凝土承重墙及框架结构等。这类结构一般用于工厂车间、机车库等空间跨度较大的建筑中。值得一提的是，中东铁路沿线大型钢结构铁路桥在结构的设计和建造工艺上已经达到极高的水准。中东铁路在技术理念上秉承俭省的工业设计思维，如建设过程中就地取材、合理利用材料特性、完善的采暖与通风设施、精细化的节点构造等，采用低技术的设计与建造策略应对寒地气候，为地域建筑技术的探索与发展提供充足的实验样本。

在文化遗产较为稀缺的中国东北地区，中东铁路作为一条完整的文化线路所具有的价值弥足珍贵。对这份遗产的历史信息与保存现状的调查、价值评价体系的建立以及保护策略的制定等一系列工作是建筑历史及文化研究者迫在眉睫的任务，也是不容推卸的责任。

# Preface
# The Diversity of Architectural Heritage along the Chinese Eastern Railway

Located in northeastern China, the Chinese Eastern Railway (CER) was built by Tsarist Russia in the late 19th and the early 20th century. The total length of the railway is 2,489.2 km. The main line runs from Manchuria to the Suifen River and the southern branch goes from Harbin to Lüshun across four different Chinese provinces. In the course of decades, thousands of transportation, industry, military, public, residential buildings as well as various railway projects and municipal facilities have been developed along the railway. After a hundred years of history, the architectures preserved along the Chinese Eastern Railway are undoubtedly a valuable cultural heritage with far-reaching significance and unique features.

There is large amount of architectural cultural heritage along the Chinese Eastern Railway, containing a great diversity of representations and strong regional characteristics in the application of functional types, art forms and technical materials. This is because of distinct architectural traditions among various ethnic groups living along the route, (b) experimentation with and exploration of new technology and materials during the modern transformation, (c) the historical dynamics of each particular time and place, (d) various forms of cultural diffusion, and (e) the vast and rich natural environment surrounding the railway. Therefore, it is important to comprehensively analyze the level of technological development as well as the social and cultural environment of the time when to interpret these architectural heritage.

## 0.1 Historical development

The Chinese Eastern Railway was a transnational railway born out of the political demands at the time, thus faithfully recording a snapshot of world history. On the one hand, the macro-strategy of Tsarist Russia's geopolitics established its leading style and basic pattern; on the other hand, the changing times and varying ownership greatly increased the diversity of the architectural heritage. In the same period, under the impact of industrialization, the world entered a time of technological and cultural transformation, either practicing new knowledge or clinging to tradition, either piecemeal improvement or cutting a new path altogether. The crossroads of civilization evolution creates a complex but vibrant scene. These developments were like a surge of electric current flowing through the rail of the Chinese Eastern Railway into the land of Northeast China, which made this cultural marginal zone join into the tide of world development.

### 0.1.1 Manifestation of geopolitical change in the modern world

The Chinese Eastern Railway as a transnational railway began with the construction of the Siberian Railway in Tsarist Russia. In the 1830s, as capitalism developed in depth, Russia urgently needed to open its markets and acquire more raw materials. Therefore, it was proposed to construct the Siberian Railway to the east where industrial and commercial development was backward but rich in mineral resources. In the 1840s, along with the gradual maturity of railway industry, the worldwide construction of the railway network began, which reached a climax in the 1850s and 1860s. This attracted a lot of capital investment and accelerated the development of cities and the accumulation of wealth. At the same time, the global focus turned to the Pacific coast, which was of strategic significance to establish a transportation connection between the central region and the Far East of Russia. In the 1860s and 1870s, the Great Powers went into a frenzy to carve up the world, and the European and American countries rushed into the Asian market, presenting Russia with unprecedented competitive pressure. In the 1880s, the competition between Russia and the Western powers in the Pacific coast and Central Asia became increasingly sharp. To deal with possible conflicts and control the border areas, a convenient railway line was necessary to provide strong military support.

It could be seen that before the 1880s, the Siberian railway scheme originated with the big landlords and the bourgeoisie, emphasizing their economic benefits. In the mid-1880s, following the changes in the international situation, the emphasis came to lie on the national military strategy, when this railway turned into the transportation route for military supplies. The raw material supply to the Russian defense industry finally became the international strategic tool, in which Russia would mastered the initiative by strengthening the trade advantage and the competitive confrontation in Pacific region on political, economy, military between Europe and Asia. Thus, the construction and operation of the Siberian Railway, as a national project, were combined with military expansion, economic planning and political strategy. Under this situation, the Siberian Railway by using the National Funds began the construction project from the eastern and western ends of both Vladivostok and Chelyabinsk in 1891. This railway was opened to traffic in 1904, but the work continued until 1916.

In the actual operation of the railway construction project, due to many difficulties, the original planned route was abandoned because the distance was proved too far with much long revenue cycle. Hence, the project plan needed to be revised (for further control the northeast region of China). "It is more economical and advantageous to link Vladivostok and Siberia through Manchuria", so the Russian government decided "to borrow land for building roads" from the Chinese government, via the northeast China connecting the Far East town and Vladivostok.

In the middle of the 19th century, Tsarist Russia terminated the Treaty of Nerchinsk, instead signing Aigun Treaties and Beijing Treaties between China and Russia with the Qing government, incorporating the north of the Heilongjiang River and the area to the east of the Wusuli River into Russia, which made the eastern part of Russia more closely connected with the northeast of China. The Qing government then signed the Sino-Russian Treaty so that both could "resist their common enemy and help each other". This treaty allowed Russian warships to enter any Chinese port in a state of war, to build a railway through northeast China to Vladivostok, and to use the Chinese Eastern Railway to transport soldiers and supplies. The signing of the Sino-Russian Treaty ensured the legitimacy of this cross-border railway. In 1897, Germany occupied Jiaozhou Bay and Russia forced China to lend Lüshun Dalian Bay on the basis of "fulfilling the mutual aid agreement against the enemy" in the same year. In 1889 the Treaty of Land (Lüshun Dalian) concession was signed, giving permission to build railway from Harbin to Dalian. Given the vicissitudes of the international situation, Russia was constantly adjusting the national strategic direction and its trade policy with China, which determined the spatial pattern of the Chinese Eastern Railway and affected the final direction of its route in a large part.

In June 1898, the Chinese Eastern Railway Engineering Bureau, sited in the Xiangfang district "Tianjiashaoguo" of Harbin, announced that construction of the whole line of the Chinese Eastern Railway would officially start that Harbin would be the center with three branches—east, west and south. The construction started at the same time at six different points and on July 14, 1903, the Chinese Eastern Railway, crossing mountains and rivers for more than 2,000 km, was opened for traffic.

In Feburary 1904, Russia lost the Japan-Russia War and Japan thus incorporated the southern branch of the Chinese Eastern Railway (from Kuanchengzi to Dalian). Russia continued to control the branch line north of Kuanchengzi and the main line. At this point, the Chinese Eastern Railway was thus divided in a north and south part, the main northern line being dominated by Russia, and the south controlled by Japan, that is called, the South Manchuria Railway. The process of construction and development of the two sections of the railway was also on a completely different track, forming their own characteristics. The architectural culture on the main line was dominated by the western classical style and partly blended with the trend of the Chinese tradition and the northeast marginal culture. The southern branch line was developed in the trend of the Japanese style and Chinese tradition with modern exploration. Under control of Russia, the administration of the Chinese Eastern Railway held the power of executive management, judicial management and garrison in the subordinate area. The railway subsidiaries had formed their own "country within China" which was far larger than the ordinary leasing land, including many cities and towns that depended on the railway station. In the negotiations over the end of the war between Japan and Russia, the United States put forward an "open door policy", calling for the opening of subsidiaries of the Chinese Eastern Railway to western countries. Soon, goods from all over the world gathered in Harbin, making it the largest trading city in northeast China and the most prestigious cultural center in the Far East, absorbing technical achievements, art forms and cultural traditions of the world, thereby greatly expanding the cultural gene pool throughout the region.

In 1917, the "February Revolution" and "October Revolution" in Russia led to large-scale migration. Russian aristocrats, landlords, rich merchants, artists and engineers fled the country and traveled along the Chinese Eastern Railway to Harbin, Dalian, and even Shanghai. The arrival of these immigrants brought a great deal of money and technology, as well as the life patterns and cultural concepts of the Russian upper class society. The architectural culture and urban landscape of Harbin changed accordingly, tending to be clearly structured and representing luxuriant central city features. The immigrant population of other cities and towns along the route also increased greatly, and the development of the CER subsidiary towns had never been more prosperous.

The disintegration of the Russian Tsarist regime also made the Administrative Bureau managed by Russia government lose control of the Chinese Eastern Railway. On September 23, 1920, the President of the Republic of China declared the establishment of the Eastern Province Special Administrative region along the railway, which would take over the Municipal power of Harbin and the cities along the railway. On October 3, the Republic of China government temporarily took over the Chinese Eastern Railway. Regions along the railway began to establish governments and judiciaries at all levels, and the Russians living there no longer enjoyed extraterritorial jurisdiction. On May 31, 1924, the Republic of China and the newly established Soviet Union signed the "Sino-Russian framework agreement to resolve outstanding issues" and the "Interim Agreement on the Administration of the Chinese Eastern Railway", which stipulated the joint ownership and management of the Chinese Eastern Railway by China and the Soviet Union, that the railway was purely commercial in nature and under the control of both countries. The third country would be no right to interfere in the Chinese Eastern Railway affairs, that the future of the Chinese Eastern Railway could only be decided through consultation between China and Russia. With the aid of this treaty, the Soviet Union formally restored the rights and interests of the Chinese Eastern Railway and diplomatic relations with the Republic of China, after that the Central Government of the Republic of China approved the Eastern Province Special region as a special administrative region parallel to the province.

In January 1925, the Soviet Union under a private deal with Japan unilaterally declared to recognize the provisions of "the Treaty of Portsmouth" against "Sino-Russian framework agreement to resolve outstanding issues". Although Zhang Xueliang launched the Chinese Eastern Railway incident in May 1929, aiming to recover railway sovereignty, it ended in failure. In 1935, the puppet government of Manchukuo, controlled by Japan, bought the Chinese Eastern Railway and its branch lines from the Soviet Union with 140 million yen. So far all the political, military and cultural forces of the Russia had completely withdrawn from northeast China, where the urban economy along the Chinese Eastern Railway had also changed from prosperity to decline, and construction activities had stagnated. Japanese immigrants and railway workers made adaptive use of the original Russian buildings, only partially reconstructing and expanding to meet their own living habits. Therefore, the urban structure and architectural form of the CER trunk line almost maintained the characteristics and features in the period of Russian rule. The traditional Russian and Art Nouveau architectural style were nearly all preserved as the main tone of the architecture.

On November 5th, 1937, Japan and the puppet Manchukuo signed the "Treaty on the Revocation of Extraterritorial Jurisdiction and the Transfer of Administrative Power of the Railway Adjunct" in order to transfer all civil buildings, sanitation, roads and Chinese schools to the government of Manchukuo, except for the type of buildings used by Japanese subjects, such as shrines, education and military facilities. On February 11, 1945, the United States, Britain and the Soviet Union signed the "Yalta Agreement" in Yalta of the Soviet Union, which seriously damaged Chinese sovereignty. It stipulated that the Chinese Eastern Railway should be jointly operated by China and the Soviet Union. In August, the Government of the Republic of China and the Soviet Union signed "the Agreement on the Changchun Railway in China", which merged the Chinese Eastern Railway and the South Manchuria Railway into the "Changchun Railway", controlled by China and the Soviet Union. On December 31, 1952, the Soviet Union completely returned the Chinese Eastern Railway to China.

The modern world situation of ups and downs, as well as the local political environment of China gave birth to the Chinese Eastern Railway, which also shaped the cultural connotations and actual features of the CER dependency territory (which is the deep reason to form the Architectural Cultural Heritage of the Chinese

Eastern Railway). Its main body is composed of Russian architectural culture, and also contains a great diversity from variation and integration of different architectural cultures and their coexisting characteristics through the time passing.

### 0.1.2 Characteristics of technological exploration in the period of civilized transformation

In the second half of the eighteenth century, the Industrial Revolution in England and the democratic revolution in France led to a transformation of Western civilization, which then spread from the center of origin to the whole western world, and to the rest of the world during the expansion of Western civilization. The Industrial Revolution had brought unprecedented technical support to commercial production, so that the invention and application of different kinds of machinery had greatly improved the production capacity and efficiency. The coal and steel industries provided the raw material based on large-scale mechanized production, whose transportation industry supported by railways and ships had met the demand for the expansion of industrial production in depth and breadth.

Because the traditional handicraft products gave way to the industrial standardized products produced by machine, social and economic relations also began to change. Agriculture and construction turned to commercialization, where the attention of the industrialists turned to capital accumulation and capital operation. The further development of the bourgeoisie required the establishment of a regime and discourse system conducive to their own to adapt to the social organization and lifestyle of the industrialized economy. The democratic revolution would completely change the old and anachronistic social, cultural and political models. This was the most important step in the self-transformation of Western civilization, since then the West and even the whole world had entered a new era.

In the process of civilized transformation, the development of science, technology, art and culture had entered a confused period. On the one hand, the new function needed to match the new spatial form, and the new spatial form needed to seek new technical support. On the other hand, when the new technology had not been formed, the form of traditional structure and materials had to be maintained. In the same time and space, the maintenance and improvement of the existing technological tradition and the keen innovation supported by new science coexisted, where and when there was an infinite possibility in all directions, and impossible to label.

The construction of the Chinese Eastern Railway coincided with the comprehensive period of civilized transformation after the Industrial Revolution, during which technology adapted to the development of the new era had achieved some results, but was not yet fully developed and matured. At the same time, the traditional technology had not been completely abandoned. Under the demand of rapid construction, the systematic and experienced structural forms and construction methods of the architecture displayed more operational use and practical significance.

In terms of quantity, the structure and material types of the architectural heritage along the Chinese Eastern Railway were mainly in the traditional form, including brick (stone) masonry structure, wooden structure, arch structure and so on. Under the guidance of the concept of standardized design and construction, these kinds of structures ensured the rapid completion of railway engineering. At the same time, the architectures with the traditional structure as the main body were also the most representative of Russian architectural culture and tradition. Improvement and perfection of traditional structural forms supported by industrial technology could often be used in the buildings along the railway, such as the general use of corrugated arch structure in the basement or ground floor of multi-storied buildings. This kind of structure usually takes steel rail as the beam and has small brick arches between two steel beams. When to arrange them next to each other, a wave-like surface would be seen. The prototype of this structure is a common traditional structure in Europe, but in the traditional methods, where wood is used as the beam and the dome material is relatively random. This structural form was more clear and complete, which function after improvement was strong and unique in the construction along the Chinese Eastern Railway.

In all kinds of construction and engineering facilities along the Chinese Eastern Railway, many new structural forms had been used, including metal frame structures, metal truss structures, reinforced concrete structures, and suspension cable structures, etc. The new materials included metal, concrete, glass and so on. The investigation and application of these new technologies and materials were in different levels and ways. There was not only the direct application of modern technology, but also the experimental study of new materials and structures, most of which were used in the railway engineering facilities with highly technical requirements such as bridges and tunnels. For a large number of metal railway bridges along the route, the material selection, structural form and joint construction mode were all given in standardized treatment, and the use of material characteristics and specific expression forms were better considered, which had become a quite mature technical system. Until now, most of the bridges are still in function and the main structure is well preserved, which fully proves their high technical level. Because the large span structure was used in some rectangular locomotive depots and other industrial buildings along the railway where the traditional wooden roof truss was unable to meet the needs, most of the buildings adopted steel roof trusses, without a uniform style. For example, the roof trusses in various types along different branches of the Chinese Eastern Railway were used, such as fink roof trusses, composite roof trusses and right angle triangles. A large number of bunkers along the railway were built that looked like a laboratory of new materials. Since such defensive buildings were built with high structural and low functional requirement, they were all constructed of concrete with a little or no reinforcement. This building wall was extremely thick with much low space and material utilization ratio.

Another common way of exploring technology in the construction along the railway line was to amalgamate the new materials and technologies with traditional ones. This kind of architecture generally took the traditional construction as the main body, and then to partially joint some new technology or materials together. For example, the fan-shaped locomotive depot is in masonry, whose exterior wall with a buttress wall is the main body of the structure. The roof is a cylindrical structure made by reinforced concrete, but the structure unit are repeatedly arranged, the metal roof is overlaid, and steel columns form a steel frame structure supporting the inner space. Although the exterior form of the depot is in the traditional masonry style, its internal structure type, material application and the space form express the strong industrialization characteristics. There are some new materials and technologies just using in a small scale without obvious features. For example, steel beams (mostly rails) are used to replace wooden beams in the local space of the buildings, or steel beams are used in cantilevered parts such as staircases and balconies of multi-storied buildings, where some floor slabs are poured with reinforced concrete.

Both the skilled application of Russian traditional technology and the experimental exploration of modern structures come along the rich and diverse natural environment of the Northeast region, and are all expressed regionally according to the climate and geological conditions. A few adjustments in technical adaptability also enriched its diversity. The Northeast China was a closed and backward society at that time, so that combination of the new technology and old tradition was a remarkable achievement.

**0.1.3 Development of artistic diversity**

The change of the technology and tradition in the period of civilized transformation was rapid and violent, the form of social organization and ideology took second place, and the transformation in art was left behind, which typically requires a longer period of adaptation than that of the first two. Therefore, the exploration of artistic expression seldom goes hand in hand with technological exploration. In architecture, the new technology and structure often match the classical art style in order to adapt to fit the mainstream aesthetic demand in society. However, the new materials and structures inevitably represent their unique artistic characteristics, so that various local or global attempts at new artistic expression come into being.

In the construction period of the Chinese Eastern Railway, the exploration of pre-modernism had made some progress. Metal materials were widely used in construction, whose characteristics and standardized production trait had broken through the aesthetic framework of the original classical style. In addition, the Art Nouveau Movement and the Art Deco Movement also became in vogue, which opened the way for the later emergence of the modern architecture. In the 1920s, when the railway construction was completed and the affiliated towns developed rapidly, it was just the embryonic period of modern architecture. However, this wave did not enter the areas along the railway, so the main architectural style in the town construction was still the traditional western style at that time. In this context, some architectural styles could just come along with the Chinese Eastern Railway, including Russian traditional rural pastoral architecture, classical style represented by Classicism and Eclecticism, Art Nouveau and Art Deco style, and modern industrial architecture style.

Among many styles, the traditional Russian architectural style is the main style, and the church buildings with the typical Russian Orthodox style is the best represented. Due to the dominant position of the Orthodox Church in the secular and spiritual life of Russia, church buildings are essential in any settlements, that were built in almost all station area in different scales along the route. In the small and medium-sized towns formed by the second and low graded stations along the route, the church buildings are mainly in wooden structure, which are built in standardized design drawing according to the scale of different site, such as the Sherafim Church in Manchuria, the church of the Virgin Mary in Hengdaohezi, and the church of Sergei in Yimianpo. These kinds of church buildings are exquisite and complicated in decoration, picturesque disorder in shape, rich in Russian national flavor, which generally become the most magnificent building in town. The St. Nicholas Cathedral in Harbin was constructed in a wooden structure and with an unique onion-style dome, which appearance was fitted into a central city. The buildings combined Orthodox masonry with the onion domes are relatively rare, mostly concentrated in Harbin and other large cities, and only a few scattered in small and medium-sized towns. Russian traditional pastoral architecture is the largest and most widely distributed, which is the main part of the CER architectural heritage, including masonry, "Mukeleng" and plate wooden buildings. These buildings have simple sloping roofs, with brick, stone and wood as the main materials, brick making patterns and wood carving as the main decoration, most of which are the residential buildings and small public buildings. From the quantitative point of view, these buildings are the main part of the CER architectural cultural heritage, setting the main style trend. The western classical architecture style mainly concentrates in the trunk line around Harbin and Dalian of the southern branch line and other big cities, but still a few exists in the other cities and towns, whose style includes classicism, baroque, Renaissance, Gothic, and some rare foreign architectural styles like Jewish, Islamic, German, American, Italian, etc. These styles are limited in number, rarely presented as an independent style, hardly mixed with other styles. Those architectures are generally used for the public and commercial buildings along the city street, which are an important part of the city. Although those buildings are the product of the economic development stimulated by the railway and have become a part of the architectural cultural heritage along the Chinese Eastern Railway, it is not directly related to the railway, for instance, different kinds of business buildings, banks, theatres, shopping malls, consulates, office buildings, and so on.

The architectural styles springing from the CER construction included modern industrial architecture style, Art Nouveau, Art Deco and so on. The style of modern industrial architecture is mainly manifested in the large-scale industrial buildings along the route. The application of new materials and technologies on the buildings embodies the technological concept and construction logic of industrialization, which also maintain the traditional masonry expression in appearance. This feature is evident in the locomotive depot buildings of different sizes along the route. Although their internal space and structure are to meet the industrialization demand, it is the traditional brick style that dominates the external appearance. The biggest difference between the locomotive depot and other masonry buildings along the line is in the building size, where the extraordinary scale of the railway industry is represented in both the whole and the part components. The railway locomotive depot has the characteristics of unit space, external outline is unified with the interior space, and the mansard roof on the facades is repeated many times, which becomes a typical form symbol. Another type of building with the characteristics of industrialization is the railway factory workshop, the famous example of which is the Harbin Railway General Factory.

The most outstanding architectural achievement of the CER subsidiary is the building style of the Art Nouveau Movement. This style is characterized by romantic and free curve decorative elements, which are often shown in the shape of doors and windows or handrails and other metal components. Although the Art Nouveau style only lasts a short time and is soon replaced by a new architectural trend in the true sense, there are still a number of Art Nouveau buildings along the Chinese Eastern Railway with high (artistic) quality. This kind of building includes small senior official residences and large public buildings, such as Administration Building of the Chinese Eastern Railway, Harbin Railway Station, Manchuria Railway Station and Suifenhe Railway Station.

Several senior official residences located in the Nangang District of Harbin greatly reflect Art Nouveau style feature in both overall outline and local details. The most typical example in formal language of the building is the Harbin Railway Station. However, all kinds of metal components in Art Nouveau decorative pattern are widely used in many buildings, which are also combined with other styles, forming a special architectural performance in unique characteristics. The Art Nouveau style is mainly concentrated in more developed cities along the line as Harbin, and is rarely found in other low-grade sites where to use this kind of decoration just as symbol of embellishment, for example, the wall decoration of a small house in Yimianpo as well as the typical Art Nouveau language of three vertical lines used at the entrance of Fulaerj sanatorium.

Another characteristic of the CER architecture is how to express the Chinese traditional architectural language within the Russian style buildings. At the same time, Chinese native craftsmen also actively studied modern technology and created unique artistic forms by combining the local traditions with western styles.

## 0.2 Cultural diversity in architectural heritage along the Chinese Eastern Railway

The construction and operation of the Chinese Eastern Railway is a typical process of cross-cultural communication, including a collision and combination of different democratic cultural traditions, different ways of life, different levels of social development and geographical environments. The architectural heritage of the Chinese Eastern Railway is the objective evidence and phenomenon of cultural spread and diffusion, which reflects the diversified cultural choice and acceptance mode of the cultural subjects, as well as the cultural transfer mechanism under the different traditions. The inclusive cultural ecological environment ensures the richness of the cultural gene pool and provides the basic foundation for the cultural fusion and variation, which is the deep reason for creating the diversity of cultural phenotype and regional styles.

### 0.2.1 Cultural migration and diffusion in the marginal wasteland

Before the Opium War, China was a typical agricultural civilization country with a long historical culture and slowly backward evolution. The closed door policy leaded the marginalization of China during the transformation tide of the modern world. The failure of the Opium War in 1840 marked the collapse of modern China's defense against the West. Facing the war failure as well as advanced science and technology, the traditional Chinese culture almost lost its competitiveness. The Westernization Movement set off a conscious and active exploration aimed to make China a more powerful country, while to introduce new technology and study the Western system. This technological worship formed a situation of overall acceptance of "western technology". Traditional technology and culture were set aside, even blindly denied and abandoned. This modern exploration, accompanied by cultural loss and transformation pains, is the evolution epitome of modern Chinese culture.

Northeast China, where the Chinese Eastern Railway is constructed, has always been a culturally marginal area of Chinese civilization. The native culture of the region is a subspecies of the orthodox culture of the Central Plains, where the cultural environment is relatively simple. The background of its traditional culture is weak, so that even no subject culture can compete with the foreign culture, causing it to be a cultural wasteland as a whole. This is why the CER culture with the typical characteristic of the region could be spreading. For example, before the construction of the Chinese Eastern Railway, some towns developed along the railway lines were still primitive villages, with farming, fishing and hunting as the main mode of production. Some towns were even uninhabited then.

Therefore, the original population along the CER trunk railway area was thin and the local construction was wild. After the later developments, the population was mainly Russian technicians and workers immigrated from Russia and other foreign countries, craftsmen and coolies gathered from the Central Plains of China. By comparison, the southern branch area had a stronger connection with the outside world, and the local towns had a certain population scale and construction foundation, where the local traditional characteristics were also more pronounced.

In general, the survival pressure, the instability and the cultural isolation in the marginal areas make it more active and changeable than that of the core areas. In this regional condition, the competition pressure of foreign culture was small, which allowed it to be more easily accepted and widely spread out, thus providing favorable soil for dispersing diversification of the railway culture along the Chinese Eastern Railway. Under the influence of the route construction, the modern transformation in this region was getting ahead, instead of originally backward.

The spread of railway culture in the Chinese Eastern Railway is a typical case of migration and diffusion. Due to the specific construction mode, the railway had completed the main project and opened for traffic in a very short time and an astonishing speed because of sophisticated early planning, functional design and construction concepts, as well as a cohesive national force and all available resources that could be mobilized through national efforts.

In the practical operation, the rapid construction mostly requires technical support of modern engineering, while the standardized design concepts is used in the most effective way. Some elements of the buildings along the route, such as door and window joints, wooden beams, timber columns and metal structural parts of bridges, have all in standardized design characteristics, whose specifications, sizes and patterns follow a certain rule to use for transportation and installation. The size, spatial form, functional layout, structural and external form of a building are also referenced by standard drawings in this approach. For different size of stations, there is a corresponding type of housing, which are designed according to the actual needs of different settlements. The functional layout of the town also has a standard planing pattern related to the site's function and the demand. This kind of rapid construction reflects the styles and features of most main cities and towns, that has greatly affected their final form.

On the other hand, due to the topographic complexity of Northeast China, the standardized urban layout model can only be used as a reference, which needs to be adjusted and modified in facing different natural environments. For example in the Yimianpo and Zhalantun stations, because of the flat terrain and beautiful scenery, the urban structure surrounding them can be arranged according to the standard design. At the same time, depending on the natural landscape, the town park has been opened up for the local citizens, workers and officials near the site. But in Hengdaohezi, the buildings cannot be arranged in chessboard pattern due to the mountains. So, the church is sited in the high place of the town, and the locomotive depot is put in the flat place next to the railway lines. The military clinic and other buildings are located in the periphery. Residences are either on the hill or at the riverside, with a relatively free layout. Since there are the different resources in different regions, the buildings are constructed according to the rules of obtaining raw material locally, including stone, wood, or brick. Therefore, although the idea of standardized design is used in the CER construction, towns and buildings still show a variety of styles and features due to the complexity and diversity of the actual circumstance.

Because of the rapid construction process, the short reaction time and weak local culture, the technicians and designers of the railway construction became the direct carriers of culture. Therefore, as a source of culture, the architectural tradition of Russia was transplanted to the cultural wasteland of Northeast China.

In the early days of the CER construction, there was a most serious cultural resistance called the Boxer Rebellion. During the movement, the railway lines and many related facilities were damaged and engineers were attacked, causing the project at a standstill, and then the Russian side sent more troops to guard the railway. This strong response to the local culture conflict would serve as a wake-up call to the engineering construction party, prompting them to make corresponding countermeasures. The most direct effect was that the building type and their macro-functional layout along the line had been changed by strengthening the military deployment. This cultural conflict was also a prelude to the cultural penetration and integration in the subsequent development.

After the railway opening, the construction did not stop and the various ancillary facilities along the line were made for further improvements. The process gradually transformed into the construction and development under the promotion of railway economic benefits. The station construction activities including the related industry, transportation and trade, attracted mass domestic and foreign immigrants, and some of the stations were gradually developed more and more prosperous, becoming important towns with considerable scale. In this process, the railway built and operated by the Russian side became a solid skeleton, along which the immigrants enriched the railway attachment like flesh and blood, making the affiliated places along the Chinese Eastern Railway full of popularity and vitality. In the prosperous period of the Chinese Eastern Railway, the route culture changed from foreign culture to integration and acculturation among different nationalities and different types, which is to influence each other and to make the culture into a new evolution process. Finally, the construction culture of the Chinese Eastern Railway was formed with strong regional characteristics.

### 0.2.2 Models of cultural choice

As the main carrier in the process of cultural transmission, the population is the main expression and container of cultural genes. For the Chinese Eastern Railway, there are two main types of population involved. The first is Russian immigrants, including technical engineers (and their families) involved in the early construction of the railway, workers and officials during the railway operation, and ordinary immigrants and businessmen in the later stages of development. The second type comprises native residents, including artisans and workers recruited from all over Shandong and Hebei Provinces for the construction, as well as later migrants. Different cultural subjects carry different cultural genes who have different selection and acceptance criteria.

The early designers mainly determined the technical and construction directions of the Chinese Eastern Railway. The technicians and designers from Russia carried authentic cultural genes and excellent professional ability, who could more accurately express their architectural tradition. It can be seen in the church buildings along the route, whose external form is relatively pure and construction technology is extremely sophisticated. It is a complete and accurate transplant of Russia traditional culture. During the booming period of the town development along the route, a large number of aristocratic capitalists made large investment in the city and employed professional architects and engineers to design these buildings, which usually was reflected in various traditional Western architectural styles, whose form and expression were also relatively sophisticated.

In the process of transplanting Russia's tradition directly, the designers and engineers also had a strong desire to learn and create new formal languages in architectural design, and to practice the former's art and technical forms of the times, such as Art Nouveau, Art Deco , and industrial architecture in various technical forms.

Besides, the designers at that time were also aware of the regional expression of architecture, and consciously explored it in practice. It can be seen in early design drawings that in almost all kinds of design scheme, the traditional Russian style is main part in which the Chinese traditional architectural symbols is involved, which is a typical example of Russian architects consciously selecting and drawing lessons from the elements of the Chinese architectural tradition. Only the designers received professional training in architectural design can be able to complete this kind of active exploration of architectural culture fusion, which is so valuable in design thinking.

In early construction, the architectural form was much uniform because of the fast speed and high standardization. After the opening of the railway, the construction activities of the ordinary Russian immigrants were carried out in the towns along the route, usually for residence purposes. The style of these buildings is relatively individualized, more dominated by personal interest, but still unified with the original urban architectural style and features on the whole. In this kind of architecture, the Chinese architectural elements are seldom found, most of which is generally to meet the needs of the traditional flavor of the Russian people.

The main labor force during the construction of the Chinese Eastern Railway was Chinese, including a large number of craftsmen recruited from the Central Plains. These artisans themselves had mastered the techniques and practices of traditional housing, who were familiar with the construction process and had rich construction experience. Compared with local residents and artisans, craftsmen from the Central Plains mastered many orthodox architectural techniques and art forms. In the construction activities, Chinese artisans naturally expressed their own architectural traditions within a new architecture system. For example, red brick walls are inserted with the gray brick to form Chinese character of " 喜 " in double, and other traditional Chinese patterns are carved on wooden elements, such as the beam head, the eaves board and so on. This is an unconscious culture expression of Chinese artisan and a concrete manifestation of cultural consciousness. Since Chinese craftsmen have no right to speak for decision-making of the railway construction projects, this kind of expression in the construction is only randomly reflected on the buildings.

In the fusion experiment design of Russian architects, Chinese traditional architectural elements is also a symbol extraction and stiff combination, which seldom reflects the deeper traditional dialogue. But in practical engineering, Chinese simple elements and practice was possible to be used in the actual structure and construction by Chinese craftsmen participating. For example, the combination of the Chinese traditional tile roof with Western masonry structures can be seen in the historical photos where some station verandas are covered by the tile roof, where the roof surface forms the inverse curve. This kind of construction can only be built with the participation of Chinese craftsmen. In whole process of the railway construction, Chinese craftsmen have always been the object of cultural transmission and passive recipients of technology and formal learning. For these Chinese craftsmen, the new architectural systems, unprecedented architectural style, modern construction methods and organization, as well as management modes greatly impact their original knowledge system, which provides a new way for them to actively reshape their construction thinking.

In the prosperous period of urban development, Chinese residents gradually gathered to form the cities and districts with strong local characteristics, such as Daowai District in Harbin. Within these areas, the Chinese craftsmen displayed their skills where Western architectural structures, material usage, spatial forms and artistic symbols were also used in the design and construction of all kinds of buildings. At the same time, their mature traditional skills were expressed freely, forming a clear personal architectural features of mixed Chinese and Western architectural culture. The design and construction of such buildings might still be done by those craftsmen participated in the railway construction, who could create new expression because of free design condition and different target audience. Here, Chinese craftsmen had the initiative to choose the necessary technical and artistic elements that showed a dual result through combining advanced technology with their own cultural tradition.

When the commerce became dominant factor in the development of the towns, the personal preference and owner's taste who had different professional features, nationalities and ethnic backgrounds had a great effect on the architectural style, which also represented person's national cultural tradition to a certain extent. This type of buildings are mostly commercial and public buildings along the street, not directly related to the railway. In addition, the emergence of the information media, such as architectural drawings, picture albums, photographs and even film images, the pattern of cultural communication had been changed to a large extent, promoting the flow of different cultural genes and making cultural choice and acceptance spreading in large environments, over longer time and wider spacial scale. One of the internal driving forces for diversity of the architectural cultural heritage is an information carrier in culture transmission along the Chinese Eastern Railway, as well as the reaction mechanism, public types of active selection and passive acceptance.

### 0.2.3 Cultural expressions with equal emphasis on inclusion and innovation

The architectural style of the Chinese Eastern Railway embodies the characteristics of multi-cultural juxtaposition and free synthesis. This dialectic idea is directly reflected in all architectural activities and the local artistic expression. The artistic features of architectural culture along the CER line show in two characteristics as tolerance and innovation. Tolerance is displayed through the diversity of architectural culture, mainly reflected in the multiple artistic styles as above mentioned. Innovation is the result of cultural exchange and a unique style from the participation of different cultural subjects and the integration of different cultures. One of the most important manifestations of Sino-Russian innovative cultural dialogue is the "Russian-Chinese combination" architecture which is the mixture of the traditional architectural styles of Russia and China, and made up the original architectural style of the Chinese Eastern Railway. This kind of "combined" performance vividly represented two kinds of culture interaction from shallow to deep fusion processes.

The early fusion architecture directly transplanted Chinese traditional architectural symbols and symbolic language to the main body of the Russian masonry architecture, which has achieved the result of "combination" by visualization. The internal space structure of the building is for meeting the needs of the modern function or Russian life style, but the material selection is mostly based on local materials.

In the aspect of concrete building style, most of these buildings draw lessons from the way of Chinese traditional big roof practice. The buildings adapt the overhanging gable roof, where the roof and ridge is straightness with the two ends different from each other. The roof of many important buildings has the inverse practice, where the main ridge has a pattern, such as dragon grain, the two ends have the tail of an owl. There is a specious vertical ridge, on which the decoration is indicatively used of an indeterminate number of immortals and animals. These practices do not have a fixed model or rules, which allows free combination, forming a variety of image effects. The most direct combination of typical elements between two architectural traditions is the Chinese roof and the main body of Russian masonry, many examples of which can be found in the records of engineering drawings and historical photographs. However, there are a few examples of actual remains, presumably because this kind of method is not mature in construction technology and practical application, and do not stand the test of time. Chinese traditional decorative motifs also appear on the eaves, such as wooden cross vertical bands at both ends of the roof, half header in shape of pomegranates and peach (symbolizing longevity and fertility) on the canopy, carved lotus flowers and birthday cake, as well as other Chinese traditional auspicious patterns. Individual buildings also have stone walls with carved peach shapes, or with different colors of brick masonry showing Chinese character in the double " 喜 ".

Another kind of combination is the integral insertion of the unit space, where the small volume unit space in traditional Chinese style is directly attached to the main body of Russian style building. For example, the greenhouse in Russian masonry building is built in a Chinese wood structure. This type of building is rare, but can be found in design drawings and historical photos. Compared with extracting single elements, the utilization of this complete space unit indicates the Russian architect's growing understanding of the Chinese wooden frame building style, referring to the demand for spatial forms and artistic elements. The actual frame is still constructed like the sunshine room in Russian-style. Nevertheless, it is a further step towards integration of architects and engineers in their architectural culture. Another example is to add a Chinese anteroom, pavilion or archway in front of a typical western-style building. It can be seen from historical data that the Chinese elements in the combination are relatively independent and pure in style, where they do not appear in the architectural drawings on which they are attached. It is supposed to be completed by Chinese craftsmen, forming a simple juxtaposition of two kinds of traditions. These practices are often used as above mentioned, such as western style buildings with Chinese greenhouse and the main roof with some Chinese elements.

The deep integration of the CER architectural culture also includes the combined utilization of Chinese and Russian architectural structure and construction technology, which are displayed as references and enrichment at the spatial level. Technically, the designer had investigated the structure of the Chinese roof truss and eaves, the practices of Chinese large roof, and learned the material properties and using methods of the fired tile. As designers know well these practices and techniques, Chinese traditional elements are more and more integrated into Russian architecture organically and naturally. For example, on the roof structure of some Russian buildings, the Chinese beam-lifting roof trusses can be seen. This phenomenon takes place in all actual construction process, as a result of the interaction between Russian designers and native craftsmen. On the space, the roof of some station buildings is connected with the rain shed, which makes the roof an extending arc, which is very similar to the eaves corridor space of traditional Chinese building. But it is hardly to be remained because the roof is too long and the structure can not withstand the heavy snow in Northeast China in winter.

Although the above-mentioned integration, the buildings are still mainly in the Russian style. However, with deep understanding of Chinese traditional architecture and practice of the basic technology, Russian architects start to design the buildings in Chinese traditional way, such as Harbin Puyu Middle School, the twin castles and Ashhe station (rebuilt in 1920s). From function point of view, the buildings were designed in modern plane pattern instead of the regular axis layout model. The appearance of the building is just in Chinese architectural style, with a little foreign cultural symbol. These buildings in combination of Russia design principles with Chinese traditional architectural language is the witness of the deep integration of architectural thinking under the different cultures. Therefore, Puyu Middle School was considered as being "an unprecedented architectural style" in the newspaper of the time. It is the first successful attempt to integrate the traditional Chinese architectural style with the European architectural style.

At the same time, native craftsmen start to learn foreign culture rapidly and make conscious attempts at integration of Chinese construction. They are not limited to the original structure and decorative logical framework in the construction, and actively utilize advanced architectural technology to select and reconstruct various architectural patterns and artistic styles according to their own understanding and preferences. Meanwhile, a unique, vibrant architectural style is created by adding the traditional cultural elements. The most typical example is the buildings in the historical and cultural blocks outside Daowai District of Harbin, which are generally in brick-and-concrete structures, with various western elements freely added to the brick wall, but the styles of each element have been redesigned with Chinese folk symbols inserted. Behind the street lined with the multi-storied buildings, there is a large space in multi-depth courtyards with the outlay pattern of Chinese traditional Chinese courtyards. As a whole, it gives people a familiar, active and unique feeling.

The cultural communication in the Chinese Eastern Railway subsidiary is a process of two-way selection. In terms of cultural expression, integration ensures sufficient raw materials of cultural elements that is the basis of the fusion in subsequent developments. And the innovation is from the interactive process of imitation, learning and deep communication. Through collage, juxtaposition, reconstruction and other operation methods, the unique artistic style and regional specific outlook are generated.

# ARCHITECTURAL CULTURAL HERITAGE OF CHINESE EASTERN RAILWAY

## 0.3 Origin of diverse functions of the CER architecture

Railway industry is a huge and complicated modern technology system. The construction and operation of railway industry need the cooperation of many departments and professions. Despite strong technical and professional properties, it is also linked with ordinary life and economic activities of human being. The functions of the Chinese Eastern Railway architecture are complete, reflecting the social environment and artificial scene of the the railway subsidiary region, in which the different architectural types emphasize the different sides of the CER architectural culture. The railway stations along with their subsidiary buildings and the railway industrial buildings along with their engineering facilities both represent the characteristics of modern traffic industry and the level of industrial technology. The buildings of military and police station are the reflection of the turbulent international political environment and the violent cultural situation in the process of cultural communication. The residential buildings of the railway community embody the characteristics of the immigrant culture of the railway-associated area at the lease land and immigrant settlement. The city streets, public and comprehensive service buildings outline the speed and level of the urbanization of the railway dependency.

### 0.3.1 Comprehensive functional requirements of the railway industry

The supporting facilities along the railway line needed in operation mainly include railway industrial buildings, stations and ancillary buildings, roads, bridges and other engineering facilities. These buildings were firstly constructed which had become the basic element needed for the railway opening. Some buildings, such as low-grade stations, locomotive depots and so on, were built as temporary buildings in simple form at the beginning of construction, which were rebuilt and improved gradually after the railway opening to traffic, forming the present appearance. Other buildings and facilities were designed to meet the special operation requirements under the technical constraints of that time, such as water towers for steam locomotives and fuel filling points. Although such buildings have lost their original functional significance in the context of modern technology, they still reflect the characteristics of the CER era and technology well.

A railway station and its ancillary buildings mainly include a station building, machine garage, locomotive depot, management building, freight yard, water tower, work area and other ancillary facilities. These buildings are the main part of the railway's operation, management, maintenance and repair, which are also the basic elements and the core contents of the line. There are some other buildings as the supporting houses of the station main body, which are set up around the station. The station house is the marked building of the railway, which is not only a best carrier of the architectural style but also a window to directly reflect the architectural culture of the CER railway. In the CER construction, the stations were divided into five grades from high to low, which scale and shape were determined according to their importance and main functions on the basis of the standardized drawings. Later, along with the development of railway traffic, some new stations were constructed and the grade of the existing stations were also adjusted. Many temporary stations in the early stages of the CER construction were rebuilt on a large scale. The new buildings, with the higher quality and rich artistic level, came into being. Some important buildings in Harbin, Suifenhe and Manchuria station, are in typical architecture style of the Art Nouveau with beautiful shape, advance structure and high application value. A beautiful building is a artwork that can enhance the image of the city. In the existing historical document, a non-constructed design drawing of Dalian station on the southern branch line can be seen, where the building is in large scale and the exterior details are gorgeous, the style is as good as Harbin Railway Station of that time.

Railway is the symbol of industrial civilization, where the buildings greatly reflected the characteristic of industrialization is the locomotive depot. This kind of building is a large store space for storage and maintenance of the train locomotives, which consists of three parts: storage room, radial track and circular tank platform. The mechanical storehouse is constructed of large number of modern materials, such as metal and cement, where to form high, deep and large-span space units by modern structural support systems, and then according to the needs of scale, many units are combined together in a fan-shaped plane pattern, which shows a clear tendency of the standardization design for construction. The locomotive repair house is also a special mechanical storehouse, which is a place for repair and maintenance of the locomotives, normally in the small numbers with rectangular plain layout and no need to borrow the circular tank platform.

The water tower is an important type of building attached to railway station along the Chinese Eastern Railway, whose function is to replenish water for the train and to supply water for the railway factory and the residential area. The water tower in Russian style along the CER line is basically a standard design product built according to two sets of final drawings. There are narrow and long lighting windows on the base of the water tower, whose function is to serve for observation and shooting, so the water tower also plays a certain role of military defense. The water tower, with its concise outline and rich decoration, is an marked symbol of the architectural cultural heritage of the Chinese Eastern Railway.

Some auxiliary buildings, such as work-area houses, are built for the line maintenance and protection. These buildings appear in groups, usually in the form of a courtyard layout, which can be divided into two types: walled and non-enclosed. Other buildings, such as freight houses, management rooms and locomotive depot offices, are mostly located in large scale stations, most of which are satisfied with freight trade, storage, station management, with the similar type to the local buildings. There are also some small types of buildings mostly close to the railway line, but not nearby the station, such as water pump house, road guard room and other buildings.

Railway industrial buildings are mainly some factories related to the material manufacturing, machinery manufacturing and maintenance. The large industrial buildings are not only to promote the development of industrial technology, but also to exhibit the level of construction technology at that time. The earliest industrial buildings along the Chinese Eastern Railway were the large factories where to produce railway materials, to assemble and repair machinery and equipment. Because the production mode of modern industry emphasizes the continuity of mechanical operation and the flexibility of space, the basic requirement of the factory space is tall, broad and far-reaching. Due to its large scale, high investment and advanced space technology, Harbin General Plant of the Chinese Eastern Railway became one of the comprehensive complex with much high modernization level at that time, which included 11 branches, such as the steam locomotives, passenger cars, truck maintenance and so on.

Railway engineering facilities mainly include a large number of bridges, culverts and tunnels along the route, which are the technical support of the construction and continuous operation of the CER route. Their distribution characteristics depends on geographic environment along the railway area, which is the best evidence of human wisdom against natural resistance. The CER construction with great skill and high technological level shows a great value in the cultural heritage of the Chinese Eastern Railway. There are many types of bridges along the Chinese Eastern Railway, all representing modern technology, either traditional stone arch bridges or steel bridges. According to the span numbers, the stone arch bridges are divided into single arch, multi-span and continuous arch structure, both ends of the bridge body would be designed one or two small steep arch for reducing self weight of main bridge structure and against flood waters. The metal bridge with small span is a plate iron bridge without bearing column in the middle, which is built directly on both sides of the foundation. Large and super-large metal bridges usually use steel truss structures and masonry piers with concrete or stone. Most of the bridges were built between 1899 and 1903, when much advanced structure and new materials were used, becoming one of the highest achievements of the construction technology along the Chinese Eastern Railway at that time. Culverts are engineering facilities to protect the railway foundation, most of which are built in masonry by stone materials and very large in number. Part of the culverts with much large scale and clear vertical space also play the role of walking corridor for the people on both sides of the railway. There are many mountains in Northeast China, where many tunnels have been dug along the Chinese Eastern Railway. Among them, a spiral line at the entrance of the Daxing'anling tunnel was built to raise the rail elevation within a limited distance. Some tunnels were decorated with Art Nouveau patterns, where the blockhouses were built at the important entrance of the tunnels.

These buildings and engineering facilities are the physical Heritage of the Chinese Eastern Railway, which reveals the complexity and comprehensiveness of the railway industry self.

**0.3.2 Requirement of urban life and management in the railway dependency**

Railway construction and management is a huge and lasting systematic engineering, the technical workers and the specialized managers are also needed even after opening to traffic. At that time, because most of the land along the CER route were wild areas without any construction background, the basic and urgent things was to create comfortable living conditions to meet the need of builders and their family when to construct the railway infrastructure. Therefore, a large scale of the residential buildings and communities of the railway came into being.

Houses in the largest proportion of the CER buildings, are all coming together with transportation facilities in all the stations. Because large numbers of immigrants flooded into the area, the residential buildings were more and more needed. There are many kinds of residential buildings in dependent territory of the Chinese Eastern Railway, which has become a unique cultural phenomenon. Those buildings are classified into three basic types: single-family residence, joint-family residence and collective residence.

Single-family house is a relatively high-grade residential form that most officials of the CER administration own. The houses in two stories were located in the superior parts of the city, with well-designed, rich functional and the most popular style in Art Nouveau at that time, some of which had official use. This type of residence is mainly located in Harbin, representing the architectural culture characteristics of the central city. Other towns also have a few number of single-family house, in relatively low grade and small scale, but the style is also unified with other residential buildings in the town.

Joint-family house is the main residence types of the CER buildings, not only in the largest number but also in the highest level of standardization. This kind of residence generally has low building density, flexible layout and strong adaptability to the environment. It can be arranged both as a courtyard to form "garden house" in pastoral landscape, and also in a linear type along the street to form a beautiful street space. In some small stations, it is mostly distributed freely. The typical combinations of the Joint houses are: two families type, three families type, four families and multi-families type. The plain layout of these houses is very compact, where usually all household unit is tightly jointed into a compact rectangle, and only some small parts protrude out the plane outline, such as anteroom and sunroom, making the building in lower area of the outer wall, also lower heat consumption and cost, that is easy to build. This plane structure is divided into many different patterns according to scale and standard. There are many standard design schemes for joint house, which make them easily to combine with the sunroom, door bucket, corner stone and architrave skintle with different decorative patterns and different matched materials. Therefore, the outline of joint residential buildings looks consistent with each other, but different in detail, each of which has its own characteristics.

The number of the collective houses along the Chinese Eastern Railway is relatively few, but the style is more distinctive. The simplest type of the collective residence is an apartment or a dormitory with much simple space composition. In addition to the public toilet and receipt room, it is mainly consist of repetitive living units, most of which is located in the railway station area, such as the railway staff dormitory at Yimianpo station. There is another resident type with the characteristic of typical modern unit house, which can be divided into two or four families. The space and function of the house are able to meet all the daily needs, such as the collective houses for the engineers at Hengdaohezi station. This kind of residence provides a modern living mode and presents a new way of life and concept for the residents of Northeast China at that time.

Through further construction and operation of the Chinese Eastern Railway, more engineers, technicians and workers, as well as their families were stationed in the dependent territory where was gradually developed into a certain scale of immigrant settlements. In order to meet the needs of daily work and secular life of the citizens, as well as to perfect the city construction, abundant public buildings were built along the line, including office and municipal facilities, such as hospitals, schools, clubs, churches, baths, public toilets, parks and so on. These buildings directly or indirectly serve the railway construction and operation during the railway development. Despite no big amount, they greatly expanded the function types of the buildings, which also reflected the urbanization process of some important stations along the CER route.

In the early days of the railway construction, hospital buildings were the earliest types of public buildings because of accidents, diseases and conflicts with Chinese residents. The hospital of the Chinese Eastern Railway has been built in different sizes according to the station grade and population amount by the standard design drawings. General hospitals in large scale and full function were established in some important stations, such as Harbin Central Hospital of the Chinese Eastern Railway. This kind of hospital is consist of a medical building group in middle or large sized stations, with standardized design of single building or building group, such as Hengdaohezi medical building group. The small station usually has a simple clinic. Hospital buildings in superior circumstance also serve with recreational functions, such as Yimianpo sanatorium.

There are a large number of cultural and leisure buildings along the Chinese Eastern Railway, such as clubs, leisure hotels and sanatoriums. Most of these buildings are located in the relative big towns with beautiful landscape and excellent natural environment by hills and rivers. At the same time, the buildings are rich, active and diverse in style, forming an important urban landscape. Among them, the clubs have the most complex function that is also the most common, which brings citizens a western style of life, advanced cultural facilities and modern leisure idea of the railway line. In order to improve the urban landscape and enrich the leisure life of the residents, some parks are built in combination with the local environment, including corridor, water pavilions, hanging bridges, sculptures, etc.

Educational buildings along the Chinese Eastern Railway can be divided into specialized technical schools for training railway technicians or engineers and general schools for railway staff's children. Professional and technical schools are located in the large and major cities, such as Harbin, Dalian, Manchuria, and so on. General schools are usually combined with the church buildings in small towns, in a church school model. In larger cities and towns, general schools are built independently by special site selection and classified to primary schools and secondary schools, such as the Zhalantun Tsarist Primary School.

Bath is a building where to serve for the railway staff of the route. There were different sized bathes in different scale station which was built on the basis of corresponding standard design drawing. At some stations far away from the town, such as the train meet place and the work area, the bath is a kind of railway auxiliary building with standardized configuration in small size. Common bathing pool in the town is much large in scale and capacity. Other public facilities are generally small, which can provide great convenience for the daily life of residents, such as public toilets, boiled-water rooms, cold storage, cellar and so on. Though the public toilets are small in size and simple in function, the heating facilities and ventilation had been arranged.

The administrative office buildings in the railway dependent territory are mainly "the official buildings and administrative organizations of the CER headquarter and subordinate", such as railway negotiation bureaus, official mansions, business or law offices and so on. Most of these buildings are located in Harbin, Manchuria, Suifenhe and other important towns. Harbin Railway Bureau is the largest visible building in Art Nouveau movement style. The office buildings in the secondary towns are usually unified with the towns in architectural characteristics.

Orthodox church is the main religious buildings along the Chinese Eastern Railway and also the most representative of the Russian architectural culture which is mostly located in center of the town. Although there is no directly relationship with the railway construction and operation, these churches are indeed the most important spiritual place for Russian immigrants. Even in the early stages of railway construction, some temporary churches were still built for use, and large military churches were also needed by garrison.

In addition, after implementing the open door policy, the consulates were established in some important cities. At the same time, with the increase of commercial activities, a number of public buildings were constructed, such as finance, department stores, hotels and other business buildings, which were greatly enriched the architectural form along the CER.

As a historical carrier, these buildings delineated the life style of the residents and social development level of the cities in the dependent territory of the Chinese Eastern Railway at that time, and were also the strong evidence of the modern transformation of Northeast China driving by construction of the Chinese Eastern Railway.

### 0.3.3 Diversification of military functions at a special time and circumstance

Because of the special status of the CER line in politics, military, economy and local management, there was always a special troop sending by Russian to protect the railway, called the road guard. During the war or local war, there were a large number of troops on the way of the Chinese Eastern Railway. The Guards of the Chinese Eastern Railway were formed in 1897. Since Tsarist Russia had no right of garrison and railway guard given to protect the CER in articles of association of the Sino-Russian Joint Eastern Railway Corporation, the number of the railway guard as the first team was not a lot and also not the regular army, which could not meet the protection requirements of the railway line. With the acquiescence of the Qing government for the garrison of the first team, Russia began to expand the guard teams who were send to the other railway subsidiaries in batches. With the construction of the southern spur line in 1898, the demand for military force increased, and the number of the railway guards had reached more than 4,500 in 1900. In response to the 1900s Boxer Regiment Movement, Tsarist Russia continued to send more troops about 11,000 soldiers to guard the Chinese Eastern Railway, including artillery, which also changed the functions of the railway guard from defensive to offensive. This transformation was also reflected in the later building construction.

Because there were more and more Russian soldiers of the railway guard after the first expansion, according to the strategic position of the different stations, Administration Bureau sent different scales of troops to the stations with corresponding arms. The military personal and facilities were assigned to different echelons and gradually established the military force distribution system in different levels, for instance, in Harbin as general headquarters, in Fullerji, Yimianpo, Tieling and other places as sub-headquarters, after that appropriate adjustments would be made with the changes of the situation. At the same time, in order to ensure the safe transportation of all goods needed for the railway construction, some troops are sent to the key areas far from the railway line where the buildings were constructed to meet the living and storage needs of the soldiers.

During the Russo-Japanese War, the Chinese Eastern Railway undertook the task of transporting and supplying the main materials and troops, which became the lifeline of the Russian army. In order to strengthen the protection of the lines, additional protective facilities and fortifications were built in the Outer Amour military region. Meanwhile, the auxiliary buildings were built, such as first aid stations and storage. This period was the golden age of the military building construction along the route, whose scale and style are basically formed. At the end of the war, Russia lost most control of the southern spur lines, and began to strengthen the military deployment of the railway trunk line, reaching a maximum of 70,000 soldiers in the Outer Amour military region.

Since then, domestic turbulent situation of Russia also impacted and weakened its military strength in the CER subsidiary areas. After the October Revolution, the number of the railway guards decreased greatly, and almost disappeared in 1920. The construction of military buildings and fortifications had basically stalled, the remainder of Russian forces tried to reorganize the railway guard teams, but no success. For a long time, the railways were jointly managed by Russia, China and Japan, when the large-scale military construction along the Chinese Eastern Railway by Tsarist Russia also stopped. It can be seen that the construction scale and layout of military buildings along the Chinese Eastern Railway are greatly influenced by the international and regional environment at that time, also reflecting the complicated historical pattern of modern Northeast China. At the same time, the CER Administration Bureau was in judicial autonomy of the dependent territory, where the police agencies along the railway were set up. In this context, the military buildings and facilities, such as headquarters, barracks, stables, ammunition depots, bunkers, police stations, prisons and so on, emerged in large numbers and become unique architectural types along the railway line.

The headquarters is the highest ranking military building along the Chinese Eastern Railway. In 1901, Russia attributed the CER guards into the "Amour military region", which general headquarter was set up in Harbin. The guard army also had headquarters in some key military garrisons, such as Boketu and Hengdaohezi. The headquarter provides office or assembly space for officers and soldiers, where to serve for both a military administration and an official business comprehensively. Unlike barracks and other military buildings, the headquarter is generally located in center of the town, such as the headquarter of the Outer Amour military region, which was located in the administrative center of Harbin, Nangang District, and Boketuu Command was also located in the central area of the town. Headquarter buildings are generally multi-storey buildings, which tends to be unified with the public buildings of the cities.

Barracks is a group of military buildings, where is normally located outside of the town, including stables, officer's residences, canteens, confinement rooms and storage buildings. The barracks of the Chinese Eastern Railway was used for the railway guards, which were the resident buildings with military nature and a standard design drawings, whose architectural scale and pattern tend to be consistent. There were also a large number of barracks in non-standardized design, whose building floor number was not limited to single-storey, such as Manchuria East Camp. The size of barracks could be adjusted according to the number of soldiers and usually by width reduction or increase in direction. The form of small barracks may be similar to ordinary residences, while large barracks may be up to 90 meters wide, such as Ang'angxi Barracks. The stables are a kind of nearby buildings in the cavalry barracks for the railway guard and also a unique type of architecture. Formally, the stables are similar to simplified barracks, whose walls are usually arranged with high windows, and roofs are often provided with ventilation windows. The interior space is simple and the standardized stable is arranged with two rows of stub pillar. In small cavalry barracks, stables are generally simpler, similar to a storehouse. If necessary, some common civic buildings are temporarily able to be used as the stables. Another type of military building with a strong characteristic is ammunition depot. According to the plan drawing, it can be found that the layout and orientation of the ammunition depot are a little far from the barracks, where not only easy to access, guard and manage, but also to prevent unnecessary casualties and incidental losses caused by the explosion. Its architectural form is much unique, generally with outline in semi-circular and internal space in barrel-shaped. Other storage rooms for military materials and equipment are generally simple in space form and non-distinctive in external form. The officer house is not very different from the ordinary railway house.

There were a large number of the work areas and small subcamps within a certain distance along the railway line. The work area far from the town is usually the same as the small camp, with defensive walls and functional buildings arranged as a courtyard space. There are tall and strong bunkers at the ends of bridge or tunnel entrance, such as Xing'anling Bunker, Fularge bridgehead, etc. These bunkers are of concrete, with thick walls and unadorned surface. In addition, there are watchtowers and outposts along the line, and water towers also have the functions of observation and shooting, all of which belong to military buildings to a certain extent.

The police station and prison buildings are mostly located inside the town. The police station is similar to the barracks, whose building is similar to a civil buildings which is in harmony with the urban architecture style, such as the Boketuu Police Department, Zhalantun Forest Police Brigade, and so on. Prison buildings are usually built as a closed courtyard surrounded by a group of buildings, all cells with masonry, thick and unvarnished wall, such as Manchuria prison, Lü shun prison, and so on.

## 0.4 Regional and diversified architectural technology and material expression

Anthropologists generally believe that technological progress leads to social change and also influences ideology. Important scientific and technological inventions and discoveries are able to propagate and spread themselves, which is the direct driving force of cultural expansion. The architecture along the CER line embodies the diversity of architectural techniques and the way of material expressions, which includes both of the creative idea of the traditional construction activities accumulated from generation to generation, and the tentative application of modern materials and structural forms. The introduction of these two aspects is an important link in modernized transformation of Northeast China, not only in architecture but also in society. While loading this kind of diversified technology and material expression, native natural environment and the social cultural situation reshape them to a certain extent, forming a strong regional characteristic.

### 0.4.1 Requirement of construction technology facing complex environments

Application of diversified technology in architectural heritage of the Chinese Eastern Railway reflected a coping strategy facing special needs of the actual construction activities on the basis of the social background and the technical level at that time. Firstly, in order to meet the time requirements of large construction, the existed and fairly well-improved technical system should be used, such as the traditional wood and masonry structure, as well as their various deformation, which were normalized by the form of the standardized drawing to ensure easy operation against time-consuming by specific form design. Secondly, in order to meet the need of large span space structure of the railway industry, a mixed technical expression method was developed by introducing the steel frame structure system and various steel structure roof truss forms, combining with the traditional masonry method. Finally, the specific geographical environment and climatic conditions of Northeast China also affect the practical application of the technology, such as wall thickness, foundation depth, roof truss practices, and so on.

The traditional structure of the CER buildings is mainly a mixed structure with brick, stone and wood, in which a wood house made of round log and stone is the main wood frame style. The mixed structure is a frame system where the wood roof truss is supported by masonry wall. In some buildings of indoor space in large span or semi-open space with air corridor, the columns with brick and stone or wooden columns are used as load-bearing structure. For example, in barracks and stable buildings, a composite structure system is formed with a load-bearing exterior walls and a whole interior frame that the wood roof truss is supported by two rows of wooden columns. In the low-rise buildings with multi-spacial separation and small span, the wooden beams are generally used to support the floor or roof truss and exposed to outside, and the edges are cut. In some buildings, steel rail is used to replace the wood beam and flat arch is built between the rails. This form is mostly used in parts of the basements and stairways, without large scale and wide application. The actual practice of masonry wall is also flexible, such as solid masonry, hollow masonry and wall built in fill. The structure form of solid masonry wall is the best, the wall built in fill is simple, material saving and widely used, while the hollow masonry wall is not generally used for load bearing. Masonry walls are so thick and solid that they are used in almost all military buildings. Because of simple in construction technology, convenient in space separation, single and easy in material selection, low cost, small site and low floor, the masonry structure is adopt by most civil buildings along the line. In addition, as a traditional structure type, brick (stone) arch structure with long history is used mostly in bridges and culverts, generally in doors and windows of the buildings, as well as the entrance to a cave.

There are two kinds of wooden structure: wooden corrugated and wooden frame, among which the wooden corrugated structure is the traditional Russian residential structure style, which has the advantages of original ecology, simple construction, warm in winter and cool in summer, strong durability and so on. The wooden Mukeleng building is generally built on a stone foundation, whose wall is stacked of the log (or half round wood, square wood) by the tenon and mortise joint structure, being a typical log cabin construction. Most of this structural type is used in residential and church buildings. Wooden frame structure is similar to wooden beam-column structure system mostly used in the building door bucket, warehouse and toilet, which is generally built in single layer board as its maintenance structure. This structure can display a transparent and bright architectural expression with decorative effects, which is often used in air corridors, sunshine rooms, landscape pavilions, church bell towers and other architectural parts. The wood structure wall of the building itself has good stability because of light weight, low height and small load-bearing. The connection between the wall and the foundation of the wood structure building in mortise and tenon work is relatively flexible, where a certain deformation and movement could be produced under the condition of external forces, and also could be diffused. Many existing masonry walls have been cracked, damaged and deformed in different degrees, but the wood structure building is still in good looking, which directly reflects the advantages of the wood structure system.

New structural style is generally applied to the modern and special construction. For example, a typical steel frame structure is used in the internal support system of the fan locomotive depot. It is a special form of the reinforced concrete structure in a distinctive characteristic of large-arc and semicircle vault, which wavy continuous vault built-in steel keel is supported by hollowed-out steel columns. Metal truss structure is much advanced form of structure and widely used. The steel truss structure is firstly used in roof structure of the large span buildings such as railway factory and waiting hall of high-grade stations. The roof truss structure includes the luxury roof truss, the Fink roof truss, the composite roof truss, the right triangle roof truss and so on. It can be divided into single span, double span, three spans and multi span. The steel truss structure also has the typical application in the large-scale railway bridge, whose metal truss beam includes the top chord truss, the under chord truss, the conventional straight truss and so on. The early top chord truss is divided into curved top chord truss and straight top chord truss, which are mainly used for large railway bridges with large span and multiple spans. The whole structure of the railway bridge in metal truss usually shows the composite characteristics, with stone masonry as the pier, steel truss beam as the basic stylobate carrying the rails and deep tank foundation as the bridge basis. The large railway bridge in steel structure is one of the most great and typical industrial landscapes along the Chinese Eastern Railway. Small steel trusses are also found as a vertical structural components as the supporting structure outside the water tank of the tower. It can be divided into reinforced and non-reinforced concrete structures, including steel-concrete load-bearing wall and steel-concrete frame structure. Concrete structures were not widely used at that time, which was only used in buildings and engineering facilities with high strength requirements, such as the railway bridges and large bunkers beside the tunnels in non-reinforced concrete structures. Reinforced concrete structures are often used in construction as parts of the buildings, such as floor and roof, which are usually mixed with other structural forms. In addition, the steel suspension structure is a special case of the existing structure of the Chinese Eastern Railway, which is used on the suspension bridge of Zhalantun Park. A typical example of the comprehensive application of modern structure and construction technology was General Factory of the Chinese Eastern Railway. During construction of the 11 branch factories, two structure forms had been used, such as the wall and roof truss bearing, column and roof truss mixed bearing. The roof truss of the factories includes wooden roof truss and steel roof truss, the building wall includes brick wall and concrete wall, and the column has different types such as wood, reinforced concrete, steel column and so on. There are single span, two spans, three spans and even more span of the factories. The roof truss forms are also very diverse. Different roof truss forms are adopted to meet their respective needs in different space of the same building. The factory building has good natural lighting and ventilation design in full of technical rationality.

### 0.4.2 Suitable material selection supported by rich resources

Because the Chinese Eastern Railway line is located in the most prosperous area of natural resources in Northeast China, the rich forest and coal not only provide sufficient guarantee for railway operation, but also supply abundant materials for the construction of the buildings and facilities in the dependent territory. The extensive use of natural materials in building construction, such as wood, bricks and stones, has also become a major feature of the Chinese Eastern Railway architecture. The regional architecture combined local materials with the traditional Russia architectural techniques makes the buildings along the CER line with much rich exotic customs and distinctive regional color, which affects the landscape and characteristics of many towns along the line, and also becomes a decisive part of the architectural culture of the Chinese northeast region. In addition to these natural construction materials, the steel and concrete, which represented the advanced materials and technology at that time, also began to be used in construction of the Chinese Eastern Railway in different levels.

Timber is the most classical material in building construction of the CER line because there are the most abundant forest area in Northeast China. as structural materials,the wood is used as sleepers, walls, piles, columns, beams, roof trusses, also as wall panels, floors, insulation layers and other materials for enclosure systems, as well as decorative panels, embossed components, and other internal and external decorative materials. The wooden doors and windows are the most common use of the buildings, including all kinds of wooden doors, mosaic wooden doors and various windows. In addition, wood is also widely used as the construction modules of the railway engineering facilities and the scaffolding. Most of the wood components have splendid mosaic texture and fine decorative patterns, which makes the building much beautiful. For example, the outside wall of a Mukeleng building made of logs is usually covered with a layer of laminated planks, which are arranged regularly to form a beautiful rhythm, in which some of the strips are ended in a sharp, semicircular or other repeated forms, or placed on the middle of the wall or the gable wall, making the wall changeable in unity. Flooring in the interior space is a typical way to use wood as an enclosure material. There are two types of flooring, one is strip flooring, and the other is mosaic flooring. In the subsidiary building of the Chinese Eastern Railway, the strip wood floor is popular and common in the residence bedroom of ordinary staff, with long and unequal width, the aperture appears on the floor by flat connection. Another kind of flooring called parquet flooring is a relatively advanced method in interior floor decoration, which is often found in the official residence buildings of the Chinese Eastern Railway. Because of floor block in small size and having bevels, the floor connection is much closed when the floor panels are clicked together.

The wood's portability makes it one of the most decorative materials in the architecture of the Chinese Eastern Railway. No matter what is a wooden wall skirt of interior space or some decorations of exterior space, such as a veneering of the door and window frame, a canopy, an eaves board under the eaves, a staircase railing, a fencing board and other additional decorative components, they are made into different elements not only in beautiful silhouette ends, but also in ordinary decorative pattern of Russian folk houses with hollowed-out carving and lively fairy tale color. It is the most attractive part, both the building in pure wood structure and in brick (stone) mixed wood. During the construction process, wooden buildings or wooden components are often painted on different bright colors to protect wood materials, then giving wood buildings a rich Russian folk architectural characteristics.

There are rich natural stone resources in the area of the Chinese Eastern Railway, especially in the mountains of Daxing'anling, Zhangguangcailing and Laoyeling, where are full of granite and limestone. Stone is another important natural materials in the railway construction. A large number of quarries and gravel processing plants have been set up along the route, which is the main way of obtaining stone materials in the construction of the railway and different kinds of the buildings. Stone materials are an important structural materials, such as subgrade gravel, pier, building foundation, wall and ground paving materials, especially in bridge, tunnel and railway engineering. In architecture, stone is used not only as fundamental materials, but also as block materials of the bearing wall. The stone, as exterior wall material, can be assembled to display a splendid effect on the facade according to different stone quality, shape and color. In large scale public buildings, processed stone is also used as decorative surface materials. In stone masonry method, there are regular masonry and irregular masonry. The regular masonry of the stone materials is similar to the brick masonry, which is mainly divided into two ways. One is a horizontal masonry joint with staggered stone, and another one is a wedge-shaped vertical masonry joint with coupons. Irregular masonry can form similar honeycomb textures, ice cracks and other random forms, a typical example of which are tiger skin stonewalls. Generally, the wall surface made of the processed stone is flat, but the inner wall is usually filled with crushed stone, gypsum, lime and mortar, which are blended to a whole.

Clay brick is the most common artificial material in the CER construction, which is used to build the foundation of the buildings, bearing or separating wall, indoor and outdoor paving materials and so on. The bricks used in the building construction are divided into red brick and black brick. Russian-made red brick are mostly used in the buildings of the trunk line, in which the local black brick is only used in special positions, such as shadow decoration and corner coign, forming red brick as dominant materials and black brick as ornaments. A large area of red brick wall inlaid with black brick displays a strange color and decorative effect. On the southern branch line from Harbin to Changchun section, buildings are especially built with black brick, which is supplemented by red brick. Brick structure buildings occupy the largest proportion of the cultural heritage of the CER buildings, mostly bare walls with a paintcoat. According to the characteristics of brick size and modulus, the wall with different patterns and light-shadow effects can be built by simple brick-repeated masonry and complicated and changeable constructive combination. In practically processing, the brick is mostly used to build the flat wall, which is mainly in the form of horizontal brick masonry in different directions. This form is also used in construction of brick foundation, buttress, pedal, and so on. In addition, brick and stone materials are often combined to build the masonry walls. Generally, the main body of the wall is built with stone materials, and red bricks are used in place such as doors, windows and other openings, where to form regular shapes. Good result is obtained not only by using different materials themselves, but also by showing dramatic color with two material texture. Another kind of masonry composite wall is built of the outside wall with stone and the inside wall with brick, between which is filled in white ash as cohesive body.

Some buildings along the Chinese Eastern Railway also use the original Chinese tile as construction materials in Manchuria, representing an outlook of the Chinese traditional building, which is not used a lot in Russian style buildings. Other artificial materials, such as pottery, glaze and glass sheet, are relatively expensive and less used as building materials, which only appear on large public buildings with inner and outer eaves as a decorative elements.

The most important modern material in construction of the Chinese Eastern Railway is metal, which is widely used in railway engineering facilities and buildings, except for the rail laying the railway. During process of the railway bridges, rain shelters, overpasses, water towers and other engineering facilities, steel profile is the main or partial structural material, while the utilization of steel profile in buildings includes beams, columns, roof trusses, staircases and platform beams, etc. Besides, the decorative fence, staircase and balcony railing of the parapet, roof slab, protective roof, metal tile, drainpipe, vent, hinges, handles and other connectors are mostly made of cast iron or sheet iron. Metal railings are often decorated with Art Nouveau patterns, which represent a new art form of the CER architecture, while a large number of cast iron components and steel beam frame structures composed of steel column and beam embody the characteristics of industrialization and production. Concrete, as a new high-strength material and a typical representative of modern technological civilization, is also used in the Chinese Eastern Railway, but not widely. Generally, it is largely used in the railway engineering facilities and military facilities such as bunkers. In early construction of the large-scale public buildings and industrial buildings such as residential buildings and locomotive depot, concrete as an experiment material is often used to make floor slabs, which is often mixed with other materials. Glass has a large number of applications in building construction along the Chinese Eastern Railway, such as light window, roof light window, lighting ceiling and residential sunshine room. In addition, the surface of brick and wood buildings are often brushed with coatings or oil paint, not only to decorate the buildings, but also to protect the material decaying.

### 0.4.3 Multiple measures to deal with the geographical climate

In order to cope with the special regional climatic conditions in Northeast China, some constructive technology and special design method of the CER buildings were developed. These attempts, on the one hand, shape the personality of the buildings along the route, on the other hand, increase the diversity of building space and technology.

Considering the influence of high altitude, low temperature and other climatic factors, most of the towns along the Chinese Eastern Railway are located in plain areas where the terrain is flat and conducive to urban construction. Because the cities are mostly surrounded by mountains on east, west and north of the region, winter is less affected by cold monsoons, which could weaken the disadvantage of cold weather. The building layout in cold region has generally two types, including determinant and peripheral. To the determinant residence, the buildings in southeast-northwest orientation makes a parallel with direction of the dominant monsoon in winter, then giving building the best orientation and decreasing the direct influence of the northwest monsoon on housing. To the peripheral residence, the buildings in introverted layout show a relatively "private" inner space, where a closed microclimate environment is created to properly control wind and sand.

In the space treatment, brick, stone and wood are normally used to build the door bucket as a buffer space. After entering the room, the hallway is used as the next layer buffer. The design of multi-layer transition space greatly reduces the possibility of living space attacked by low temperature and snowstorm in winter. The entrance design to some large public buildings of the Chinese Eastern Railway is even more ingenious, where the height difference of indoor and outdoor is solved in the hallway instead of the steps outside. This is a very humanized design because the outdoor steps are prone to ice skidding in snow and ice environments, and the indoor steps are able to prevent people from falling over by snow and ice. At the same time, the indoor height difference can prevent the direct attack of the outdoor cold wind, which makes the cold wind accumulate in the sinking space and avoid the interference to other space. In order to reduce the proportion of the outer wall and avoid the excessive "cold mountain" wall, the shape of the building is relatively simple, and the plane of the ordinary building is usually in a regular rectangle. The buildings are linked each other in function, especially the contiguous houses which can makes full use of the heat exchange between households in winter and reduce the heat dissipation.

The building wall of the Chinese Eastern Railway is much thick up to the width in 1.5 m. In addition to the basic load bearing requirements, it is more important for demand of cold heat preservation. The composite walls in different forms are also structurally improved to enhance cold resistance. The building wall in brick and wood block appears more frequently used, whose outside wall is built with red brick and the real wall is built with two layers of wood block filled in sawdust. In general, the supporting structure of this wall is the two layers of wood block, whose external brick layer is later built as a "protective and decorative" material. According to the existing examples of more than 100 years, some sawdust within two layers of the wood blocks is still intact and dry, with good insulation properties. Sometimes, in order to improve the bearing capacity of the wall, the sawdust was partly replaced by some broken bricks. Another composite wall is called as "sandwich" wall, whose brick wall on both sides is filled in sawdust, or sometimes with mixture of sawdust and soil. This kind of the filling materials have advantages of low specific heat capacity and good adhesion, which are able to strengthen the insulation ability of the wall. At the same time, it is impossible to see its "sandwich" attribute outside the wall. Compared with the other two composite wall forms, this kind of wall has good performance both of the thermal insulation and structure. No matter what kind of wall, one side of the house surface is generally covered with a layer of slanted wood strips in mesh structure, on which a layer of plaster is covered to improve the wall insulation performance at the same time. In addition, in the Mukeleng wall, the gap between logs is stuffed into felt, hemp and other fibers, on which white mud is coated to prevent wind and cold, so that good insulation effect is ensured.

The roof trusses of most buildings along the Chinese Eastern Railway are wooden, in the form of single slope, double slope, four slope, compound inclined type and fold type, among which the truss roof frame with double slope is the most common. The sloping roof of the building, on the one hand, can meet the requirement of snow discharge in winter of Northeast China. On the other hand, this kind of wooden roof frame has created a triangular space as a air layer between the roof and the indoor ceiling, which is called as "stuffy roof". In order to keep the dry and ventilation of the stuffy roof, the ventilation window opening all year is often set up at the two sides of the gable wall. Meanwhile, the ceiling is covered with sawdust, wood chips and other materials in order to protect the winter cold wind.

The basement also plays a positive role in preventing cold and heat preservation, although there are different purposes to build the basement, such as storage function, equipment installation and other safety aims. However, as a transitional medium between the main body of the building and the earth, the basement, which is warm in winter and cool in summer, could greatly decrease the direct influence of the ground on the room temperature. At the same time, there is a certain air inter-layer formed by the wooden beams as a keel support between the indoor floor and the ground against moisture and cold.

In conformation of the building node, many detail designs can reduce energy consumption simply and effectively, such as the most typical structure of windows and doors. The gaps between the wood door-frame and the wall are sealed with felt and then is covered by triangular strip to prevent cold wind. For a unequal double door, when the door is closed, the bigger side of the double door has a cover plate to seal the door gas. Through different processing in details, some structural disadvantages of the doorplate are avoided for cutting off cold wind at the entrance. The building windows are generally small in size, with double-layers to form an air inter-layer. In order to increase the indoor lighting area, the window is usually designed to an inward bell window. There is a small vent window on the upper part of the window, which can avoid a massive loss of indoor heat and quickly get the air exchange at the same time. Both outside the middle sill and the low sill of the window are set up a wood strip, which inclines downward to make rain and snow water flowing directly to the windowsill so as to avoid heavy frost when the water enter the window. At the same time, the outer frame of the window like the door is also set a cover strip, so that the window seam after closing can be cover by it, to avoid the cold air directly entering the room.

At that time, the building interior was mainly heated by fireplace, wall heating and central heating system. Fireplace heating is a traditional heating method in Europe. It is an important facility and also an important decorative element of a family, which is introduced into the CER dependent territory by the line construction. Because the buildings were all built at a relatively fast speed, and the most residents were the railway workers with strong mobility and changeable habit. Therefore, a kind of closed fireplace in simple style, few decoration and multi-room heating was built instead of an open fireplace in the exterior gorgeous and strong belongings. This type of fireplace can be roughly divided into three types: round, square and corner. Firewalls can be divided into two types, the stove type and the independent type. The independent firewall was set separately up in a large wall area with fast heat dissipation and surface decoration, which mainly appeared in the corridors of public buildings and some official residences of the Chinese Eastern Railway. The stove firewall was a special design that combines the stove with firewall together. The stove was able to meet the daily needs of cooking, baking and boiling water, while to warm the rooms through the firewall. These heating methods awereonly used in the residential buildings. Most of the centralized heating systems were used in large public buildings, where the boilers are generally placed in the basement, and the heating radiators are built in the living space, which is a relatively modern heating method.

In addition, the ventilation system is generally designed in combination with the heating system in the building. The ventilation passage is set up next to the exhaust passage. The remained temperature of the cooking fume in the exhaust passage heats the air of the ventilation passage for air exchange by the principle of hot air rising.

### 0.5 Conclusion

During Qing Dynasty, Republic of China, Russia and Japan, as well as puppet Manchuria, the Chinese Eastern Railway has been more than a hundred years, bearing a historical rising storm, a lot more ups and downs in modern China, and recording the magnificent experiment of the regional modern transformation along the line. Culturally, on the basis of the railway industry civilization and as the representation of Russia-Japan immigrant culture, the construction of the Chinese Eastern Railway has a profound impact on the social structure, life mode, architectural style and settlement pattern of Northeast China, which has also formed an edge culture in difference from the key circle of the Chinese traditional culture. The inherent cause and the external form of an Architectural Cultural Heritage of the Chinese Eastern Railway have created a strong localized characteristics which has a very high historical and cultural value.

The architectural cultural heritage along the Chinese Eastern Railway, both in content and in form, all shows an extraordinary richness, integrity and uniqueness, which constitutes a complex and meticulous system with different cultural factors in the region. In terms of structures and patterns, the CER architectural complex includes almost all the types of buildings involved in human production and life at that time, where each building has own spatial form and combination method, blending of the classical axisymmetric feature in plane layout and large-space machinery factory representing industrial civilization. In terms of architectural style, the Russian architectural style with the railway industrial characteristics is the main type, combining with the Art Nouveau Movement, Japanese traditional and modern culture, classical, Islamic, Jewish and other styles, some of which are presented in an independent one and some are in the compromise or mixing style, while a mixed style of Chinese and Western from the cultural exchange has become a typical representative of the original architectural culture in Northeast China. On the whole, most of the buildings in non-central city stations show in a Russian style with standardized design trace, which ensures the consistency of the architectural community along the line. In the technical form, the traditional skill is practiced parallel to modern technology. The main structure form of the Chinese Eastern Railway is an mixed bearing pattern with brick, stone and wood, as well as "Mukeleng" building. Stone (brick) arch structure is used in bridge. The exploration on the new structural forms includes metal frame, metal truss structure, reinforced concrete load-bearing wall and frame structure, which are generally used in large-span spacial buildings such as factory workshop, locomotive depot and so on. It is worth mentioning that the design and construction technology of the railway bridge in large steel structure along the Chinese Eastern Railway have reached a very high level. On the technological concept, the thrifty industrial design thinking have been created, such as to obtain materials from local sources, to use material characteristics reasonably, to perfect heating and ventilation facilities and to design fine node construction, etc. The low-tech design and construction strategy are used to deal with the cold climate, which provides sufficient experimental samples for the exploration and development of the regional architecture technology.

In Northeast China where is originally short of the cultural heritage, the Chinese Eastern Railway is even more valuable as a complete cultural route. A series of works need to be done, such as investigation of the architectural historical information and conservation status, the establishment of the heritage evaluation system and protection strategies, which are an urgent task and important responsibility for the researchers of architectural history and cultural heritage.

# 1 站舍

中东铁路建成初期原有火车站点 104 个，按照级别分为一等站、二等站、三等站、四等站、五等站及会让站，这些站点留存有大量铁路站舍建筑。中东铁路全线竣工时，满洲里与绥芬河之间的主线和哈尔滨至旅顺的支线上共有 96 个客货营业车站。其中客运站舍占绝大部分，即铁路客运站房，指旅客候车和运营管理所使用的建筑。随着铁路交通的发展，一些新的站点陆续增补建设，原有站点也出现了级别变化。中东铁路建设初期的许多临时站点纷纷新建了规模更大、建筑空间质量及艺术水平更高的新站舍。

## 1.1 站舍的选址及平面布局

作为公共交通建筑，站舍通常选址在紧邻铁路且和城镇保持适度距离的位置。站舍建筑的功能涵盖了售票、候车、安检、办公休息等多项内容。级别较高的火车站会增加一些划分更精细的专用空间，如豪华候车室、寄存、茶饮等，站舍建筑的平面布局就是围绕这些功能展开的。整体来看，为了便于缓冲和疏导旅客人流，中东铁路的站舍平面大都以平行于铁路的方式一字排开。这些站舍从平面形式上看，主要可分为"山"字型和"一"字型两种。简洁的平面布局模式使站舍建筑的功能分区明确，交通流线组织合理，便于灵活调度。

高等级站舍的平面具有明显的中轴线，呈"山"字型布置，内部空间较大，平面布局舒展开阔，其形式体现了公共建筑空间的严整与恢宏。一般来讲，站舍建筑规模最大的主入口位于建筑的正中央，两侧有供工作人员和出站旅客使用的次入口。平面以入口处候车大厅作为大空间组织两侧不同功能的辅助用房。较高等级的站舍建筑会有多个空间较大的候车厅，一般以穿插辅助空间的形式将其连接，这样可使人群合理分流，节约空间且方便使用，如哈尔滨站站舍的空间处理就运用了这种手法。

中东铁路沿线最普遍的站舍平面形式为"一"字型，没有明确的中轴线。这种平面类型一般应用于等级较低的站点和规模较小的会让站以及站舍与轨道线退距较小的站区。内部空间没有明确的中心，一般集站内工作人员的使用空间以及乘客的候车空间于一体。这类站舍一般客流量较小，因此建筑体量也不大。主入口供站内工作人员与旅客同时使用，由于客流量较小，不需要较大的候车空间，其平面组织上结合站区工作人员的使用，站舍建筑功能复合化。部分站房还在室外设置灰空间作为临时候车空间，如安达站、昂昂溪站等。

## 1.2 站舍的标准化设计

标准化设计还被中东铁路工程师们称为定型设计。在进行标准化设计时，建筑师们主要控制两个方面：一是哪些级别的站舍需要标准化设计；二是设计的标准化控制在什么程度。从实际情况看，中东铁路站舍的标准化设计主要针对二级与二级以下站点的站舍建筑，这些站舍数量众多，适宜采用统一设计。其他一些大型站点的站舍则采用定制设计，如当时哈尔滨站、大连站的站舍，其规模、体量、形态在中东铁路沿线都是独一无二的。

中东铁路初创时期的铁路站舍是严格按照等级来修建的，初建成时期共设 104 个车站，分为五个等级。其中 1 个一等站，9 个二等站，8 个三等站。在形制上，除哈尔滨、大连以及满洲里、绥芬河等特殊位置的站舍外，大部分站舍建筑根据等级不同采用了相应的定型方案和模件化设计，采用统一设计标准。标准化设计是中东铁路建筑中的普遍现象，但在站舍建筑中体现得最为明显。一般来讲，二、三等站是按照同一种标准样式建造，四、五等站是按照同一种标准样式建造。采用定型设计的站舍在规模体量、平面布局、立面形态乃至建筑装饰等方面都大致相近，在一些细节方面根据所在站点的具体需求和实际情况进行灵活调整。

目前，中东铁路沿线站点还保存一些较标准的二、三等站标准化设计模式的站舍，如铁岭站、德惠站、扎兰屯站、昂昂溪站、安达站、一面坡站、穆棱站、海拉尔站等。按照标准设计图纸，二、三等站站舍为局部二层的小建筑，集转运、站长室、候车室于一体。候车室占据了一层不足 30 平方米的一部分。建筑立面上采用非对称式构图，楼梯间突出山墙，具有辨识性，也使建筑的形象中心非常醒目，变化丰富的坡屋顶使建筑轮廓生动灵活。建筑墙身和门窗部分分别装饰以精美的砖砌图案，机械化的标准化设计并没有减损建筑的艺术价值。

### 1.3 站舍风格的多样化

虽然中东铁路站舍的标准化设计现象十分普遍，但它们的建筑风格并不单一。相反，这些站舍更多地呈现出了风格多样化的特点：以铁路建筑风格为主，兼有俄罗斯民族传统、新艺术运动、折中主义、中国传统等多种风格与元素。如横道河子站舍是典型的带有俄罗斯民族元素的铁路建筑风格，哈尔滨、大连、满洲里及绥芬河的站舍设计采用了当时流行的新艺术运动风格，香坊站舍是以古典主义建筑风格为主的折中主义风格，双城堡和尚志站舍则以中国传统建筑风格为主。值得一提的是早期站舍建筑设计中均糅合了中国传统大屋顶的元素，极具地域化特征。

从近代发展的历史来看，中东铁路沿线相当一部分城镇的产生和发展都得益于火车站舍的兴建。因此，中东铁路的站舍建筑不仅仅是近代重要文化遗产的中东铁路的代表，也是依托铁路而形成的近代中国东北城镇体系的重要标志。部分中东铁路时期的站舍建筑经过改、扩建，当前仍然发挥着其功能，应该得到应有的保护。

## Train Stations

With the construction of the Chinese Eastern Railway(CER), 104 railway stations were built and ranked from 1st to 5th class, as well as the stops with passing loop. Soon after the completion of the entire railway line, 96 stations of them ran for passengers and freight, along the main line connecting Manzhouli and Suifenhe, and the south branch connecting Harbin and Lushun. Most of the station buildings were used for passengers and consisted of waiting rooms and administration offices. Following the development of the CER, new stations were gradually built, while some original stations' rank altered. Thus, many temporary stations built at the beginning of CER construction were transformed into those with large size, high-qualified space and high artistic level.

As built for public transportation, station buildings of CER were usually sited near the railway while keeping proper distances with cities and towns. They contained multiple functions, which determined the layout of the buildings, such as ticket office, waiting room, security check, offices and lounge, as well as some specialized spaces like luxurious waiting room, left luggage and bar in high-rank stations. Holistically, the station buildings stretched parallel to the railway line so that passengers could buffer and evacuate more easily, therefore their plans were mainly designed in two simple shapes of "I" and "E", providing clearly functional zoning, rational organization of traffic flows and flexible uses.

Standardization design, also named as stereotyped design by CER engineers, was largely applied in the railway design and construction, especially in the station buildings. Engineers mainly focused on two aspects, one was the rank of the station, the other was the degree of the standardization. In fact, standardization design was usually applied on the second and lower rank stations for their large quantity and high feasibility, while large stations as Harbin and Dalian adopted customization design in their station buildings for their unique size, volume and forms. Generally, the second and the third rank stations were in one stereotype, while the fourth and the fifth rank stations were in another. And those stations in the same stereotype were similar in scale, layout, facade, and decoration, but flexible in the details according to specific needs and certain situations.

Although standardization design was considerably common in the design of CER stations, the building styles were more diversified than monotonous, based on the railway building pattern and mixed with styles and elements of traditional Russian, Chinese, Art Nouveau, and eclecticism. For example, Hengdaohezi Station was a typical railway building in Russian folk style; Harbin Station, Dalian Station, Manzhouli Station and Suifenhe Station presented the fashionable Art Nouveau style; Xiangfang Station was characterized by eclecticism with classicism elements; Shuangchengpu Station and Shangzhi Station were figured by Chinese traditional style. It was worth mentioning that stations built in the early period of CER all assimilated the elements of Chinese traditional gable roof, which were extremely regionalized.

# ARCHITECTURAL CULTURAL HERITAGE OF CHINESE EASTERN RAILWAY

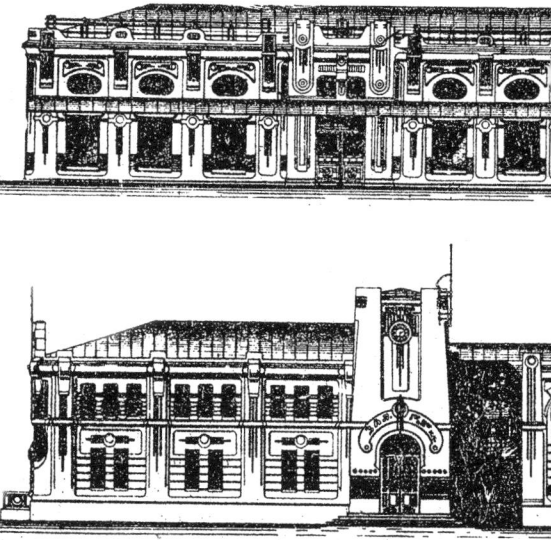

哈尔滨站历史照片 Historical photos of Harbin railway station

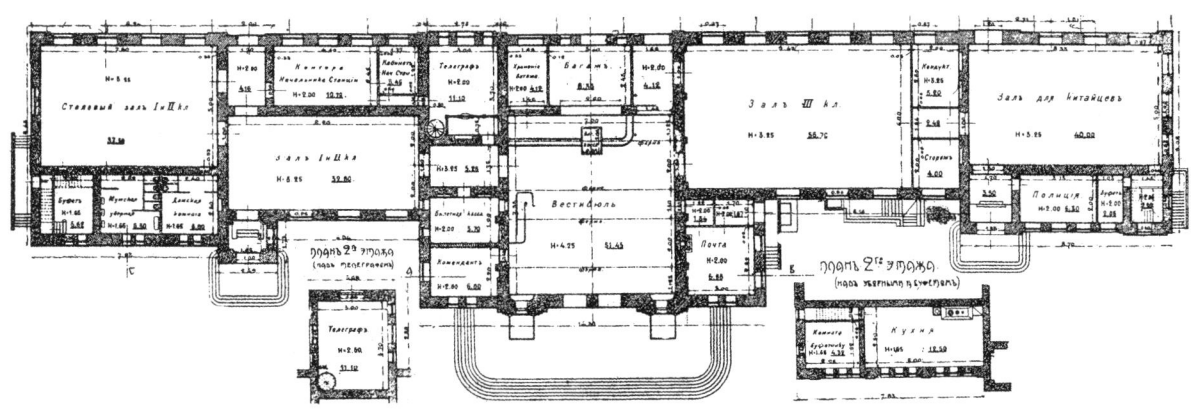

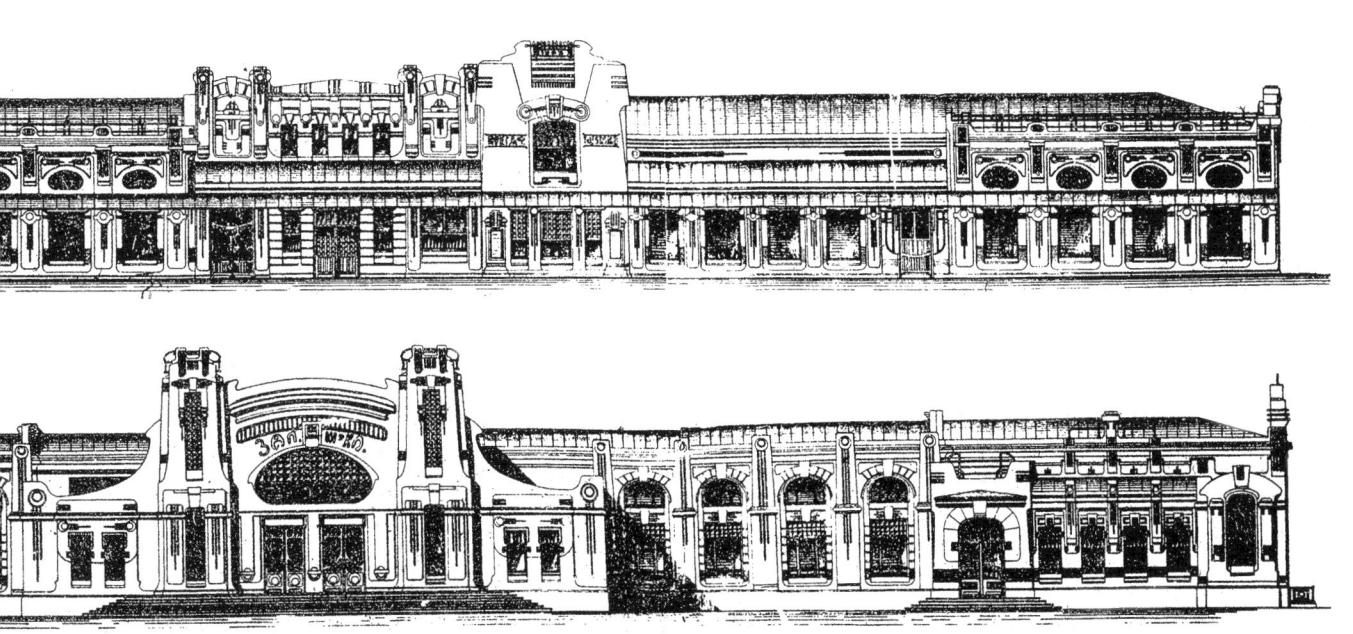

哈尔滨站设计图 Drawings of Harbin railway station

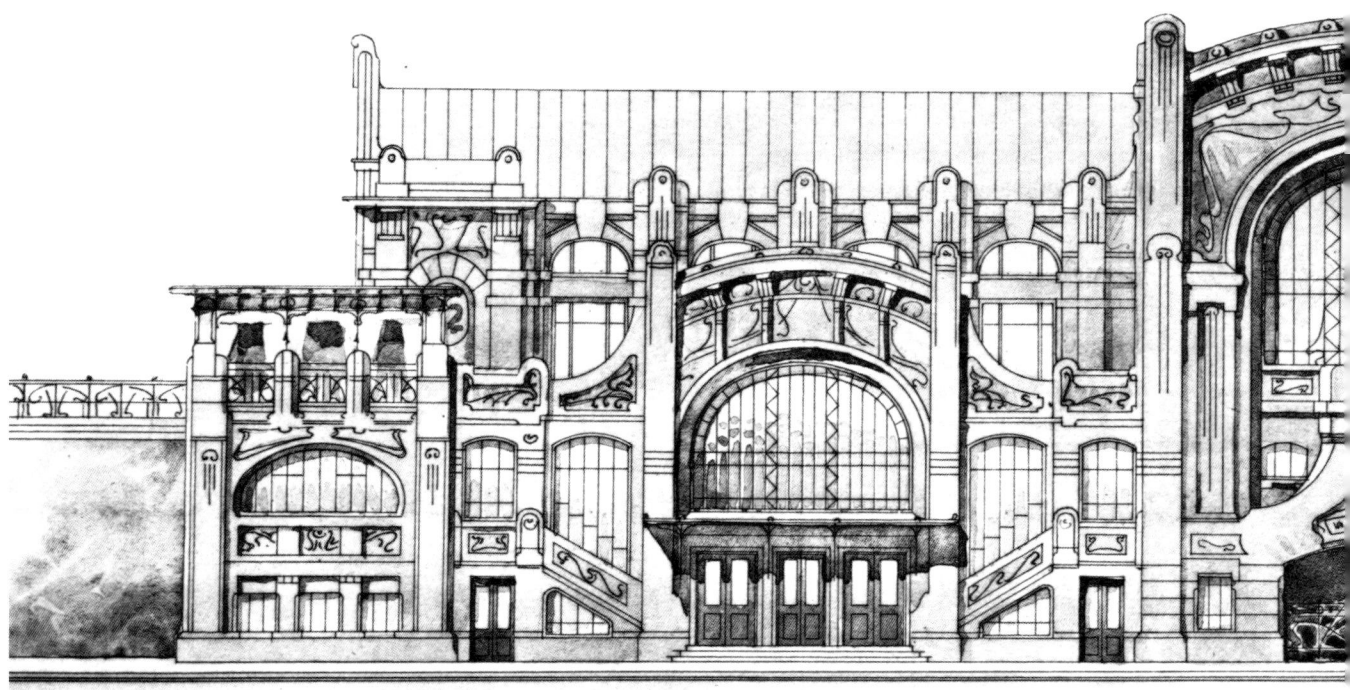

大连站设计图 Drawings of Dalian railway station

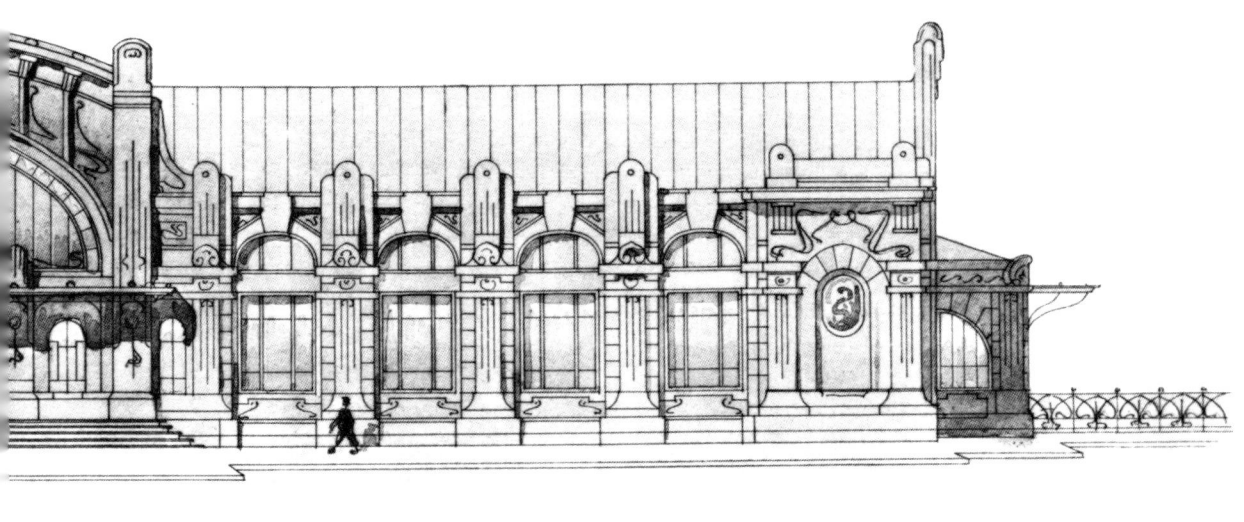

# ARCHITECTURAL CULTURAL HERITAGE OF CHINESE EASTERN RAILWAY

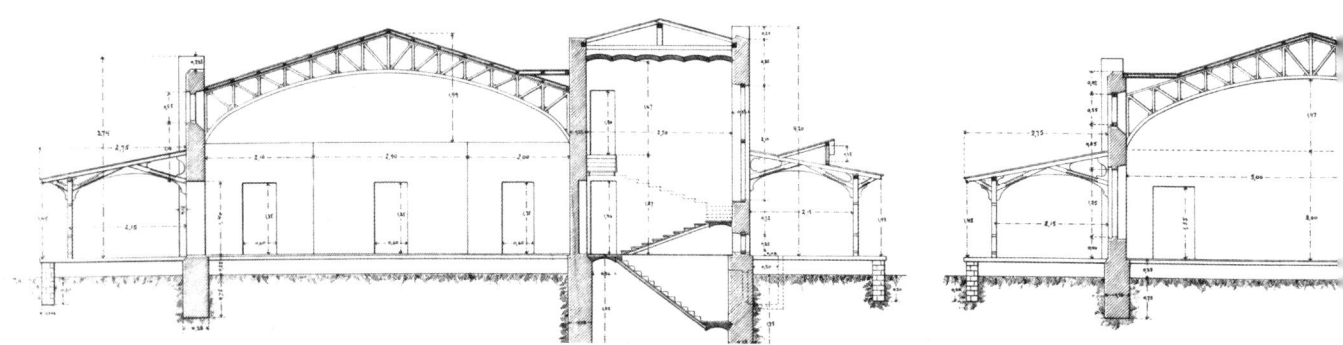

满洲里站设计图 Drawings of Manzhouli railway station

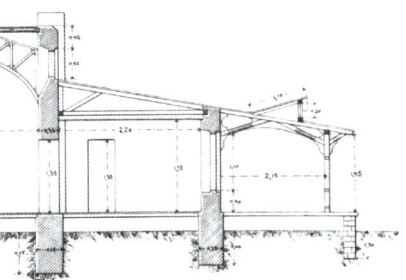

满洲里站（1995年拆除）Manzhouli railway station（demolished in 1995）

满洲里站历史照片 Historical photo of Manzhouli railway station

1 站舍

ARCHITECTURAL CULTURAL HERITAGE OF CHINESE EASTERN RAILWAY

绥芬河站历史照片 Historical photo of Suifenhe

绥芬河站 Suifenhe railway station

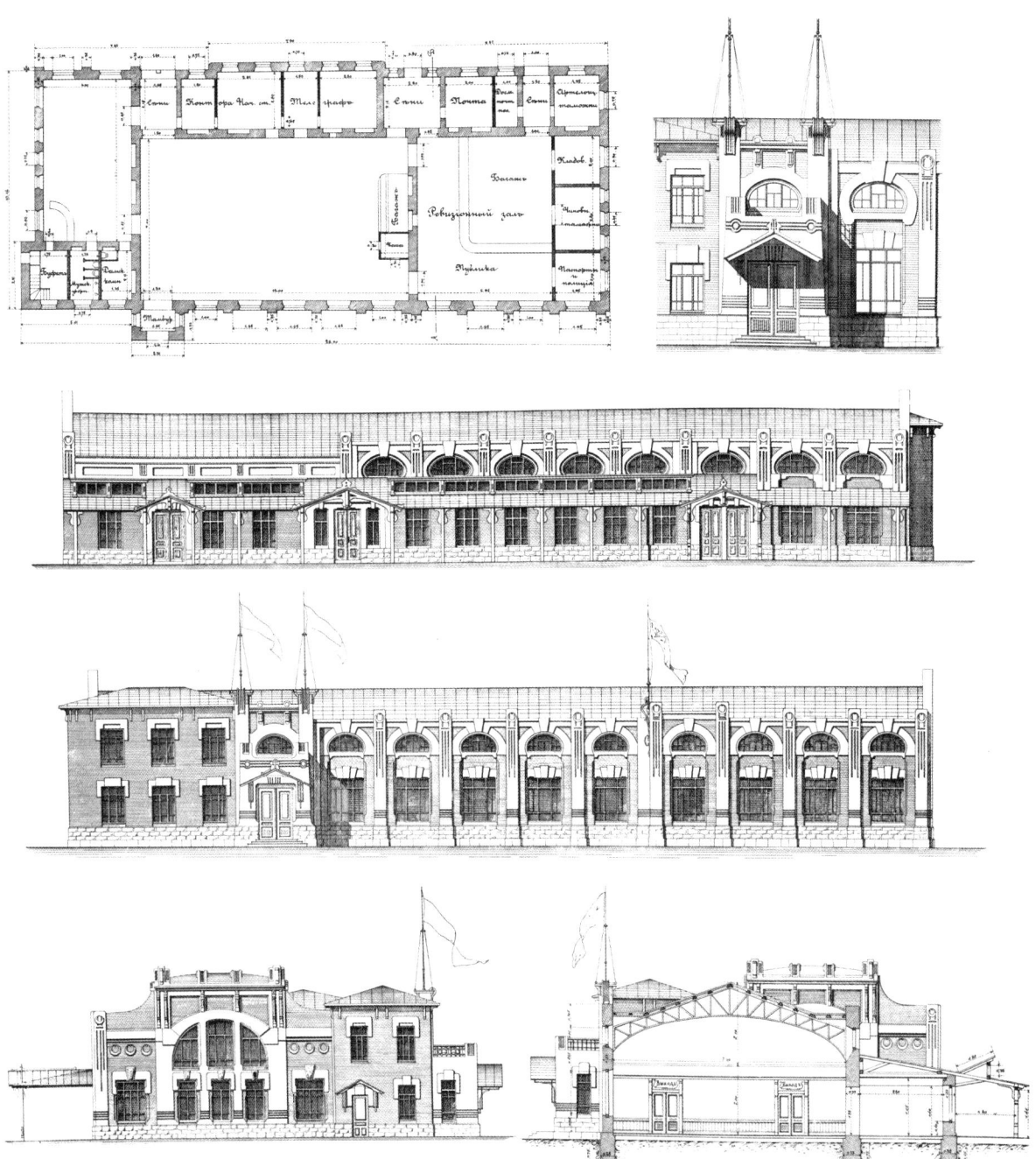

绥芬河站设计图 Darwings of Suifenhe railway station

ARCHITECTURAL CULTURAL HERITAGE OF CHINESE EASTERN RAILWAY

横道河子站历史照片 Historical photo of Hengdaohezi railway station

横道河子站 Hengdaohezi railway station

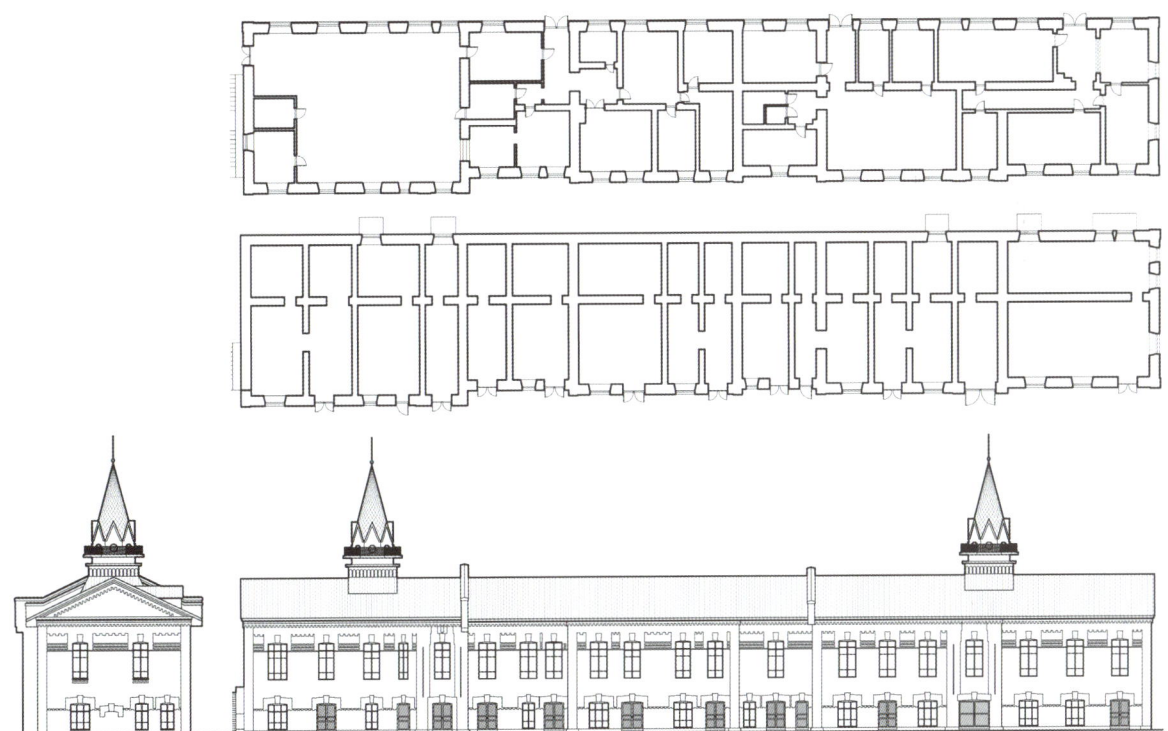

横道河子站测绘图 Drawings of Hengdaohezi railway station

1 站舍 | 67

# ARCHITECTURAL CULTURAL HERITAGE OF CHINESE EASTERN RAILWAY

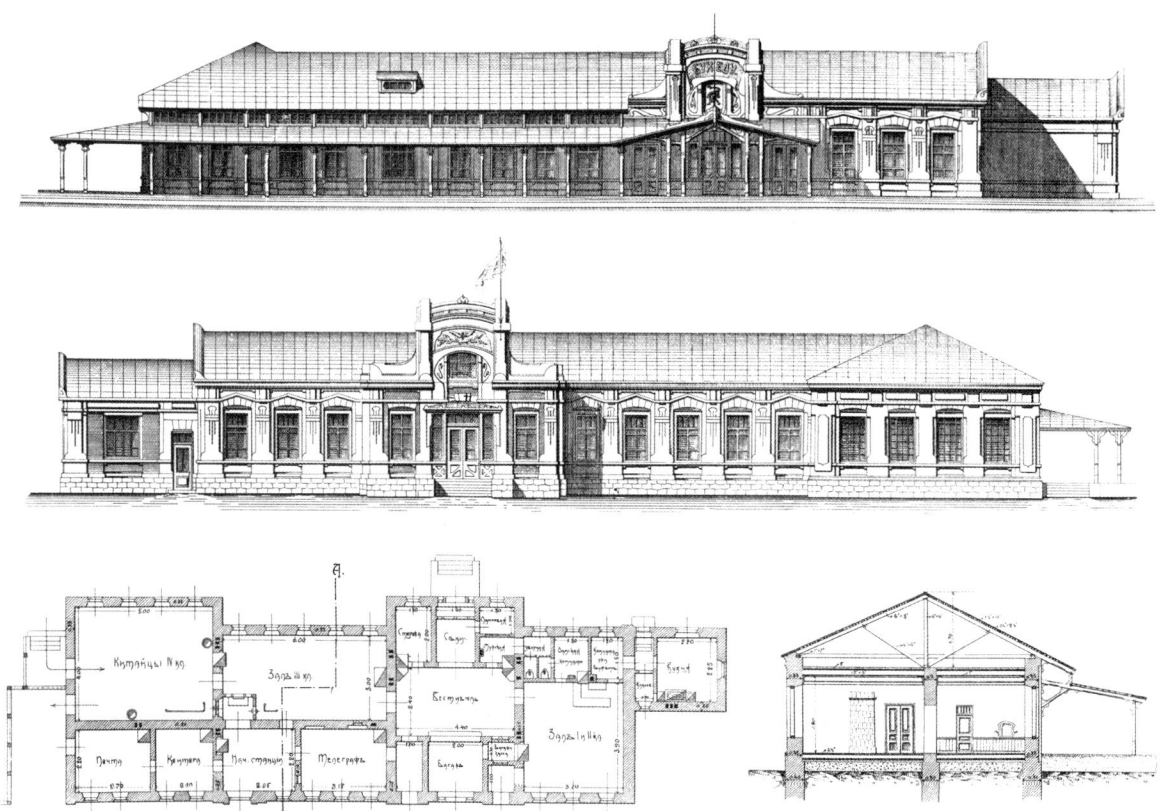

博克图站设计图及历史照片 Drawings and historical photo of Boketu railway station

公主岭站历史照片 Historical photos of Gongzhuling railway station

# ARCHITECTURAL CULTURAL HERITAGE OF CHINESE EASTERN RAILWAY

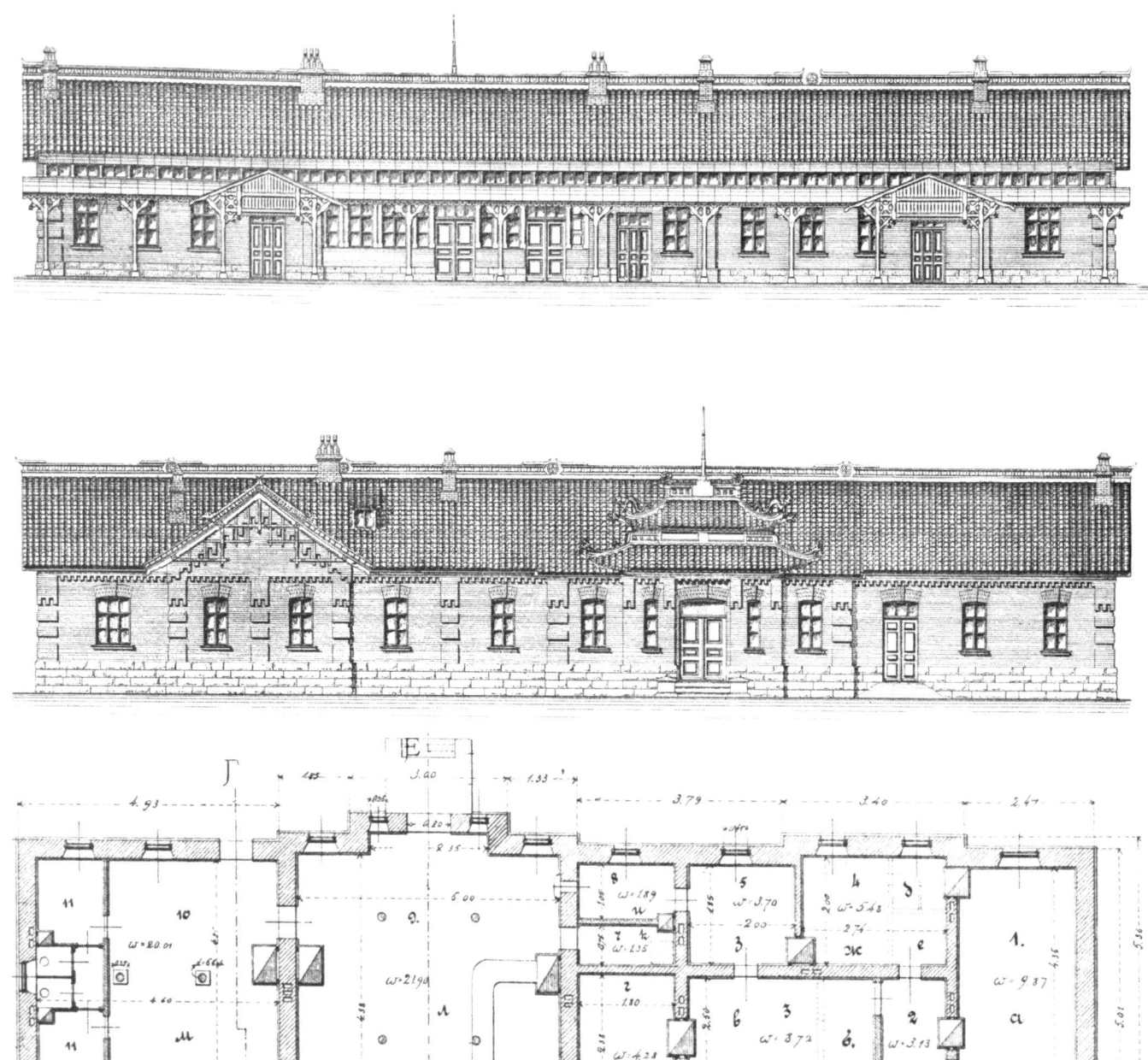

二、三等站标准设计图纸 Standardized drawings of 2nd and 3rd railway station

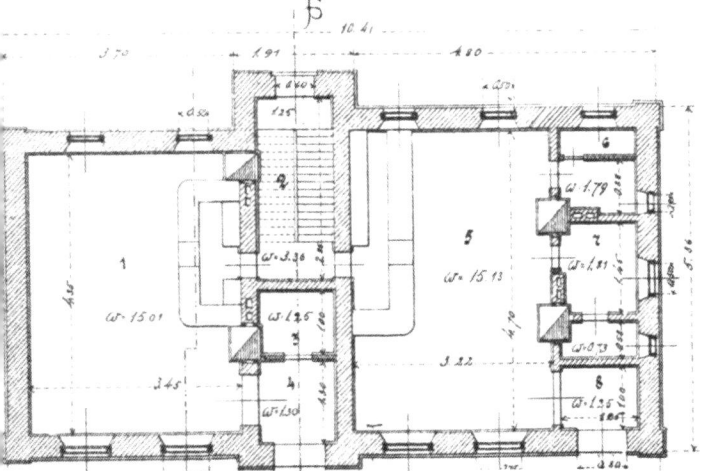

辽阳站历史照片
Historical photo of Liaoyang railway station

瓦房店站历史照片
Historical photo of Wafangdian railway station

1 站舍

昂昂溪站历史照片 Historical photo of Ang'angxi railway station

昂昂溪站 Ang'angxi railway station

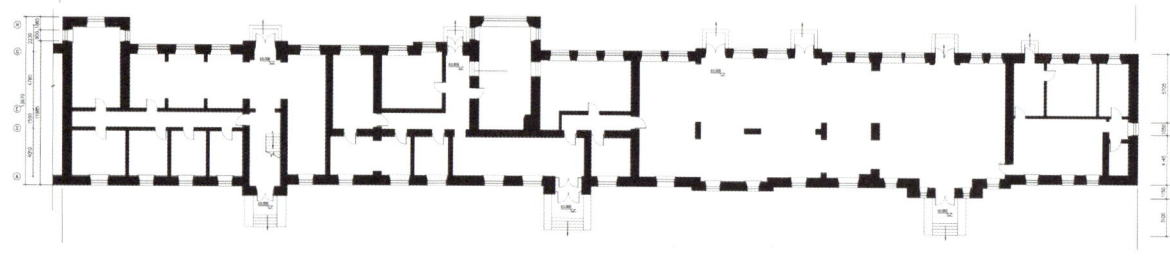
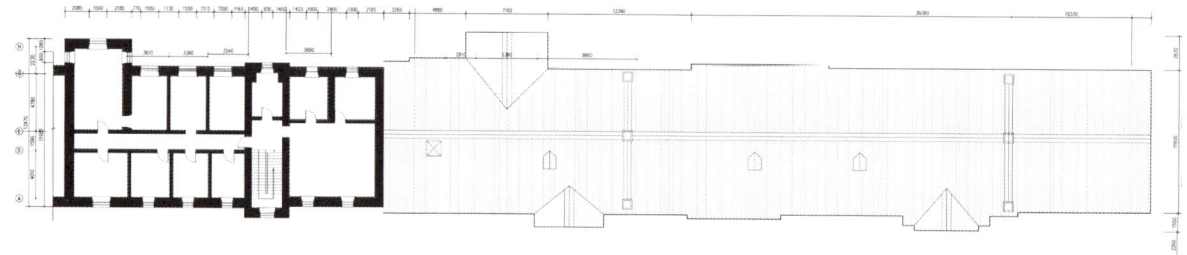

一面坡站历史照片、测绘图及现状 Historical photos, drawings and current condition of Yimianpo railway station

安达站历史照片、测绘图及现状 Historical photos, drawings and current condition of Anda railway station

1 站舍 | 75

扎兰屯站历史照片及现状 Historical photos and current condition of Zhalantun railway station

海拉尔站历史照片及现状 Historical photo and current condition of Hailaer railway station

穆棱站历史照片及现状 Historical photo and current condition of Muling railway station

德惠（原窑门）站历史照片及现状 Historical photo and current condition of Dehui（former Yaomen）railway station

1 站舍 | 79

大石桥站历史照片 Historical photos of Dashiqiao railway station

铁岭站历史照片及现状 Historical photo and current condition of Tieling railway station

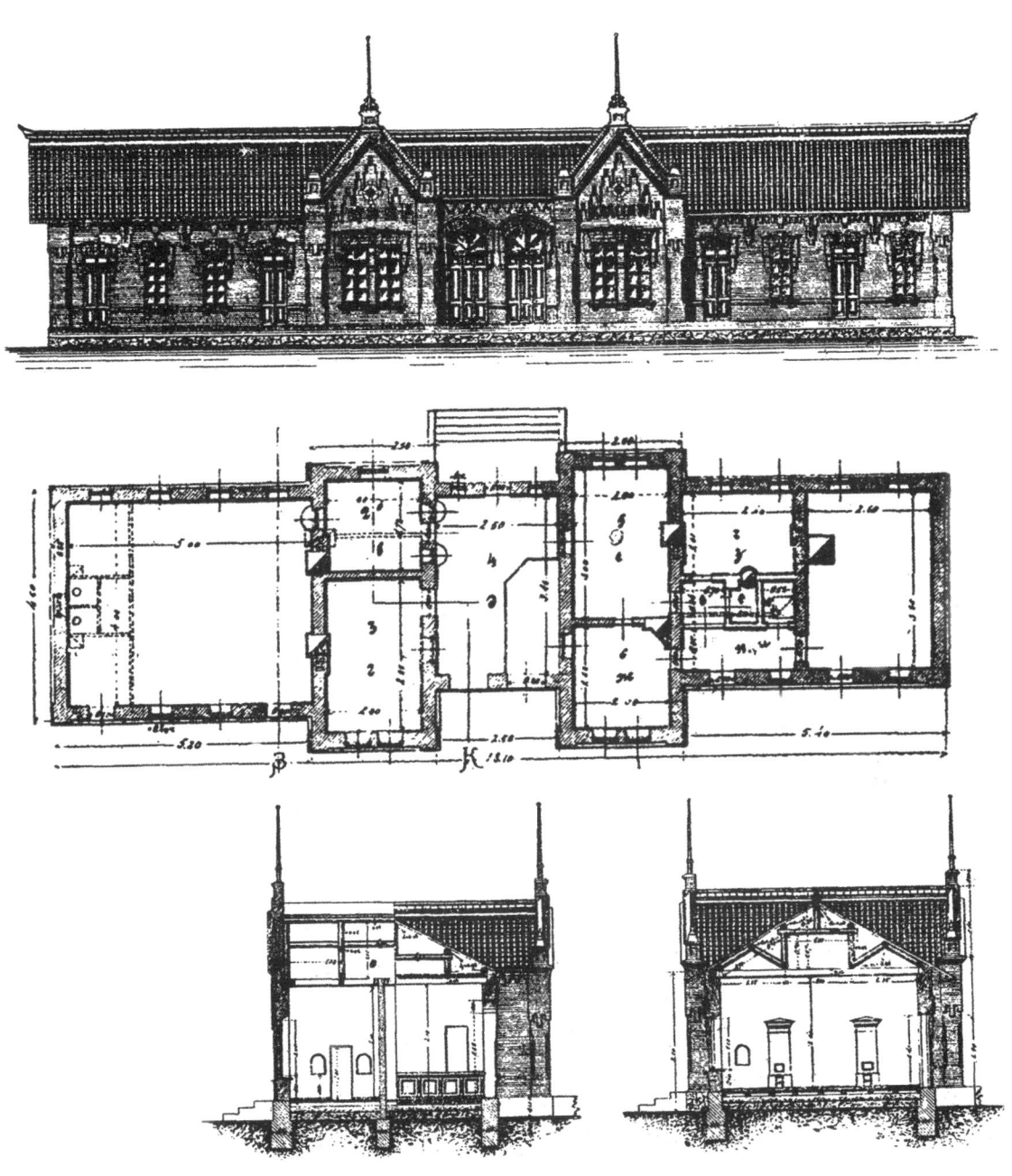

四等站标准设计图 Standardized drawings of 4th railway station

# ARCHITECTURAL CULTURAL HERITAGE OF CHINESE EASTERN RAILWAY

石头河子站历史照片
Historical photo of Shitouhezi railway station

牡丹江站历史照片
Historical photo of Mudanjiang railway station

赫尔洪德站历史照片
Historical photo of Heerhongde railway station

长春（原宽城子）站历史照片
Historical photo of Changchun（former Kuanchengzi）railway station

熊岳站历史照片
Historical photo of Xiongyue railway station

郭家店站历史照片
Historical photo of Guojiadian railway station

南关岭站历史照片
Historical photo of Nan'guanling railway station

沈阳（原奉天）站历史照片
Historical photo of Shenyang（former Fengtian）railway station

金州站历史照片
Historical photo of Jinzhou railway station

伊列克得站历史照片
Historical photo of Yiliekede railway station

阿什河站历史照片
Historical photos of Ashihe railway station

磨刀石站历史照片及现状 Historical photo and current condition of Modaoshi railway station

陶赖昭站历史照片及现状 Historical photo and current condition of Taolaizhao railway station

细鳞河站历史照片及现状 Historical photo and current condition of Xilinhe railway station

马桥河站历史照片及现状 Historical photo and current condition of Maqiaohe railway station

海林站历史照片及现状 Historical photo and current condition of Hailin railway station

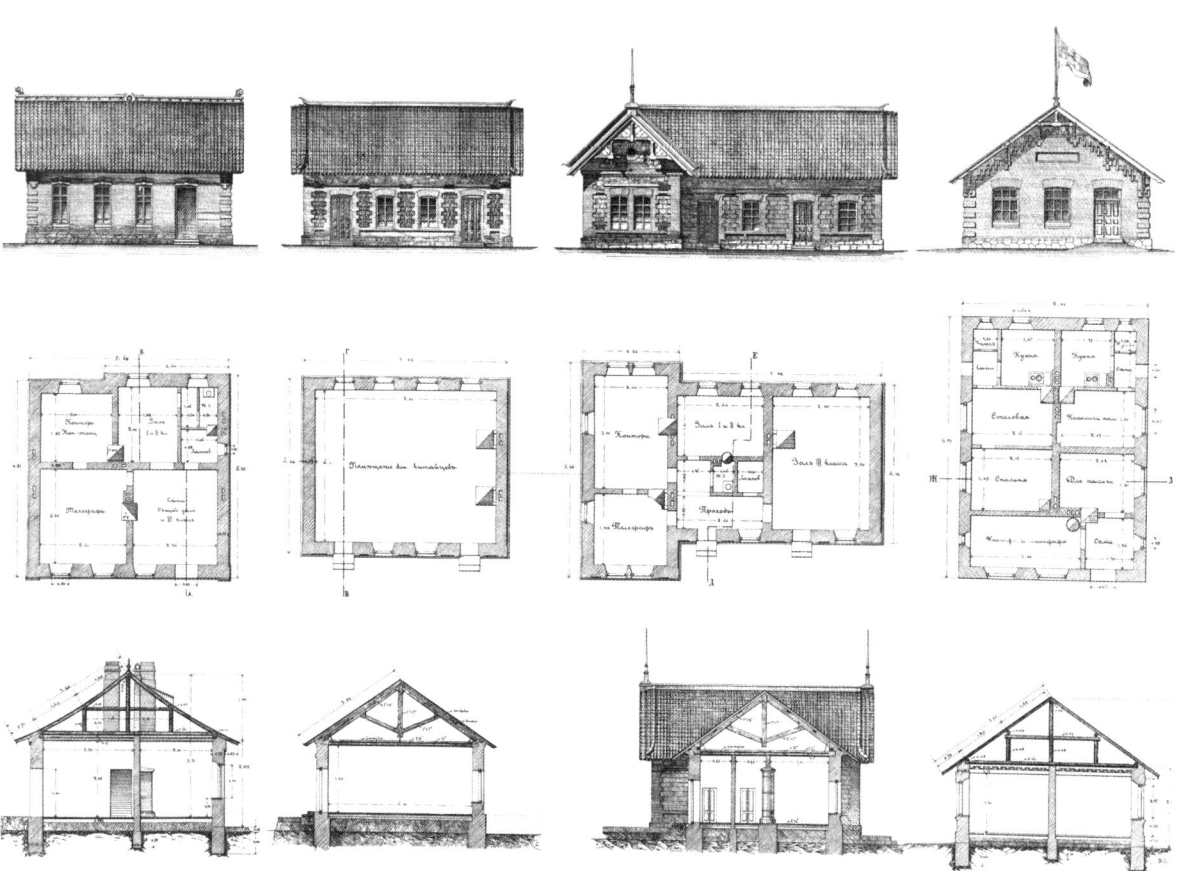

四等站以下站点标准设计图 Standardized drawings of railway stations under 4th class

太岭站历史照片及现状 Historical photo and current condition of Tailing railway station

代马沟站历史照片及现状 Historical photo and current condition of Daimagou railway station

小岭站历史照片及现状 Historical photo and current condition of Xiaoling railway station

# ARCHITECTURAL CULTURAL HERITAGE OF CHINESE EASTERN RAILWAY

哈拉苏站历史照片及现状 Historical photo and current condition of Halasu railway station

巴林站历史照片及现状 Historical photo and current condition of Balin railway station

完工站历史照片及现状 Historical photo and current condition of Wangong railway station

绥阳站历史照片
Historical photo of Suiyang railway station

肇东站
Zhaodong railway station

高岭子站历史照片
Historical photo of Gaolingzi railway station

虎尔虎拉站
Huerhula railway station

玉泉站历史照片
Historical photo of Yuquan railway station

兴安岭站
Khingan railway station

# ARCHITECTURAL CULTURAL HERITAGE OF CHINESE EASTERN RAILWAY

敖头站 Aotou railway station

姜家站 Jiangjia railway station

红房子站 Hongfangzi railway station

旧堡站 Jiupu railway station

爱河站 Aihe railway station

小九站 Xiaojiu railway station

老少沟站 Laoshaogou railway station

布海站历史照片及现状 Historical photo and current condition of Buhai railway station

大榆树站历史照片 Historical photo of Dayushu railway station

王岗站 Wanggang railway station

1 站舍

# ARCHITECTURAL CULTURAL HERITAGE OF CHINESE EASTERN RAILWAY

旅顺站历史照片及现状 Historical photo and current condition of Lüshun railway station

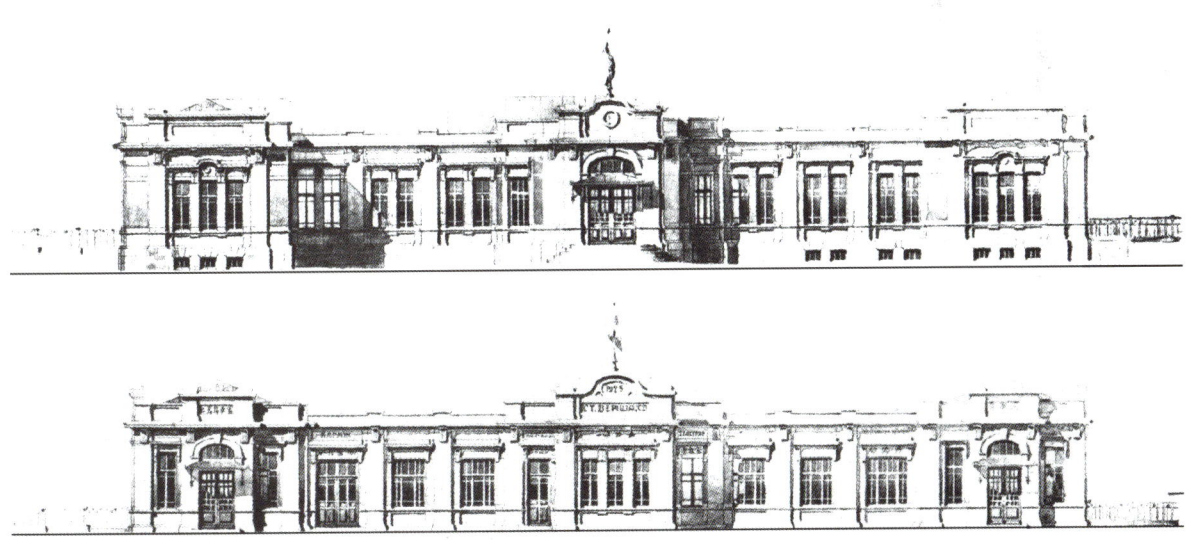

苇河站现状及设计图 Current condition and drawings of Weihe railway station

1 站舍 | 93

# ARCHITECTURAL CULTURAL HERITAGE OF CHINESE EASTERN RAILWAY

1928年重建后的双城堡站历史照片 Historical photo of Shuangchengpu railway station rebuilt in 1928

双城堡站现状及初期历史照片 Current condition and historical photo of early stage of Shuangchengpu railway station

# ARCHITECTURAL CULTURAL HERITAGE OF CHINESE EASTERN RAILWAY

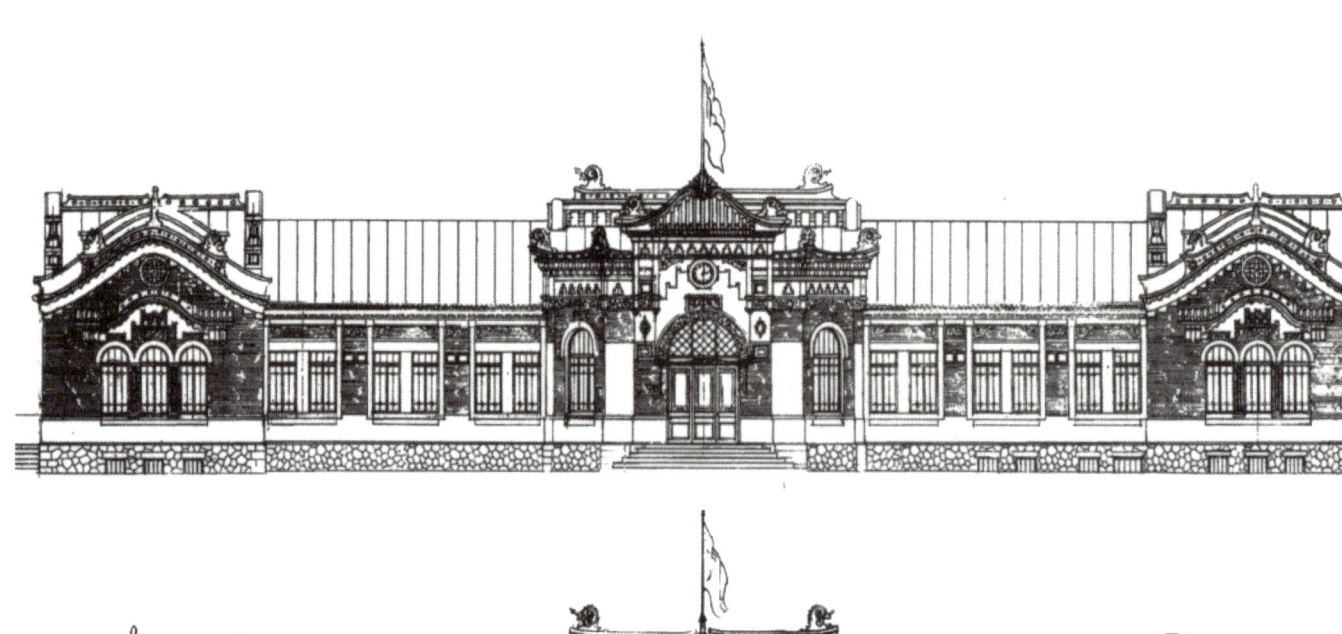

尚志站设计图 Drawings of Shangzhi railway station

尚志站（2014 年拆除）1 Shangzhi railway station (demolished in 2014) 1

初期尚志站历史照片 Historical photo of Shangzhi railway station in early stage

尚志站（2014年拆除）2 Shangzhi railway station (demolished in 2014) 2

伊林站 Yilin railway station

下城子站 Xiachengzi railway station

九江泡站现状及设计图 Current condition and drawing of Jiujiangpao railway station

初期富拉尔基站历史照片 Historical photo of Fulaerji railway station in early stage

富拉尔基站 Fulaerji railway station

1 站舍

北林站 Beilin railway station

大观岭站 Daguanling railway station

香坊站 Xiangfang railway station

# 2 机车库

中东铁路全线靠蒸汽机车进行运输，在特定地段需要加助推车或更换车头，因此，供机车停放检修的机车库是中东铁路沿线必备的重要建筑。中东铁路沿线分布着规模不一的多座机车库，其体量、形态、空间结构在中东铁路建筑群中独树一帜，极具标志性，是这一时期工业建筑中的典型范例。

## 2.1 机车库的分布特点

中东铁路各站点落成后，以客货运数量、自然地理环境以及折返车站点作为依据，在对应的站点及机务段制定了机车库的分布方式。1906 年前中东铁路管理局设机务处，下辖海拉尔、博克图、齐齐哈尔、哈尔滨、横道河子、绥芬河、公主岭、辽阳、瓦房店、大连机务段，机务段的重要配套设施之一就是机车库。一、二、三等站均配备有机车库，在一些四等站如磨刀石站、伊列克得站等设有矩形机车修理库。

每个站点机车库的规模根据实际情况灵活调整，有些多达 20 个车库单元，亦有些少于 4 个车库单元。机车库的规模主要受所在站点的客货运量、自然地理条件两个主要因素影响。横道河子站货运量巨大且地理位置特殊，其机车库多达 15 个单元库，在沿线属于相对较大的规模。处于兴安岭峰顶南麓的博克图车站为军事咽喉，中东铁路在博克图区域内的坡度较大，故在此为列车尾部加挂一辆机车作为补机，博克图机车库多达 20 个单元库。其他一些大型的机车库因位于客货运输枢纽而设置，如齐齐哈尔站，承担编组、护路、维修等重要功能。还有一些处于地域交界处的重要站点，如绥芬河站、海拉尔站以及满洲里站，都建有 12 个单元库以上的机车库。一些折返站则建有相对小型的机车库，便于更换机头方向。一面坡站是东线上的折返站，设有 5 库机车库。西线折返站为扎兰屯站，同为 5 库机车库，机车在此停留检修后返回富拉尔基或者哈尔滨。还有一些站点曾设置临时机车库，为铁路建设时期的机务需要提供重要保障。机车库规模完全按需分布，节省资源，适应快速建设及使用的需求，是中东铁路建筑标准化设计的典型体现。

## 2.2 机车库的平面布局

机车库的特种功能决定了其建筑平面布局的独特性。机车库是机头存放和检修的场所，由车库及其附属的轨道与转盘组成。机车库的功能需要使机车库必须临近铁路，一般从主铁路线引支线，再通过转盘的调转通往车库，因此在选址方面，机车库多远离城镇中心，设置于边缘地区，减弱大型工业建筑对生产生活的影响。基于机车库的功能需求，机车库的平面形态分为扇形和矩形两种。扇形平面机车库最为常见，扇形平面中包含若干个尺寸相同的车库。因为蒸汽机车只能向前行驶，故蒸汽机车需要在转盘上回转行进方向的转换。因此，机车库平面与盘转形成同心的围合式扇形，并由放射形铁轨连接。一些临时机车库与机车修理库为矩形，在山墙两侧开两到三扇门，双向出车。

沿铁道一侧的立面开窗，形体简洁且整体。在磨刀石、满洲里均可见此类型的机车库。

### 2.3 机车库的建造技术特点

无论是扇形平面还是矩形平面的机车库，车库都是其最主要的组成部分，作为基本单元，其平面尺寸主要由机车尺寸及相应操作所需空间决定。单元库的平面尺寸基本相同，这是机车库平面标准化设计的重要体现。中东铁路机车库多为砖石结构且体量巨大，就当时中东铁路沿线的技术条件而言，无论是跨度还是高度都具有一定挑战性。为实现较大的空间跨度，机车库采用以钢构支撑柱连续券屋顶的结构形式。屋面采用连续发券的形式形成较大跨度，一般沿机车库进深方向每隔 0.6 米铺设一根钢拱肋，拱肋上灌注水泥，并采用压型钢板拱结构，构成单元式发券，重复单元券的连续使用形成较大跨度。钢结构柱子作为内部支撑，在拱券交界处下端均匀排列。钢柱由四根"L"形钢条与多根短钢板斜向拉结组成，形成中空柱，在保障最低空间损耗的前提下，平衡了大面积屋顶的垂直荷载。为平衡屋面的侧向推力以及保障机车库的使用高度，外墙均为砖石砌筑，在两侧山墙窗间设置宽约 0.3 米、高近 3 米的砖砌扶壁支撑，扶壁之间距离约 2 米。每一个单元库大门之间在外墙上均匀设置约半米的矩形构造柱用以支撑檐部，有助于解决单元库界面太窄而造成的不合理受力现象。在排水、采光等方面，机车库采用有组织排水、集水井、高位窗等手段。

机车库的营建技术兼顾了功能、建筑形态等多个层面，从实际考量又兼具美感，使结构构件成为空间营造的一部分，虚实相结合体现了当时高超的建造技艺。20 世纪 90 年代，蒸汽机被内燃机取代，退出铁路运输的舞台，大部分机车库失去了其检修及调转车头的作用。

# Train Garage

The Chinese Eastern Railway (CER) applied steam trains for transportation across the entire line. It was necessary to add a booster locomotive or change the front locomotive at certain locations. In some hubs for passenger and cargo transportation, trains needed to be repaired to achieve higher standards. Therefore, train garages for trains parking and maintenance became important type of buildings along the CER. There were different scale train garages along the CER, which were remarkable and unique in their volumes, shapes and spatial structures among the historical buildings, and became the typical examples in this period.

After the construction of various stations along CER, train garages was distributed at stations and locomotive depots, based on the capacity of passengers and freight, the geographical environment and the return station points. Before 1906, the CER Bureau set up a department administrating locomotive depots in Hailaer, Boketu, Qiqihar, Harbin, Hengdaohezi, Suifenhe, Gongzhuling, Liaoyang, Wafangdian and Dalian, and the train garage was one of the important supporting facilities in the locomotive depot. The scale of train garage at each locomotive depot was adjusted flexibly according to the actual situation, which could have as many as 20 garage units or less than 4 garage units, and was mainly affected by the passenger and freight traffic and geographical conditions of the station. Temporary train garages were also built at some stations, which provided important guarantee during the railway construction. On the whole, train garages were completely distributed according to the needs, saving resources and adapting to the rapid construction, and became typical of the standardization design in the CER construction.

The special function of train garages determined their unique architectural layouts. A train garage, composed of a garage, affiliated tracks and a turnplate, was the place where the train was stored and repaired , and its function made it close to the railway. Generally, a branch line was drawn from the main railway line and led to the garage through the rotation of the turnplate. Therefore, a train garage was often sited at the marginal area far away from the downtown to reduce the impact of large industrial buildings on daily life. The train garage plans could be divided into two types based on their functions: sector and rectangle. The sector train garage was the most common type, which contained several units of the same size. As the steam train could only travel forward and needed to be turned on the turnplate for direction conversion, the train garage plan formed a concentric fan-shaped enclosure connected to the round turnplate by radial rails. The plans of some temporary train garages and repair depots were rectangular, with two or three doors on each side of the gable walls for two directions way out. Mainly used for repairing the trains, train garages appeared simple but integral with windows on the facade facing to the railway, as could be seen in Modaoshi Station and Manzhouli Station.

A train storage spot was the basic unit of a train garage. The size of the train garage was mainly determined by the size of the train and the space required for operations. The unit sizes were basically the same. The CER train garages were mostly of masonry structure and large volume, and continuous vaults supported by iron pillars were adapted to obtain a larger span. In order to balance the lateral thrust of the vaults and ensure the use height of the train garage, the outer wall was masonry, and brick buttresses, each about 0.3 meters in width and nearly 3 meters in height, were placed between windows on the gables, and the distance between buttresses was about 2 meters. Organized roof drainage, wells for collecting water and high windows for day lighting were also applied.

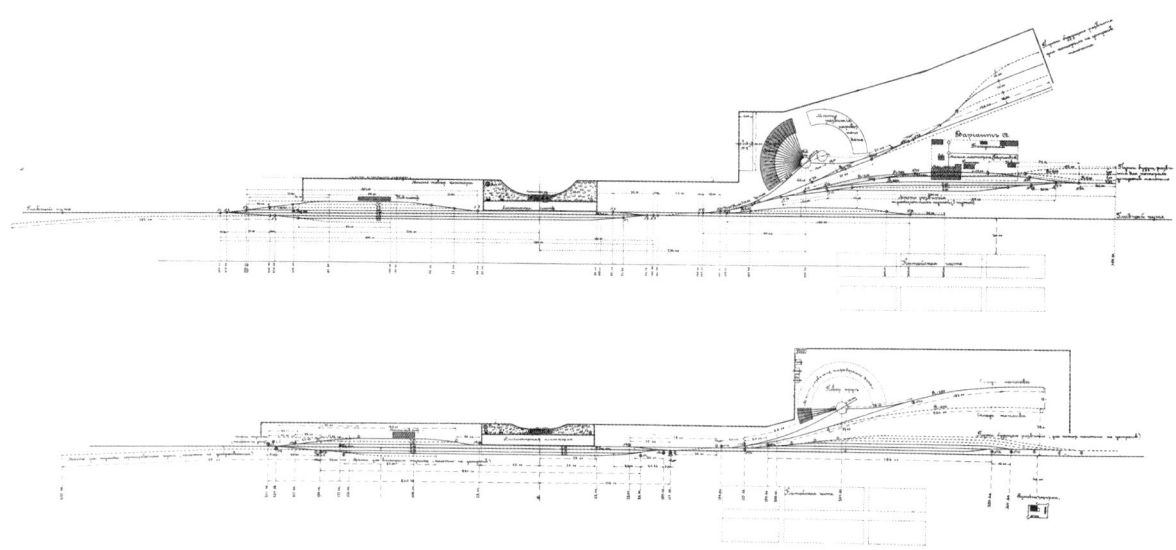

二、三等站铁路站区标准设计图 Standardized drawings of 2nd and 3nd train station areas

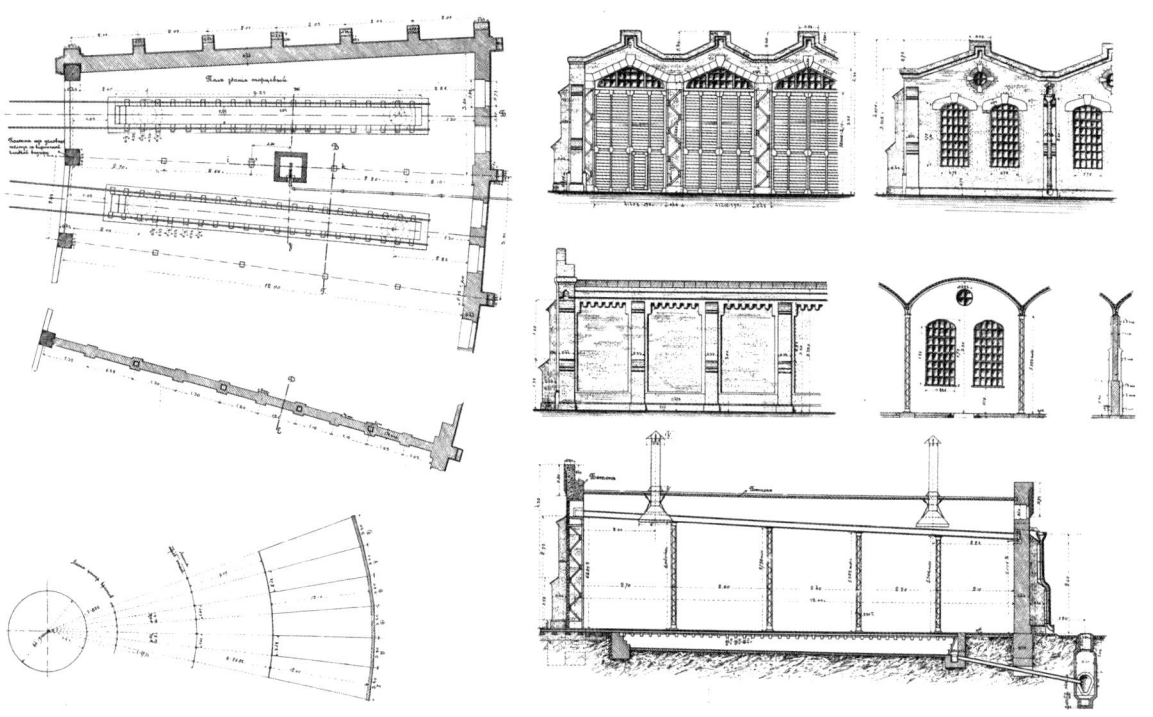

扇形机车库标准设计图 Standardized drawings of fan-shaped train garage

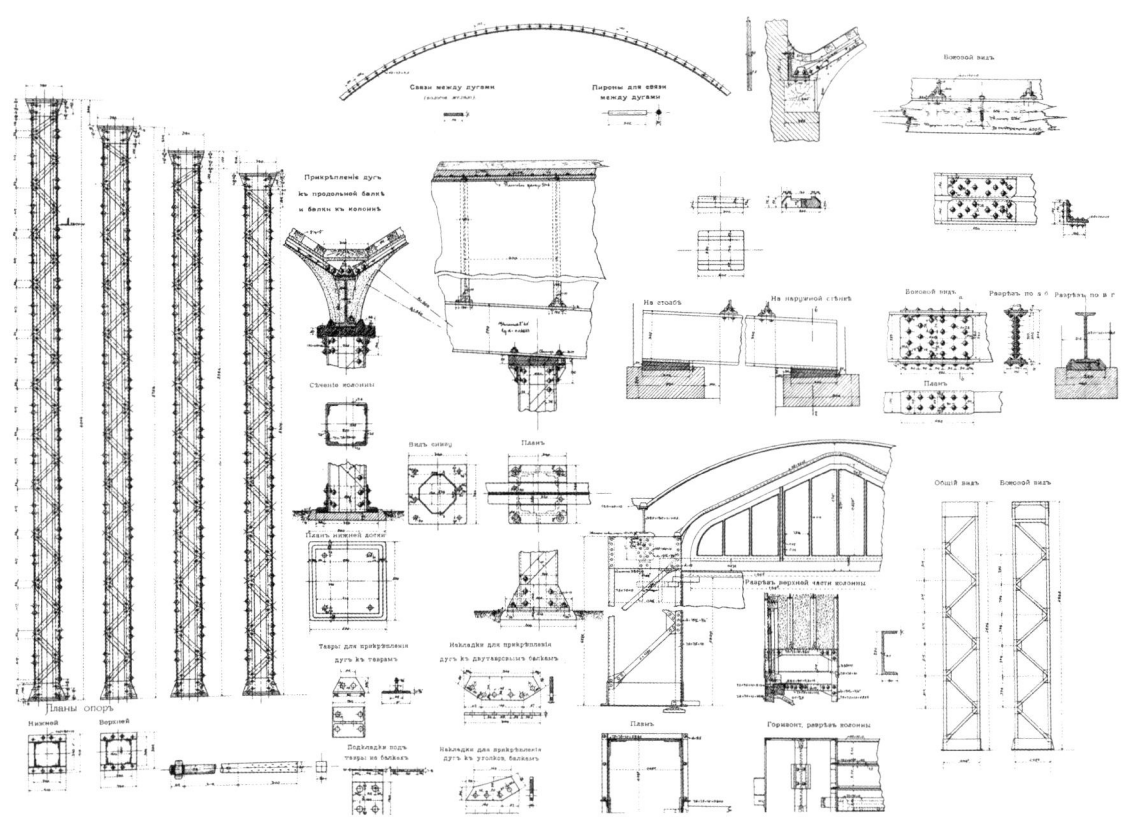

机车库结构细部标准设计图 Standardized drawings of details of train garage

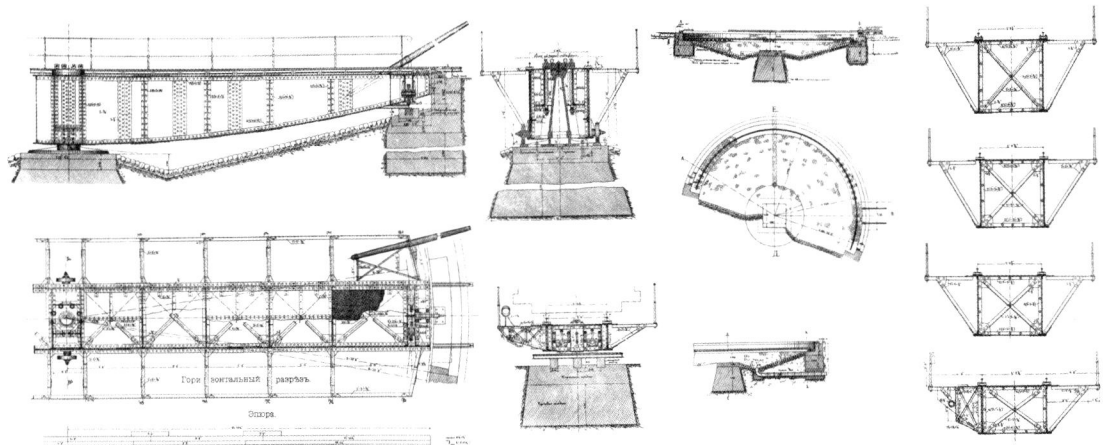

机车库转盘标准设计图 Standardized drawings of turntable

2 机车库

横道河子机车库历史照片 Historical photo of train garage in Hengdaohezi

横道河子机车库 Train garage in Hengdaohezi

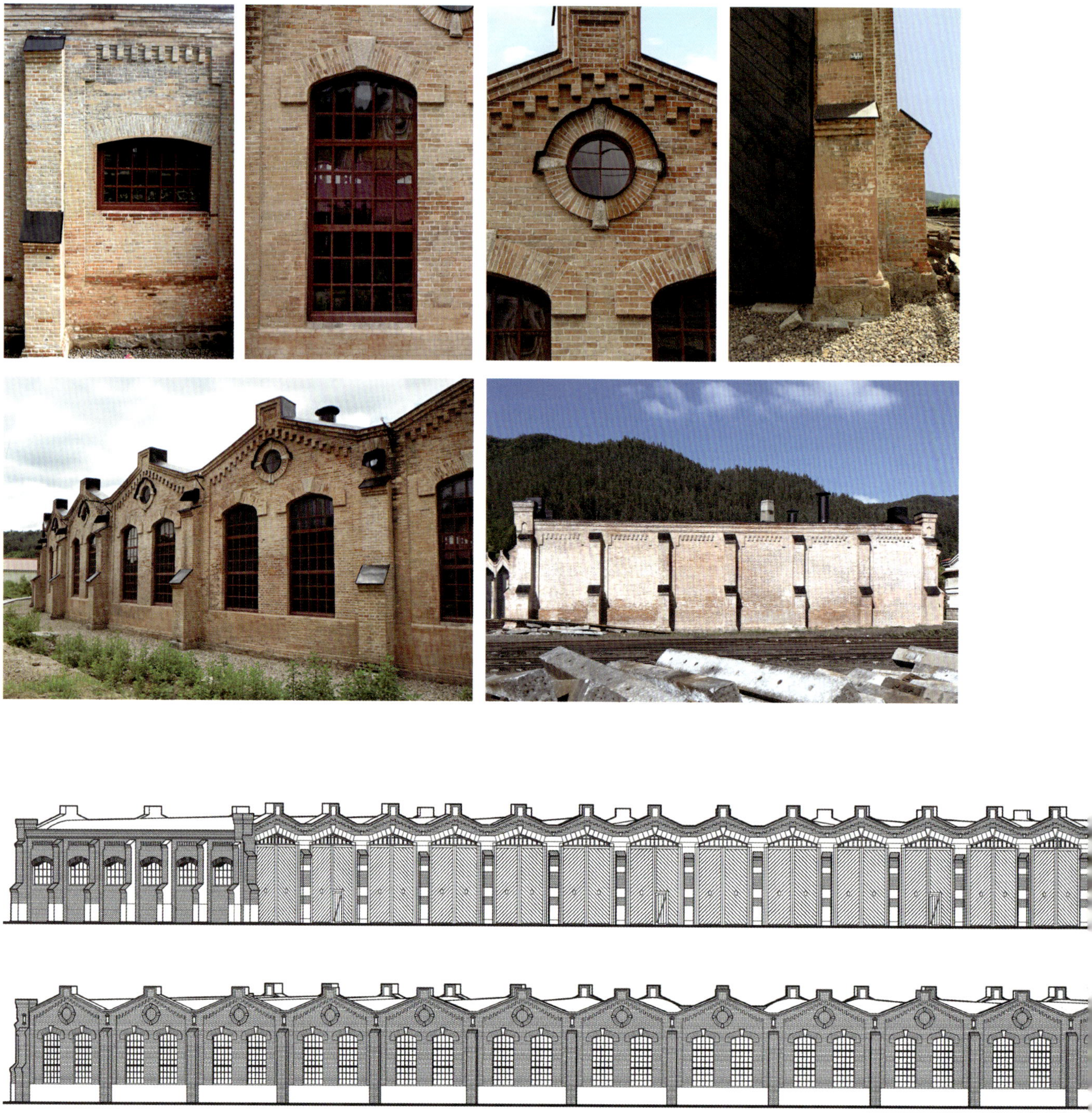

# ARCHITECTURAL CULTURAL HERITAGE OF CHINESE EASTERN RAILWAY

横道河子机车库现状及测绘图 Current condition and drawings of train garage in Hengdaohezi

扎兰屯机车库测绘图 Drawings of train garage in Zhalantun

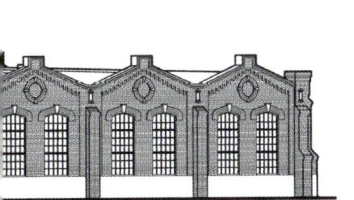

扎兰屯机车库 Train garage in Zhalantun

海拉尔机车库历史照片及现状 Historical photo and current condition of train garage in Hailaer

一面坡机车库历史照片及现状 Historical photo and current condition of train garage in Yimianpo

2 机车库

绥芬河机车库历史照片 Historical photo of train garage in Suifenhe

公主岭机车库历史照片
Historical photo of train garage in Gongzhuling

安达机车库历史照片
Historical photo of train garage in Anda

穆棱机车库历史照片
Historical photo of train garage in Muling

满洲里机车库历史照片
Historical photo of train garage in Manzhouli

德惠机车库历史照片
Historical photo of train garage in Dehui

2 机车库 | 117

# ARCHITECTURAL CULTURAL HERITAGE OF CHINESE EASTERN RAILWAY

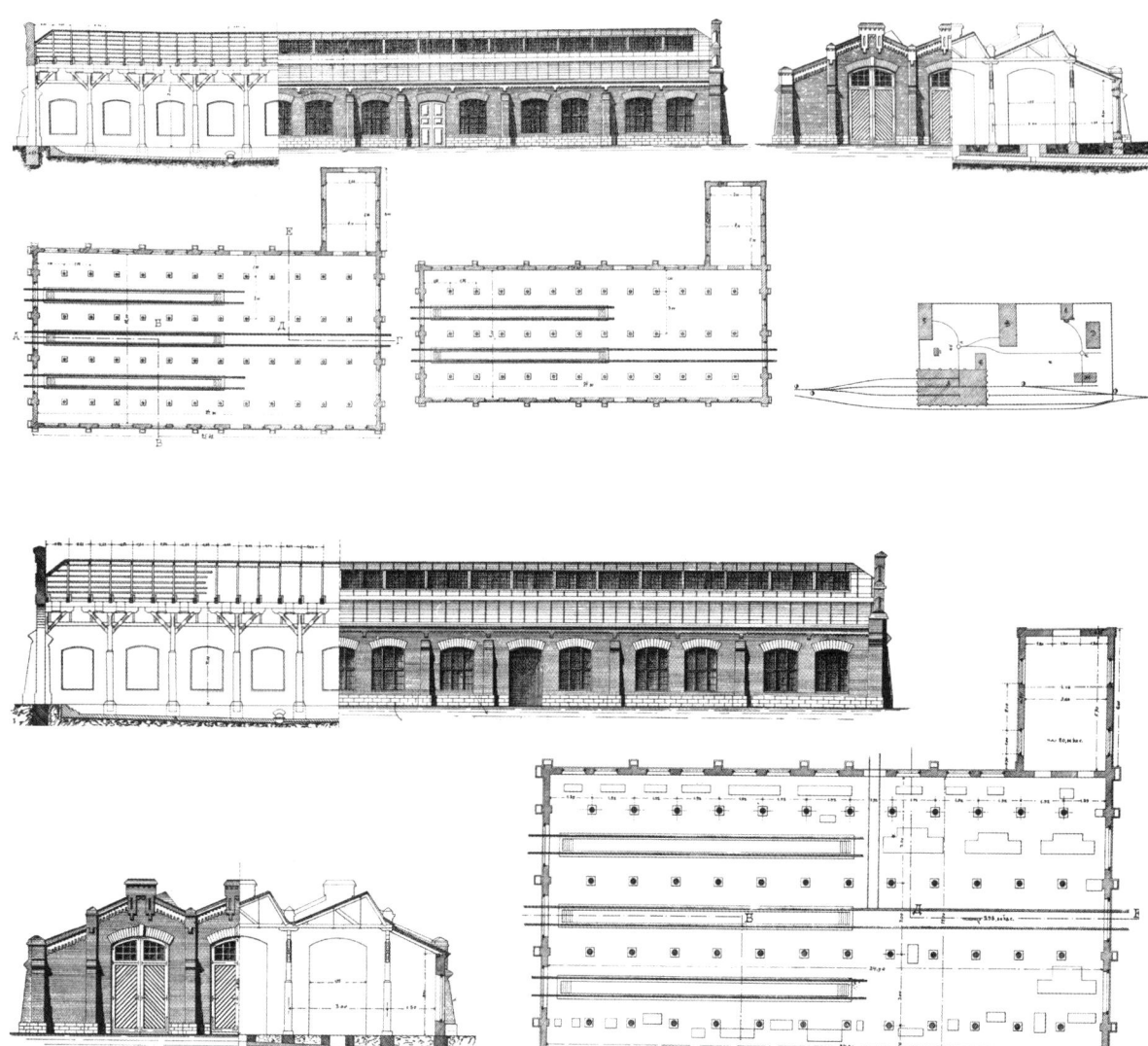

中型机车维修库设计图 Drawings of train garage in middle scale

哈尔滨中型机车修理库历史照片 Historical photos of middle scale train garage in Harbin

公主岭中型机车库修理库 Middle scale train garage in Gongzhuling

昂昂溪中型机车维修库
Middle scale train garage in Ang'angxi

绥芬河中型机车维修库
Middle scale train garage in Suifenhe

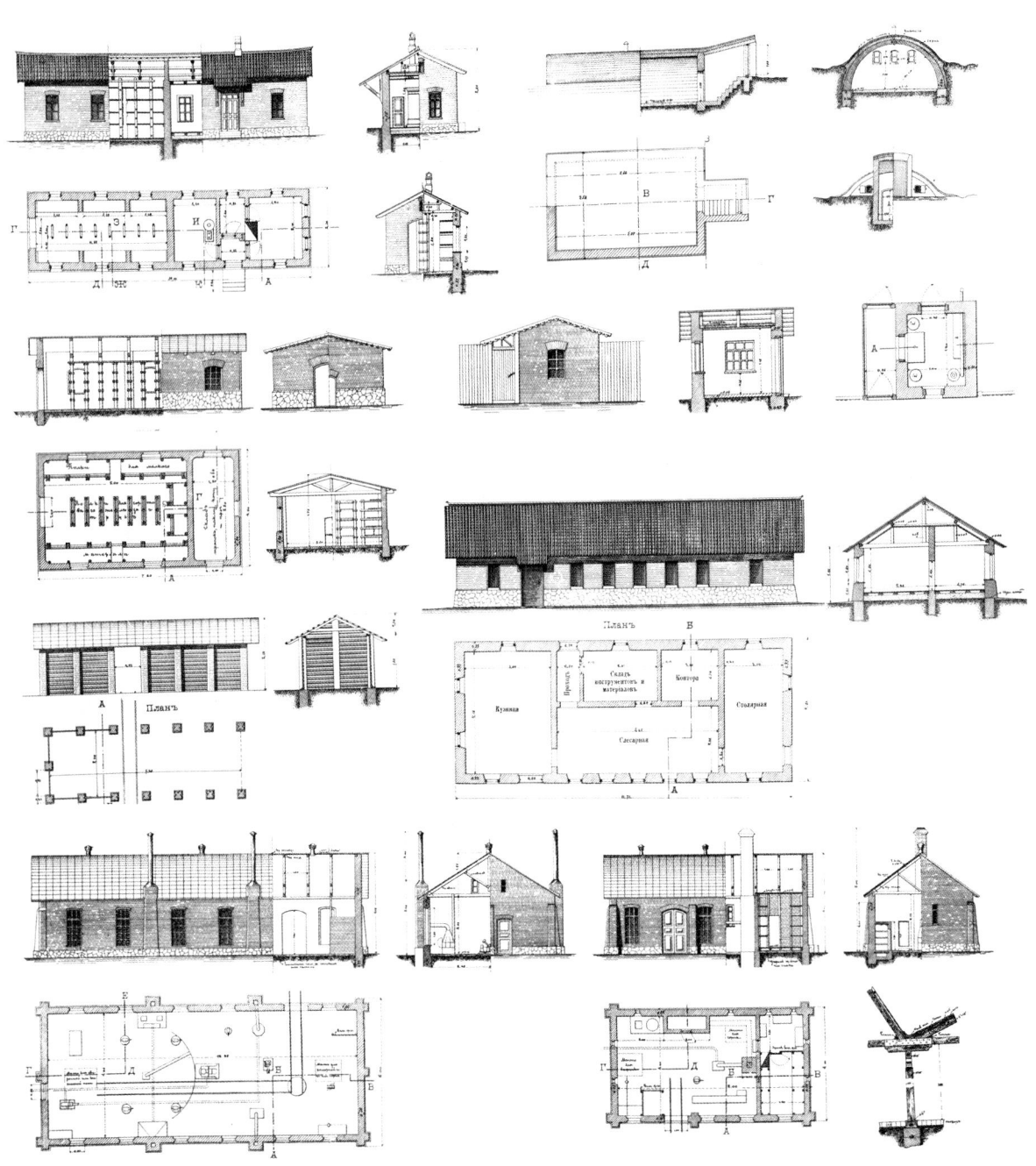

小型机车维修库设计图 Drawings of train garage in small scale

# ARCHITECTURAL CULTURAL HERITAGE OF CHINESE EASTERN RAILWAY

满洲里小型机车修理库 1
Small train garage in Suifenhe 1

满洲里小型机车修理库 2
Small train garage in Suifenhe 2

满洲里小型机车修理库 3
Small train garage in Suifenhe 3

满洲里小型机车修理库 4
Small train garage in Suifenhe 4

齐齐哈尔临时机车库
Temporary train garage in Qiqihaer

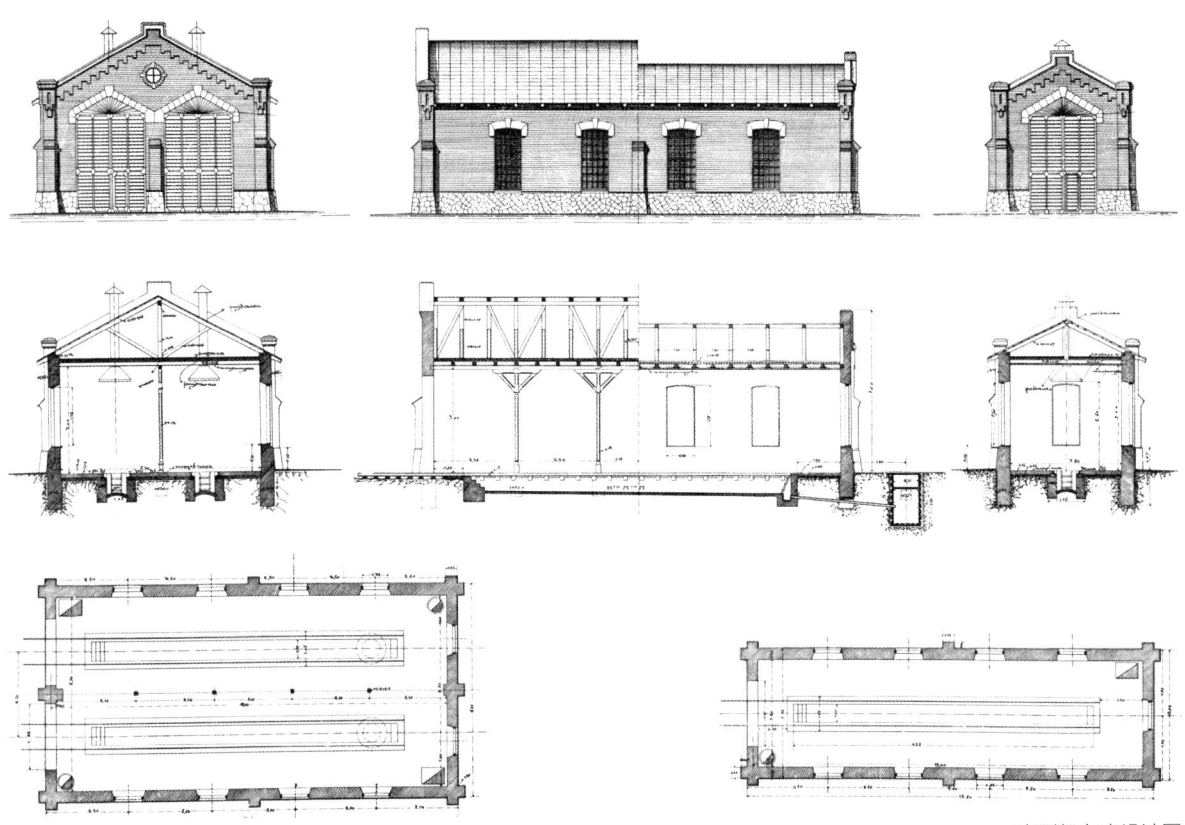

方形机车库设计图
Drawings of rectangular train garage

磨刀石方形机车库
Rectangular train garage in Modaoshi

伊列克得方形机车库
Rectangular train garage in Yiliekede

2 机车库 | 123

# 水塔

水塔是中东铁路沿线一种独特的建筑类型，常见于铁路沿线车站内部，为供给蒸汽机车、客运列车、站段生产、沿线职工生活用水而设置，是铁路运行所必须的基础设施。虽然仅是一种功能性设施，但中东铁路沿线水塔的建造却凝聚了大量的技术手段与艺术匠心。

## 3.1 水塔的空间与结构特点

中东铁路的标准水塔分为两种容量，分别是250吨和360吨。在中东铁路沿线，根据机务段的地点和机车用水量，每25—30公里设立一个给水站，给水站内设给水所（水源地和水塔），站线设水鹤和清灰地沟等，在铁路枢纽或沿线给机车上水，较大的给水站均设有水塔，位于机务段和机务折返段。1935年之前，中东铁路全线已经有57处给水站，均匀分布在铁路沿线。

水塔的平面为正多边形或圆形，形态分为两种。一种水塔的外部形态上下保持一致，均为相同直径的圆柱体，上部水箱不挑出，荷载垂直落于下部墙体之上，水柜底部采用球形壳，塔身多采用石材建造。另一种水塔的下部为砖石砌筑的向内收分的圆锥体承重墙，上部水箱部分挑出，水箱柜壁为圆柱形壳体，属于圆柱壳式水柜。柜底的外伸段是倒锥形壳，中间段采用球形壳，水箱的荷载通过钢结构传递至下部的墙体。从水塔的剖面看，水箱部分采用钢结构框架，塔体由厚重的砖石砌筑承重，没有额外的柱子等支撑构建。第一种水塔，由于上下垂直相连，上部水箱由钢结构支撑，其压力直接传递给下部塔身，没有过多的横向荷载，因此构造较为简单。而第二种水塔的水箱由大面积的桁架结构支撑，为防止双层铁皮强度不够，在柜底的外伸端局部增加小型桁架。而且这种水箱充满水后对锥形塔身端部形成侧向压力，容易造成塔身失稳，致使整个构筑物坍塌。为此，在水箱下部，即水箱外表皮与塔身连接点之间砌拱形支撑体，与锥体塔身形成稳定的空间结构，使塔身四周受力均匀，达到整体平衡，巧妙地解决了这一问题。水箱外层是双层的木质保温层，其中间加入棉毡，木质外皮与水罐体之间又留有半米距离的空气保温层，水罐体的外表皮亦为双层钢板，铁皮的防水屋面采用白灰锯末保温，以此来防止寒冷地区冬季水箱的结冻现象。开窗形式为竖向窄长窗，面积很小以减小室内墙面的冷桥现象，窗洞采用喇叭口的形式，最大限度地接受阳光，同时减少热损失。这种砖石、木材、钢几种材料搭配的建构和保温处理的方式完全符合俄罗斯传统建筑的建造特点。

## 3.2 建造技术与艺术的高度统一

水塔立面分为屋顶、水箱、塔身和基座几个部分。基座由规则的方条石排列，砖石尺寸远大于塔身砖石尺寸，给水塔以坚固的基础保护。水塔的塔身高度有限，无论是圆锥体还是圆柱体都显得整体粗壮而有力。墙的厚度亦要兼顾上部水箱的荷载和寒冷地区的保温隔热，而墙上只开狭长的几扇长条窗，加之塔身由砖石砌筑而成，显得建筑物整体更加厚重而踏实。而水箱部分，虽以木材为外皮，但仍沿袭了塔身稳重的风格。长条木板或横向或竖向地紧密排列，在面与面的相接处及水箱腰身部分配以彩色的钢板或木板加固。水箱上半部开方形的小窗，显得清新而跳脱，避免水塔给人以头重脚轻之感，却仍未破坏其整体的厚重内向的性格。利用不同材质的不同性格特质互相搭配，使其发挥所长，同时避免单调和乏味。圆柱壳式水塔的塔盖为正圆锥形壳，塔顶中央升起一座小的采光庭，双层屋盖呈重檐之态；而通体为圆柱体的水塔塔盖则多为单层的正圆锥形壳。极为特殊的是穆棱站的水塔，塔顶是十字交叉的坡屋顶，使得水箱部分看起来像是一处小型的俄式民宅。这种俄式传统的坡屋顶，不仅可以分解屋顶积雪的荷载，方便屋顶的排水，还丰富了建筑的轮廓线。

在中东铁路水塔中，木材的装饰性被发挥得淋漓尽致，利用其易于雕画的性格为建筑装饰加入新的活力，并且使建筑气质更为温和。一些水塔屋檐边缘和水箱的下边缘由木板雕刻出锯齿状与阶梯状来装饰。而水箱的上端部，则是在横向木板表皮外叠加紧密排列的竖向短木板，木板端头被雕刻成倒挂的圆角三角形。水箱每个面重复出现相同的装饰母题极其精美。砖石用于水塔的墙体砌筑，有的利用石材的颜色和形状来装饰塔身，有的以其叠加的砌筑方式形成线脚。细致的腰线利用砖砌层层出挑的手法做出锯齿状线脚，使腰线呈现出富有节奏的凹凸变化。有的还在水箱与塔的连接处增加牛腿装饰，转角处也采用俄式传统房屋转角处的装饰做法，用蘑菇石的饰面叠砌在塔身上面。明艳的建筑颜色成为中东铁路建筑特有的标志性风格。有的塔身会在底部叠加几层不同形状的五彩石头，别有一番异域风情。与民用建筑相比，通常工业建筑更注重其特殊的功能要求，往往不会将重心放在装饰上，而中东铁路时期的诸多水塔，立面均充分发挥不同材料的肌理、质感、色彩的特点，这是后来出现的水塔无法企及的。

水塔是蒸汽机机车时代的标志性设施，作为一种独特的工业建筑遗产见证了近代的工业变革。中东铁路沿线水塔以其独特的形体结构，稳重温和的立面形象和富有韵律感的装饰构造，成为了一道亮丽的风景线，其体量虽小，却浓缩了这一时期沙俄建筑的传统构造技术与民族性装饰风格，展示了很高的建筑艺术魅力与文化韵味。

## Water Towers

Water tower was a unique type of building along the CER and usually located in the station area. As a kind of infrastructure which provided water for steam trains, passenger trains, stations, and workers' daily life, water towers along the CER were built not only for functions but also with technical and artistic conceptions.

There were two capacities of standard water towers of the CER, 250 tons and 360 tons. Considering the site of locomotive depots and water consumption of the trains along the railway, water supply stations were set up every 25—30 km and equipped with water supply spot (water source and water tower), together with water crane and ash removal trench along the line, so as to water the locomotive at a railway hub or along the railway line. Water towers were built in larger water supply stations which located in the locomotive depots. Before 1935, there were 57 water supply stations evenly distributed along the railway.

Water towers had regular polygon or round plans and two types. One was a cylinder with the same diameter from bottom to the top. The upper water tank would not stretch out, and its load fell vertically on the lower shaft. The bottom of the water tank adopted a spherical shell, and the tower shaft adopted stone. The other type water tower had a masonry cone shaft in the lower part, and the upper water tank streched out and formed a cylindrical shell. The outer of the water tank was a double-layer wood insulation with cotton felt in between the wooden layers. There was a 0.5 meter air insulation between the wooden skin and the water tank body whose outer skin was also a double-layer steel plate, and the iron-sheet waterproof roof adopted white ash and sawdust as the insulation layer to prevent water frozen in the water tank in winter. Windows on the tower were narrow and long so as to reduce the thermal bridge on the interior wall. The window hole was wedged outwards to let much sunshine in and reduce heat loss, and could also be used as an embrasure serving as a temporary military facility.

A water tower consisted of roof, water tank, tower shaft and the base. Various wooden carvings on the facade added new vitality to the decoration and made the building gentler. Jagged and stepped wooden elements were decorated on the edge of some water tower eaves and the lower edge of the water tank. At the upper end of the water tank, vertical short wooden boards with their rounded triangle ends were closely arranged outside the horizontal wooden boards. The same delicate decoration motif was repeated on each side of the tank. The water tower shaft was of masonry structure applying the shape and color of stones or moldings created by masonry itself as the decoration. The waistline on the shaft showed a changing rhythm by stringcourses of the brick masonry. Corbels were sometimes used as the decoration at the junction of the water tank and the tower shaft. In regular-polygon-plan water tower, the corner was also decorated with traditional Russian house details, and the tower shaft was covered by mushroom stones. Bright colors had created a typical feature of the CER buildings. Different shape and color stones were sometimes used on the lower part of the tower shaft, thus created an exotic flavor. Unlike normal industrial buildings that focused more on their special functions than on decorations, water towers in the CER period presented high architectural and cultural charm with their facades full of characteristics of the texture and color of different materials.

# ARCHITECTURAL CULTURAL HERITAGE OF CHINESE EASTERN RAILWAY

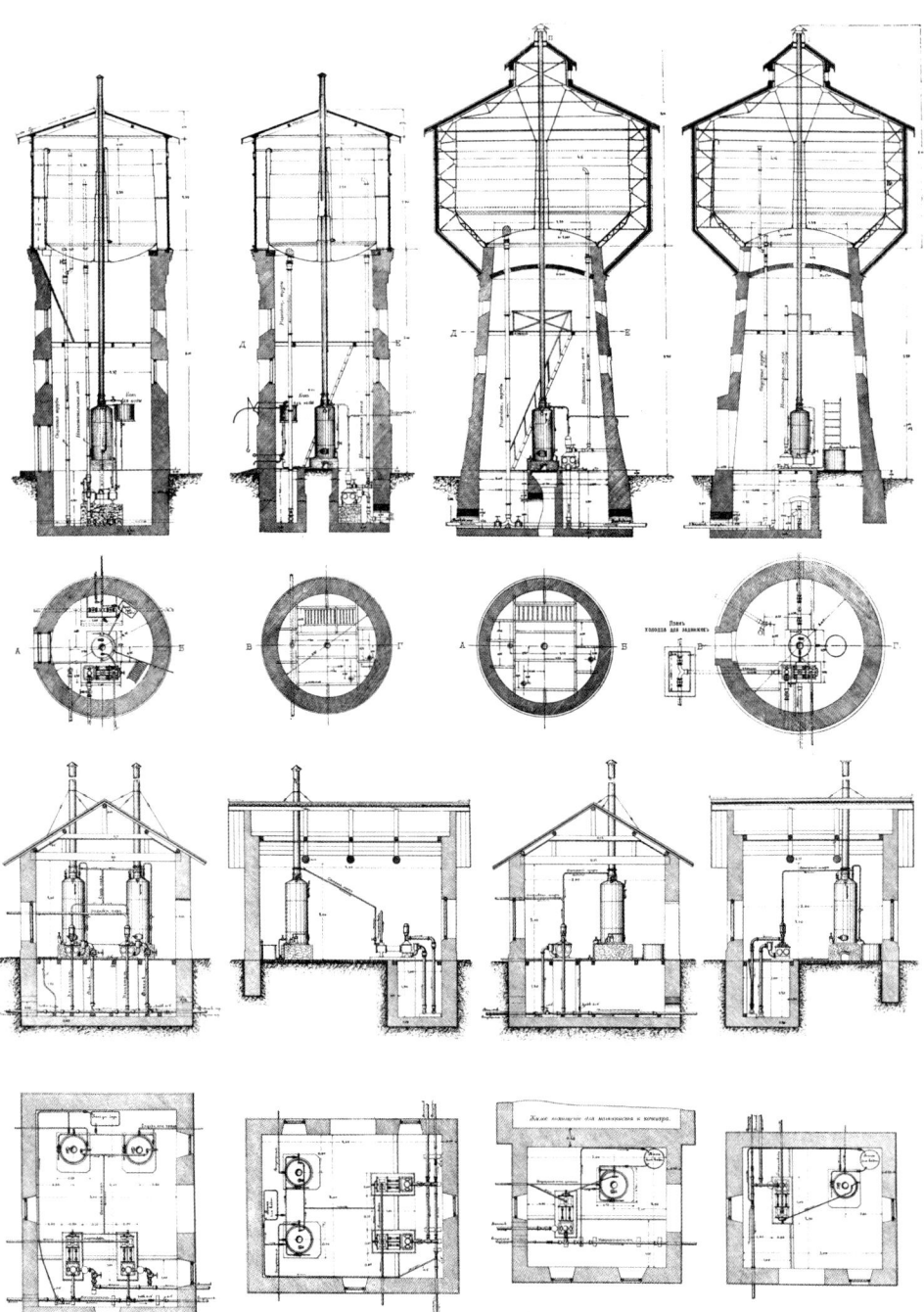

水塔及辅助建筑设计图 Drawings of water tower and affiliated facilities

穆棱站水塔历史照片
Historical photo of water tower in Muling

赫尔洪德历史照片
Historical photo of water tower in He'erhongde

砖石水塔历史照片 1
Historical photo of water tower 1

砖石水塔历史照片 2
Historical photo of water tower 2

哈尔滨水塔历史照片
Historical photo of water tower in Harbin

磨刀石水塔安装过程历史照片
Historical photo of construction process of water tower in Modaoshi

3 水塔 | 129

 满洲里道南水塔 Water Tower in north Manzhouli

 满洲里道北水塔 Water Tower in South Manzhouli

 巴林水塔 Water tower in Balin

 扎赉诺尔水塔 Water tower in Zhalainuoer

3 水塔 | 131

# ARCHITECTURAL CULTURAL HERITAGE OF CHINESE EASTERN RAILWAY

乌固诺尔水塔
Water tower in Wugunuoer

完工水塔
Water tower in Wangong

碾子山水塔
Water tower in Nianzishan

香坊水塔
Water tower in Xiangfang

博克图水塔
Water tower in Boketu

扎兰屯水塔
Water tower in Zhalantun

牙克石水塔
Water tower in Yakeshi

哈克水塔
Water tower in Hake

成吉思汗水塔
Water tower in Chengjisihan

伊列克得水塔
Water tower in Yiliekede

雅鲁水塔
Water tower in Yalu

龙江水塔
Water tower in Longjiang

中德水塔 Water tower in Zhongde

# 4 工区

工区是中东铁路沿线较为常见的小型功能性聚落，主要功能是线路养护与检修。其选址较注重距离的安排，需保证工区所辐射的工段之间的连续性，既可位于各等级站点之中，也可独立布置于没有建设基础的铁路线旁，均临近铁路。从具体职能、建筑布局以及形态表现方面的区别可分为有围墙工区与无围墙工区两类。

## 4.1 普通工区

普通工区不带有围墙，一般仅有铁路检修与维护职能，因此多位于各等级的站点附近，如哈尔滨、博克图等。除没有围墙外，建筑的形式、体量以及布局方式与带有围墙的工区差别不大，三栋建筑也呈半开敞的院落式排布。由于没有围墙，这类工区的地形适应性更好，可以建于有地势起伏之处。如博克图工区，建筑顺应地势，主体位于最高处，辅助建筑分布在下方，但整体上还是符合两横一纵式的排列方式与朝向选择。

## 4.2 防御性工区

防御性工区带有围墙，具有一定的军事职能，同时也是小型的驻扎营地，因此一般独立布置，距离站点较远。建筑呈封闭的院落式布局，以围护墙体围合成矩形院落，内部三栋建筑沿三面墙体布置，另一侧则为院落的主入口。三栋建筑规模不等，体量最大的建筑一般置于院落北侧的长边上，是工人与士兵的居住空间，另两栋建筑则尺度较小，各仅占主体建筑的约一半大小，功能主要是马厩、水泵房等。围墙以砖石砌筑，墙体较厚，主体内外均用石材，中间填充碎石、碎砖及泥土等混合材料。墙面上均匀排列狭窄射击孔，平面呈八字形，是军事功能性格最为典型的体现。另外，在院落的对角处设有两个圆形的小型碉堡，这也成为其最具识别性的特点。

这类工区是一种标准的建筑聚落，是标准化设计的一种具体类型。标准建筑聚落是指一些铁路附属设施中必不可少的、具有标准化配置的建筑功能组团，其功能单元类型与形式较为固定，因此可以用一个定型的布局形式进行批量化的建造。其具体特点为聚落都是由不同的几座单体建筑组合而成，这些建筑分为功能性主体建筑和辅助建筑，按照固定的功能关系及交通联系整合在一起，并通过室外路径、庭院、绿化，甚至带有防护性堡垒的围墙形成一定规模的院落。相同功能的建筑组团使用同样的标准设计和规划图纸，只是在适应不同的地貌条件或在针对不同需求时做适当的调整。工区具有固定的建筑类型配置和空间模式，外部带射击孔的石质围墙具有高度的封闭性和军事防御体系特征，因此只要规模没有变化，可以在不同的站点间大量复制。

工区建筑均为砖石砌筑，建筑形象与沿线主要的建筑风格相一致。很大一部分工区位于山区，距离城镇较远，使其得以在现代城镇建设中幸存，同时也多处于荒置的状态，急需保护。

## Work Areas

Work area was a small-sized and more common functional working and living place along the Chinese eastern railway line, with the function to maintain, examine and repair the railway. The distance among the work areas was more important in the site selection, where the continuity between the work area and the processing block surrounded must be guaranteed. No matter where the work areas were located in different graded stations as well as independently in the side of the railway route without fundamental construction facilities, all of them were not far from the stations. According to the difference in specific function and architectural layout as well as form properties, the walled and non-walled work areas are divided.

The non-walled work area was normally located nearby the station of different grades, with function of the line maintenance and repair, such as Harbin and Boketu station etc. Except for the wall, there was no great difference between walled and non-walled work areas in architectural form, size and layout pattern. Generally speaking, this kind of work place included three buildings, presenting half-open courtyard type. Since there was no wall surrounding, the work area became more suitable for the land, even to be constructed in undulating terrain. Boketu work area was an example in the terrain utilization of the site, the main building was constructed in the high part of the location and subsidiary buildings were arranged in the low part. The general layout, the range pattern and orientation selection of the buildings were coincident with the distribution in two horizontal and one vertical.

The walled work area, also called defence work area, had a certain military function, where was garrisoned a small number of troops and normally constructed independently and a little far from stations. The buildings presented a closed courtyard type, with a rectangular court surrounded by the wall. The wall was built by bricks and stones in much thickness, and the dimension stones were placed on both outsides of the wall and some mixed materials were filled inside in gravel, bricks and clay and so on, the shooting holes were well distributed on the wall. In the courtyard, three buildings were built along the adjacent three walls and the main entrance is on the rest side of the wall. These three kinds of buildings were different in size, where the largest building was normally located in the long edge of north side of the courtyard as the living space for workers and soldiers. The other two buildings was about half size of the main building, mainly as stable and pump house.

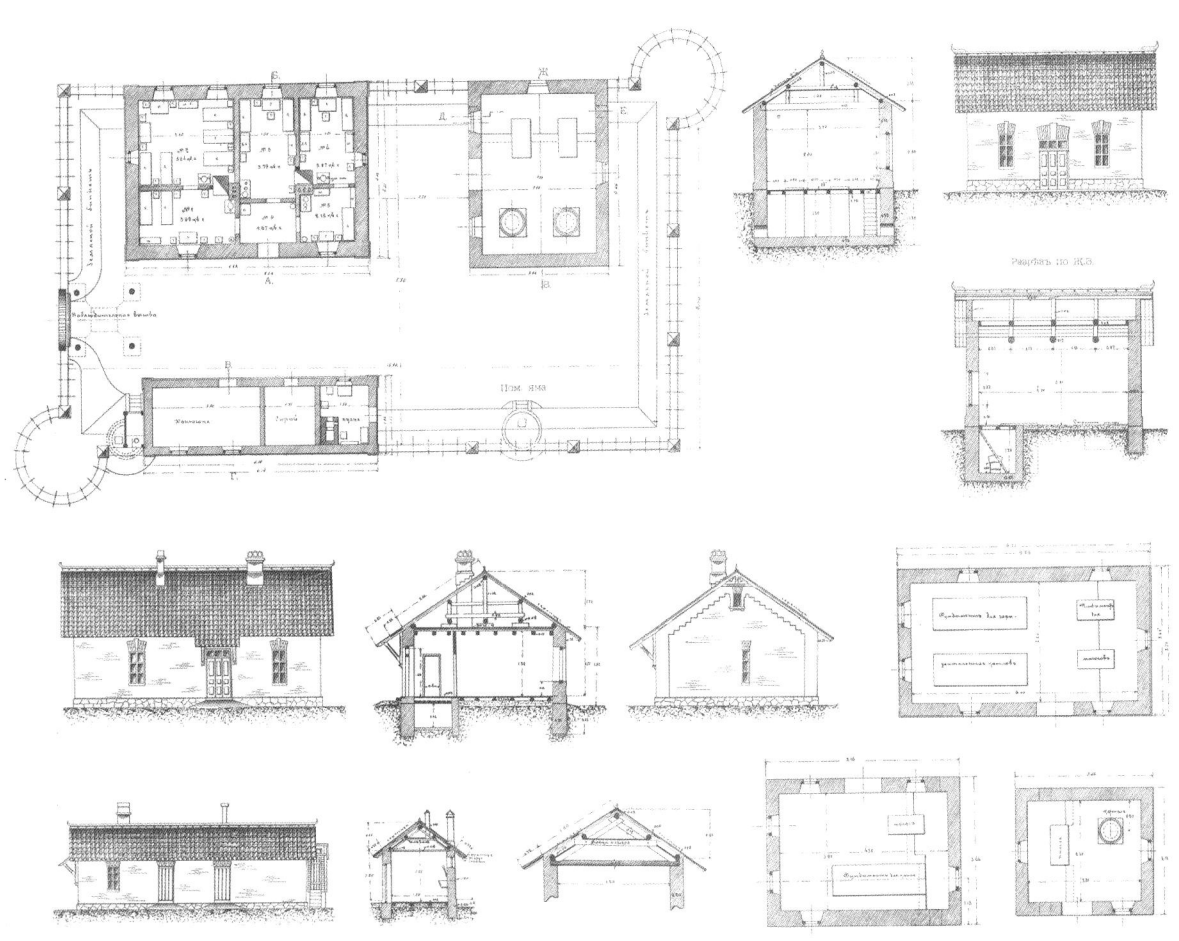

防御性工区标准设计图 Standardized drawings of defence work area

穆棱河工区历史照片 Historical photo of defence work area in Mulingr river

东线工区历史照片 Historical photo of defence work area on east line of CER

东线哨所历史照片 Historical photo of defence work area on east line of CER

南线哨所历史照片 Historical photo of defence work area on south line of CER

横道河子防御性工区 Defence work area in Hengdaohezi

老少沟防御性工区 Defence work area in Laoshaogou

戈达木防御性工区 Defence work area in Gedamu

一间堡防御性工区 Defence work area in Yijianpu

达家沟哨所 1 Defence work area in Dajiagou 1

拉古防御性工区 Defence work area in Lagu

磨刀石防御性工区 Defence work area in Modaoshi

达家沟哨所 2 Defence work area in Dajiagou 2

山市防御性工区 1 Defence work area in Shanshi 1

山市防御性工区 2 Defence work area in Shanshi 2

石河防御性工区 Defence work area in Shihe

中德防御性工区 Defence work area in Zhongde

代马沟防御性工区 1 Defence work area in Daimagou 1

代马沟防御性工区 2 Defence work area in Daimagou 2

下城子防御性工区 Defence work area in Xiachengzi

哈拉哈防御性工区 Defence work area in Halaha

东线工区历史照片 Historical photo of work area on east line of CFR

伊列克得工区历史照片 Historical photo of work area in Yiliekede

扎兰屯工区历史照片 Historical photo of work area in Zhalantun

大庆让胡路工区 Work area on Ranghu Road, Daqing

土塔河子工区 Work area in Tutahezi

帽儿山工区 Work area in Mao'ershan

雅鲁工区 Work area in Yalu

三道桥工区 Work area in Sandaoqiao

高台子工区 Work area in Gaotaizi

舍利屯工区 Work area in Shelitun

博克图工区 Work area in Boketu

喇嘛山工区 Work area in Lamashan

卧牛河工区 Work area in Woniuhe

中德工区 Work area in Zhongde

齐家工区 Work area in Qijia

赫尔洪德工区 Work area in Heerhongde

高家工区 Work area in Gaojia

前后代工区 Work area in Qianhoudai

南木工区 Work area in Nanmu

万乐工区 Work area in Wanle

# ARCHITECTURAL CULTURAL HERITAGE OF CHINESE EASTERN RAILWAY

小九工区
Work area in Xiaojiu

红房子工区
Work area in Hongfangzi

九江泡工区
Work area in Jiujiangpao

青云工区
Work area in Qingyun

高岭子工区
Work area in Gaolingzi

山底工区
Work area in Shandi

鲁河工区
Work area in Luhe

龙江工区
Work area in Longjiang

黑岗工区
Work area in Heigang

哈拉苏工区
Work area in Halasu

成吉思汗工区
Work area in Chengjisihan

乌川工区
Work area in Wuchuan

白山工区
Work area in Baishan

小扎泥河工区
Work area in Xiaozhanihe

小五官工区
Work area in Xiaowuguan

# 5 厂房

铁路的修筑与机械制造、建材加工及原料开采等工业行业息息相关,随着中东铁路的修建以及铁路运输系统的不断完善,大量的铁路附属工厂为满足运输需求便选址于铁路沿线附近以实现其生产需求,并且也可以降低货物的运输成本。中东铁路附属地内各类厂房的建设不仅推动了工业技术发展,也是当时建筑技术水平的最佳见证。

## 5.1 铁路机械厂

铁路车辆与设备的维修和加工需要在铁路沿线设立必要的机械工厂,工厂的选址需要充分考虑多种要素,便利的位置可以既使工厂靠近城市,又为其扩建和发展留有余地。交通方面,尽量使工厂与码头和火车站距离较近,水陆运输都很便利;水源是选址的另一个重要因素,靠近江河的位置可以有效地解决工厂的供水和排水问题。在中东铁路附属机械厂中,无疑哈尔滨总工厂是规模最大、设立最早、最为先进的典型代表。

中东铁路哈尔滨总工厂是由中东铁路公司投资兴建的,在资金和技术方面都有良好保障,从1898年兴建临时工厂到1903年扩建新厂,直至1907年新厂建成。中东铁路哈尔滨总工厂选址在埠头区(今道里区)临近松花江一带的水运码头西侧的平坦地段。中东铁路哈尔滨总工厂以其庞大的规模、先进的空间技术成为当时具有现代化水平的工业建筑群。据史料记载,中东铁路哈尔滨总工厂新址"占地面积84万平方米,建筑面积3.8万平方米,安装机械设备324台",5条主运输线中有2条可以直通哈尔滨站。整个工厂有11个分厂,是"集蒸汽机车、客车、货车维修、加工"为一体的综合性工厂。中东铁路哈尔滨总工厂的结构形式包括墙体承重和墙体与柱混合承重两种方式,屋架有木屋架和钢屋架,墙体包括砖墙和混凝土墙,柱则有木、钢筋混凝土、钢柱等不同类型。厂房的跨度有单跨、双跨、三跨以至更多跨,屋架的形式也很多样,同一座厂房的不同跨空间采用不同屋架形式来满足各自所需,充满技术理性。总工厂厂房还有良好的自然采光和通风设计,建筑形象更是充分利用俄罗斯砖砌装饰语言实现了技术和艺术的高度统一。

## 5.2 电力工厂

铁路的运营和附属工业设施的使用需要充足稳定的电力供应,发电厂的选址一般位于机械制造厂附近,便于电力及时、安全的输送。中东铁路沿线及铁路附属地中都会设立若干不同等级规模的发电厂或电站。中东铁路发电厂,原名为中东铁路电灯厂,始建于1903年,是中东铁路设立最早的发电厂。该厂房构造方式与锻造厂房如出一辙,皆为砖墙砌筑与钢架屋顶相互组合构成。不同的是,为了满足厂房室内空间的采光,锻造厂利用屋顶中央采光带来采光,而发电厂则利用建筑立面开大窗形式采光,厂房内部设有4台25千瓦的汽轮机发电站,不仅可以供厂区内部设备运转、照明,同时也可供哈尔滨站及铁路各部门用电。发电厂车间厂房之外同样配有烟囱等附属设施,形式与锻造厂烟囱形式相似，同样为方形基座上方有平面形式为八角形的烟囱主体，主体上方附有层层铁箍缠绕以加固主体结构的稳定性。

### 5.3 煤矿与船舶工厂

在中东铁路众多附属工业中，原料开采业是比较特殊的一种类型，而其中煤矿工业又最为典型。根据文献记载，中东铁路修建之初，就考虑到矿产资源的攫取利用，因此在铁路线路的规划中，往往选择靠近煤矿的位置以便于资源的开采和运输。1902 年初，沙俄与清政府签订《黑龙江开挖煤斤合同》，取得了在黑龙江省境内中东铁路沿线附近开采煤炭的权利。同年 8 月，中东铁路理事会批准波洛尼科夫的开采煤矿计划，并于 9 月 1 日正式建立一号矿井，时名"波洛尼科夫矿场"。1902—1910 年，中东铁路公司直接经营期间，煤矿陆续开凿，形成系统化管理模式，并建成了我国首个露天煤矿。《中俄解决悬案大纲协定》签订后扎赉诺尔煤矿随之成为中苏合办企业，归中东铁路管理局经营。煤矿周边还建起了医院、学校、商店、俱乐部、图书馆等。煤矿矿井的厂房多以平房为主，双坡屋顶，局部有二层尖屋顶阁楼，旁边耸立一座高大烟囱，在另一侧有一座金属构架开采设施，运煤轨道将不同矿井连接。

中东铁路跨度巨大，沿线江河众多，因此在铁路附属工厂中有一特殊类型的工厂——船舶工厂。船舶厂早期主要承担修筑码头与修建船所的任务，后期也可以修理及制造各类船舶和船用机器。中东铁路桥梁组装厂始建于 1898 年，原为中东铁路航务处松浦船坞，位于道外区松浦镇航务街 1 号，1926 年建修船所，设南北两港，南港可泊船 40 余艘，北港可泊船 60 余艘。

时至今日，中东铁路沿线的铁路工业建筑所剩无几，但仍能从中窥探出当时工业建筑的发展水平。这些铁路工业厂房现已成为各类建筑遗产中独具特色的一类，记载着中东铁路修建那段轰轰烈烈的历史。

## Plants

With the construction of CER and the improvement of the railway transportation system, a large number of factories were located near the railway line, to meet with their production needs using the transportation conditions and reduce the cost of goods transporting, therefore the construction of the railway was closely related to such industrial sectors as machinery manufacturing, building materials processing and raw material mining. The industrial buildings along the CER included railway machinery factories, ship factories, power plants, coal mines, etc. The construction of various types of factories not only promoted the development of industrial technology, but also witnessed the construction standard of the period.

Machinery factories were founded along the railway line to maintain and process the railway vehicles and equipments. The site needed carefully selected to keep the factory not only close to the city but also have spaces for its future expansion. Being close to the dock and the railway station, the factory could occupy convenient water and land transportations. Meanwhile, water source was another important factor for the factory site, and a location close to a river could effectively solve the problem of water supply and drainage in the factory. Among the machinery factories along CER, the Harbin General Railway Works was undoubtedly the largest, earliest and most advanced one, with high standards in investment, site and technology due to its"sustained factory"standard of construction. Load-bearing walls or pillars compound wtih load-bearing walls were the two main structures of its factories, with roof trusses in wood or iron, walls in brick or concrete, and pillars in wood, reinforced concrete or iron. Spans of the factories were in single, double, triple and even more, as well as various forms of roof trusses. Technical rationality could be seen when different spans in one factory adopted different forms of roof trusses to match with their needs. Natural lighting and ventilation were also well designed in Harbin General Railway Works, and its architectural image achieved the perfect unity of technology and art by fully using of the Russian brick decoration languages.

Power plants, which provided sufficient and stable supply of electricity to the railway and industrial facilities, were generally located near the machinery manufacturing plants to facilitate the timely and safe electricity transportation. Power plants or power stations in different scales were founded in CER and CER Zones. The CER Power Plant was the earliest one, originally named the CER Electric Lamp Factory founded in 1903. The plant adopted brick masonry wall and iron roof truss as same as the forge factory in the Harbin General Railway Works, only different from that the forge factory used central skylights on the roof for interior lighting, while the power plant used large windows on the building facade. Chimneys outside the power plant was also similar with that of the forge factory, with a square base and an octagonal chimney shaft, whose upper part was hooped with layers of irons to strengthen the main structure.

The CER line was so long and it crossed so many rivers that a specific type of factory was built along CER—the ship factory, which was in charge of the construction of dock and shipyard in the early time, and later repairing and manufacturing various ships and ship machines. Among other industries along CER, raw material mining industry was a particular type, especially the coal mining industry. During the years between 1902 to 1910 when directly operated by the CER Company, coal mines were successively excavated, forming a systematic management mode, and the first open-pit coal mine in China was built. Hospitals, schools, supply and marketing cooperatives, clubs, libraries, etc. were also built around the coal mines which gradually developed into resource-based settlements.

# ARCHITECTURAL CULTURAL HERITAGE OF CHINESE EASTERN RAILWAY

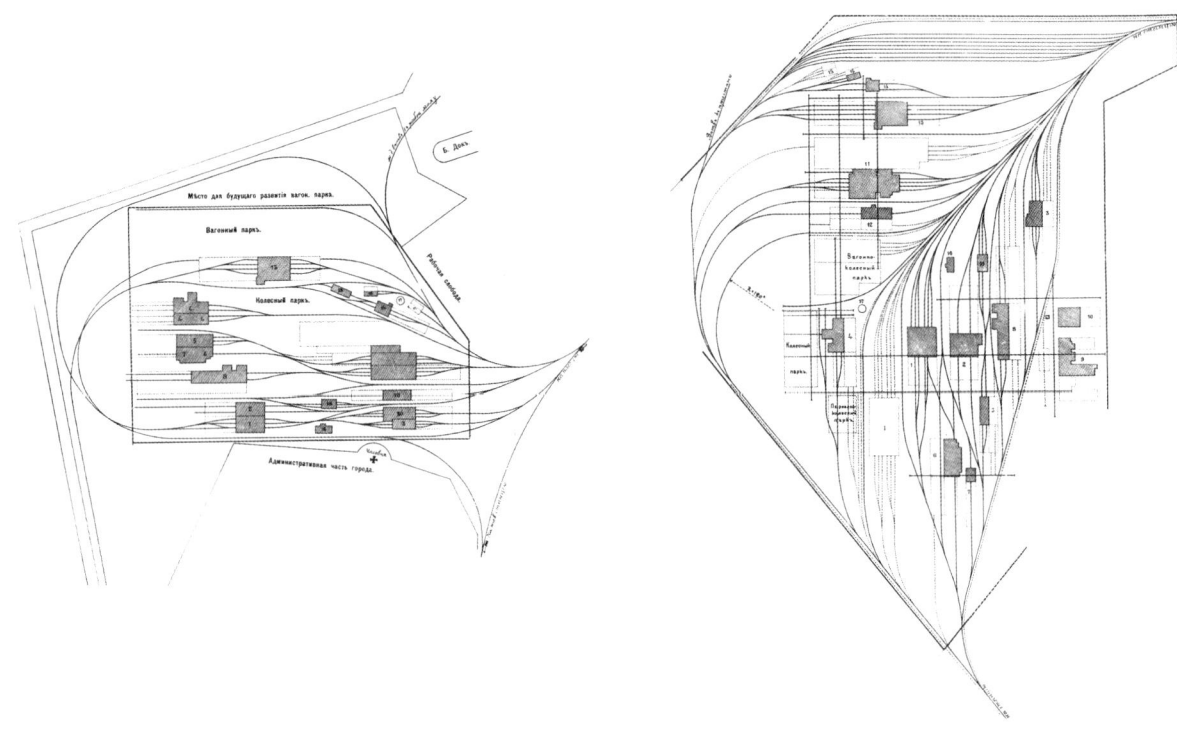

中东铁路大连工厂规划图
Planning of the factory of CER in Dalian

中东铁路哈尔滨总工厂规划图
Planning of the general factory of CER in Harbin

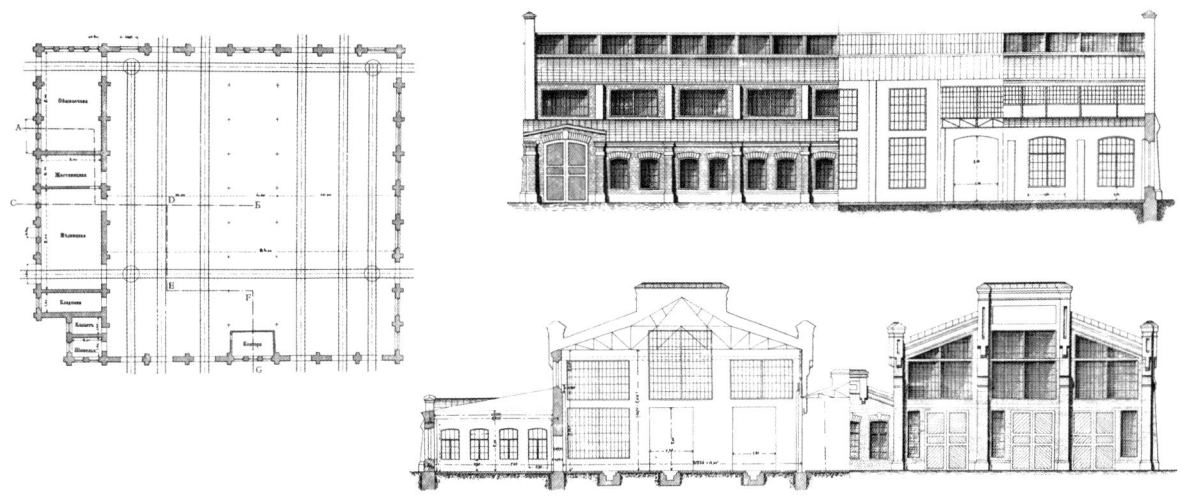

中东铁路工厂厂房设计图纸 1 Darwings of buildings of the factory of CER 1

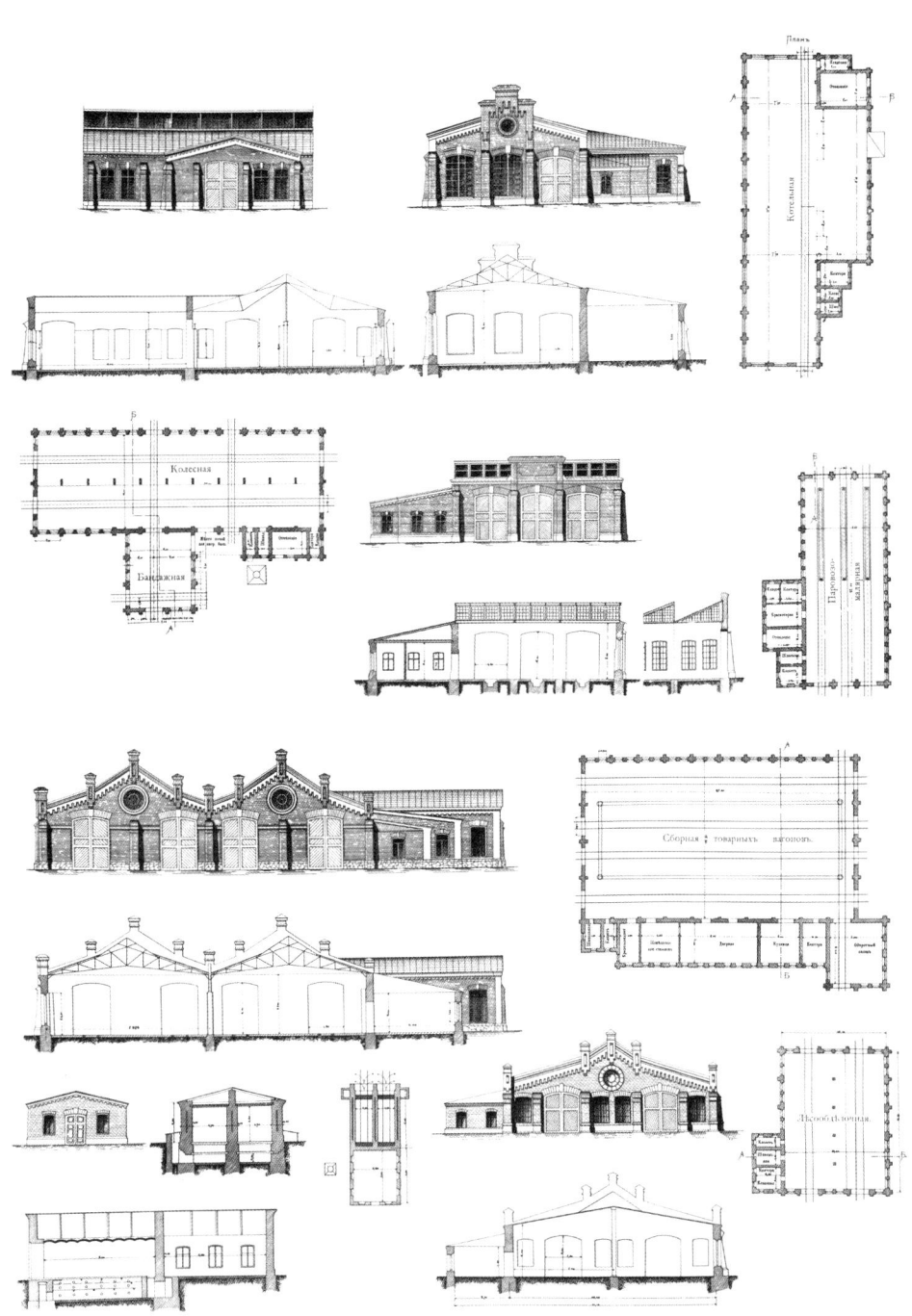

中东铁路工厂厂房设计图纸 2 Darwings of buildings of the factory of CER 2

# ARCHITECTURAL CULTURAL HERITAGE OF CHINESE EASTERN RAILWAY

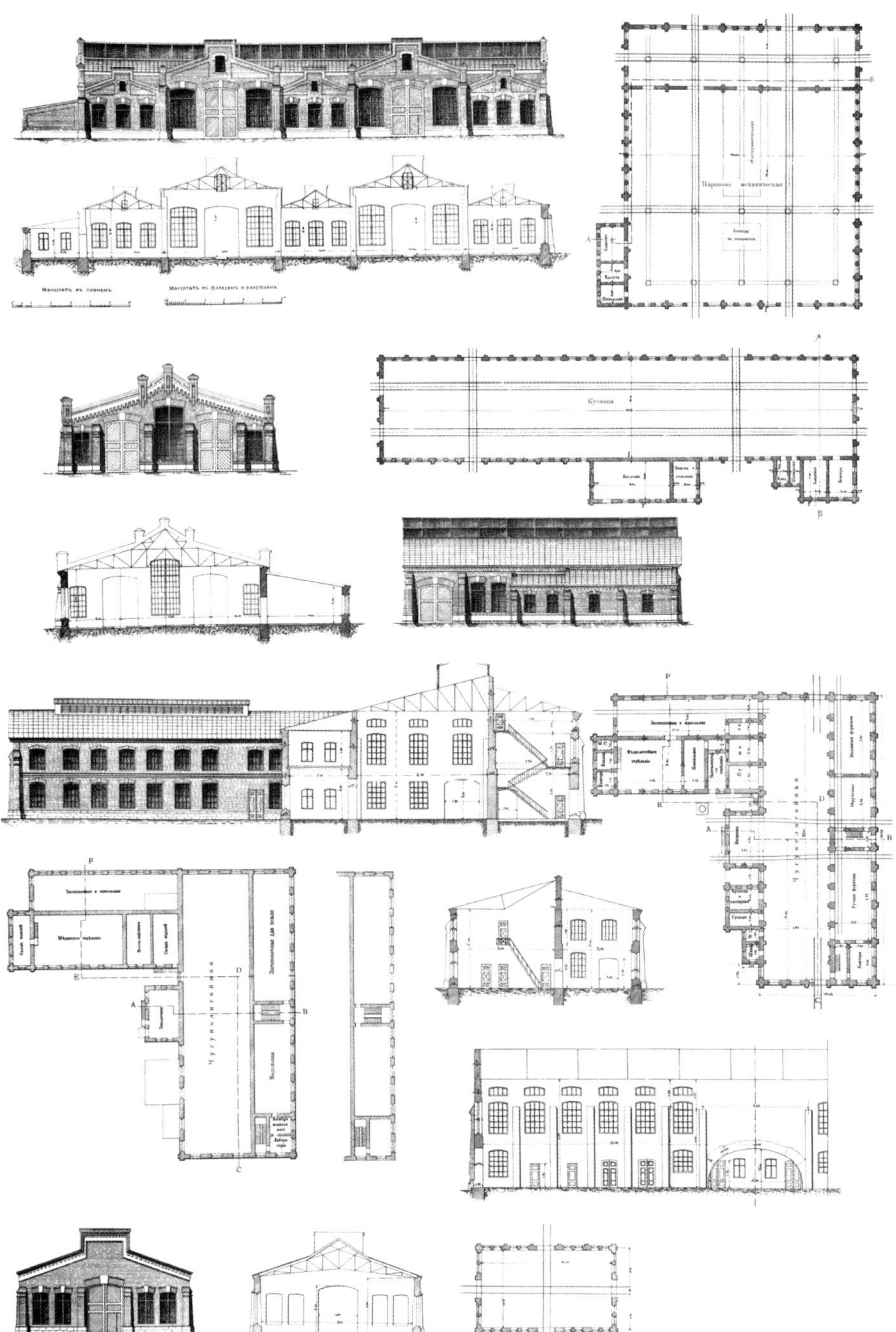

中东铁路工厂厂房设计图纸 3 Darwings of buildings of the factory of CER 3

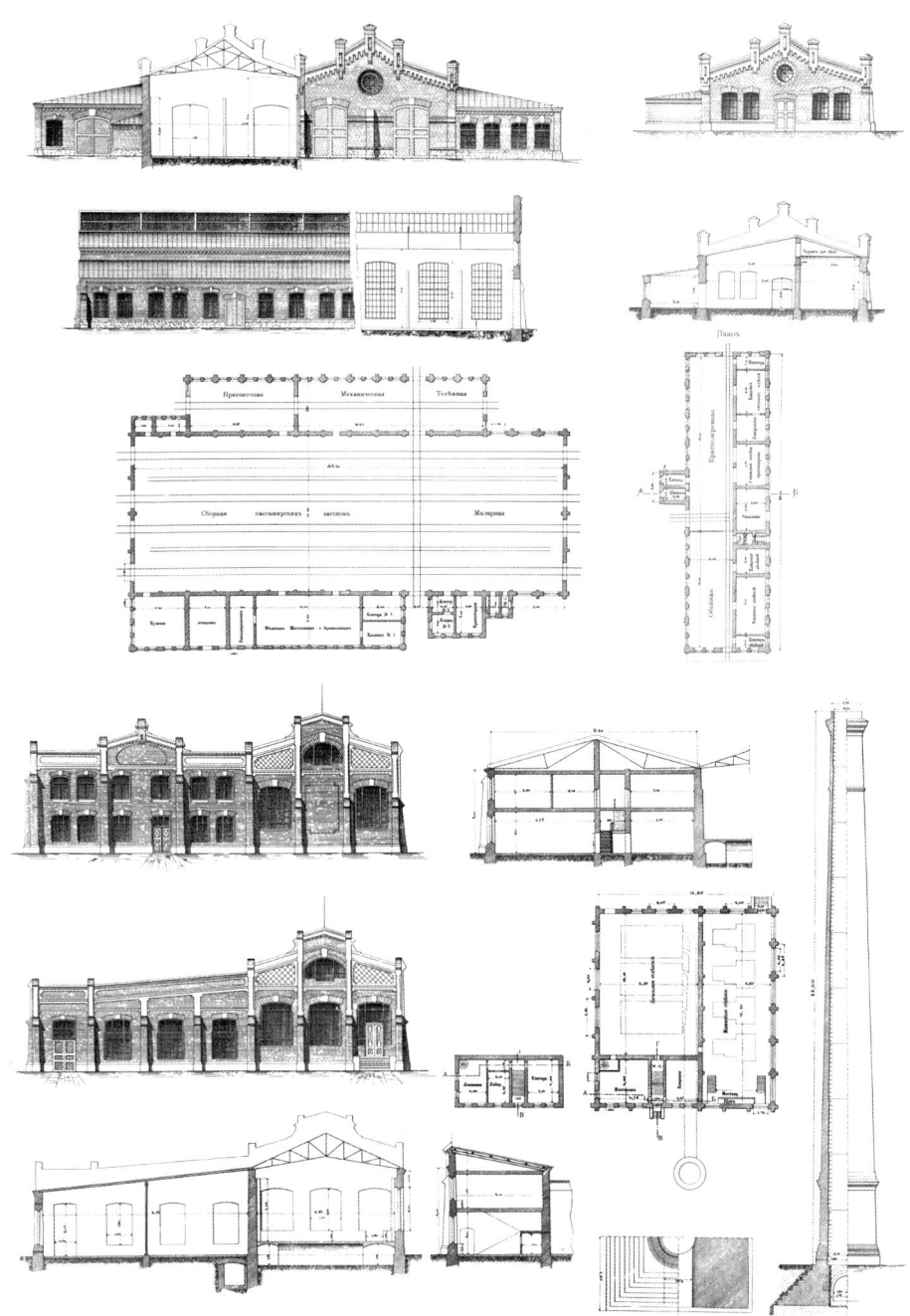

中东铁路工厂厂房设计图纸 4 Darwings of buildings of the factory of CER 4

中东铁路哈尔滨总工厂全景历史照片 Historical photo of panorama of the general factory of CER in Harbin

中东铁路哈尔滨总工厂厂房历史照片 Historical photos of buildings of the general factory of CER in Harbin

中东铁路哈尔滨总工厂厂房 Buildings of the general factory of CER in Harbin

中东铁路哈尔滨电厂历史照片 Historical photo of power station of CER in Harbin

# ARCHITECTURAL CULTURAL HERITAGE OF CHINESE EASTERN RAILWAY

辽宁灯塔煤矿历史照片 Historical photos of coal mine in Dengta, Liaoning province

扎赉诺尔煤矿历史照片 Historical photos of coal mine in Zhalainuoer

# 6 仓库、厕所及其他辅助用房

仓库和厕所是站舍、住宅、兵营等建筑群的重要附属建筑，在中东铁路各个站区、营区、住区均有分布。一些公厕和仓库采用了标准化设计，但在具体的建造中，多样的细部样式被添加其中，这使厕所和仓库的建筑形象朴素而不单一。其他辅助建筑设施还包括开水房、水泵房、石质蓄水池等。

## 6.1 厕所

中东铁路公厕的设计展现了高超的水平，在工艺技术层面也有突出成就。中东铁路沿线主要使用较为原始的旱厕，气味较重，这就要求公共厕脱离其服务的建筑主体单独建设，其结构形式为砖木结构、石木结构或全木结构，很注重粪尿的收集处理和通风排气的工艺设计。厕所按照使用对象不同可分为：住宅附属厕所、兵营厕所和公共厕所。住宅的附属厕所位于住宅院落中，并不与住宅毗邻，主要供住户使用。这类厕所多为木构，矩形平面，四角设置木柱，柱子上开凿凹槽，柱间用木板条垒砌作为墙体，屋顶采用俄式的单坡屋顶，其椽子密集，封檐板厚重。根据家庭人口的数量，木构厕所多采用1—3个蹲位，每个蹲位独立设置厕门，蹲位间用隔墙分隔，蹲位地板垫高，下部挖坑设有贮存便溺的空间，并配备有通风烟囱或通气窗，将厕所内浊气抽到室外，厕所的便溺贮存室后墙设有可开启的盖子，可收集便溺用于耕作。站区的公共厕所修建标准较高，蹲位较住宅厕所有所增加，多采用砖石砌筑，矩形平面，内部通过隔墙分隔成男厕和女厕，男女厕分别设置独立的门斗，门斗在遮蔽视线的同时还能防风保温。厕所内部地板抬高，蹲位下部设置便溺贮存室，一些等级较高的厕所还设置了专门的采暖设施，在中东铁路西线的宋站、扎赉诺尔，东线的磨刀石站等地均存有这种形制的厕所。兵营附属厕所根据营区人数而设，人数较少的设木厕所，与住宅厕所相同；人数稍多的则近似公共厕所，随着人数增加蹲位。

## 6.2 仓库

仓库按照其服务对象不同大致可分为住宅附属仓库、货运站场仓库两类。住宅附属仓库大多设置于住宅院落中，少数住宅附属仓库位于院落外部，主要供住户作为日常生活仓储之用。住宅附属仓房规模不大，平面大多为矩形，有些仓房内部分为若干个仓储间，供不同住户分别使用。每个仓储间都分别开门，门轴、门闩等构件为生铁铸造，用道钉与木质门框固定。这类仓房一般为木构，和木构厕所相似，采用木柱上开凿凹槽，榫接木板条形成墙体，屋顶大多采用单坡屋顶，便于雨水倾泻。一些住宅附属仓库向地下拓展空间，外部墙体堆土，达到控制室内温度的效果，既可在冬季存粮储菜，又可在夏季贮冰。中东铁路一些站点配有货场，货场以仓库建筑为核心，货场仓库主要用于粮食、木材等物资集散的临时仓储空间，一般设置在站区内部或附近。货场仓库的长度和跨度都比较大，大多以砖石结构结合木构屋架建构而成，一般为单层建筑，举架较高，便于货物流通。如哈尔滨货场，每间仓库长40—50米，横向跨度约 13 米，十多个仓库串联起来达到 670 余米。仓库一侧紧挨且沿着铁路线平行布置，采用砖墙围合成矩形平面，横向双向开门，基座与车站站台同高，便于货车卸货，不挨着铁路线一侧的门设有坡道，便于货物转运，2016 年哈尔滨货场拆除。此外一面坡、德惠等车站附近也遗存有货场仓库。

中东铁路仓库和厕所具有数量多、分布广等特点，作为基本的生活配套设施，其重要性不言而喻。厕所和仓库的使用性质决定其平面布局和建筑样式的简洁性和质朴性，其朴素简洁的建筑特点使其在种类众多的中东铁路建筑并不凸显。但正是这些不显现的建筑体现了对生活细节无微不至的关心，这也是保障中东铁路顺利建设运行的重要条件。

## Storehouse, Lavatory and Other Assistant Room

Storehouse and lavatory were important subsidiary buildings in the railway architectural complex, such as the station, residence and barracks etc., which were built in all places of each station, barracks and residence. The standardizing design was adopted in construction of some lavatory and storehouse. In specific construction, many detail constitutive pattern made the architectural form more simple but no single. The subsidiary buildings also included boiling water house, pump house, stone impounding reservoir and so on.

Lavatory was an important and specific building type along the railway line, which were divided into the resident toilet, barracks toilet and latrine according to the using object. The latrine design along Chinese Eastern Railway was in much high level, with distinguishing feature in process engineering. Primitive dry toilets with heavy smell was mainly used in the railway line, which required latrine to be constructed separately from main buildings, normally in brick-wood, stone-wood or wood structure. Some latrines have heating system in winter.

Storehouse was roughly divided into two types, including resident affiliated facilities and freight yard storehouse. Most of resident affiliated facilities were located in the resident yard and a few of them was outside, which were used as a store space of diary supplies, normally in wood structure. Some stations along Chinese Eastern Railway line had freight yard, where the main building was storehouse and provided a temporary distributing area for food supplies, wood and other material collection, normally within the station or nearby. The length and span of the freight yard storehouse were much large, which were mostly constructed in masonry combined with wood roof structure.

Along Chinese Eastern Railway line, large number of storehouses and lavatories were constructed and also distributed widely. The simplicity in plane layout and construction pattern made them less prominent in many kinds of buildings of Chinese Eastern Railway. It dose these ordinary buildings that not only meet the needs of their function but also present solicitude for the user in detail, then becoming one of their important requirements to ensure the smooth construction of Chinese Eastern Railway.

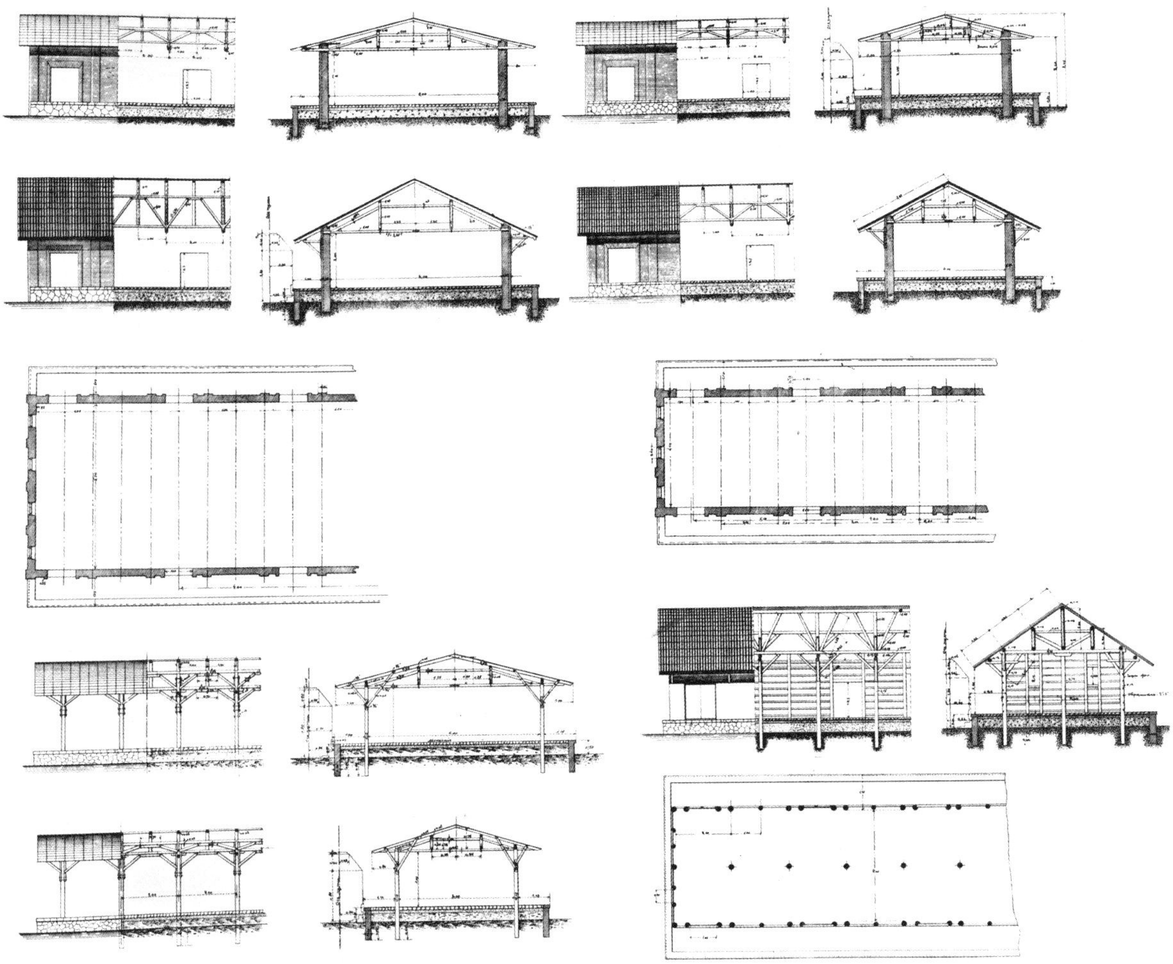

货运站台和堆栈设计图 Drawings of freight yard

扎兰屯货栈历史照片 Historical photos of freight yard storehouse in Zhalantun

6 仓库、厕所及其他辅助用房

# ARCHITECTURAL CULTURAL HERITAGE OF CHINESE EASTERN RAILWAY

扎兰屯货栈
Freight yard storehouse in Zhalantun

马桥河粮仓
Granary in Maqiaohe

一面坡粮食仓库
Granary in Yimianpo

齐齐哈尔货栈历史照片
Historical photo of freight yard storehouse in Qiqihaer

横道河子住宅仓库
Residence storehouse in Hengdaohezi

里木店仓库
Storehouse in Limudian

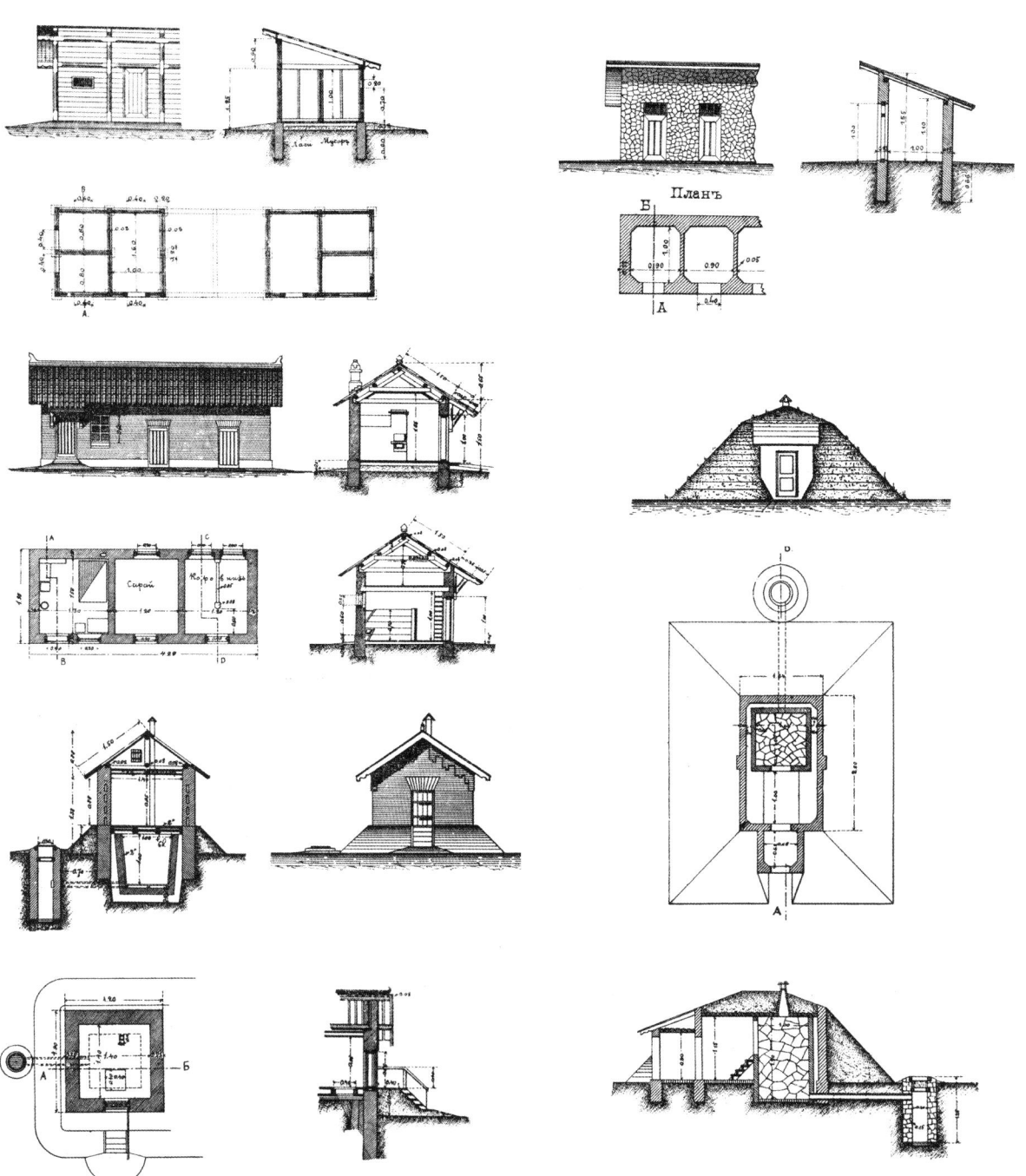

住宅附属仓库设计图 Drawings of residence storehouse

6 仓库、厕所及其他辅助用房

# ARCHITECTURAL CULTURAL HERITAGE OF CHINESE EASTERN RAILWAY

扎兰屯住宅仓房
Residence storehouse in Zhalantun

石头河子木仓房
Residence storehouse in Shitouhezi

满洲里住宅仓房 1
Residence storehouse in Manzhouli 1

满洲里住宅仓房 2
Residence storehouse in Manzhouli 2

满洲里住宅仓房 3
Residence storehouse in Manzhouli 3

庙台子冰窖
Icehouse in Miaotaizi

虎尔虎拉住宅拉仓房
Residence storehouse in Huerhula

乌奴耳住宅仓房
Residence storehouse in Wunuer

嵯岗住宅仓房
Residence storehouse in Cuogang

哈拉苏车站仓库
Storehouse in Halasu station

代马沟仓库 1
Storehouse in Daimagou 1

代马沟仓库 2
Storehouse in Daimagou 2

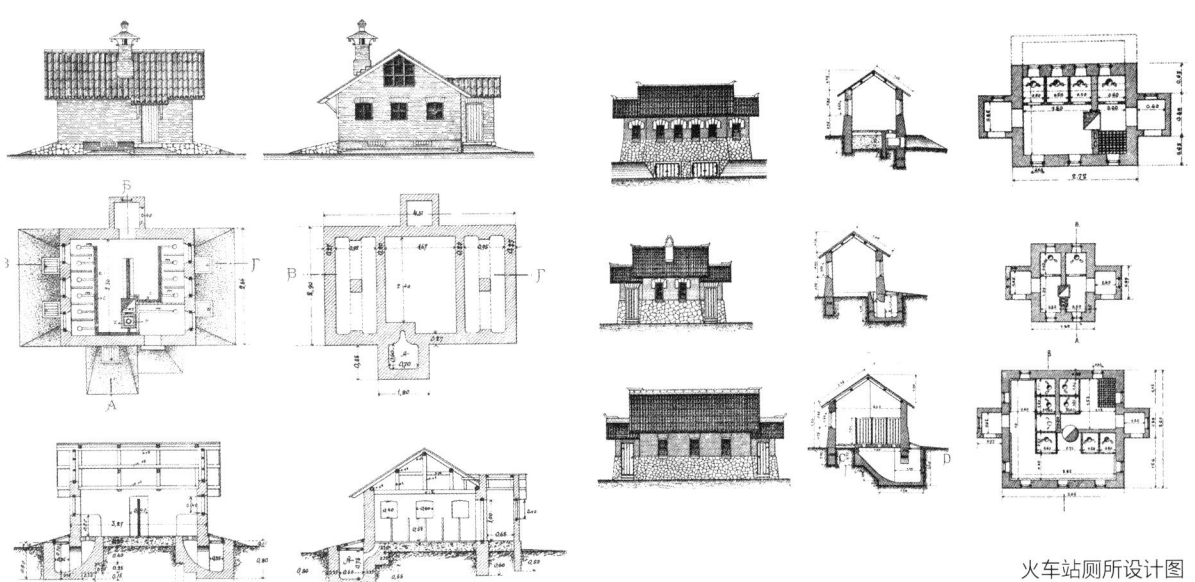

火车站厕所设计图
Drawings of lavatory in train station

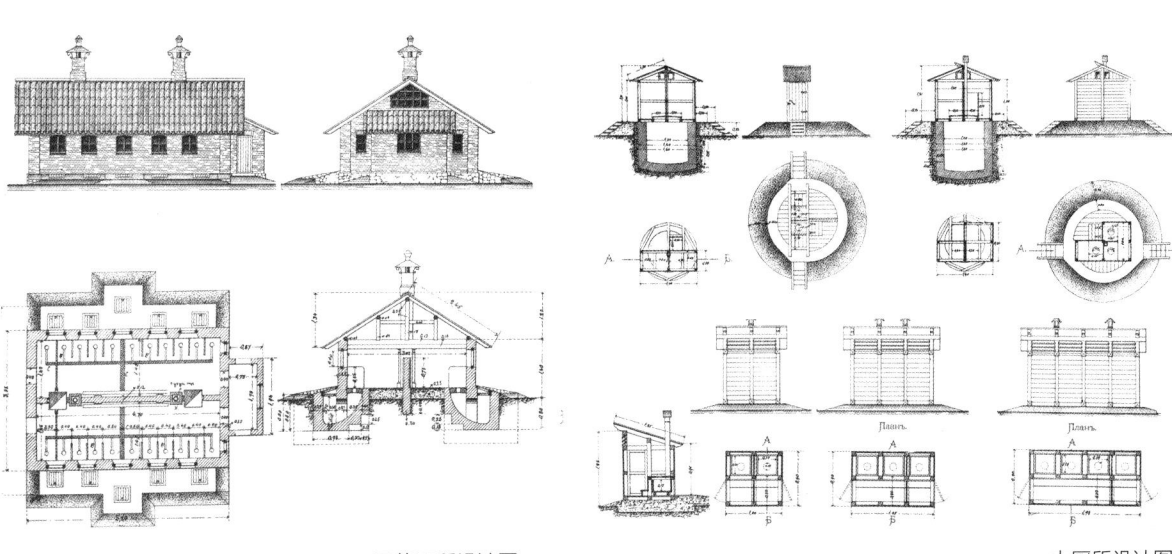

军营厕所设计图
Drawings of barrack lavatory

木厕所设计图
Drawings of wooden lavatory

6 仓库、厕所及其他辅助用房 | 173

# ARCHITECTURAL CULTURAL HERITAGE OF CHINESE EASTERN RAILWAY

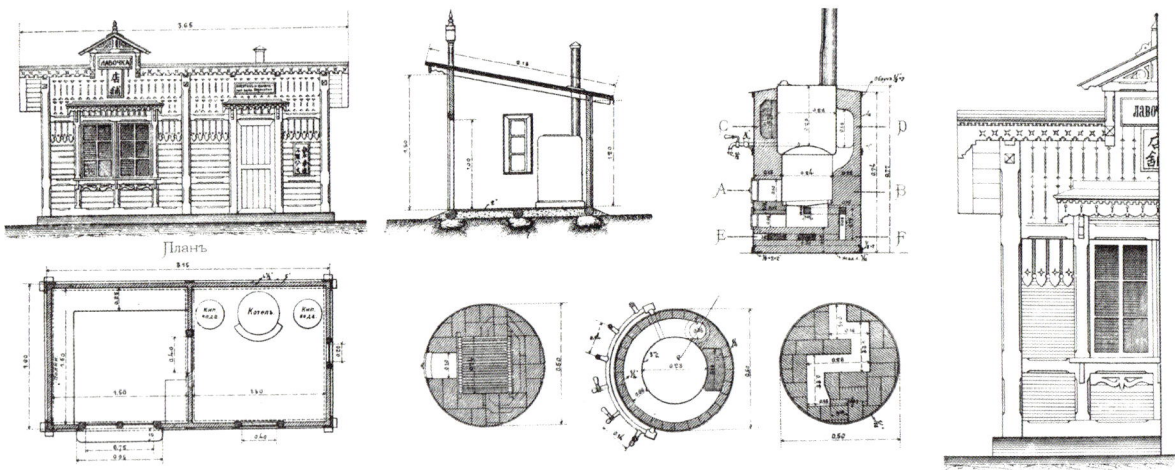

开水房设计图纸 Drawings of boiling water house

博克图厕所历史照片
Historical photo of lavatory in Boketu

博克图开水房历史照片
Historical photo of boiling water house in Boketu

哈拉苏木厕所
Wooden lavatory in Halasu

满洲里木厕所1
Wooden lavatory in Manzhouli 1

满洲里木厕所2
Wooden lavatory in Manzhouli 2

扎赉诺尔厕所
Lavatory in Zhalainuoer

宋站厕所
Lavatory in Song

九江泡厕所
Lavatory in Jiujiangpao

赫尔洪德厕所
Lavatory in Heerhongde

磨刀石厕所
Lavatory in Modaoshi

细鳞河厕所
Lavatory in xilinhe

# ARCHITECTURAL CULTURAL HERITAGE OF CHINESE EASTERN RAILWAY

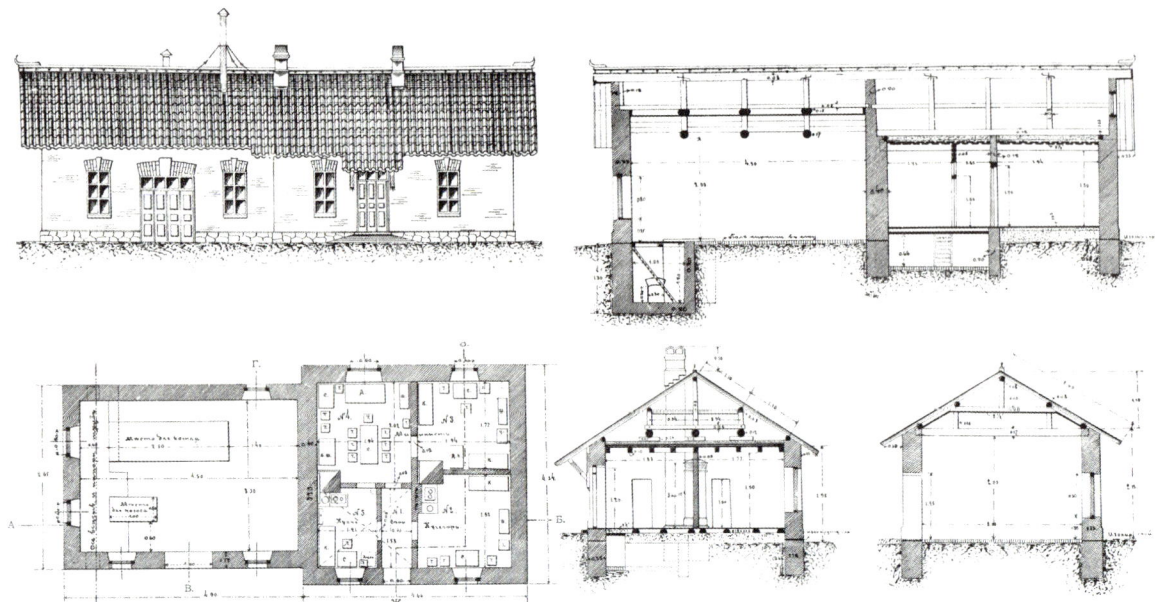

汲水房设计图纸
Drawings of pump house

汲水房历史照片
Historical photos of pump house

虎尔虎拉汲水房
Pump house in Huerhula

成吉思汗汲水房
Pump house in Chengjisihan

哈克汲水房
Pump house in Hake

免渡河汲水房  
Pump house in Mianduhe

嵯岗汲水房  
Pump house in Cuogang

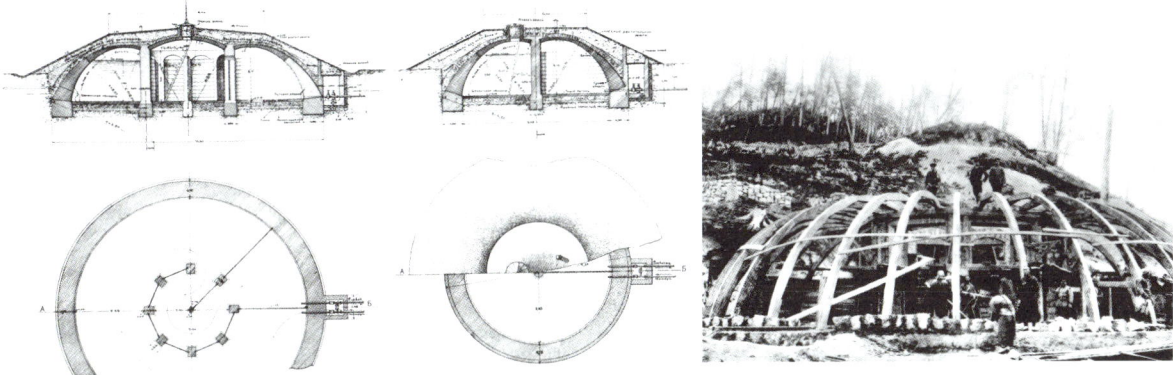

石质水池设计图及建设过程历史照片  
Drawings and historical photo of construction process of stone reservoir

北林铁路油库  
Oil depot in Beilin

一面坡机车库附属建筑  
Assistant building of garage in Yimianpo

# 7 浴池

中东铁路浴池建筑是一类重要的生活服务性建筑，广泛分布于中东铁路沿线各个站点，其主要职能是为中东铁路职工提供洗浴服务，为人们的生活需求和卫生需求提供必要保障，提高铁路员工的生活质量。而由于功能的特殊需求，浴池建筑在具有铁路沿线其他建筑的共性特点外还有其自身的特征。

## 7.1 中东铁路浴池的规模和分布

中东铁路修建之初进行了标准化的浴池设计，对不同规模的车站，配置相应规模的标准设计图。从平面上来看，浴池的标准化设计主要分为小型浴池和大型浴池。小型浴池建筑面积在 50 平方米左右，大型浴池建筑面积在 100 平方米左右。小型浴池建筑一般设在会让站与工区，标准较低，现存数量最多，如马延、万山、青云、姜家、成高子、里木点、舍利屯、清岭子等站点的浴池。大型浴池建筑设在级别较高、规模较大的站点，这类浴池设计标准较高。由于规模较大，因此平面布局也比小型浴池更为舒展。大型浴池的典型实例是中东铁路绥芬河站浴池与横道河子站浴池。大型浴池建筑的功能配备也是标准化的。除了必须的门厅、更衣室、浴室、设备房等标准化配备外，大多数大型浴池建筑都配有蒸汽室，一方面是受俄罗斯人的蒸汽浴传统影响，另一方面也表明中东铁路浴池建筑在功能配备方面的标准化程度很高。

## 7.2 中东铁路浴池的平面布局与形态特点

从历史资料与现存建筑实例来看，中东铁路浴池平面功能的组织完备而合理，流线清晰明确，空间布局紧凑简洁。建筑功能包括门厅、更衣室、浴室、蒸汽室、设备房等。进入浴室门厅，面对一间服务室，之后经更衣室进入到洗浴空间与桑拿房。浴室与蒸汽室旁是设备用房，为整个浴池建筑提供热水。大型浴池在功能更加完善的基础上，相应的每个功能区面积都有增加。小型浴池建筑有两条交通流线，一条是人们的洗浴流线，另一条是后勤流线，男女共用门厅，自门厅经更衣室、浴室到达桑拿房。规模更大的浴池建筑平面中，男女两条流线完全独立，分设出入口。后勤流线则与洗浴流线分开，直通设备房。三条流线互不干扰，有序合理。浴池建筑平面轮廓简单，利于取暖安排，减少热量损失。建筑形态与中东铁路建筑的整体风格相一致，但也有其自身特点。因内部空间需求，立面形态错落，洗浴部分设小高窗。

## 7.3 中东铁路浴池的建造技术

中东铁路浴池在建筑技术方面，针对铁路沿线寒冷的气候和建筑功能的特殊要求，采用简单实用的技术措施，取得了良好的效果。从防寒角度来看，浴池建筑的外墙厚重，有些墙体最厚的部分达到 1 米有余，这使其具有较好的保温效果。墙体下部逐渐加宽以增加墙体的稳定感，墙体材质多为石头，起到防水的作用。墙体上开双层喇叭窗，以隔绝冬季的冷空气并让更多的阳光进入室内。从采暖角度来看，浴池建筑有专门的供暖设备间，主要空间配有壁炉和较长的烟道，这些采暖措施保障了浴池建筑在冬季有温暖的室内环境。建筑一般依靠室内或者室外建筑顶部配有的蓄水池供水；排水则依靠建筑的每一个房间内都设有的排水口，地面设计有合理的排水坡度，经由排水管道将废水由地下排到室外预定的区域。在当时的条件下，中东铁路浴池建筑的给排水系统是相当完善的。

浴池作为中东铁路附属建筑类型之一，承载了当时实现建筑特殊功能需求所采用的技术手段，在克服保温、防水、排水等技术难题上显示出卓越的技术理念与操作能力，在功能与形态上也有着自身的特点，对构成中东铁路建筑的遗产多样性和地域性特征有着重要的价值。

## Common Bathing Room

Bathrooms of the CER were an important service building, which were widely distributed at each station along the railway. Their main functions were to provide bath service and necessary garantee for living and health for staff, which could improve their life quality.

At the beginning of the CER construction, bathrooms were built in a standardized design, which meant different scaled standard design drawings for different size of stations. The standardized design was mainly divided into small bathroom and large bathroom according to the plane layout. The area of the small bathroom was about 50 square meters, and the large one was about 100 square meters. Small bathroom buildings in lower standard was generally located at the passing stations and work area, with much large number at present, such as the bathrooms at Mayan, Wanshan, Qingyun, Jiangjia, etc. The large bathrooms in higher design standard were constructed in some important stations, for instance, the Suifenhe station and Hengdaohezi Station.

The plane function of the CER's bathrooms was reasonable and clear, and the space layout was efficient and simple. In addition to the standard space, the bathroom buildings were equipped with the foyer, locker room, bathroom, equipment room, etc., in most of which the steam room influenced by the Russian tradition was set up. It showed the bathroom buildings along the CER in much high standardized level.

About technologies, some simple and practical technical measures had been adopted in bathroom construction according to the cold weather along the railway and the special requirements of the building's function. And they had achieved good results. Water supply of the bathroom relied on the reservoirs at the roof of indoor or outdoor buildings. Besides, building drainage depended on each rooms' sewer outfalls, and the ground was designed with a reasonable slope where the waste water was discharged from the underground to a predetermined area outside through the drainage pipes.

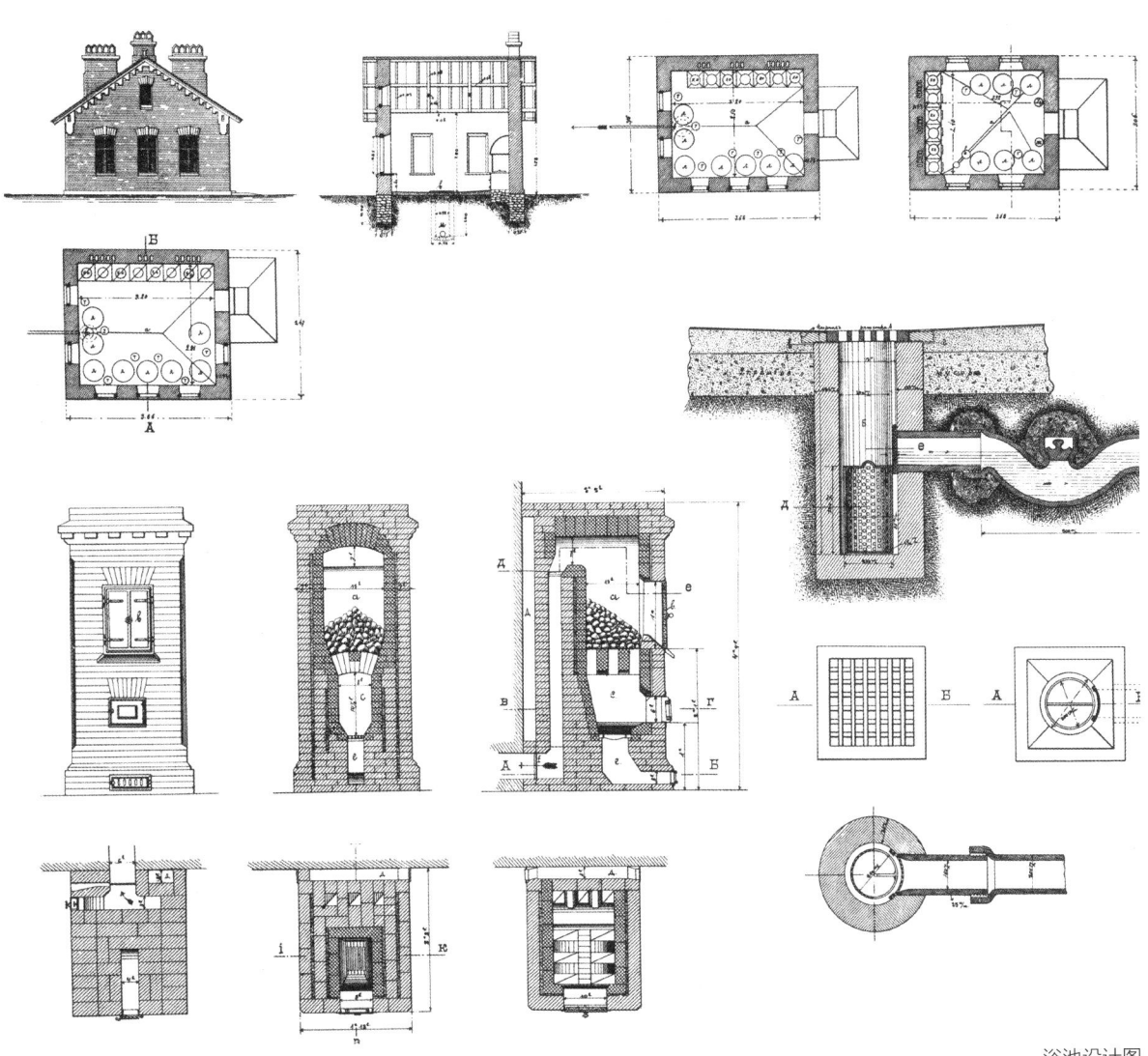

浴池设计图
Drawings of common bathing room

# ARCHITECTURAL CULTURAL HERITAGE OF CHINESE EASTERN RAILWAY

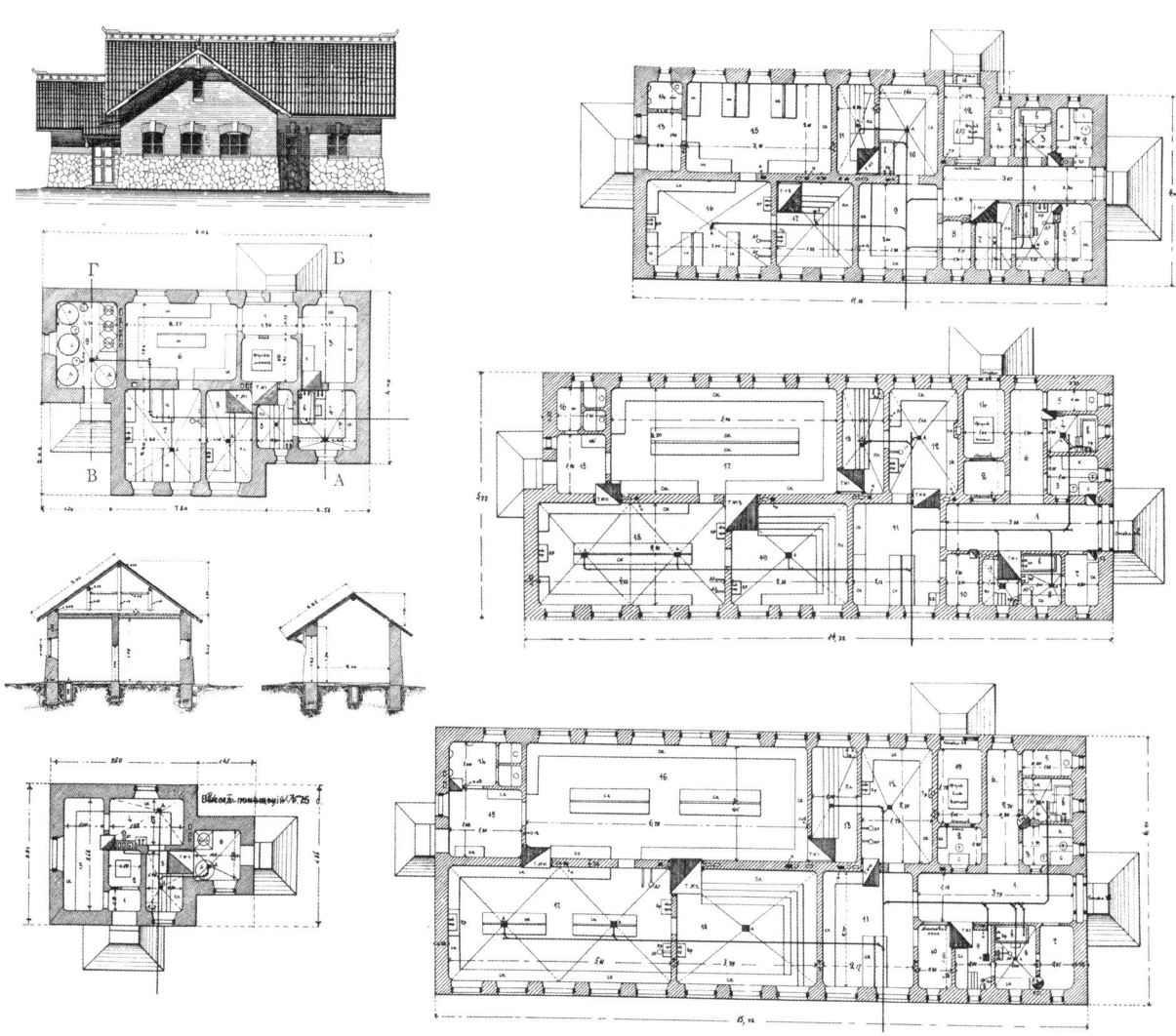

浴池设计图及不同规模浴池平面设计图
Drawing of common bathing room and planning map of common bathing room in different scales

横道河子浴池
Common bathing room in Hengdaohezi

横道河子浴池与住宅历史照片
Historical photo of common bathing room and residence

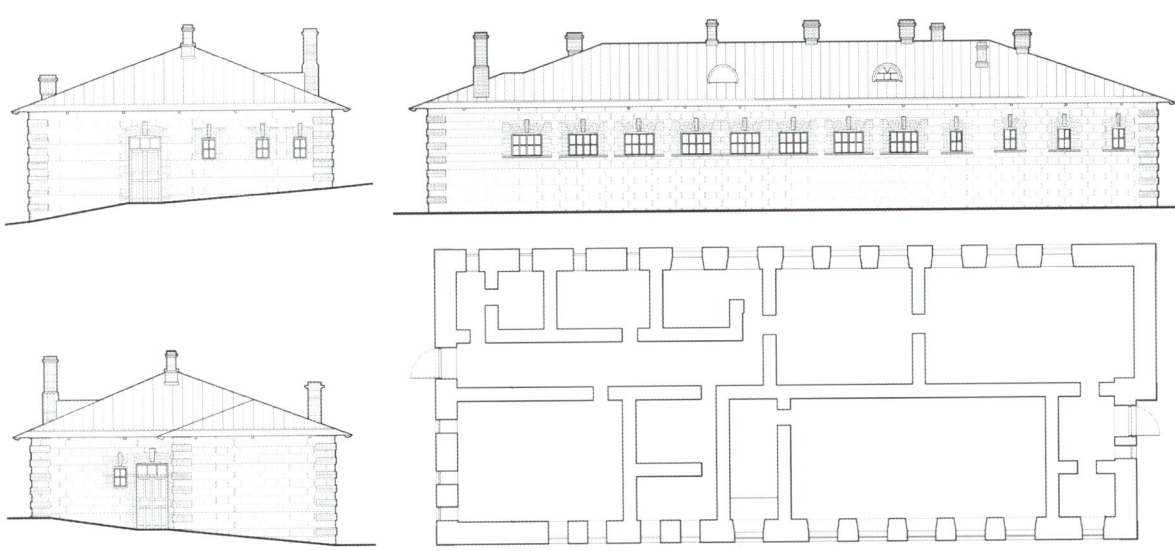

横道河子浴室池测绘图 Drawings of common bathing room in Hengdaohezi

7 浴池 | 183

# ARCHITECTURAL CULTURAL HERITAGE OF CHINESE EASTERN RAILWAY

绥芬河浴池 Common bathing room in Suifenhe

五里木浴池 Common bathing room in Wulimu

里木店浴池 Common bathing room in Limudian

红房子浴池 Common bathing room in Hongfangzi

奇峰浴池 Common bathing room in Qifeng

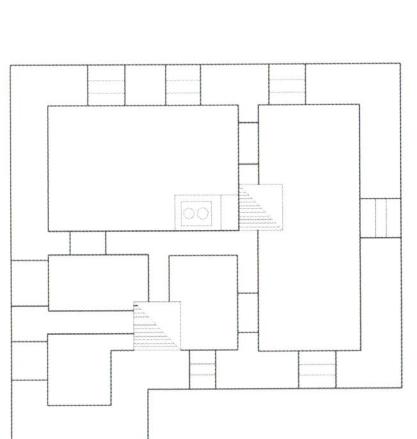

九江泡浴池现状及平面图 Current condition and drawing of common bathing room in Jiujiangpao

7 浴池 | 185

# ARCHITECTURAL CULTURAL HERITAGE OF CHINESE EASTERN RAILWAY

马延浴池 Common bathing room in Mayan

山洞浴池 Common bathing room in Shandong

姜家浴池 Common bathing room in Jiangjia

冷山浴池 Common bathing room in Lengshan

道林浴池 Common bathing room in Daolin

尚志浴池 Common bathing room in Shangzhi

青岭子浴池 Common bathing room in Qinglingzi

小九浴池 Common bathing room in Xiaojiu

成高子浴池 Common bathing room in Chenggaozi

舍利屯浴池 Common bathing room in Shelitun

富林浴池 Common bathing room in Fulin

雅鲁浴池 Common bathing room in Yalu

# 8 兵营

在中东铁路修建初期，沙俄政府以"筑路工人众多，无兵保护，不免发生危险"为由，以中东铁路公司理事会的名义单方面组建了中东铁路护路队。伴随着护路队规模的发展，针对不同的驻军规模与兵种，围绕其防卫职能，配套建设了大量的满足一般生活与特殊军事需求的建筑，形成兵营组团。

## 8.1 兵营的类型与布局方式

兵营在功能上是驻扎军队的营地，在中东铁路沿线军事建筑中占有最大比重。建筑包括营房、马厩、马匹医院、食堂、禁闭室、指挥部、高级军官住宅及厕所等，根据军队的规模大小与兵种不同而配合不同的功能。兵营建筑中具有代表性的是营房、马厩及司令部。兵营建筑一般成组布置于附属地重要城镇的边界，也有些位于铁路两侧，沿对角线方向布置。如宽城子站共有4个军队营区，营区布置在铁路两侧，其中两个营区分别布置于宽城子附属地的边界处，且每两个营区之间均保持一定的距离，形成营区最大的监管范围。在较为重要的城镇还建有以指挥办公职能为主的司令部建筑，这类建筑一般不驻扎军队，是一种军事管理的办公建筑，不与营区混在一起，多位于城镇的中心区，如哈尔滨外阿穆尔军区司令部。

从空间组合形式上看，兵营的布局大致可分为行列式、散点式及院落式三种。其中，行列式是规模较大的军队营区普遍采用的形式，即规模形制几乎完全相同的建筑以相同朝向与间距排列，数量较少时，一般为并联式，数量较多时则成方格网式布局。行列式布局的兵营多设置在城镇中俄人居住区附近用地较充裕的边界处。

散点式布局兵营一般以单栋营房为主要建筑，周边自由零散地配以仓库、禁闭室、厕所、食堂等附属建筑。这种布局方式既可以根据地形的变化进行灵活的布置，也可以通过调整兵营尺度来满足不同规模的驻军需求，是最为常见的布局形式，在磨刀石、烟筒屯、成吉思汗、昂昂溪、扎兰屯、宽城子等站点均可见到。院落式布局应用于防御性工区和小型驻扎营地，这类建筑是散置在铁路沿线的小规模护路队的哨点，距离铁路不超过50米，主要担任保护筑路工人、器材给养、修补通信设施、侦查、护送、邮递信件和保障居民点安全等工作。小型驻扎营地一般由营房、马厩与附属建筑组成，三栋建筑与带有圆形堡垒的围墙围合成封闭院落。

## 8.2 营房建筑的空间形式与建造特点

营房建筑是士兵的起居场所，是一种特殊的集合住宅，其功能构成与空间组织形式独具特点。中东铁路沿线的营房以一层为主，部分大型营房有地下空间，并开设一些洞口，来满足地下空间的通风要求，这些洞口开设位置较低，推测也可作为射击孔使用，具有防御作用。平面基本形式为简单的一字形，但室内空间高，建筑进深也很大，一般在15米左右。开间宽度根据驻军人数的规模需求确定，以容纳一定数量床位的空间为基本单元进行增减。营房建筑内部空间一般分为三部分，中间大厅部分为食堂，两侧尽端处为盥洗室、医务室、禁闭室等辅助空间。食堂与辅助功能之间的空间则为居住空间。居住空间不用墙体分割，成组的布置床铺，以线状的交通空间做基本的分隔，这种对一个相对较大尺度的空间进行整体利用，而功能划分上具有一定模糊性的处理方式在沿线其他建筑类型中较为少见。无论兵营规模如何，一般均在建筑上开多个出入口。建筑主要出入口多设于两端山墙及正立面中心部分，门前以砖石砌筑门斗。随着规模扩大，会在增加的居住单元之间增设两个相对的穿套式辅助入口。由于建筑进深与净空高度较大，因此达到一定规模时多采用天窗辅助采光与通风。单层营房的形式多为这一基本型在尺度上的变体，少数营房在中间部分有附加功能空间，形成 T 字形平面。

司令部建筑具有办公功能，一般为多层建筑，室内空间的结构布局多为鱼骨式，即以内廊贯穿连接各个小的功能单元，一字形的平面一般两侧与中间设有大空间，服务于各类集体活动。作为重要的辅助建筑，配备的大型食堂平面呈"L"形，短端为大厅空间，剖面与巴西利卡式近似，长端为中小用餐单元，形式较有特点。营区中的禁闭室为临时拘押犯人的场所，主要特点为建筑尺度很小、平面多为方形、立面开小窗或不开窗。

营房建筑的结构主体也是防御性工程设施，建造材料以石材为主，以红砖辅助，较少使用现代材料。墙体很厚，多为填充式，即以砖石砌筑内外两侧，中间填充碎砖、碎石及灰土的混合物。当建筑面宽过大时主入口设置于建筑中间部分，如阿城兵营、昂昂溪兵营。中东铁路沿线多数的兵营建筑主入口均设置于山墙面，门斗也多是砖石砌筑，双坡屋顶的形式呼应整体轮廓，形象的特征明显，也是整栋建筑的主要装饰所在。兵营建筑的装饰语言与一般住宅建筑相似，但在尺度、比例与秩序上适合自身的体量。由于建筑体量大、空间简单、在铁路建设初期需求量大，因此其建筑标准化程度相对较高，且形象统一。

### 8.3 马厩

马厩是中东铁路护路队骑兵营的附属建筑。由于 20 世纪初骑兵营大规模扩编，因此一些普通的民用建筑也会被临时充作马厩使用。马厩主要功能是畜养马匹，体量上与营房相近，但在形态与空间上更加简单。在已有的马厩设计标准图中可以看到，其平面均为一字型，沿进深方向布置 4 排马槽，马槽之间设柱，可作为拴马设施。马槽尺寸约为 1.7 米 ×2.7 米，室内过道宽约 2 米，室内使用空间的进深均在 15 米左右。马槽沿开间方向依次排列，根据其所需的数量规模确定建筑的开间尺度。建筑空间流线为完整的环形，在两侧山墙尽端各开有三个门，与各条通道相连接，这种入口的处理形式在实例中较少见。实际马厩多在山墙面开设一个主入口。当需要畜养的马匹数量很多，建筑的面宽过大时，如同兵营一样，会以一个长度适当的环形交通所连接的空间为一个基本单元，两个或者多个单元连接成更大规模，在单元相交处也开设出入口，方便使用与疏散。小型的马厩平面接近方形，规模越大形体越狭长，但总体模式与形态基本不变。

马厩同营房一样具有较大的空间尺度，因此结构形式相近，也以砖石结构为主体，内部搭配木梁柱框架以承托屋顶。马厩的室内空间朴素，以实用性为主，梁柱的用材相对粗糙，细节上不做过多修饰。柱子下面设有石质的柱础以避免柱子受潮，柱子上部与大梁之间有有垫板或托手。马厩为双坡屋顶，举架较高，并在两侧屋面上分别设有多个换气天窗。马厩的天窗为木质结构，在现有资料中尚未发现马厩中有采暖设施。马厩建筑的外部形态更加简单，墙面多开高窗，窗口为狭长矩形，尺度很小；门窗洞口等处也比较朴素，除山墙面檐下有少量线脚外少有复杂装饰。马厩建筑朴拙的形式反而形成其自身的形象特点。

### 8.4 马匹医院

马匹医院一般设置于骑兵驻扎的地区。根据现存设计图纸可见，其建筑平面为 L 形，内部功能分为两个大部分，其中一部分也如马厩一样布置马槽单元，另一部分则为其他辅助空间，推测可能是治疗室、手术室、药房等。建筑功能分区明确，为人与马分设入口能够做到两条流线互不干扰，以满足管理与使用要求。马匹医院的立面与马厩有相似之处，同时兼具一般建筑的特点：在马槽单元，墙面设高窗，屋顶有换气天窗；治疗部分则为铁路沿线通用窗的尺度与形式，内部空间与外部形式的逻辑比较统一。

# Military Camp

In the early period of the Chinese Eastern Railway (CER) construction, Russia unilaterally founded the CER Escort (CERE) in the name of the Board of CER Company, to ensure the safety of railway workers and the construction process, as well as enhancing its control over the railway and the CER Zone. With the expansion of the escort, a large number of buildings were constructed to fulfill basic living and special military needs, based on the size, type and duty of defense of the garrisons. Military Camps were then set up.

Military camps occupied the largest percentage among the military facilities along CER, containing buildings in a variety of functions like barracks, stables, horse hospitals, canteens, confinement rooms, headquarters, senior officer residence and toilets, based on the garrison size and type. Barracks were usually located in groups near the border of important town in the CER Zone, or on both sides of the railway line in a diagonal position to protect the town and the railway. Moreover, headquarters were built in more important towns, which functioned as military administration and offices without troops stationed nor mixed with barracks, and were mostly located in the downtown, for instance, the Headquarter of Russian Outer Amur Military Region.

Barrack, a special kind of apartment with some unique features of functions and space, was the core element in the layout of the camp. Barracks along CER were mainly in single-story, while some large ones had basements with some holes used as airshafts. The holes were drilled at rather lower positions that, as a hypothesis, might have also been used as embrasures for defense. The barrack plans were long rectangles, but had large heights and depths (15 meter in common). The widths of the bays were determined by the number of garrisons, and were adjusted by the units containing certain numbers of beds. As unique apartment, barracks had to deal with the evacuation of large number of people. Therefore, despite of the size, a barrack had normally multiple exits. The main exits were mostly located at the gables of both ends or at the center of the front elevations. For barracks had some certain sizes as big depth and height, skylights would be adopted for better lighting and ventilation.

Stables were the affiliated buildings of the CER cavalry battalions. Due to the large expansion of cavalries in the early 20th century, some civil buildings were temporarily used as stables. As the place to store and raise horses, stables were similar in size with barracks, but had simpler shapes and spaces. As can be seen from the standardization drawings, stables had a long rectangular shape, with 4 rows of mangers in the depth, and pillars in between the mangers to tie horses. The manger's size was around 1.7 m × 2.7 m, and the corridor between manger rows was 2 m in width, thus the total depth of interior space was commonly around 15 m. The mangers were lined up along the bays whose size was determined by the number of mangers needed. The traffic flow in a stable was a closed circle, and three doors connecting with the corridors were opened at each gable, which could seldom be seen in realities yet. In fact, most stables had only one main entrance at the gable. In case of large number of horses (to breed) which might give a too long façade to the stable, like in barracks, the stable would be divided into several units, each with a moderate length and a closed circle traffic flow. When two or more units were connected to form a large stable, entrances were also placed at the junctions of units for use and evacuation. A small stable's plan was nearly a square, and much bigger the stable, much narrower and longer the plan. However, the overall layout remained the same. As barracks, stables had large space and masonry structure with wooden frame to support the roof, and high gable roofs with a number of skylights on each slope for lighting and ventilation. The exterior of the stable was much simpler, with high and narrow small windows on the walls.

Horse hospitals were normally located close to cavalry battalions. As could be seen in the drawings, the plan had an "L" shape and was divided into two major sections. One had manger units as in the stables; the other was an auxiliary space, which might have been used as treatment rooms, operating rooms or pharmacies. With clear functional zoning and reasonable arrangement of traffic flow by separate entrances for soldiers and horses, the plan fulfilled the demand of administration. The horse hospital façade was similar with the stables, but had some features of an normal building in the meantime: long and narrow windows on the walls and skylights on the roofs in the horses section, while normal scale and shape windows were used in the treatment section. The interior space matched exactly well with exterior forms.

满洲里军官宿舍 Dormitory for military officer in Manzhouli

# ARCHITECTURAL CULTURAL HERITAGE OF CHINESE EASTERN RAILWAY

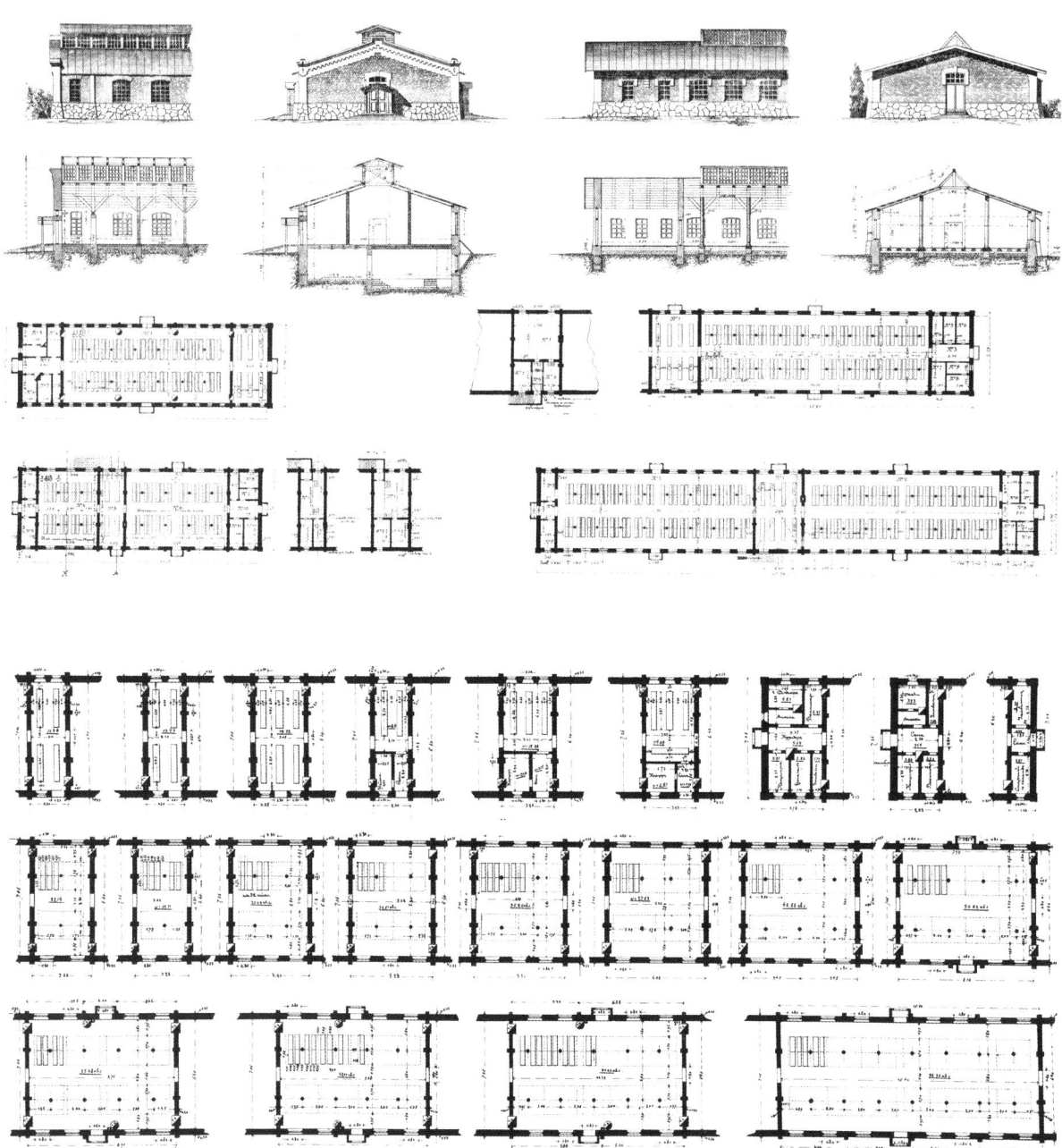

营房设计标准图 Standardized drawings of barrack

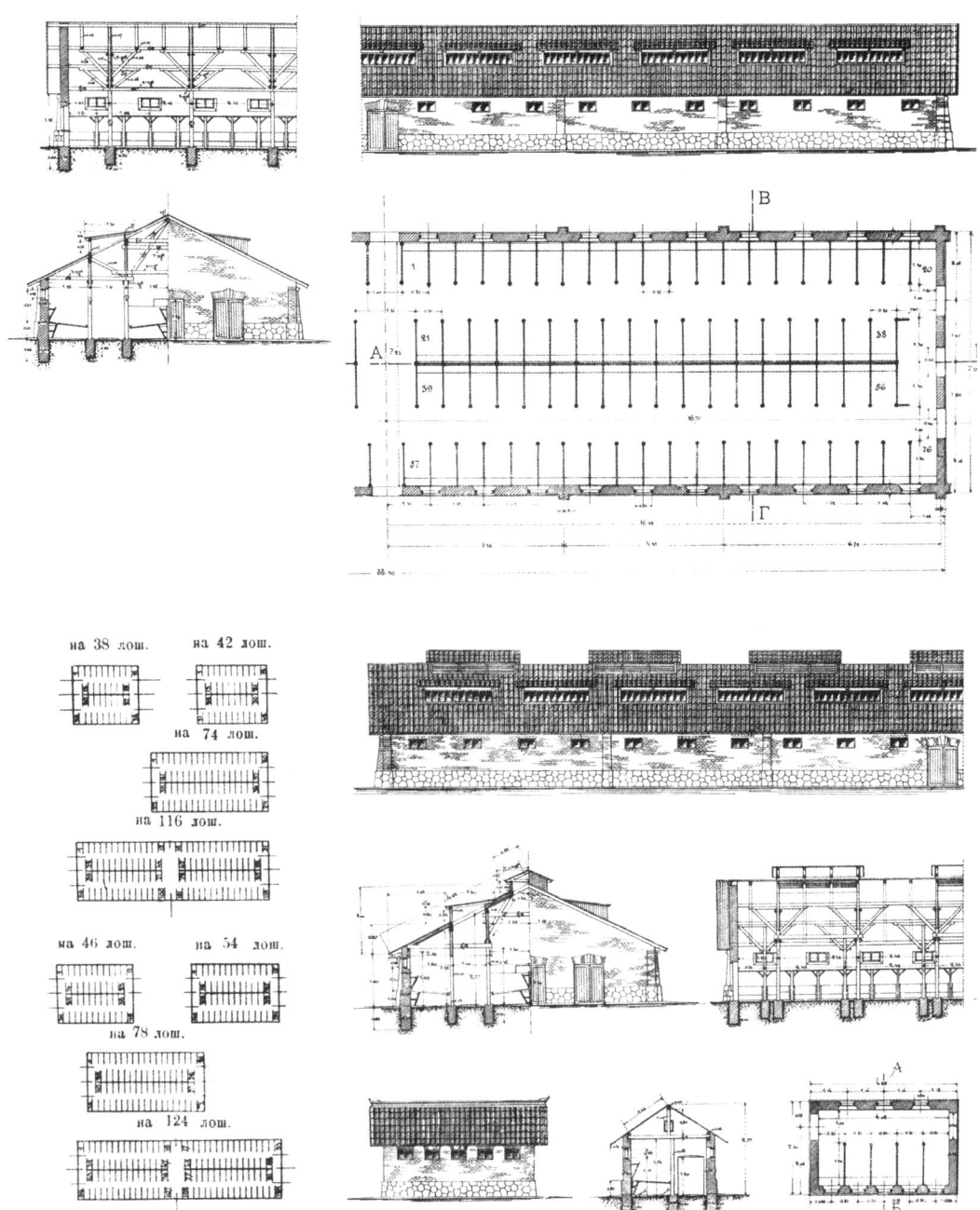

马厩标准设计图 Standardized drawings of stable

# ARCHITECTURAL CULTURAL HERITAGE OF CHINESE EASTERN RAILWAY

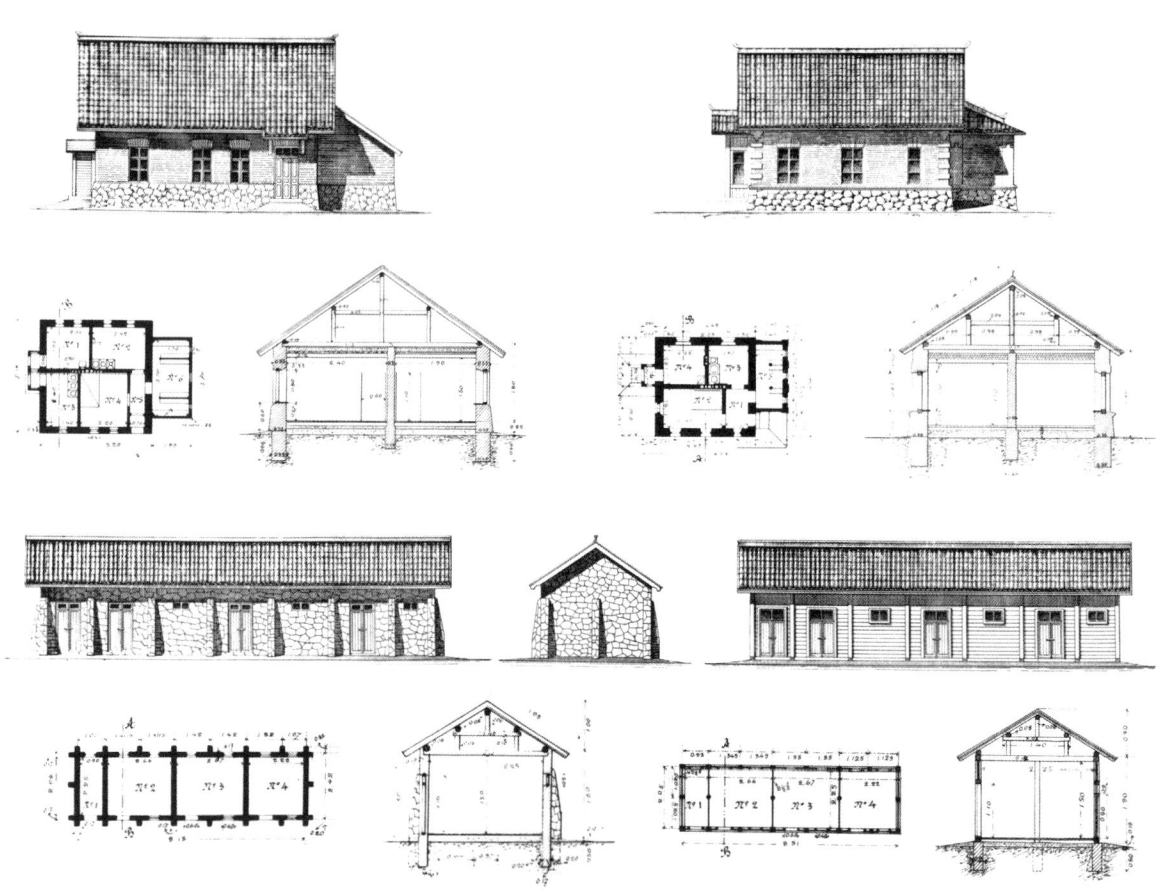

散兵营房设计图 Drawings of barracks

完工兵营历史照片（37 骑兵）
Historical photo of cavalry camp in Wangong
(37 cavalrymen)

巴林兵营历史照片（74 骑兵和分队指挥官）
Historical photo of cavalry camp in Wangong
(74 cavalrymen and commander)

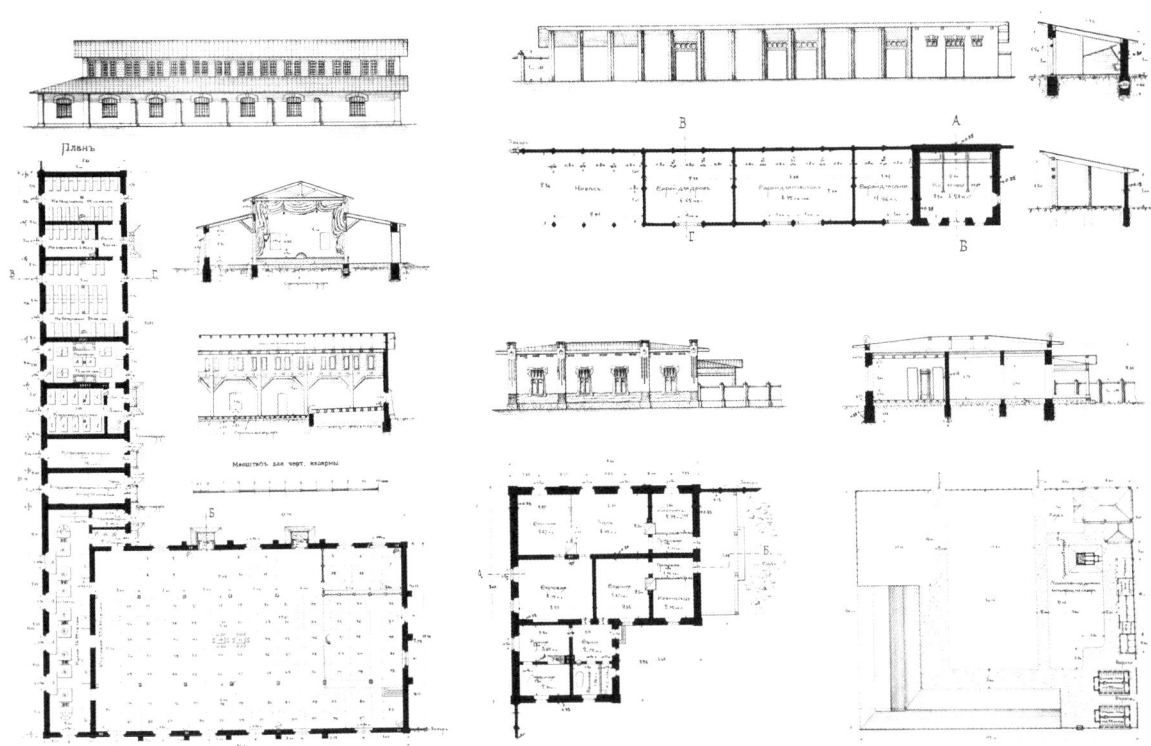

兵营食堂设计图 Drawings for military canteens

博克图兵营食堂历史照片 Historical photo of military canteen in Boketu

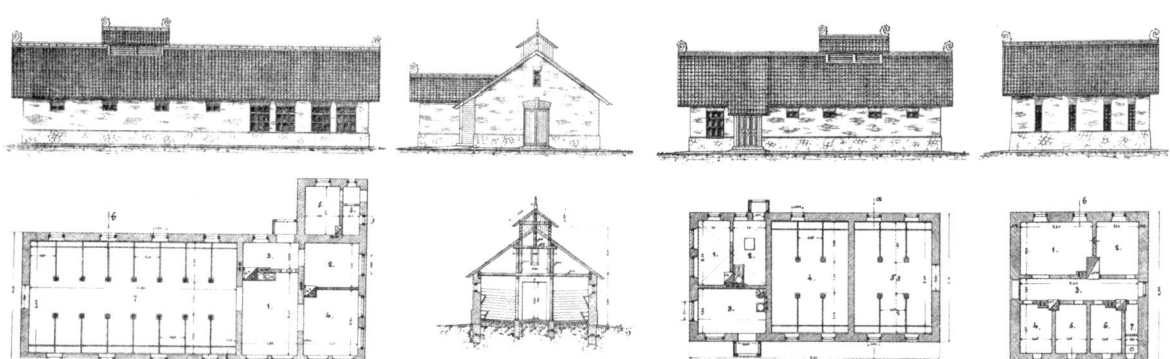

马匹医院标准图纸 Standardized drawings of horse hospitals

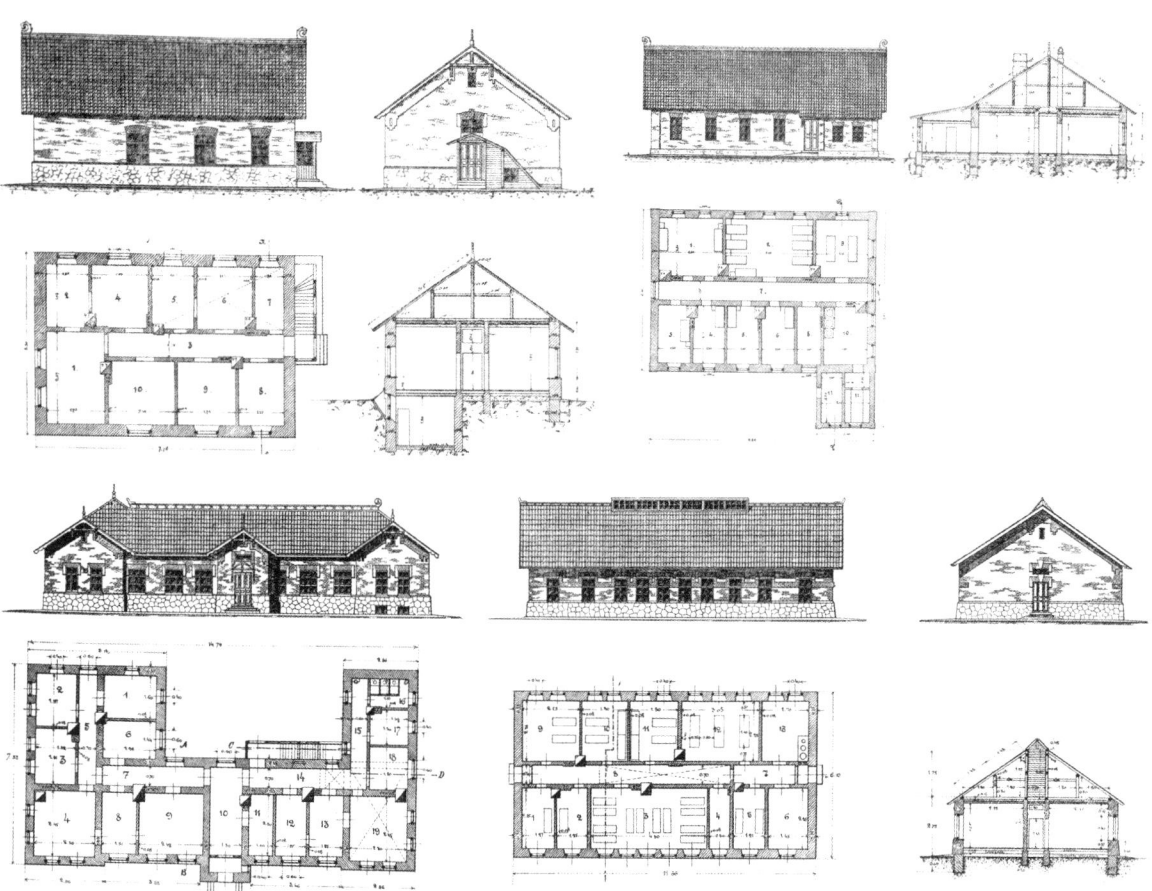

指挥部设计图 Drawings of headquarters

兵营会议室设计图 Drawings of military conference rooms

# ARCHITECTURAL CULTURAL HERITAGE OF CHINESE EASTERN RAILWAY

磨刀石兵营历史照片（37 骑兵 42 步兵 3 军官）
Historical photo of military camp in Modaoshi (37 cavalrymen, 42 infantrymen and 3 officers)

东线兵营历史照片 Historical photo of military camp on east line of CER

扎罗尔得兵营历史照片（48 步兵） Historical photo of military camp in Zhaluoerde(48 infantrymen)

松花江大桥边兵营历史照片 Historical photo of military camp alongside the Songhua River Bridge

海拉尔兵营历史照片 Historical photo of military camp in Hailaer

横道河子兵营历史照片 Historical photo of military camp in Hengdaohezi

齐齐哈尔兵营食堂历史照片 Historical photo of military canteen in Qiqihaer

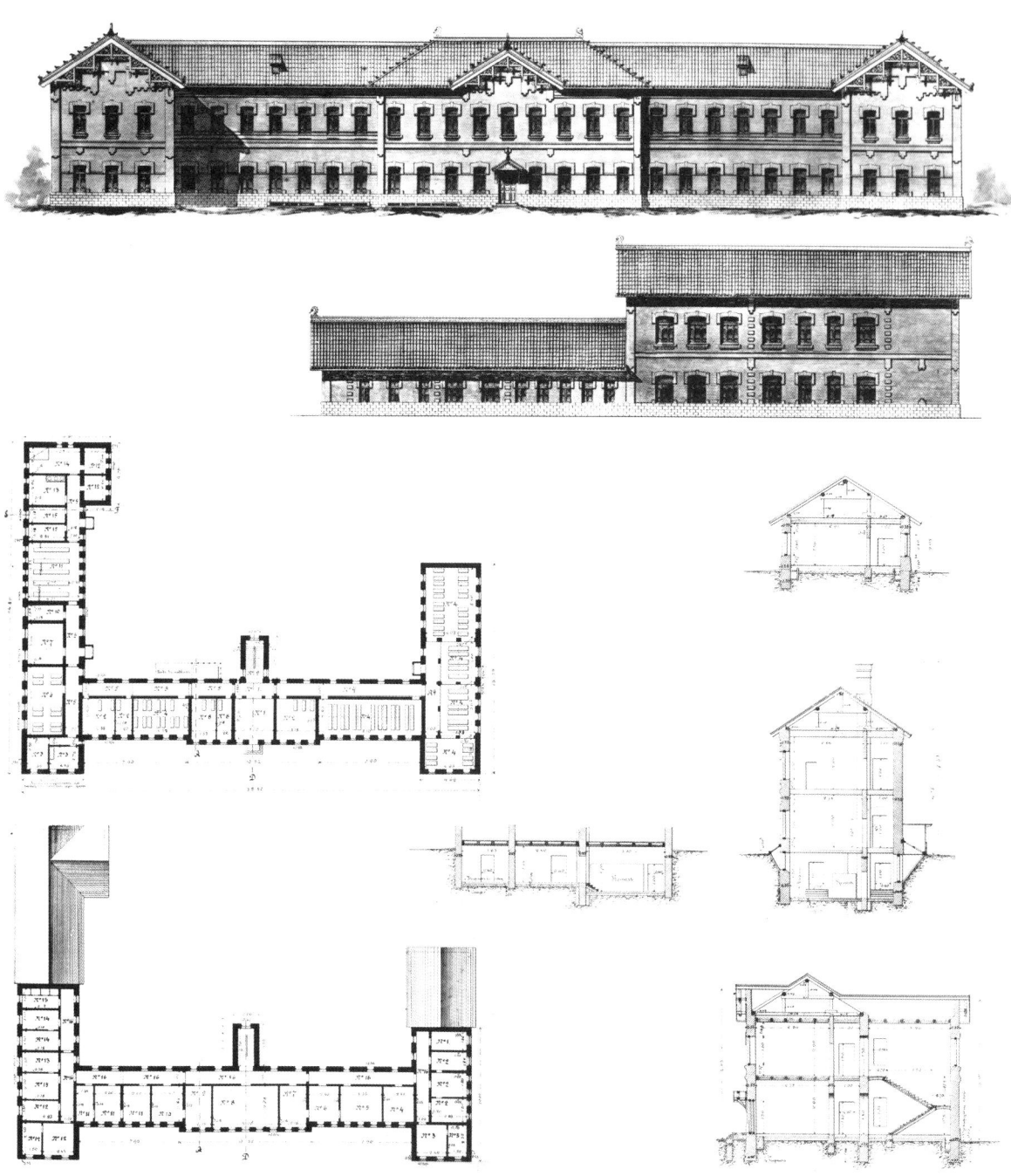

外阿穆尔军区司令部设计图
Drawings of headquarters of outer amur military district

外阿穆尔军区司令部现状及不同时期历史照片
Current condition and historical photos of headquarters of outer amur military district in different periods

# ARCHITECTURAL CULTURAL HERITAGE OF CHINESE EASTERN RAILWAY

扎兰屯营房
Barrack in Zhalantun

扎兰屯兵营附属建筑
Affiliated facilities of Zhalantun military camp

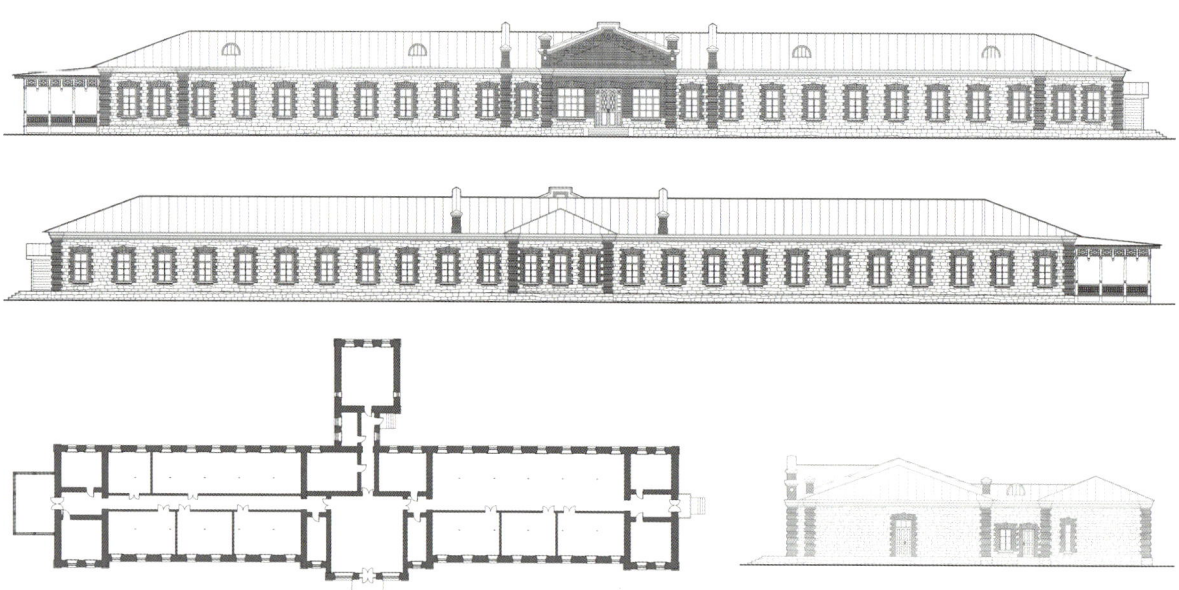

扎兰屯营房测绘图 Drawings of barrack in Zhalantun

扎兰屯马厩现状及测绘图 Current condition and drawings of stable in Zhalantun

富拉尔基兵营 Military camp in Fulaerji

富拉尔基兵营营房1 Barrack in Fulaerji 1

富拉尔基兵营营房2 Barrack in Fulaerji 2

阿城兵营营房现状及测绘图 Current condition and drawings of barrack in Acheng

昂昂溪兵营营房 Barrack in Ang'angxi

昂昂溪兵营附属建筑 Affiliated facilities of Ang'angxi military camp

横道河子兵营营房 Barrack in Hengdaohezi

横道河子兵营建筑群 Mititary buildings in Hengdaohezi

# ARCHITECTURAL CULTURAL HERITAGE OF CHINESE EASTERN RAILWAY

昂昂溪兵营食堂 Military canteen in Ang'angxi

博克图镇内兵营历史照片 Historical photos of military camp in Boketu

博克图镇内营房 Barrack in Boketu

博克图镇外营房 Barrack outside Boketu

博克图镇内营房 Barrack in Boketu

满洲里兵营历史照片 Historical photo of military camp in Manzhouli

满洲里兵营 Military camp in Manzhouli

满洲里兵营营房 Barrack in Manzhouli

满洲里东大营历史照片 Historical photo of military camp in Dongdaying, Manzhouli

满洲里东大营营房 Barrack in Dongdaying, Manzhouli

扎赉诺尔马厩 Stable in Zhanlainuoer

一面坡护路队营房 Barrack for garrisons in Yimianpo

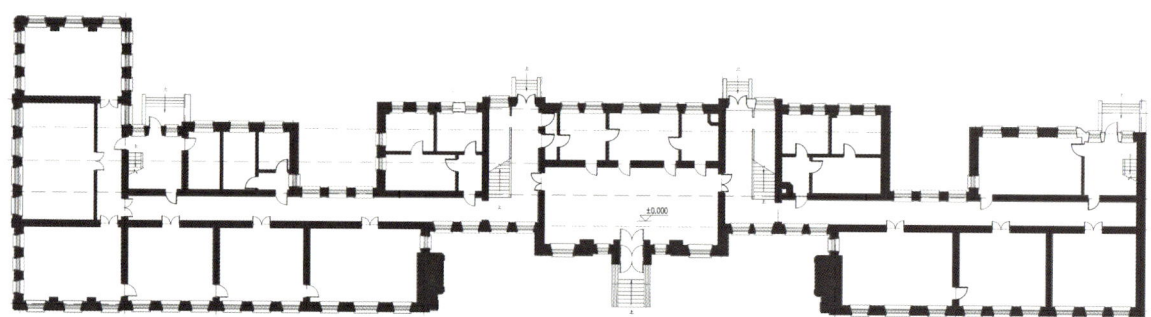

一面坡护路队营房平面测绘图 Drawing of barrack for garrisons in Yimianpo

一面坡护路队营房现状及立面测绘图 Current condition and drawing of barrack for garrisons in Yimianpo

巴林兵营 Military camp in Balin

哈拉苏兵营 Military camp in Halasu

南木兵营 Military camp in Nanmu

肇东兵营 Military camp in Zhaodong

雅鲁营房
Barrack in Yalu

对青山营房
Barrack in Duiqingshan

苇河营房
Barrack in Weihe

穆棱营房
Barrack in Muling

德惠营房
Barrack in Dehui

磨刀石营房
Barrack in Modaoshi

双城营房
Barrack in Shuangcheng

成吉思汗营房
Barrack in Chengjisihan

8 兵营 | 223

# 9 碉堡及其他军事设施

除兵营建筑组团外,中东铁路沿线还有碉堡、弹药库及瞭望塔等军事设施,对重要的铁路节点加强守御,具有典型的军事建筑性格,形式与功能都极为独特。

## 9.1 碉堡

碉堡多设置于隧道口、桥头等铁路重要的节点上,如哈尔滨段的第一松花江大桥、牡丹江、富拉尔基江桥、新南沟、兴安岭隧道等地均设有碉堡。一方面这些位置对铁路来说至关重要,一旦遭到破坏影响很大,且易破坏而难修复;另一方面,这些节点又有极强的军事战略地位,在滨江或倚山之处设置防御设施能最大化地起到阻击作用。碉堡通常成对出现,分别置于江桥或隧道两侧,以加强其防御功能。碉堡的平面形态有八边形、十二边形、P形等,层数则二至五层不等,且均带有地下室。建筑平面无直角转折,多为圆弧状,在顶部中间位置还设有方形塔楼。内部空间狭小,无采暖设施,功能较为完善,有休息室、厨房、卫生间、菜窖、煤仓等空间,能保持相对长时期的守戍要求。平面布局紧凑,对交通空间进行最大程度上的压缩,走廊宽不到1米,楼梯间也仅有约2米宽,内部采光不足。碉堡建筑中大量使用混凝土材料,是中东铁路沿线建筑中较特殊的现象。出于防御强度的考量,碉堡建筑墙体极厚,下部约为1.5米,部分碉堡的底部以毛石砌筑,上部墙体约为1.1米厚。混凝土浇筑的墙体并未配筋,仅在局部,如楼板处,用钢轨加强结构性能。建筑表面为素混凝土,不做装饰处理。立面上均匀分布形式相同的洞口,尺度较小,且层层叠涩,呈外大内小的喇叭状,以利于采光、射击及观察活动。顶部女儿墙为雉堞形式,雉堞上面的垛口呈内大外小状,可作为炮孔或射击孔使用,同时也具有排水功能。典型的江桥碉堡,如哈尔滨松花江大桥碉堡,两岸共有3座,均建成于1916年。以松花江北侧的碉堡为例,其平面为P形,共三层并带有地下室,占地面积约150平方米。主入口位于面向江边一侧,内部仅有一部置于建筑中部的楼梯。三层的平面形式相同,均划分为尺度相当的4个空间,内部沿墙面设置一圈重机枪滑轮。除一般交通空间外,还在其靠近江桥一侧布置一条撤退的通道。兴安岭隧道处的碉堡与隧道合建,建设年代也更早。兴安岭隧道是中东铁路沿线最大的工程之一,碉堡形式也更复杂,即在隧道口两侧进行对称建设,并向两侧扩展,形成线形的防御带。在规模较小的隧道口,碉堡形式与江桥碉堡类似,是独立建造的。

## 9.2 弹药库及瞭望台

弹药库是储藏弹药、物资的仓储建筑。由于弹药具有易燃、易爆的特性,容易产生爆炸事故,危险性极高,因此弹药库的设计要综合考虑结构形式以及周围环境,以保证在事故发生时最大限度地减少损失。弹药库的选址一般距离兵营营区有一定距离,同时也会保证使用的方便。由于其建筑性质上的特殊性,弹药库在形象与建造方式上均有自身的特点。弹药库为拱形结构,剖面轮廓为一个较完整的抛物线,建筑材料以石材或砖为主,搭配使用粗混凝土。

内部空间单一，平面多为长宽比接近 2 的矩形，出口设在山墙面。入口上部一般开设狭长窄窗，部分弹药库侧面也开有小窗，以避免内部因缺少采光与通风而造成弹药潮湿的问题。军事建筑还包括瞭望台，一般为借助地形在高处设置的平台。另外，水塔作为铁路机车与生活区的补给设施，形式上的特性也令其有一定的军事功能。

碉堡等军事工事与设施虽然数量不多、形式简单，但属于特种建筑类型，具有独特性和唯一性，极大地丰富了中东铁路建筑遗产的类型和文化多样性，对中东铁路这一完整的文化遗产来说不可或缺。

## Fortified Tower and Other Military Facilities

There were not only military camps but also other military facilities like fortified towers, ammunition depots and watchtowers along CER. The fortified towers were mostly located at the key nodes of the railway, such as the tunnel entrances and the bridgeheads. For example, the Songhua River Bridge in Harbin, Mudanjiang River, Fulaerji River Bridge, xinnan'gou and xing'anling Tunnels were all equipped with fortified towers. They were usually in pairs and placed on each side of a bridge or a tunnel, with plans of octagonal, dodecagon, (P-shape), etc, and they ranged from two to five storeys with a basement. The buildings adopted arcs at corners instead of right-angles, and a square tower was put in the middle of the top. Large amount of concrete were used in the fortified towers, which was rather specific among buildings along CER. The walls of the towers were extremely thick, with about 1.5-meter-thick lower parts and about 1.1-meter-thick upper parts, and bottoms of some fortified towers were constructed by rubble stones. There is no heating inside the fortified tower. The concrete walls were constructed without reinforcement bars and partly used rails to enhance the structure. The concrete surface had no decorations, only with same-sized small holes evenly distributed on the façade and corbeling out in a wedge-shape to facilitate lighting, shooting and observation. The parapet on the top also crenellated in a wedge-shape to be used as embrasures or drainage.

The ammunition depots were to store ammunitions and materials, and because of the properties and high risk of flammable and explosion of the ammunitions, they were normally located with a certain distance from the military camps. Meanwhile, due to the uniqueness of functions, ammunition depots had some different characteristics in appearance and construction with a mostly complete parabola in their vault sections. They were mainly made of stones or bricks together with coarse concrete. The interior space was simple with rectangle plan whose length and width were in a ratio close to 2, and an entrance was opened on the gable with some narrow long windows on the upper part, and also some small windows on the sidewalls.

Monitoring posts were also a kind of military buildings, which were generally designed into platforms placed at high elevations according to the territory.

第一松花江大桥碉堡历史照片 Historical photo of fortified tower beside the No.1 Songhua River Bridge

第一松花江大桥碉堡 Fortified tower beside the No.1 Songhua River Bridge

9 碉堡及其他军事设施

富拉尔基江桥碉堡 Fortified tower beside the bridge in Fulaerji

新南沟碉堡 1 Fortified tower in Xinnangou 1

新南沟碉堡 2 Fortified tower in Xinnangou 2

兴安岭隧道碉堡历史照片及现状图 Historical photo and current condition of fortified tower of Khingan Tunnel

旅顺东鸡冠山暗堡复原图 Recovery map of fortified tower in Jiguanshan, Lüshun

旅顺东鸡冠山暗堡 Fortified tower in Jiguanshan, Lüshun

9 碉堡及其他军事设施 | 231

# ARCHITECTURAL CULTURAL HERITAGE OF CHINESE EASTERN RAILWAY

弹药库设计图 Drawings of ammunition depot

富拉尔基弹药库现状
Current condition of ammunition depot in Fulaerji

一面坡弹药库 1
Ammunition depot in Yimianpo 1

一面坡弹药库 2
Ammunition depot in Yimianpo 2

玉泉瞭望塔 Watchtower in Yuquan

# 10 警察署及监狱

中东铁路管理局在铁路附属地内部私设警察机构进行司法管理，因此，铁路沿线多地建有警察署和监狱。监狱建筑是与警察署建筑关联紧密的建筑类型，二者互相配合，整合了治安维护、警务管理、护路、审讯、羁押等职能，具有类似于军事建筑的功能属性。

## 10.1 警察署

警察署的基本职能是管理中东铁路及其附属地的地方治安，防控对中东铁路和俄国居民的危害活动，侦破各种案件。1908年11月1日，中东铁路警察管理局在哈尔滨设立，下设海拉尔、昂昂溪、哈尔滨、绥芬河四个警察分局。并在扎兰屯、昂昂溪、安达、一面坡、穆棱、绥芬河等各大站设立警察署及宪兵队。警察署建筑的功能专业性不强，其内部空间的划分都为简单实用的通廊式布局，可以作为多用途的建筑使用。扎兰屯的警察署则为简单的一字形，建于1909年，建筑面积为1 020平方米，为单层建筑形式，举架较高，体量大，空间完整。根据史料记载，原建筑内部设有办公室、审讯室、羁押犯人室和囚室等功能性空间，在建筑内部北侧还设有地窖。各站点的警署建筑整体上多与中东铁路沿线建筑风格统一，局部有较为独特的处理，立面装饰较为丰富，如博克图警察署采用砌筑线脚形成凹凸变化的光影效果，局部高耸的女儿墙丰富了建筑的天际线。

## 10.2 监狱

中东铁路干线有5座监狱，分别位于哈尔滨、满洲里、海拉尔、博克图和横道河子，其中以哈尔滨监狱规模最大，可容纳500人，监狱均设于城市边缘的位置。监狱往往以建筑组群的形式出现，建筑的形象厚重朴素，包括大门、狱所及附属建筑，利用砖石砌筑成一个坚固厚实的墙体来围合成封闭院落，并在围墙转角处设置岗楼用以监视和瞭望。这样的布局形式以主体建筑为中心，监视和瞭望部分置于围墙边缘，扩大了监管的范围，提高管理效率。

在监狱建筑组群中，最主要的是狱所建筑。其功能复杂，建筑体量大，通常为带有地下室的多层建筑，包含囚室、办公室、审判厅、宿舍、焚尸房等多种功能空间。一层主要功能为囚室，地下部分会配以暗牢或水牢以关押重刑犯；二层则为狱长办公室、审判厅、候审厅等办公性质的空间，办公性的空间与囚室相比空间尺度较大，利于结构布置。狱所平面形式可分为一字形、大字形及十字形。虽然形体不同，但其主入口多置于建筑的中部，囚室集中设置在入口一侧。囚室部分被划分为多个房间，房间多为1.9米×3.5米的狭长型小空间，高度约为2.4米，开设高窗，高窗多为30度角的斜坡，既满足采光和通风要求，也可避免犯人攀登逃跑。高窗尺度较小，室内光线少，阴暗潮湿。入口另一侧为办公性质空间，如医务室、警卫室、教诲室等。特殊的功能对建筑流线的设置有较高的要求。如满洲里沙俄监狱，长度为34米余，建筑中部设有一部楼梯，便于疏散。狱所室内的流线组织采用尽端的内廊式和无廊式的结合，内廊式又可分为长内廊和短内廊。满洲里沙俄监狱一层为长内廊，这是因为一层主要为囚室部分，需要开设较多的门，以避免房间产生穿套。二层以大空间审判厅为主，另一侧为几个独立空间组合而成，故而二层为短内廊形式。而地下空间采用串套式空间布局，形成无廊式交通流线。

  警察署和监狱建筑是中东铁路附属地内较为特殊的建筑类型，有别于军事建筑，但同时又具有部分军事建筑的功能属性。整体上看，警察署和监狱建筑都是当时特定的历史条件下的特殊产物，形式也极为独特，丰富了中东铁路建筑遗产的多样性。

## Police Stations and Prisons

  The police stations were buildings closely related to the prisons. They functioned similarly with military buildings as they cooperated to take the responsibility of public security, police management, railway protection, interrogation, and custody, etc.

  The duty of the police station was to ensure the public security of CER and the CER Zone, and to prevent possible harms to the CER and Russian citizens, as well as to solve various cases. On Nov. 1st, 1908, the CER Police Station was established in Harbin, followed by branch stations in Hailar, Ang'angxi, Harbin and Suifenhe, and police departments or gendarmeries in big towns as Zhalantun, Ang'angxi, Anda, Yimianpo, Muling and Suifenhe. The building layout of police stations was normally rather simple and practical with an inner corridor than specialized in certain functions, and could be used for multiple purposes. Police station buildings in different towns were holistically coordinated with other buildings along the CER, but had special designs in some parts and rich decorations on the facades.

  Five prisons were located along the main line of CER in Harbin, Manzhouli, Hailar, Boketu and Hengdaohezi, among which the one in Harbin was the biggest with a capacity of 500 prisoners, and all situated at places distant from the downtown. Usually prisons consisted of a group of buildings, with a heavy but simple gate, a prison and some affiliated buildings, enclosed by thick and solid masonry walls creating a closed yard with watchtowers at the corner for monitoring and observing. In the complex, the prison building was the most important one with large volume and various functions, and usually built in multi-story with a basement, including cells, offices, courtrooms, dormitories, incineration and other functional spaces. Various functions needed diversified spaces, and the organization of spaces varied from small spaces like cells to the large spaces like the courtrooms.

博克图警察署 Police station in Boketu

10 警察署及监狱 | 237

扎兰屯森林警察大队现状及测绘图 Current condition and drawings of forest police station in Zhalantun

横道河子军警建筑群 Buildings of police station in Hengdaohezi

# ARCHITECTURAL CULTURAL HERITAGE OF CHINESE EASTERN RAILWAY

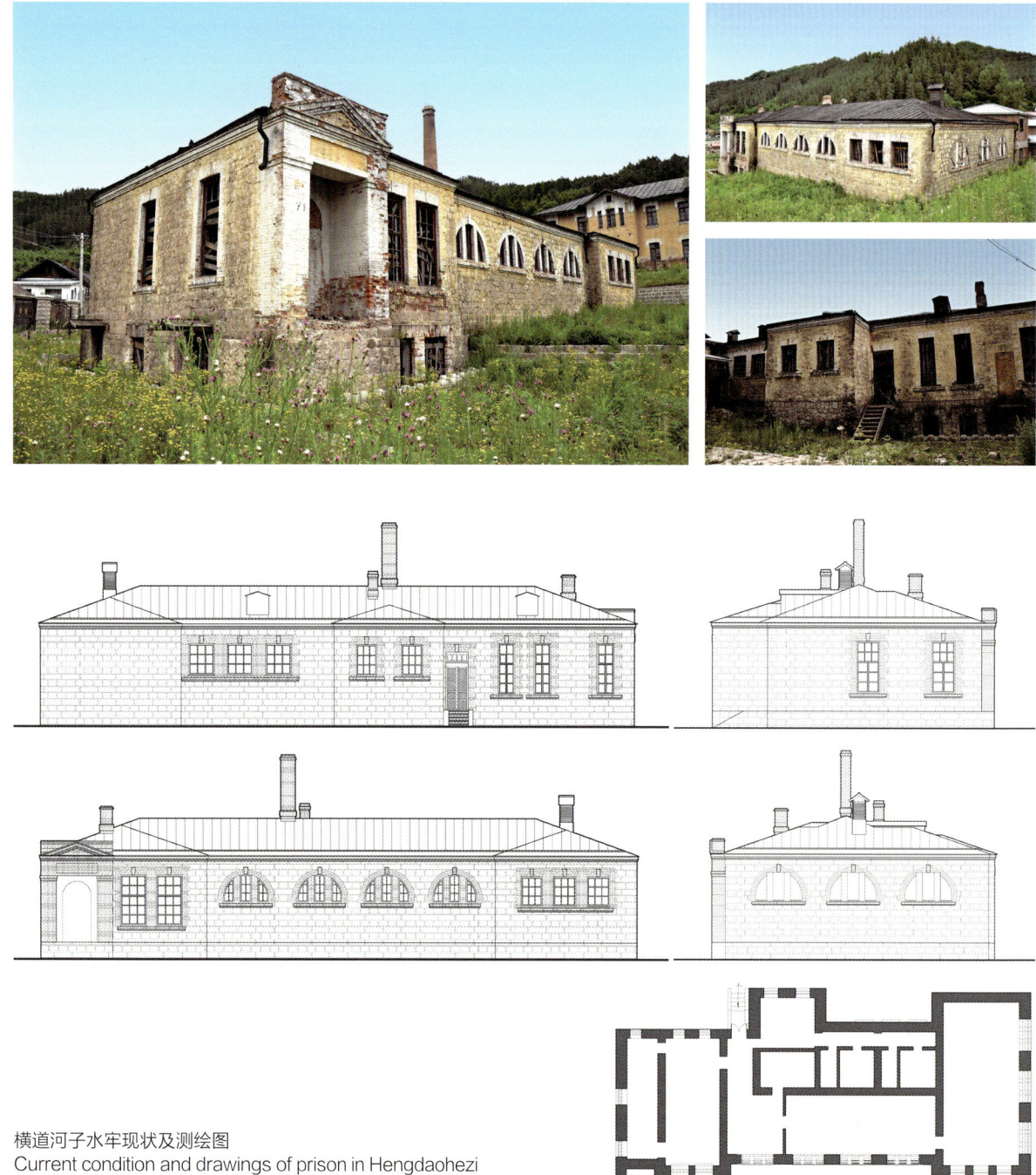

横道河子水牢现状及测绘图
Current condition and drawings of prison in Hengdaohezi

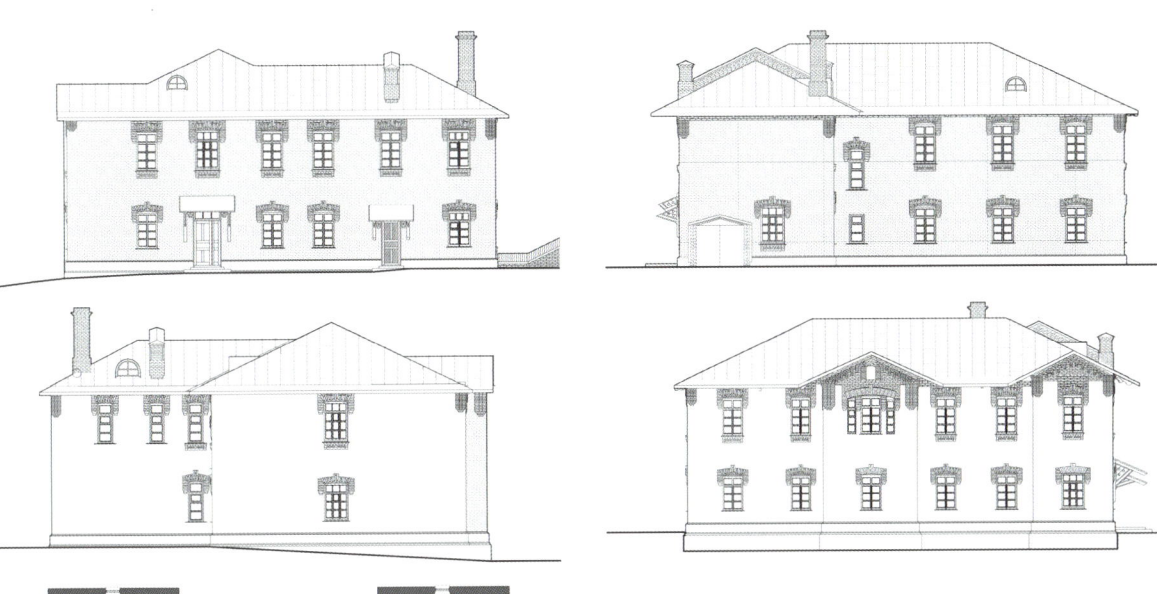

横道河子警察署现状及测绘图
Current condition and drawings of police station in Hengdaohezi

10 警察署及监狱

# ARCHITECTURAL CULTURAL HERITAGE OF CHINESE EASTERN RAILWAY

旅顺监狱 Prison in Lüshun

满洲里监狱 Prison in Manzhouli

# 医疗建筑

中东铁路医疗建筑是重要的公共服务建筑。按其职能和规模的不同主要可以分为中东铁路中心医院、集中式综合医院、卫生所、医务室、专科医院、特殊医院等。各种不同规模、等级、类型的医疗建筑共同构成了中东铁路沿线的医疗保障体系，是中东铁路能够建成通车的必要保障。

## 11.1 医疗建筑的分布方式与规划选址

中东铁路医疗建筑的分布方式与铁路站点的设置有很大关联。中东铁路的站点设置具有很强的系统性，各站点被冠以不同的等级。从一等站、二等站、三等站、四等站、五等站，一直到会让站和乘降点，每个站点都有自己的配套设施，医疗建筑就属于公共服务区的重要组成部分。按照不同的车站等级，配置设施有不同的功能构成及规模标准，以标准化设计建造完成。一等站哈尔滨站设有中东铁路中央医院，医院环境优美，占地8万余平方米，规模巨大、医疗功能完善、科室齐全、医疗资源雄厚；二、三等站设置一定规模的医疗建筑群，如在二等站横道河子站设置的医院，采用单体标准设计、整体自由组合的方式；小站则灵活地设置医务室，功能较为简单。

中东铁路医院在规划选址上，因医院的规模和性质不同而各具特点，根据各个站点的情况因地制宜。选址在保证功能合理的前提下注重与自然环境的融合。中东铁路中央医院在选址上充分考虑了哈尔滨的城市规模和性质，作为中东铁路枢纽站的主要医院，中东铁路中央医院不只服务于所在城市，还要服务于整个中东铁路沿线地区。医院选址在南岗区哈尔滨火车站的东南侧，交通位置优越，和城市衔接紧密，便于医疗资源及病人的输送和转移；医院位置相对独立，和居住区相对分离，便于医院的管理和服务。医院后退主要城市道路红军街一定距离，形成开敞空间，便于集散。二、三等站设置的医疗建筑群主要服务于该站点，医院一般选址在离生活区较远的街道尽端、空地等相对僻静和独立的地段，保障和城市紧密联系的同时减少对居民生活的影响，如二等站博克图的铁路医院就选址在离居住街区不远的一块空地上，和居住区保持若即若离的位置关系。医疗建筑群内的疫情观察、隔离、治疗所等单体建筑以及一些传染病医院的设置还会考虑风向等制约因素。在一些小站设置的卫生所、医务室服务对象较少，主要职能是对一般疾病的临时处置，所以其选址较为灵活，具体位置根据城镇的平面布局、自然环境而定，受城市交通等因素的影响制约较小。一些医务室还常常复合在其他建筑内，不单独另行设置。

## 11.2 医疗建筑的平面布局

规模和性质的不同也使中东铁路医疗建筑的平面布局有所差异，规模较大的综合性医院一般呈现自由式平面布局，这种平面布局功能分区明确，门诊、医技、住院、库房、食堂等不同功能分区按照医院的使用逻辑分配于不同的建筑单体中。各建筑之间联系紧密又留有间距，共同组成一个有机的医疗建筑群。这种布局形式为医院带来了良好的朝向及通风。建筑单体之间的空地被充分利用,大量绿化分布其间,在为患者营造一个舒适的内部医疗环境的同时也形成了宽松舒适的外部环境。一些站点设置的医院采用集中式的平面布局方式,平面布局紧凑,各功能区之间联系紧密,门诊、病房、库房、食堂等不同功能体块被整合在一栋大建筑里,各功能体块之间距离较近,便于灵活调度。这种平面布局更适于东北的严寒气候。具体的平面形式有矩形、L形、U形等样式。虽然是独栋建筑,但丰富的平面样式使建筑体量富于变化,因此建筑造型并不单一呆板。卫生所和医务室的规模较小,功能较为单一,住院床位较少甚至没有,相应的平面布局模式也较为简单,门厅结合走廊将各个房间串联整合是常用的平面形式,扎兰屯卫生所的平面布局就是这种模式。较小的卫生所和医务室功能分区相对弱化,可以整合的功能大多被设置在一起,这种平面布局模式比集中式平面布局更加紧凑精简,在管理和使用上更加灵活,与卫生所医疗室的功能性质更加契合。特殊医疗建筑,如疫情观察所、传染病医院等,平面布局上体现出严格的功能区块隔离和流线分离特点。病人使用的疫情隔离区、观察室、治疗室等空间与医生使用的空间被严格地分开,降低疫情传染和爆发的可能性。

### 11.3 先进的医疗方式及理念

中东铁路医院大量建设前,沿线各地的医疗方式相对落后。中东铁路修筑对医疗资源的大量需求催生了医疗建筑的出现。从大站的综合性医院到小站的卫生所,中东铁路医疗建筑各具特色。这些医疗建筑的修建和一批国外医生的到来使当时的东北地区成为中国境内较早普及西方医疗技术及理念的区域。中东铁路医院在为沿线地区提供一般性医疗服务的同时还兼有其他许多职能。如:工程伤害医疗、军事医疗、寒地疾病医疗、传染疫情防治等。这些职能是由中东铁路大量的相关建设活动以及特殊的地理自然条件、紧张的政治军事背景乃至大量的人员流动性所决定的。传统的医疗方式及理念无法满足这些医疗需求,因此,中东铁路各类医院的建造都是在当时先进的医疗理念指导下完成的。以中东铁路中央医院为例,其对急诊病人的处理、对外伤病人的处置、对寒地疾病的预防治疗、对传染病的控制等多个方面都有成熟的方式及先进的理念。此外,其在康复医疗方面也有所建树。这些医疗方式和医疗理念的应用直接在医疗建筑上得以体现,在建筑布局、分区、流线、室内和室外环境营造等方面都有别于原有医疗建筑。

中东铁路的修建是在相对恶劣的自然条件、落后的经济条件、不发达的技术条件下进行的,铁路修筑人员的健康和安全不断经受着各方面的考验,中东铁路医疗建筑的修建满足了他们的医疗卫生需求,为中东铁路的运营、维护和管理提供了一个稳定的后勤保障。时至今日,一些存留下来的中东铁路医疗建筑还在继续发挥其功能。

# Medical Buildings

Medical buidings along Chinese Eastern Railway (CER) were important public buildings that offered medical services for railway staffs. Medical buidings for CER could be divided into hospital center, integrated general hospitals, clinics, infirmaries, specialized hospitals and special medical care hospitals, according to their different scales and functions.They constituted the rear medical security system and guaranteed the completion and operation of CER.

The distribution of medical buildings along CER was closely related to the function, scale, and rank of the railway stations, and most of the buildings were built under the standardization design. Hospitals showed different characteristics in their site selection according to their scales and properties, and would be arranged to the local conditions of the stations. Wind direction would also be concerned in designs of epidemic oberservation building, isolation building, treatment center and infectious disease hospitals. Some clinics and infirmaries, which were located at small stations and provided temporary treatments to small group of people, were often flexibly sited according to the town plan and natrual envrionment, and seldom affacted by the town traffic. Some infirmaries were independently set in other buildings.

Different scales and properties of medical buildings along CER gave them different layouts. Large scale general hospitals usually adopted free layout and functional zoning, with their outpatient department, medical technology department, inpatient department, ware house and canteen distributed in different buildings. These buildings were closely connected but with a certain distance and formed an organic medical group.

Clinics and infirmaries were often in simple plans with rooms linked by entrance hall and the corridor, as could be seen in Zhalantun clinics, due to their small scale, single funtion and fewer or even no beds. The functional zoning in smaller clinics and infirmaries was rather weak and many functions were integrated together. Special medical care buildings like epidemic obersercation and infectious diseases hospitals showed strict isolation features in functional zoning and traffic flow. Epidemic isolation areas, oberservation rooms and treatment rooms which were mainly used by patients were strictly seperated from doctor's spaces so as to reduce the risk of infection and outbreak.

The construction of CER and its needs for medical resources stimulated the emerging of medical buildings along the railway, where the medical conditions were relatively undeveloped in the past. Medical buildings along CER presented distinctive features, from general hospitals at large stations to the tiny clinics at small stations, and their construction together with the arrival of foreign doctors made northeast China become the area where western medical technology and theory were spread much earlier. Meanwhile, the medical buildings along CER provided not only normal medical services, but also many other services, including engineering injury treatment, military injury treatment, cold region diseases treatment, and epidemic prevention and control.

ARCHITECTURAL CULTURAL HERITAGE OF CHINESE EASTERN RAILWAY

中东铁路中央医院历史照片
Historical photo of the Central Hospital of CER in Harbin

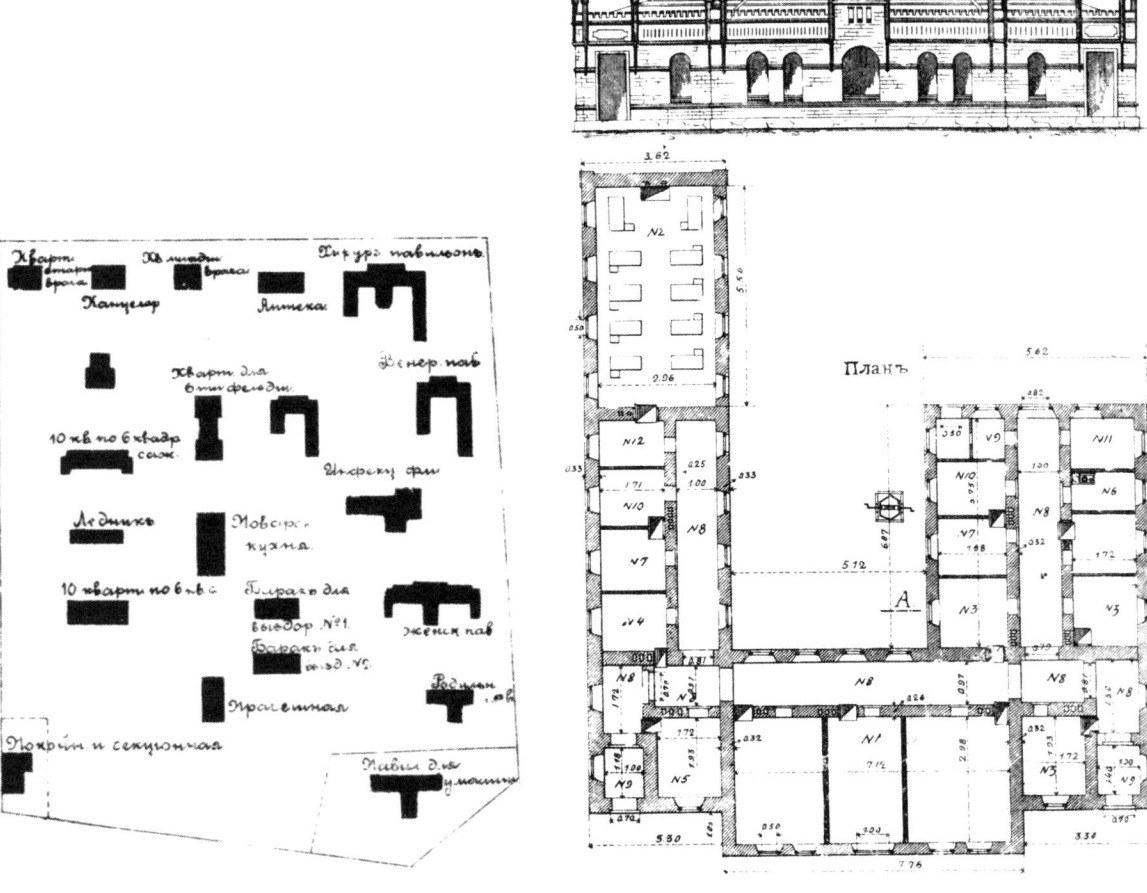

160 床位医院总平面图
Planning map of 160-bed hospital

36 床位病房设计图
Drawings of 28-bed ward

中东铁路中央医院病房历史照片
Historical photos of ward of Central Hospital of CER in Harbin

中东铁路中央医院病房 1
Ward of Central Hospital of CER in Harbin 1

中东铁路中央医院病房 2
Ward of Central Hospital of CER in Harbin 2

中东铁路中央医院病房 3
Ward of Central Hospital of CER in Harbin 3

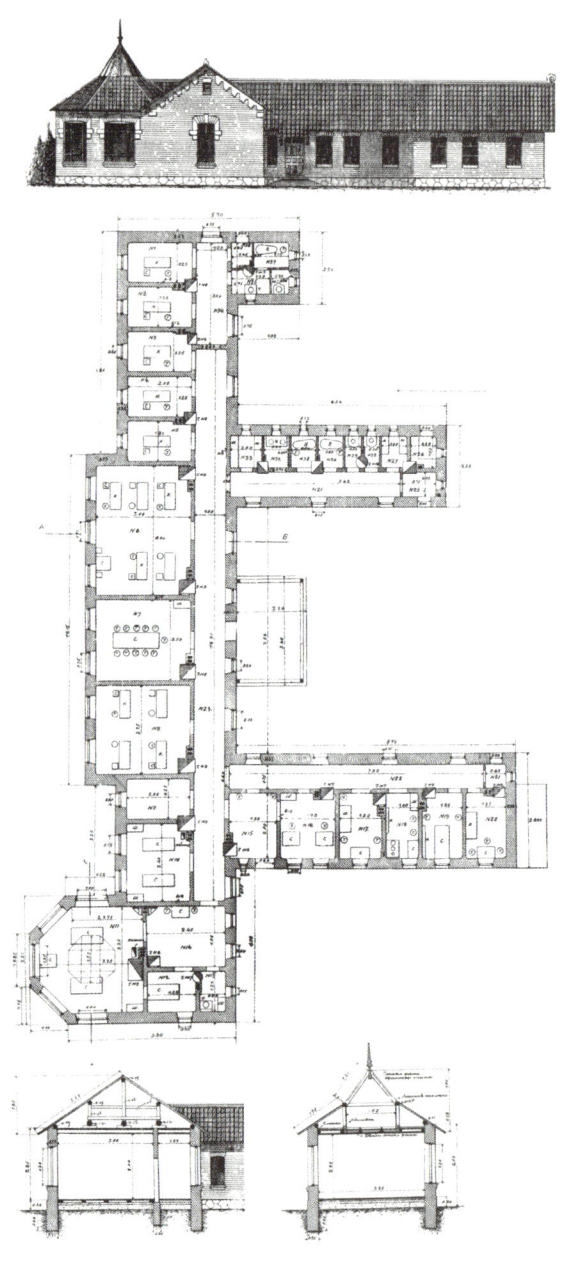

13 床位病房设计图
Drawings of 13-bed ward

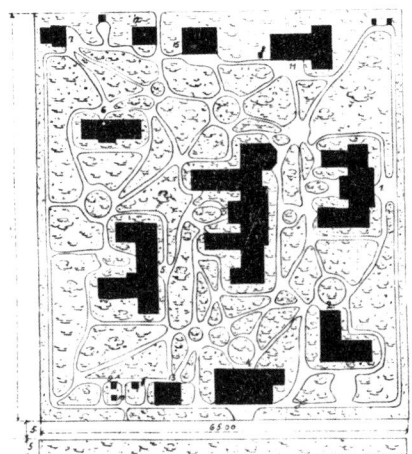

50 床位医院总平面图
Planning map of 50-bed hospital

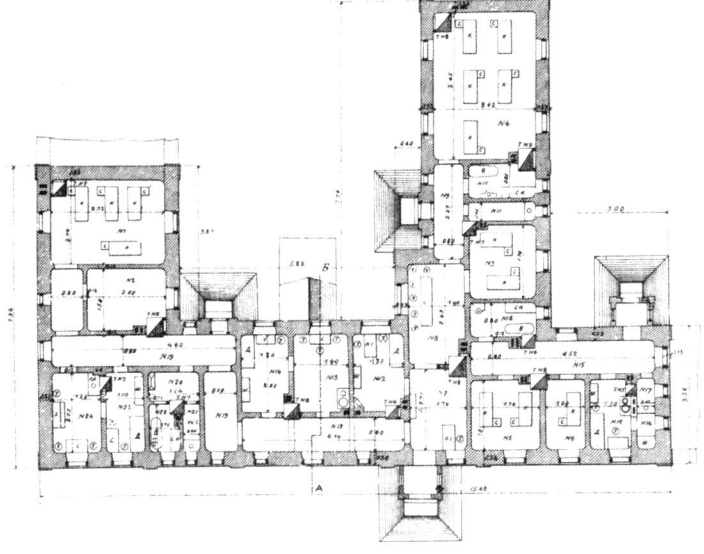

15 床位病房设计图
Drawings of 15-bed ward

海拉尔医院病房（50 床位）历史照片
Historical photo of hospital ward (50-bed) in Hailaer

11 医疗建筑 | 251

# ARCHITECTURAL CULTURAL HERITAGE OF CHINESE EASTERN RAILWAY

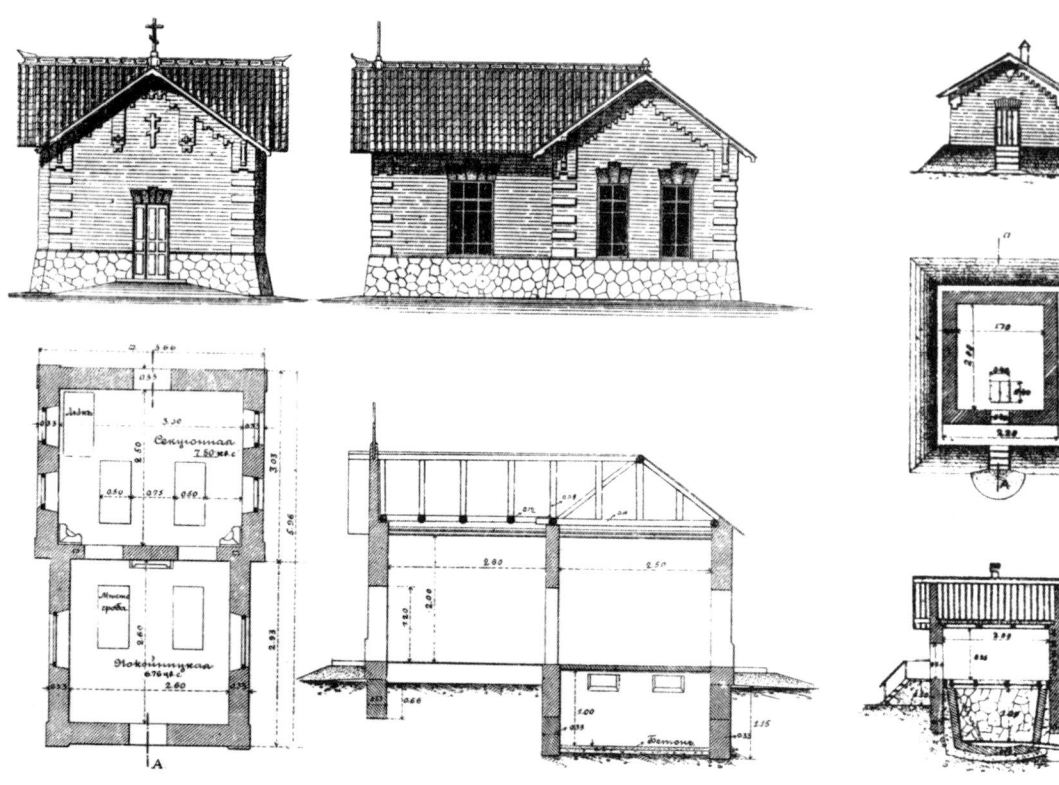

160 床位医院停尸房设计图
Drawings of morgue of 160-bed hospital

医院冰窖设计图纸
Drawings of hospital icehouse

绥芬河医院停尸房历史照片
Historical photo of hospital morgue in Suifenhe

绥芬河医院普通病房历史照片
Historical photo of ordinary hospital ward in Suifenhe

公主岭医院（130 床位）历史照片
Historical photo of hospital（130-bed）in Gongzhuling

公主岭医院病房历史照片
Historical photo of hospital ward in Gongzhuling

# ARCHITECTURAL CULTURAL HERITAGE OF CHINESE EASTERN RAILWAY

一面坡医院 Yimianpo Hospital

一面坡医院正立面测绘图 Drawing of front elevation of Yimianpo hospital

一面坡医院建筑细部 Details of Yimianpo hospital

一面坡医院室内环境 Interior of Yimianpo hospital

一面坡医院背立面测绘图 Drawing of back elevation of Yimianpo hospital

11 医疗建筑 | 255

一面坡医院主入口
Main entrance of Yimianpo hospital

一面坡医院平面测绘图
Drawings of Yimianpo hospital

扎兰屯卫生所历史照片
Historical photo of hospital in Zhalantun

扎兰屯卫生所 Hospital in Zhalantun

扎兰屯卫生所测绘图 Drawings of hospital in Zhalantun

11 医疗建筑

# ARCHITECTURAL CULTURAL HERITAGE OF CHINESE EASTERN RAILWAY

横道河子医院病房现状及立面测绘图 1 Current condition and elevation drawings of hospital ward in Hengdaohezi 1

横道河子医院病房现状及立面测绘图 2  Current condition and elevation drawings of hospital ward in Hengdaohezi 2

11 医疗建筑

横道河子医院病房
Hospital ward in Hengdaohezi

满洲里医务段
Hospital in Manzhouli

博克图医院
Hospital in Boketu

昂昂溪医院
Hospital in Ang'angxi

# 12 休闲建筑

休闲设施主要是指为中东铁路官员及职工提供休闲娱乐活动的场所,按照具体功能大致可分为三类,即铁路俱乐部、休闲公园、度假旅馆。每类设施各具特色,其中铁路俱乐部数量最多,种类丰富多样,是最具有代表性的中东铁路休闲建筑。

## 12.1 俱乐部

中东铁路沿线建有大量类型多样的俱乐部,如文化休闲类俱乐部、运动竞技类俱乐部、特定使用人群类俱乐部等。作为一种福利性设施,俱乐部一般设置在重要城市,如哈尔滨、大连、昂昂溪等,或者环境极佳的火车站点,如扎兰屯、一面坡、富拉尔基等。城市中俱乐部多位于中心区的铁路办公机构或火车站点附近,其他一般站点的俱乐部则根据自然环境条件选址于靠山滨水之处。虽然相较于一般的站舍、铁路用房及住宅等建筑来说,俱乐部建筑普遍体量较大,但其形象注重与城市氛围和自然环境的协调呼应,具有景观建筑的特征。在中东铁路沿线的各种建筑类型中,俱乐部建筑风格最为丰富,成为中东铁路附属地内城镇景观的重要点缀。如位于哈尔滨松花江畔建于1912年的中东铁路江上俱乐部,集餐厅、接待与茶室于一体,顺着江堤倚叠而起形成尖塔,并朝向江面方向挑出大面积观景平台。整座建筑形象优美轻盈、高低错落,充满滨水建筑的韵味。

典型的俱乐部建筑包含剧场、舞厅、台球厅、活动室、餐饮区、休息室、酒吧、棋牌室、书报阅览等丰富的功能分区,一些大型俱乐部还设有网球场、花园、凉亭及露天剧场附属功能分区。俱乐部本身即是一种偏向于现代化的功能类型,其平面布局多从功能出发,结构与材料也多选用能够支持电影放映厅及戏剧观演厅等大空间的形式,对于当时中东铁路沿线地区来说是相当前卫的建筑潮流,如哈尔滨中东铁路俱乐部,砖混结构面积超过 5 000 平方米;中东铁路哈尔滨总工厂俱乐部剧场通高 20 米,观众厅座席设两层楼座,共 1 000 余个座位,舞台设备装有当时远东最先进的 12 米直径旋转舞台;安达俱乐部设有双层放映厅,上层装有包厢,楼下场地 400 余平方米,能容纳 15 排座位。

## 12.2 度假旅馆

中东铁路沿线的宾馆大致可分为铁路机构特设宾馆、城市宾馆、休闲度假宾馆及疗养院所。铁路宾馆选址靠近火车站,城市宾馆大多在市街中心,而度假旅馆则选址于临近自然景观的河畔、山脚或林间。休闲度假宾馆的主要功能是为休假、疗养的中东铁路官员提供休息空间,其装修相对高档豪华,使用起来更加舒适。宾馆的平面布局具有多元组合特征,重复的客房单元、形态各异的大堂、餐厅、会议厅、多功能厅以及后勤服务空间构成宾馆的典型布局,休闲宾馆还设有豪华的外部敞廊,人们可以在长廊里用餐、沐浴阳光、远眺风景。建于 1925 年的扎兰屯避暑旅馆是典型的度假旅馆,建筑为俄罗斯风格砖木结构,建筑立面精美端庄。建筑的平面布局以直线形走廊贯穿,客房分布于两端，空间比例舒适、采光良好，建筑端部有开放式的凉廊，供客人休闲使用。

### 12.3 休闲公园

休闲公园是当时最具代表性的室外休闲场所，为铁路职工以及市民提供休闲娱乐所必须的室外场地。从分布形式上看，休闲公园可以分为城市公园与疗养公园两类。城市公园是重要城市的绿地系统规划内容，主要是为了塑造良好的城市环境。如位于哈尔滨、大连、满洲里等地的公园是重要的城市基础设施与景观资源。带有疗养职能的公园则是为铁路官员与职工提供休养福利，一般选址在植物类型丰富、群山环绕、水系充沛的站点，如位于富拉尔基、兴安、巴林等处的公园为疗养站点塑造宜人的休养环境。位于扎兰屯、一面坡、穆棱的公园则二者兼有之，一方面有疗养功能，另一方面也是城镇功能的一部分。

中东铁路休闲公园的规模尺度一般和所在城镇的规模相适配，规模较为适宜，既不像传统园林那样狭促，又不像大型城市公园那样广阔。以扎兰屯公园为例，现在的扎兰屯市吊桥公园经过加建，占地68公顷，位于城市的西北角，面积相当于城区的二十分之一。公园的构成要素与布局方式因环境与功能不同而各有差异，除一般的山水植被与建筑小品外，还有露天剧场、自然浴场、日光浴场等特殊功能。设计上以利用已有条件、顺应自然环境为主，辅以尺度较小且形态通透的亭台楼榭、雕塑、吊桥等小品，风格上也包含中、俄民族传统甚至现代元素，材质则以木、石等天然材料为主。除建筑小品外，部分休闲公园内还设有办公管理建筑、俱乐部、休闲餐厅等。

中东铁路沿线的休闲设施与日常生活息息相关，为沿线地区带来了时尚的休闲娱乐理念，也把先进的城市规划和景观理念引入铁路沿线地区。有些中东铁路休闲娱乐建筑至今仍在使用中。以这些设施为载体，一些西式的休闲文化被引入到中国东北地区，其影响至今仍有余音。

## Leisure Architectures

Recreation facility was the main space that provides leisure activities for officers and staff of CER, which could be concluded to three types, such as railway club, leisure park and holiday hotel according to their specific function. Among them, the railway club was the most representative recreation buildings in the largest number and various styles.

There were various clubs constructed in different types along CER, such as cultural leisure clubs, competitive sport clubs and clubs for special population. As a kind of welfare facilities, railway clubs were usually arranged in important cities, such as Harbin, Dalian, Ang'angxi, as well as some stations with excellent environment, such as Zhalantun, Yimianpo, Fulaerji and so on. Clubs were often built near the office buildings and the stations in central area of the city, and some clubs were also built in normal stations usually with a beautiful landscape, for instance, near the rivers or mountains. Compared with ordinary residence and station buildings, the club buildings were often in large size, and integrate them into the surroundings, which presented characteristics of the landscape buildings in form. Among all the building types along CER, the railway club was much diversified, which became the most important decorative factor of urban landscape in the dependency of CER. The typical club buildings included theater, ballroom, billiard room, activity room, catering area, lounge, pub, chess and card room, reading room and so on. There were also tennis court, garden, pavilion and outdoor theater in some large clubs.

Hotel along CER line mainly included the railway hotel, city hotel, resort hotel and sanatorium. The railway hotel was usually located near the station in site selection, the city hotel was usually located in the central part and main street of the city, the resort hotel was usually built in natural environment near the forest, river or mountain. The main function of the resort hotels was to provide the resting space for vacation and convalescent of the staff and officers, of which the decoration was much costly and comfortable. The plane layout of the hotel was multifarious, with a typical hotel pattern including guest room unit, various lobbies, catering, conference room, multifunctional hall and logistic service. Also, the resort hotel was used to set up outdoor gallery where to arrange dinner, to have sunshine and beautiful scenery.

Leisure park was the most typical outdoor recreation space, whose main function was to provide a place for outdoor activity of citizen and railway staff. It could be divided into city park and healing park according to different functions. City park was an important part in the green space system of urban planning, whose function was mainly to create a good city environment. For example, the parks in Harbin, Dalian and Manzhouli, had become an important urban infrastructure and landscape resources. The parks for resting and healing were the welfare for the railway officer and staff, which were usually located near the stations with beautiful landscape surrounded by mountains and rivers, such as the parks in Fulaerji, xing'an, Balin and so on. Parks in Zhalantun, Yimianpo and Muling had the characteristics and function of both.

富拉尔基疗养处历史照片 Historical photos of sanitarium in Fulaerji

哈尔滨中东铁路俱乐部历史照片 Historical photo of CER Club in Harbin

# ARCHITECTURAL CULTURAL HERITAGE OF CHINESE EASTERN RAILWAY

哈尔滨中东铁路俱乐部现状及设计图
Current condition and drawings of CER Club in Harbin

哈尔滨铁路竞技会馆现状、历史照片及设计图
Current condition, historical photo and drawings of sports club of CER in Harbin

中东铁路哈尔滨总工厂俱乐部  
Club of Harbin General Factory of CER

哈尔滨枢纽站俱乐部  
Club of hub station in Harbin

哈尔滨中东铁路江上俱乐部历史照片及现状  
Historical photos and current condition of Riverside Club of CER in Harbin

12 休闲建筑

ARCHITECTURAL CULTURAL HERITAGE OF CHINESE EASTERN RAILWAY

一面坡铁路俱乐部历史照片 Historical photo of railway club in Yimianpo

一面坡铁路俱乐部（已拆除）Railway club in Yimianpo (demolished)

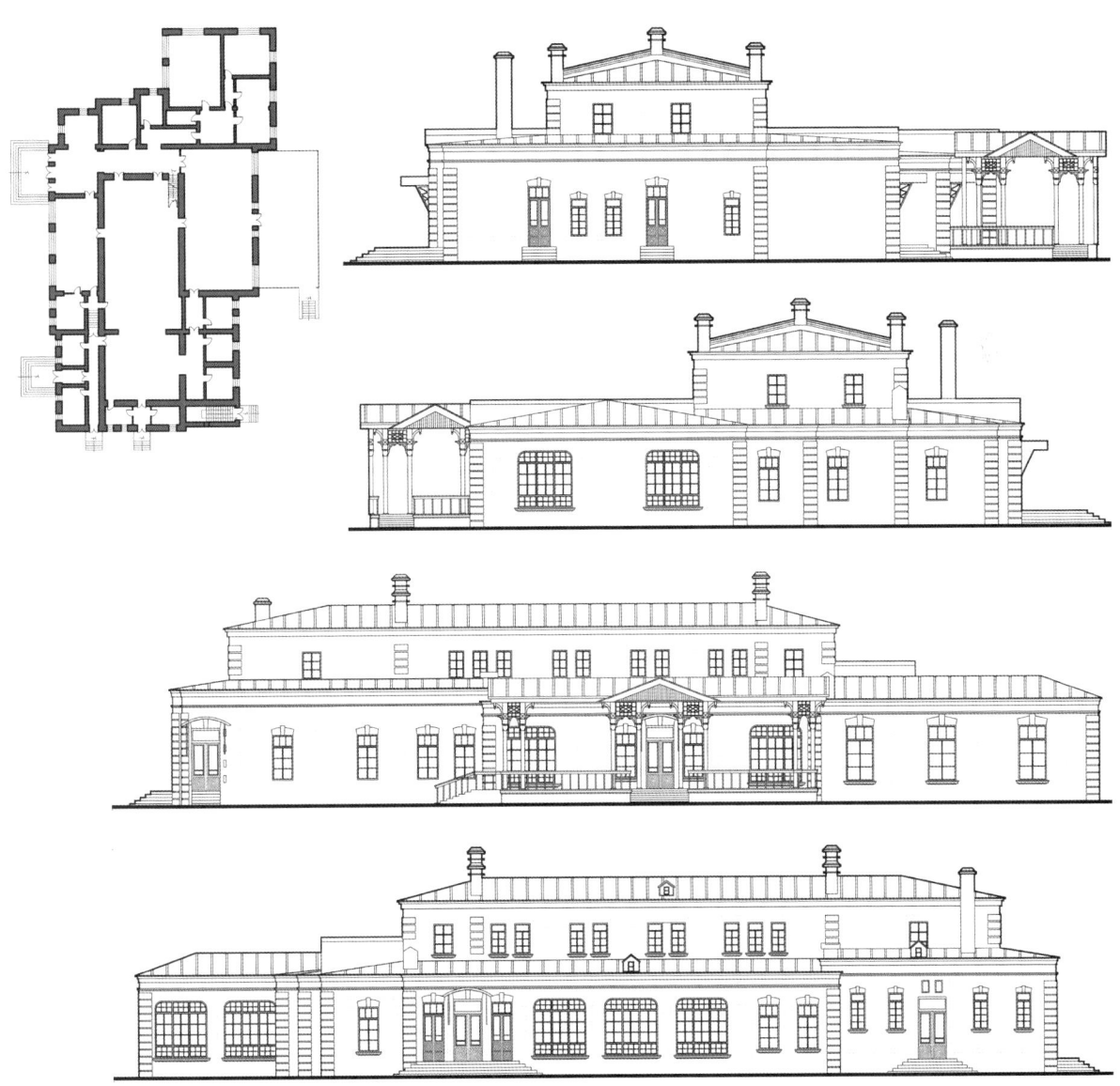

一面坡铁路俱乐部复原设计图 Restoration drawings of railway club in Yimianpo

一面坡疗养处历史照片 Historical photos of sanitarium in Yimainpo

横道河子公园凉亭历史照片
Historical photo of park pavilion in Hengdaohezi

穆棱公园历史照片
Historical photo of park in Muling

巴林疗养处历史照片
Historical photos of sanitarium in Balin

满洲里俱乐部历史照片
Historical photo of club in Manzhouli

兴安疗养处历史照片
Historical photo of sanitarium in Xing'an

12 休闲建筑

# ARCHITECTURAL CULTURAL HERITAGE OF CHINESE EASTERN RAILWAY

扎兰屯铁路俱乐部现状及测绘图 Current condition and drawing of railway club in Zhalantun

扎兰屯俱乐部 Club in Zhalantun

扎兰屯避暑旅馆历史照片、现状及测绘图
Historical photo, current condition and drawings of summer hotel in Zhalantun

12 休闲建筑

扎兰屯公园历史照片 Historical photos of park in Zhalantun

扎兰屯凉亭历史照片
Historical photos of pavilion in Zhalantun

扎兰屯疗养处历史照片
Historical photo of sanitarium in Zhalantun

扎兰屯浴场历史照片
Historical photo of bathing spot in Zhalantun

扎兰屯球场历史照片
Historical photo of court in Zhalantun

扎兰屯日光浴场历史照片
Historical photo of sunbathing spot in Zhalantun

12 休闲建筑

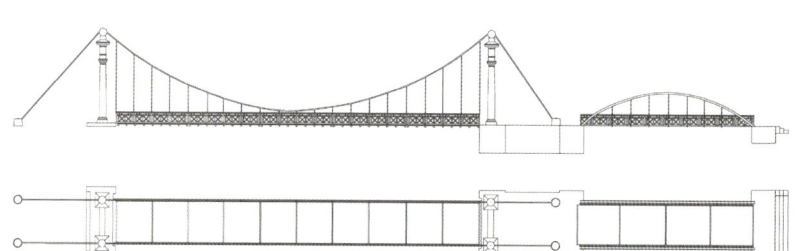

扎兰屯公园吊桥现状及测绘图 Current condition and drawing of suspension bridge in Zhalantun park

昂昂溪铁路俱乐部 Railway club in Ang'angxi

安达铁路俱乐部 Railway club in Anda

# 13 办公建筑

中东铁路办公建筑的主要职能是为中东铁路官员及职工提供办公场所，是维护和运营中东铁路必不可少的建筑类型。中东铁路办公建筑主要包括中东铁路管理局大楼和铁路下属机构的办公用房。其中，下属机构的办公用房还包括铁路站区外部与中东铁路交涉事宜相关的办公建筑和站区内部与铁路车务管理有关的办公建筑。级别较高的一、二等站，办公建筑类型较为全面，与中东铁路相关的办公建筑类型基本都有配备，在等级较低的站点，以和站区内部车务管理相关的办公建筑为主。

## 13.1 中东铁路管理局大楼

中东铁路管理局一度是中东铁路的最高权力机关，管理局大楼作为其办公场所，在所有中东铁路建筑中等级最高、规模最大，有着举足轻重的地位，也是一栋非常有特色的建筑。中东铁路管理局设置在一等站哈尔滨，管理局大楼位于南岗区西大直街。建筑后退道路边线60余米，在道路和建筑之间形成了一个宽阔的广场，方便使用的同时，还为建筑立面的展示提供了一定的缓冲距离。管理局大楼于1902年5月开工建设，1904年2月投入使用。建筑面积20 000余平方米，总长度180余米，总宽度80余米，层高超过5米。大楼为双合院"日"字形平面布局，建筑分主楼、配楼、后楼几大部分，各部分由多个拱形门洞及短廊联结而成，交通流线明晰合理，各功能区块彼此相互独立又不缺乏联系，组成了一个功能多样、体量庞大的行政办公建筑综合体，这种体量的办公建筑在中东铁路沿线可谓独一无二。中东铁路管理局大楼建筑立面构图均衡、比例匀称，正楼3层、配楼2层，体量舒展开阔，沿西大直街望去有很好的视觉效果。立面装饰以新艺术风格为主，窗洞口贴脸、门廊、阳台栏杆、女儿墙等部位都以新艺术风格的曲线做装饰。建筑饰面以青石为主要材质，色彩古朴典雅、气氛庄严肃穆，和建筑性格十分吻合。

整体来说，中东铁路管理局大楼是中东铁路建筑中的精品，建筑前面有视野开阔的广场，后面有两个尺度小巧、气氛宁静的内部院落，空间丰富、内外贯通。建筑外观庄严沉稳，这种气质也体现在空间尺度、外墙材料、装饰风格等各个方面，充分显示出统领全局的气魄，是当年哈尔滨的标志性建筑。

## 13.2 铁路下属机构的办公用房

中东铁路管理局的下属机构按其职能大致可分为行政办公部门和站务管理部门，相应的办公建筑也可以分为两类，即行政办公建筑和站务管理办公建筑。前者主要设置于站区外部，后者一般分布于站区内部。

站区外部与铁路交涉事宜相关的行政办公建筑主要包括各地铁路交涉局、事务所、官署、领事馆等。这类行政部门的职能主要是处理中东铁路运营管理及相关的行政事宜，贯彻落实中东铁路管理局的政令，办公性质偏于官方性和正式性且交涉事务较多，因此，这类建筑在装饰上一般比较精美典雅。总理绥芬河铁路交涉局就是一个典型实例。

这座建筑建于 1903 年，专门管理与中东铁路相关的交涉事宜。建筑面积为 2 100 余平方米，平面为口字形，共两层，中间设有天井，建筑立面装饰精美，形象典雅美观。二等站博克图的百年段长办公室也是一个具有代表性的实例，办公室建于 1903 年，是中东铁路满洲里至安达区段机务段长办公室。建筑平面呈矩形，南侧有一个突出的门斗与外部相连。建筑面积 290 余平方米，南北长 24 余米，东西宽 12 米，平面上布置有段长室、教育室、技术室、众务室、夫役室、仓库、卫生间等。建筑采用砖石砌筑而成，仅一层，立面造型简约大气，根据各房间的位置分布及使用性质灵活开窗，东立面中部设有突出的三角形山花，打破水平构图，檐口处设有顺砖叠砌线脚，丰富了立面的层次感。铁路站区内部的办公建筑都与车务管理有关，如：车务稽查段、扳道房、值班室等，这类建筑相对于站区外部的行政办公建筑而言规模较小，功能更加单一具体，是许多站点的标准配置。如横道河子车务稽查段。这座建筑建于 1903 年，一字形平面，单层砖木结构，属于站内标准配置。这类办公建筑体量及规模较小，主要使用对象是铁路职工，对内性比较强，因此其相对于其他办公建筑在装饰上比较简单质朴，具有标准化设计倾向，以中东铁路风格为主。

　　中东铁路行政办公建筑是和中东铁路管理运营息息相关的公共建筑，类型丰富多样，功能涵盖了与中东铁路相关的各个层面，大到中东铁路行政政策的制定，小到铁路职工的日常办公。这些办公建筑根据各个站点的不同功能需求合理分布，按照行政级别和职能的不同严密地组织起了中东铁路运行维护管理网，是中东铁路存在和正常使用的重要保障，有些办公建筑至今还在为铁路的运营管理发挥作用。

## Office Buildings

　　Administration building of the CER was functionally to provide an office space for officials and staff, which was an indispensable building type for maintaining and operating the railway. This kinds of buildings mainly included administration building and office space of the railway affiliates, in which the subsidiary office buildings also included some related negotiation buildings outside the station and the buildings related to interior station and vehicle management inside the station. In high-grade stations, such as the first- or second-grade stations, the office buildings were much comprehensive, including all kinds of building types related to the CER. While in the low-grade stations, the office buildings were mainly used to internal vehicle management.

　　Administration Bureau of CER had been the highest authority and also was management hub. The building of the Administration Bureau of CER was the main office space that plays an irreplaceable role among all the buildings and also a much distinctive building. Administration Bureau of CER was set in Harbin as the first-grade station, which was located in West Dazhi Street, Nangang District. The building was constructed in May, 1902 and came into service in February, 1904. The gross area of the administration building was more than 20,000 square meters with more than 180 meters in length, more than 80 meters in width and more than 5 meters in floor height. The building was back from the sideline of the road more than 60 meters, and the plane layout was designed as double courtyard with a shape like "日". The building was divided into several parts, such as the main building, the annex building and the back building. Each part was linked by several arched doorways and corridors, which made the building not only independent but also connective with each other, becoming a multifunctional and large-scaled administration building complex. The facade composition of the Administration Bureau of CER was balanced and well-proportioned in 3 floors with a main building and 2 floors of the annex building. Besides, the building facade was mainly decorated in Art Nouveau style, as well as other details, such as windows, porches, balcony railings, parapet walls, were all decorated in Art Nouveau curve pattern. The building surface was made of blue stone that accords with the architectural characteristics very well.

The subsidiaries of the Administration Bureau of CER could be roughly divided into administration departments and station management departments according to the function. And the corresponding office buildings could also be divided into two categories, administrative office buildings and station management buildings. The former was mainly located outside the station area, and the latter was generally distributed inside the station area. The administrative office buildings related to railway negotiations outside the station mainly included railway negotiation office, law offices, government offices, consulates, etc. The function of the administrative office buildings mainly dealt with the operation, management and administrative matters of the CER, and also implement the decrees from the Administration Bureau of CER. These buildings were beautiful and elegant in decoration because of the formal and official nature. The buildings inside the stations were mostly related to the vehicle management, such as the vehicle audit section, the switchman's cabin, the duty rooms, etc. Compared with the administrative office buildings outside the stations, these buildings were smaller in size and more specific in function, where the standard layout was used for many stops. Meanwhile, they were relatively simple in decoration with a trends in standardized design in contrast with other office buildings.

# ARCHITECTURAL CULTURAL HERITAGE OF CHINESE EASTERN RAILWAY

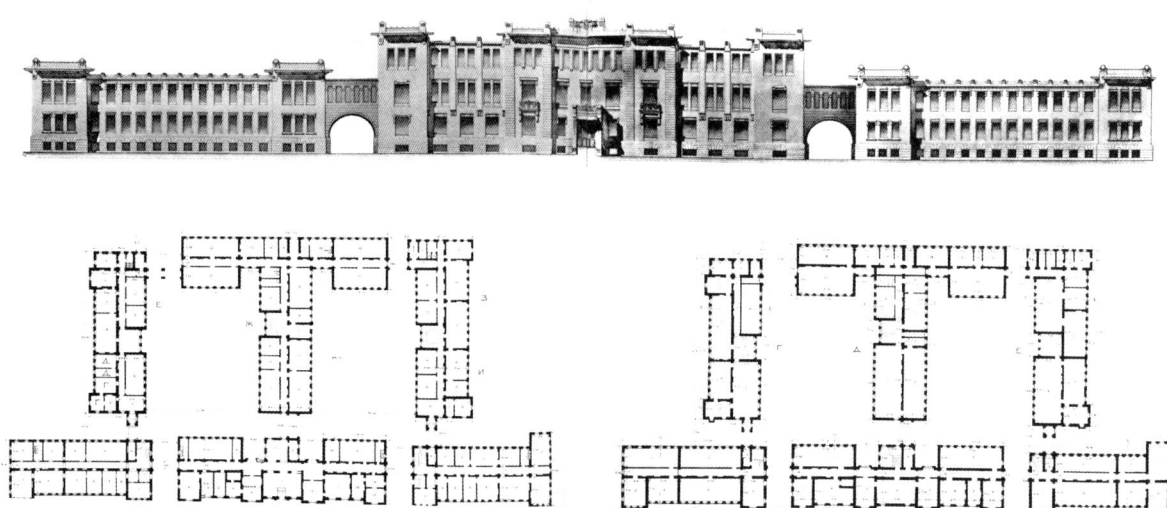

哈尔滨中东铁路管理局历史照片及设计图
Historical photo and drawings of Administration Bureau of CER in Harbin

哈尔滨中东铁路管理局
Administration Bureau of CER in Harbin

# ARCHITECTURAL CULTURAL HERITAGE OF CHINESE EASTERN RAILWAY

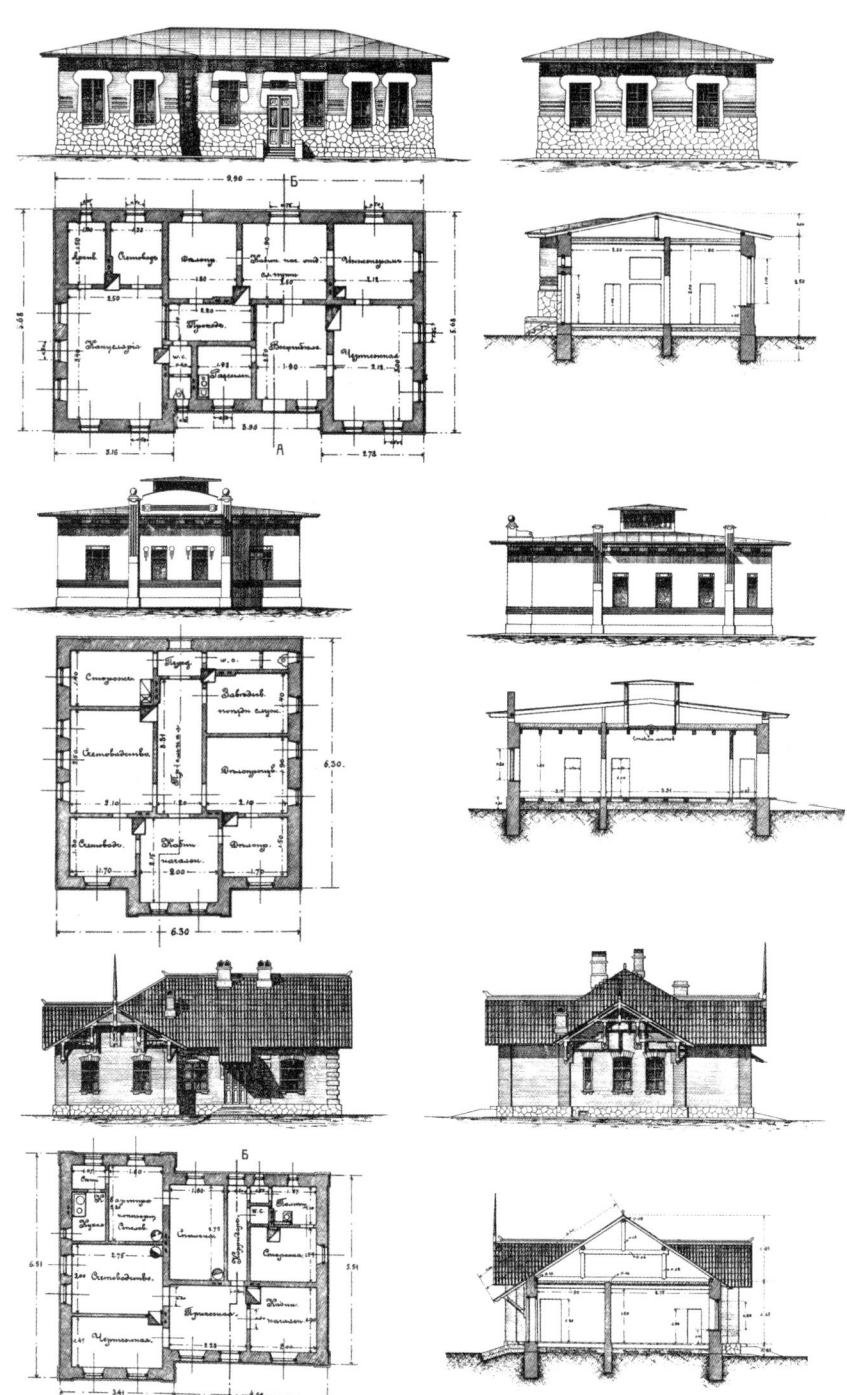

中东铁路沿线办公建筑设计图 Drawings of offices along CER

博克图站办公室 Office in Boketu Station

满洲里站办公室历史照片 Historical photo of office in Manzhouli Station

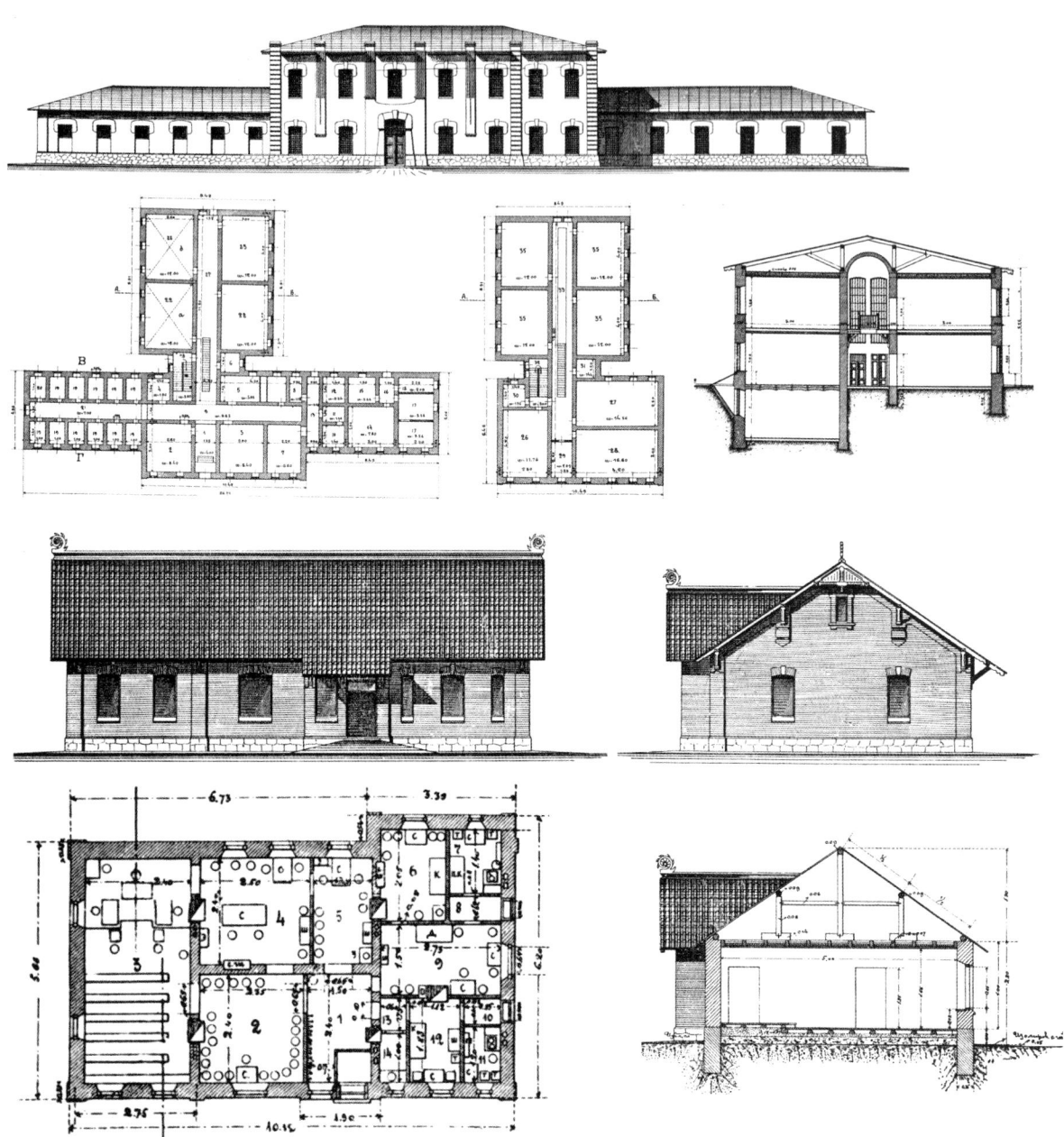

中东铁路沿线法院设计图 Drawings of courts along CER

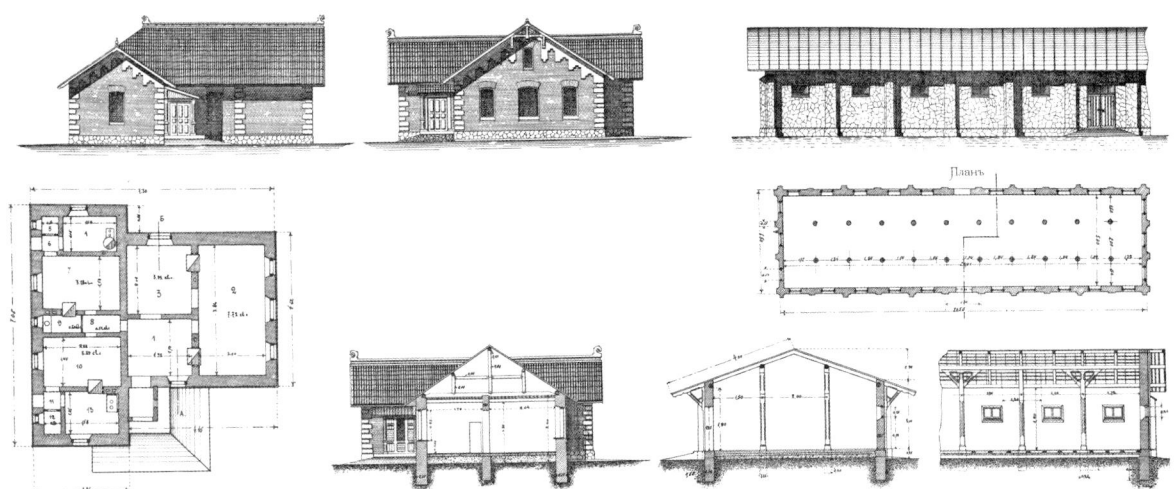

海关建筑设计图
Drawings of customs houses

满洲里中国海关历史照片
Historical photo of Chinese customs house in Manzhouli

扎兰屯地区办事处与铁路服务部门历史照片
Historical photo of office in Zhalantun

绥芬河地区办事处与铁路服务部门历史照片
Historical photo of office in Suifenhe

满洲里地区办事处与铁路服务部门历史照片
Historical photo of office in Manzhouli

满洲里商务处 Commercial office in Manzhouli

满洲里苏俄领事馆 Russian embassy in Manzhouli

满洲里日本领事馆 Japanese embassy in Manzhouli

营口俄国领事馆历史照片 Historical photo of Russian embassy in Yingkou

绥芬河苏俄领事馆 Russian embassy in Suifenhe

绥芬河日本领事馆 Japanese embassy in Suifenhe

# ARCHITECTURAL CULTURAL HERITAGE OF CHINESE EASTERN RAILWAY

总理绥芬河铁路交涉局现状 Current condition of General Suifenhe Railway Representation Bureau

总理绥芬河铁路交涉局室内外细部 Interior and exterior details of General Suifenhe Railway Representation Bureau

一面坡俄国领事馆
Russian embassy in Yimianpo

一面坡建筑段办公室
Office for building section in Yimianpo

一面坡货运段办公室
Office for cargo segment in Yimianpo

一面坡货运段工房
Workshop for cargo segment in Yimianpo

一面坡机务段工房 Workshop for locomotive depot in Yimianpo

横道河子机务段办公室 Office for locomotive depot in Hengdaohezi

13 办公建筑 | 297

# 14 校舍

中东铁路学校的主要职能是为铁路职工子女提供教育和培养与铁路工程相关的技术人才。可分成两类：提供普通教育的俄侨铁路职工子弟学校和进行铁路工程相关专业技能培训的技工学校。此外还有专门的俄人学校、华工子弟学校、商务学堂，以及数量众多的教堂学校等。在一些规模不大的城镇，学校大都与教堂建筑复合在一起，类似于教会学校的模式；而在规模较大的城镇，学校建设会专门选址，并有了小学、中学的具体分类；在城市规模更大的一等站，学校数量众多，种类齐全。

## 14.1 俄侨子弟学校

中东铁路附属地被分为四个特别学区进行管理。哈尔滨市即第一学区，哈满沿线是第二学区，哈绥沿线是第三学区，哈长沿线是第四学区。原第一学区共有高小学生 1 422 名，初小学生 5 865 名；第二学区共有高小学生 519 名，初小学生 2 778 名；第三学区共有高小学生 538 名，初小学生 2 831 名。干线上三区共有高小学生 2 479 名，初小学生 11 474 名。为了便于统一管理维护，中东铁路管理局专门设立了学务处，负责铁路职工子弟学校的教育事务。到 1926 年，中东铁路附属地内已有俄人学校 68 所，华工子弟学校 18 所。俄侨子弟学校具有附属地内建筑典型的标准化特征，根据人数规模的不同建筑有着特定的形式，形式上也采用以砖石砌筑的中东铁路风格。典型实例如扎兰屯中东铁路沙俄子弟小学，建于 1910 年。该建筑呈"L"形布局，两边分别靠北侧和东侧，为南向留出一个小院，推测为学生活动场地。这类建筑并没有特殊的形式特点，除有资料记载的几处外，其他与中东铁路一般住宅极易混淆。另外，中东铁路沿线大量建造的部分东正教堂也兼做教育场所，但此部分只描述专门的学校类建筑。

## 14.2 中东铁路职业教育学校

职业技术学校是中东铁路附属地教育的一大特色，主要为铁路及城市建设培养专业的技术人才。这类学校普遍设置于等级较高的站点，如一等站哈尔滨，二等站绥芬河、满洲里等。学校建筑规模较大，以城市建筑的规格与形式设计，风格采用折中主义、古典主义等当时仍占主流的形式，也有新艺术风格的运用。个别规模较大的学校由多栋建筑组成，形成建筑组群。其中最负盛名的是建于 1904 年的哈尔滨中东铁路技术学校，其建筑分期建设，1920 年发展为哈尔滨中俄工业学校（哈尔滨工业大学前身）。校园除教学楼外还有实习工厂与宿舍楼。教学楼为两层，砖木混合结构，转角处设有带穹顶的塔楼。建筑立面造型优雅舒展，是典型的新艺术运动风格。中东铁路管理局于 1906 年在哈尔滨开办中东铁路商务学堂，该校旨在培养致力于中俄商务关系的人才，招收了大量的中东铁路职工子女。建筑为两层，平面呈中轴对称，规模较大，包括教室、实验室、教师办公室以及后勤用房等。建筑立面上几对纤细的壁柱突破檐口形成跳跃的天际线，密集的小方格网在檐下墙壁上形成水平的装饰带，墙面及女儿墙上以植物图案和浅浮雕相结合作为装饰,形式非常独特。

随着中东铁路的修建和沿线城镇的建设,大量教育建筑集中出现,在服务中东铁路的同时,也推动了东北地区的近代教育发展。中东铁路建设时期的教育建筑不仅类型全面、功能完善,而且建筑造型典雅优美,建筑风格多样。在一定程度上体现了当时的建筑科技发展水平。

## Schools

Main function of the schools managed by the CER was to provide education and skill training, which were divided into two kinds of schools, including ordinary school for staff's children and technician school for professional skill training related to railway engineering. The schools were also divided into school for Russian descendants and school for Chinese children, as well as business school and plenty of schools possessed by church. In some small cities and towns, schools were usually linked to the church, which looked like the church school. But in large cities and towns, schools were constructed in special site which were divided into primary schools and middle schools, so that the schools in different types largely existed in most big cities. Moreover, libraries were built up along the CER, which provided reading space and document consulting for staff and students in most of time, becoming a significant part of education architecture of the railway.

The Administrative Bureau of the CER started a school project when the CER began to construct and large numbers of Russian emigrated to northeast of China. In order to offer good education to Russian children and teenagers who lived in China, the subsidiary areas along the CER line were divided into four school districts, including Harbin city as the first school district, the area between Harbin and Manzhouli as the second, the area between Harbin and Suifenhe as the third and the area between Harbin and Changchun as the fourth. The Administration Bureau of the CER also set up an office of student affairs for school's management and maintenance. The school buildings were especially available for Russian children, most of which were built in masonry structure, with typically standardized characteristics, whose size depended on the number of students.

Technician school was one the educational symbol in subsidiary areas of the CER, which mainly concerned professional skill training of railway engineering and urban construction. In general, these kinds of schools were located in the large cities with high grade stations, such as the first-grade station Harbin, the second-grade station Suifenhe station and Manzhouli station. Schools here were all in large size and harmony with the scale of city, while the form in prevalent eclecticism and classicism, and Art Nouveau style was also adopted. Moreover, some of them consisted of many buildings to form the campus.

哈尔滨中俄工业学校历史照片 Historical photo of Technical School of CER in Harbin

哈尔滨中俄工业学校历史照片及设计图 Historical photo and drawings of Technical School of CER in Harbin

哈尔滨中俄工业学校室内历史照片
Historical photo of interior of Technical School of CER in Harbin

哈尔滨中俄工业学校院内部分历史照片
Historical photo of parts of Technical School of CER in Harbin

哈尔滨中俄工业学校
Technical School of CER in Harbin

# ARCHITECTURAL CULTURAL HERITAGE OF CHINESE EASTERN RAILWAY

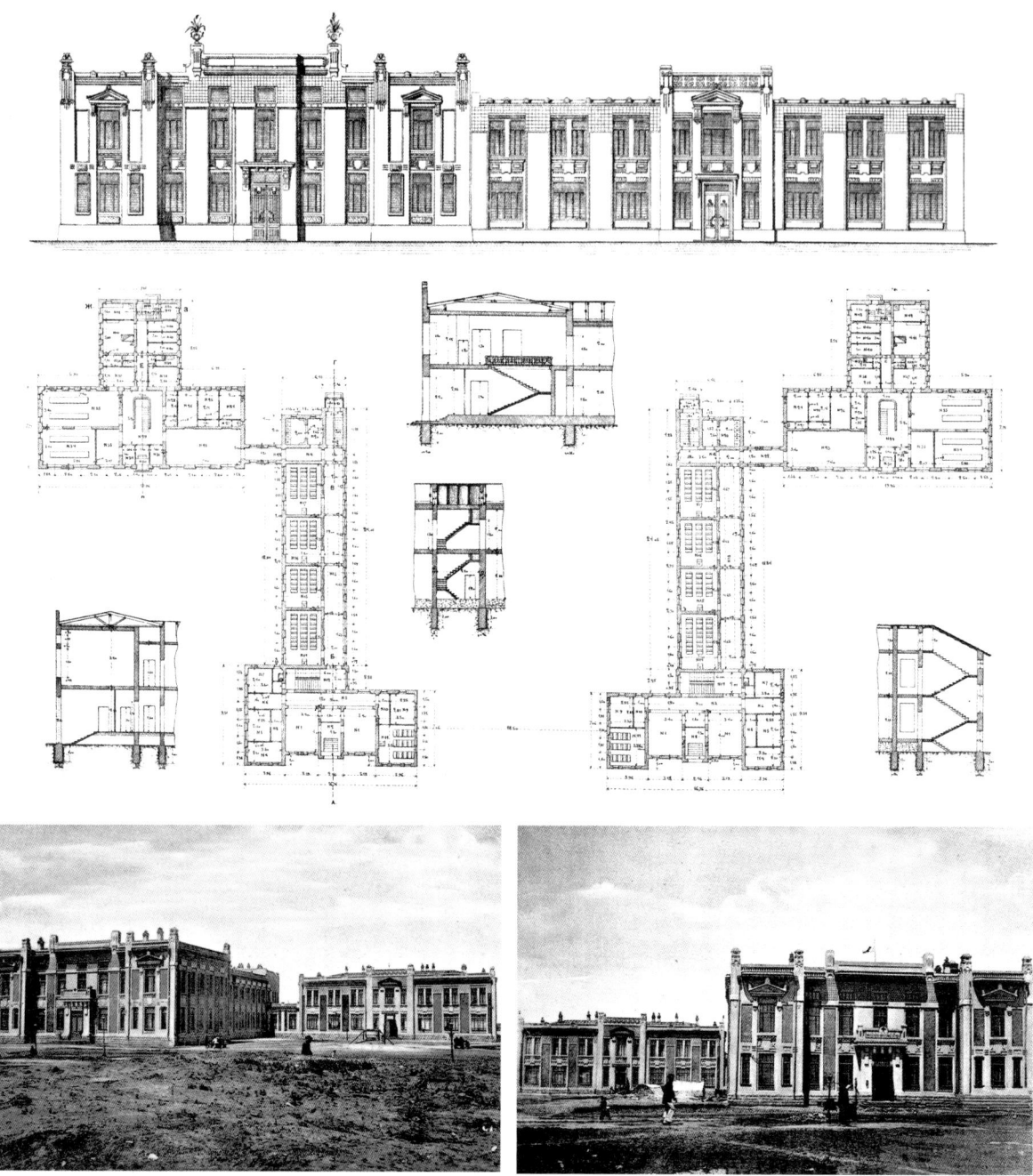

哈尔滨中东铁路商务学堂设计图及历史照片 Drawings and historical photos of Commercial School of CER in Harbin

哈尔滨中东铁路商务学堂 Commercial School of CER in Harbin

ARCHITECTURAL CULTURAL HERITAGE OF CHINESE EASTERN RAILWAY

绥芬河铁路技工学校 Railway Mechanic School in Suifenhe

绥芬河铁路技工学校细部  Details of Railway Mechanic School in Suifenhe

ARCHITECTURAL CULTURAL HERITAGE OF CHINESE EASTERN RAILWAY

满洲里铁路学校现状及历史照片
Current condition and historical photo of Railway Mechanic School in Manzhouli

满洲里铁路学校细部
Details of Railway Mechanic School in Manzhouli

14 校舍

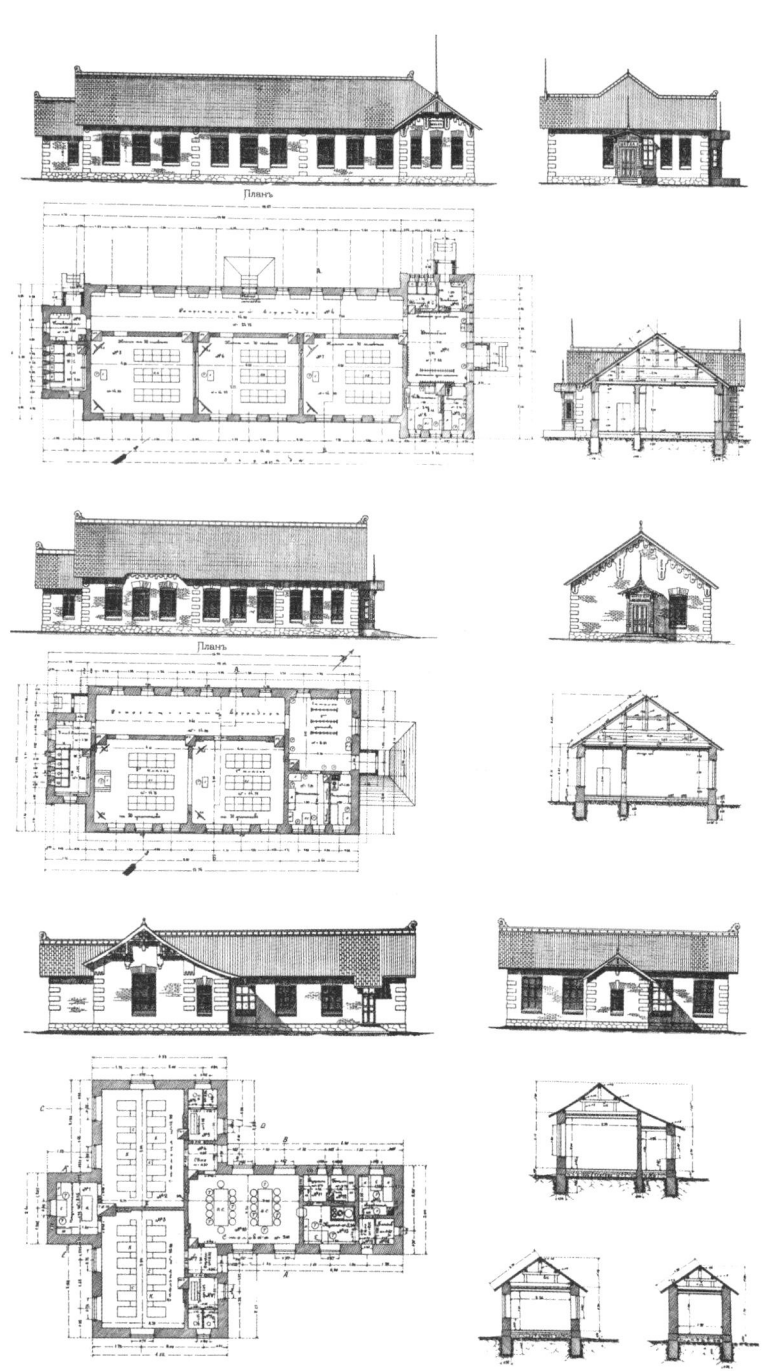

学校设计标准图纸 Standardized drawings of schools

免渡河铁道学校
Railway Mechanic School in Mianduhe

盖平公学校历史照片
Historical photo of Railway Public School in Gaiping

14 校舍 | 311

金州俄清学校 Russo-Chinese School in Jinzhou

扎兰屯沙俄子弟小学 Primary School for Russian in Zhalantun

德惠中学现状及设计图 Current condition and drawings of Dehui Middle School

# 15 教堂

从中东铁路修建伊始就有大批的俄国员工与士兵来到中东铁路沿线，教堂建筑作为远在异国他乡的俄国人的精神家园，为他们提供了情感和精神寄托，是一类很重要的公共建筑。相对于其他注重实际使用功能的中东铁路建筑来讲，教堂建筑更加注重心理和情感因素，这也使其成为一类较为特殊的中东铁路建筑。

## 15.1 中东铁路教堂的分布及选址

中东铁路教堂的修建始于中东铁路的建设，在分布上与中东铁路沿线站点级别有很大关系，也受宗教活动以及地理环境的影响。教堂在城镇中的选址则与地势、人群密度密切相关。一般来讲，站点等级越高，教堂的规模越大。在一等站哈尔滨与大连，教堂在规模和数量上都是首屈一指的，形式也更加精致华贵，如1898年即在哈尔滨修建的圣·尼古拉教堂。二等站与三等站全部设立教堂，修建时间大都在20世纪初，即在铁路修建过程中或建成之初，由中东铁路公司提供资金统一规划与修建，如1903年修建的满洲里谢拉菲姆教堂，1900年修建的绥芬河协达亚·尼古拉教堂。等级较低的四、五等站仅个别设立教堂，如免渡河教堂。教堂是城镇中的标志性建筑，一般修建在车站附近或地势较高处，墓地教堂较为特殊，常选址于城镇的边缘地带。另外中东铁路建成之初修建了一批随军教堂，这些教堂的选址则主要考虑军队所在的位置。如哈尔滨圣·索菲亚教堂，该教堂原为沙俄军队西伯利亚第四步兵师随军教堂，修建于军队所在地。

## 15.2 中东铁路教堂的类型及特点

中东铁路教堂以东正教堂为主，除为俄国居民、铁路员工及其家属服务的日常性教堂外，还包括为中东铁路护路军配置的随军教堂，这类教堂战时还作为收容伤兵的后方医院，实例如哈尔滨的圣·伊维尔教堂。中东铁路沿线最主要的教堂还是一般性教堂，其数量最多、分布最广，大部分随着铁路通车而建成，如满洲里、海拉尔、博克图、齐齐哈尔、绥芬河、穆棱、德惠等地的教堂。部分站点的教堂建筑还为中东铁路职工子女提供教育服务，如大连石筑教会学校、绥芬河的协达亚·尼古拉教堂、横道河子的圣母进堂教堂等。另外还有一类墓地教堂，是为安葬城镇病亡的俄国铁路职工及其家属而兴建的教堂，毗邻墓地，如哈尔滨圣母守护教堂，南部支线的大连圣弥哈伊尔总领天使教堂。教堂伴随着中东铁路的修建与运营陆续修建，因时间、地点、社会环境及经济条件的不同而呈现了丰富的建造特点与内外形态。

## 15.3 中东铁路教堂的建筑特点

位于中东铁路沿线重要城市如哈尔滨、大连等地的教堂，以砖石砌筑为主，帐篷顶搭配洋葱头的屋顶形象是典型的俄罗斯民族传统风格。圣·尼古拉教堂由于是第一座教堂，需要在较短时间内建成，因此为木结构，但形态上也符合城市环境特点。其他站点的大量教堂建筑则大部分以木材砌筑，采用通用的标准设计图纸，标准的教会学校平面呈十字形，分为圣坛和 3 个教室，在圣坛的两侧添加 2 个小房间，也包含厕所与厨房。虽然标准化的设计图中也有包含砖石材料的做法，但就历史资料与现状来看，数量较少。建筑形式上有典型的俄罗斯民族传统风韵，但又稍有不同，有着铁路附属地建筑自身的特点。各地教堂在建设中用材因地制宜，细节上各有自己的特点，在统一的形象中有着丰富的表情。木结构教堂装饰繁复、细节充盈，是中东铁路建筑遗产中最具艺术价值的类型之一。

中东铁路教堂是特定历史时期与社会环境的结果，在中东铁路建筑遗产中具有最强的文化内涵与人文属性，作为文化载体鲜明地呈现了宗教建筑艺术的跨文化传播过程。同时，作为沿线艺术性最高的建筑类型，教堂建筑凝结了俄罗斯民族宗教建筑的技术形态与艺术形式，具有的价值也是不言而喻的。

## Churches

Church construction of the CER started along with the railway development, whose distribution was dramatically related to the statio's grade. Churches were usually sited in consideration of the topography and population density. In general, the higher the grade of the station was, the larger the church scale was, so that it mostly turned to be the landmark of the cities or towns. These churches were often built near stations or on highlands, except for the graveyard church which were always located near the border of cities and towns.

Orthodox churches were the main religious architectural in all churches of the CER line. Besides ordinary churches for Russian residents, railway staff and their families, the churches were also built for the railway guard soldiers as military church, which was always sited near the armies. Moreover, this kind of churches could be also used as hospitals for injury soldiers in a war, for example, Saint Eve Church in Harbin. However, churches for ordinary people were the most popular buildings along the CER, which were in large number and wide distribution, most of which were built after the railway opening, such as the churches in Manzhouli, Hailaer, Boketu, Qiqihar, Suifenhe, Muling, Dehui and so on. Some of churches also provided education service for children of the railway staff.

Churches located in some important cities along the CER line, such as Harbin and Dalian, were built in masonry structure. In other cities and towns, churches were mostly made of wood and constructed by standardized design. The standardized plane layout was a cross type that divided the space into an altar and three classrooms. There were also two small rooms on both sides of the altar, including kitchen and bathroom. Considering the historical archives and remained situation, most of churches in masonry structure were built in standardized design, but still in small number. In architectural style, the church building displayed special characteristics in subsidiary areas of the railway. In addition, the wooden churches were decorated with complicated and detailed way, which resulted themselves to be the most artistic value types of the architectural heritages along the CER.

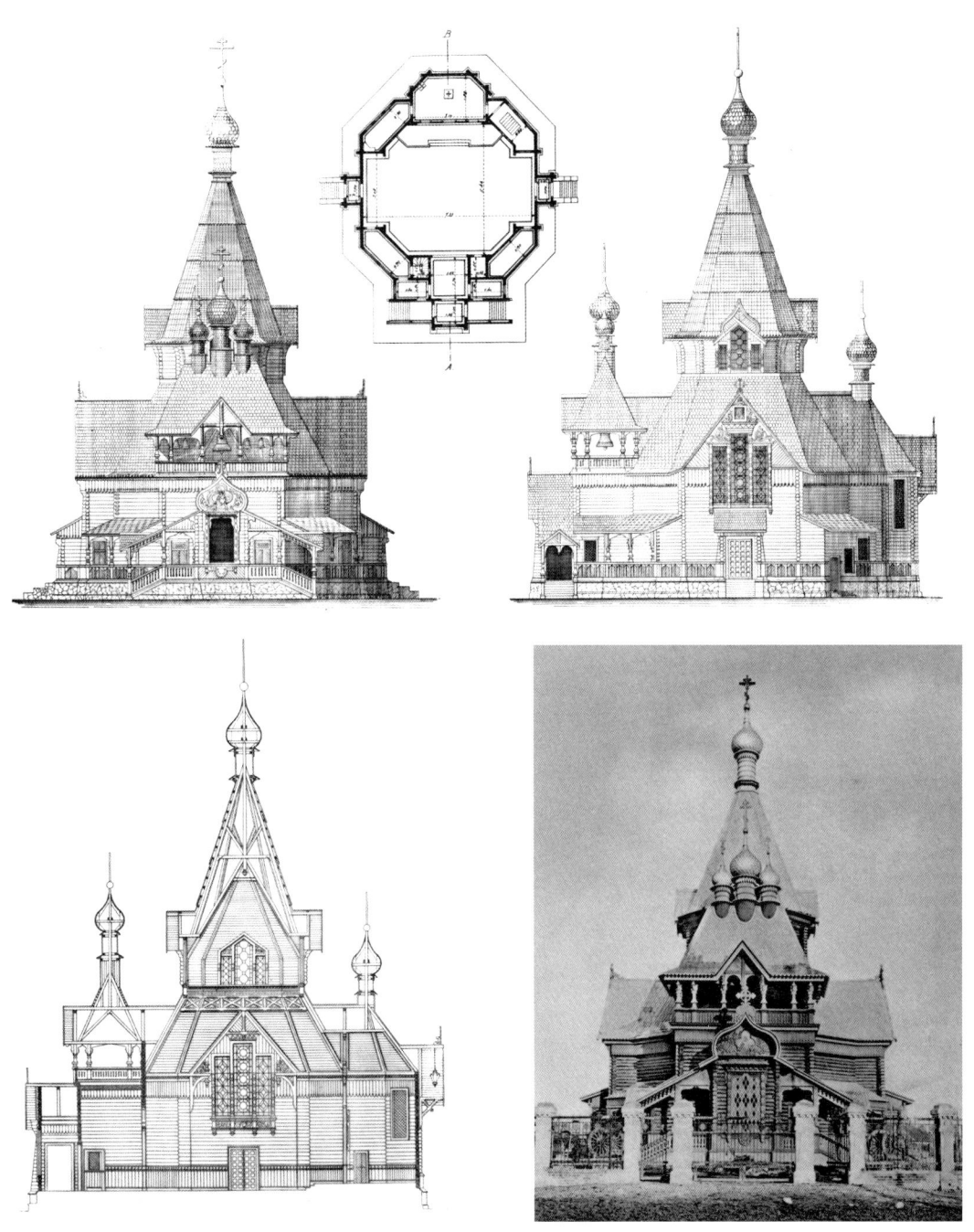

哈尔滨圣·尼古拉教堂设计图及历史照片 Drawings and historical photo of St. Nicholas Church in Harbin

# ARCHITECTURAL CULTURAL HERITAGE OF CHINESE EASTERN RAILWAY

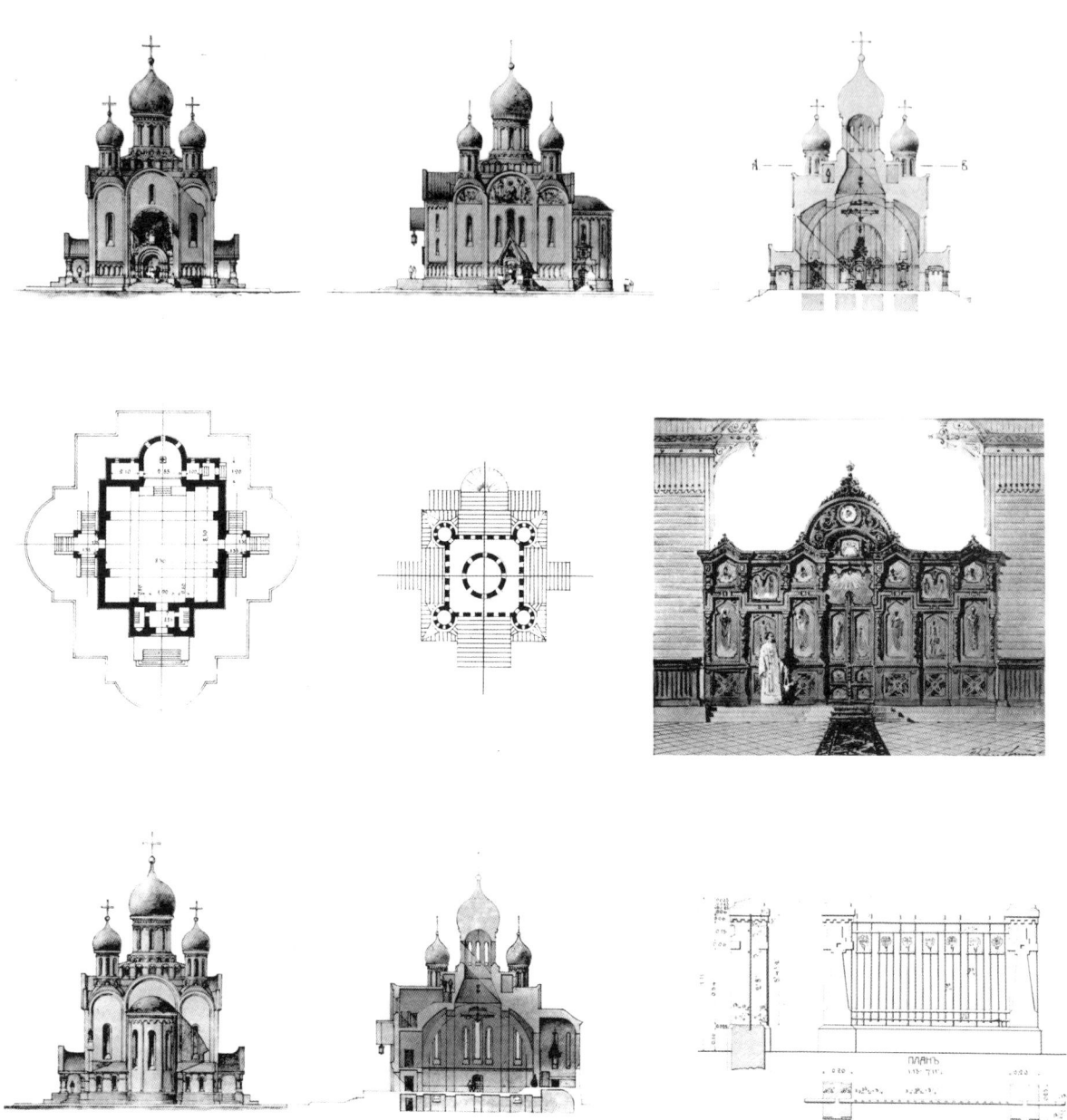

大连教堂设计图 Drawings of church in Dalian

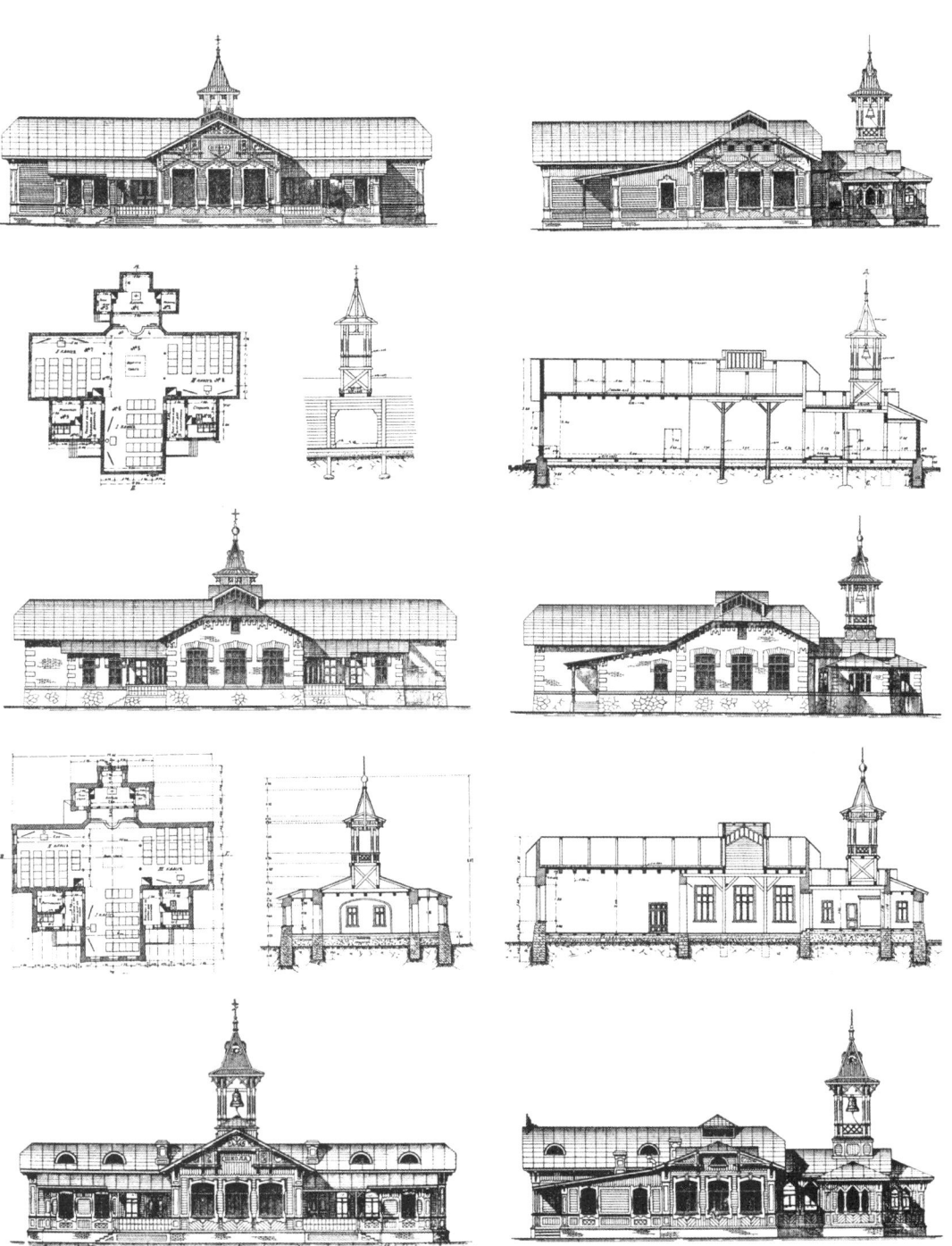

教堂标准设计图 Standardized drawings of churchs

辽阳教堂历史照片
Historical photo of church in Liaoyang

博克图教堂历史照片
Historical photo of church in Boketu

昂昂溪教堂历史照片
Historical photo of church in Ang'angxi

海拉尔教堂历史照片
Historical photo of church in Hailaer

公主岭教堂历史照片
Historical photo of church in Gongzhuling

绥芬河初期教堂历史照片 Historical photos of initial church in Suifenhe

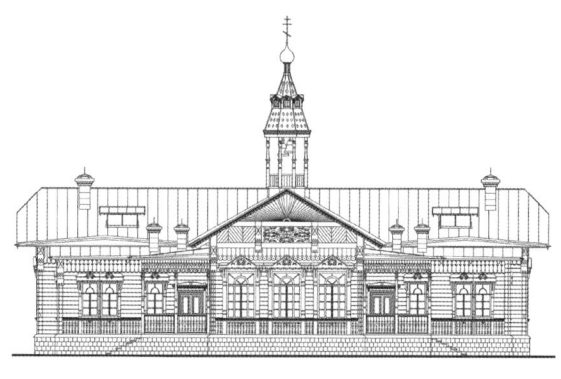
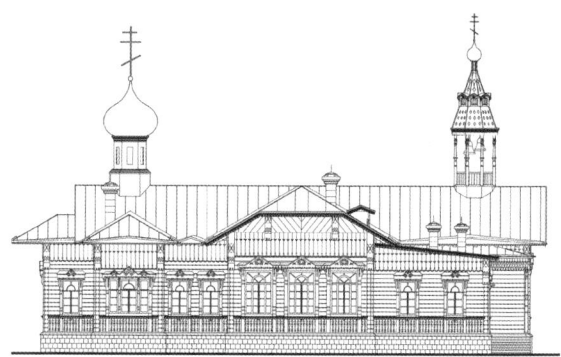
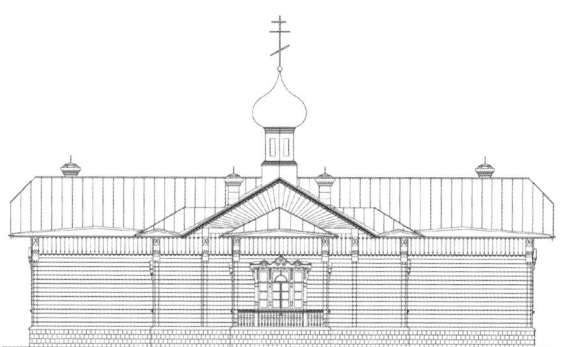

绥芬河初期教堂复原设计图
Restoration drawings of initial church in Suifenhe

绥芬河教堂 Church in Suifenhe

满洲里教堂 Church in Manzhouli

满洲里教堂历史照片 Historical photo of church in Manzhouli

# ARCHITECTURAL CULTURAL HERITAGE OF CHINESE EASTERN RAILWAY

横道河子教堂历史照片 Historical photo of church in Hengdaohezi

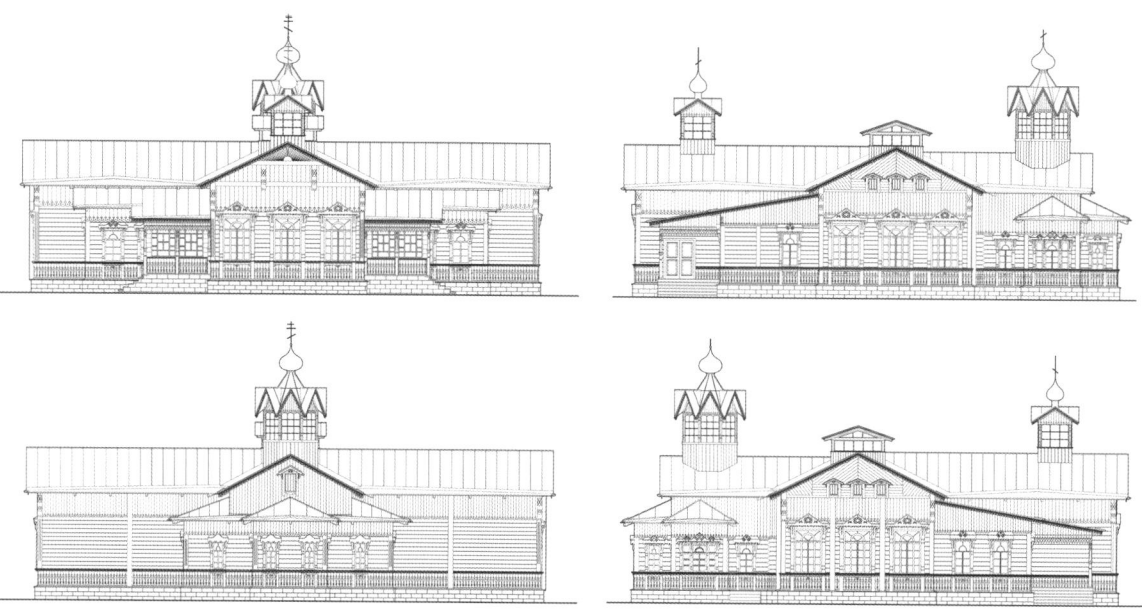

横道河子教堂测绘图 Drawings of church in Hengdaohezi

横道河子教堂 Church in Hengdaohezi

# ARCHITECTURAL CULTURAL HERITAGE OF CHINESE EASTERN RAILWAY

一面坡教堂
Church in Yimianpo

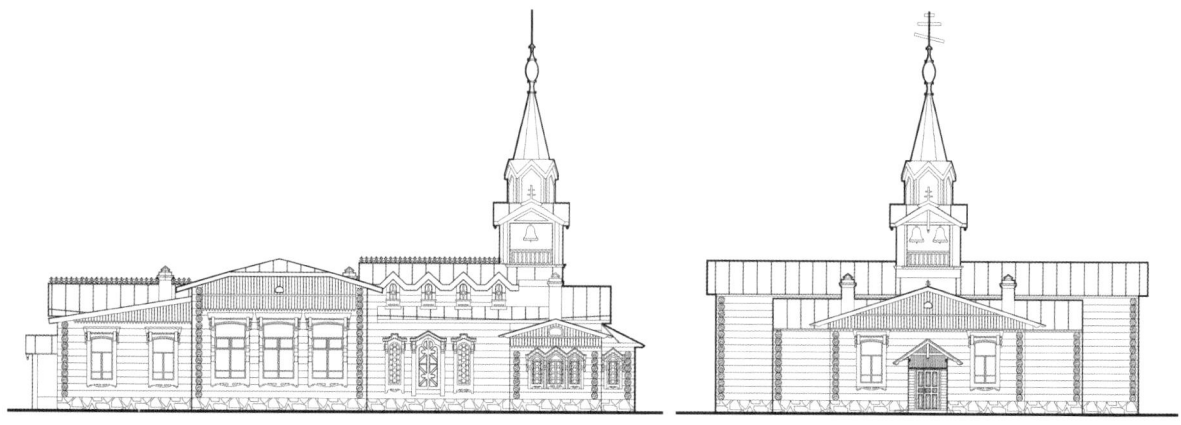

一面坡教堂复原设计图
Restoration drawings of church in Yimianpo

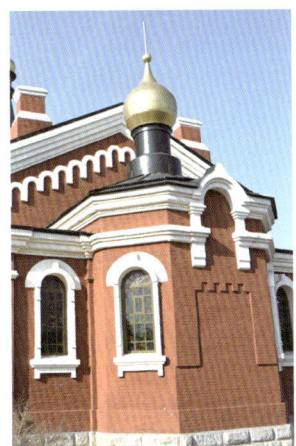

德惠教堂 Church in Dehui

扎兰屯教堂 Church in Yimianpo

扎兰屯教堂测绘图 Drawings of church in Zhalantun

免渡河尼古拉耶夫基卡娅教堂 Church in Mianduhe

# 16 居住建筑

住宅是中东铁路沿线数量最多、分布最广、类型最丰富的建筑，其主要职能是为中东铁路官员、职工及其家属提供居住和日常生活所必需的空间，是重要的建筑类型。住宅建筑在规划设计理念、平面及空间结构、建造技术、建筑艺术风格等方面都独具特色。

## 16.1 住宅建筑的类型

中东铁路住宅可分为独户住宅、联户住宅、集合住宅三种形制，不同形制的住宅按照行列式、周边式、混合式、自由式等组合方式排列成居住区。三种住宅在功能、造型等方面各具特点，呈现鲜明而多元的艺术风格，可分为三大类：具有新艺术特色的现代风格、中俄建筑文化融合的合璧式风格和追求比例尺度和谐的古典风格。独户住宅主要供中东铁路官员居住，一些高级官员的官邸还兼做接待、办公之用。等级较高的站点独户住宅比低等级站点数量多，一般独立设置。联户住宅主要供中东铁路职工居住，数量最多，无论哪种等级规模的城镇站点均有配置。按照居住户数不同又可将联户住宅分为两户型、三户型、四户型及多户型。集合住宅一般作为铁路职工宿舍使用，因平面布局的不同分为内廊式集合住宅和单元式集合住宅。

## 16.2 住宅建筑的平面布局

出于气候、工期、施工等多方面的考虑，中东铁路住宅单体的平面轮廓大多是简单的矩形，联户住宅和集合住宅的建筑平面布局都比较简单，主要包括卧室、起居室、厨房等几个功能分区，在独户住宅中会增加会客室、书房、会议室及佣人房等空间。独户住宅一般建筑面积较大，功能相对复杂，各功能空间通过楼梯、走廊、门厅等多种交通空间相连。一般起居室和厨房设置在一层，卧室在二、三层。佣人房、储藏间等辅助空间在一层朝向较差的方向，书房一般在主卧附近。联户住宅中每户面积跨越较大，从十几平方米到六十几平方米之间不等，均为单层。每一户的房间数量不等，其中卧室一般为1—3间，至少有一间卧室位于较好朝向；起居室的数量为1—2间；餐厅多与厨房或起居室联合使用。联户住宅内各个房间的使用面积较普通独户住宅要更小，平面布局模式更为简单规整。两种集合住宅的平面差异较大。内廊式集合住宅平面呈"日"或"口"字形，内部以单侧廊或内走廊连接房间单元，建筑通常为二层或以上，每层设置公共活动区域，如厨房和卫生间等。单元式集合住宅为多层建筑，由楼梯间直接进入分户门，一般每梯为2—4户。这种平面布局形式布置紧凑，户间干扰较少，同时由于公共交通面积较小，所以建筑利用率高。每户除了基本的卧室、起居室和厨房外均配置有厕所及浴室，适合小家庭式的住户使用。

## 16.3 住宅的标准化设计

中东铁路建筑设计中广泛采用的标准化设计理念也体现在住宅建筑中，具体表现在两个方面，即平面标准化与构件标准化。中东铁路住宅建筑平面标准化主要体现在联户住宅和集合住宅的设计中，尤以联户住宅最为明显。如数量众多的两户型住宅、三户型住宅、四户型住宅都有若干种不同的标准平面的混合运用，这些住宅在平面布局和面积规模上都基本相同。中东铁路住宅建筑构件的标准化在装饰性构件和功能性构件中都有体现，如檐口、墙面、门窗洞口等处的处理。构件的标准化强化了中东铁路住宅建筑的统一性，在不同构件的组装配合下，也丰富了住宅的建筑样式。住宅的标准化设计能够形成有工业化特征的生产与施工模式，提高建筑施工效率，形成的住宅具有统一的形貌特征，使中东铁路住宅建筑成为一种标志性的文化符号。

### 16.4 住宅的防寒保温措施

相对于其他建筑，中东铁路住宅的设计建造更加注重保温采暖，这些保暖防寒措施主要在以下三方面得以体现：居住区选址及单体形态控制、围护结构的构造做法、壁炉和火墙等采暖设施的运用。住宅在选址方面注意避开风口和背阳的位置，单体建筑会尽量争取良好的日照朝向，主要功能房间和阳光室等空间直接向阳而设。单体形态力求规整，简单的平面和体量形式使住宅的体形系数得到严格控制。在维护结构的防寒构造方面，为使墙体有足够的热阻，中东铁路住宅的墙体构造采用了两种措施。一是增加墙体厚度，以弥补砖石材料导热系数大的缺陷。二是采用导热系数小的材料如木材、木屑等作为墙体构造材料，在一些厚度不大的墙体中，一般采用木屑等材料形成保温层。中东铁路住宅屋顶部位一般采用坡屋顶形成闷顶构造。闷顶空间内填以木屑、草灰等保温材料形成保温层。在住宅楼地面及其他细部构造中，也都采用了相应的防寒构造以减少热量流失和冷风渗透。为应对寒冷的气候，俄罗斯工程师把俄罗斯传统的壁炉、火墙等采暖措施引入中东铁路住宅中，这些采暖技术和东北地区传统的采暖措施结合，形成了特有的中东铁路住宅采暖系统。火墙作为散热面有着类似于今天的暖气散热器的作用，而且有其独特优势，火墙面积较大，内部构造曲折利于储存热量，这样热量可快速持久地向室内传递。

中东铁路住宅建筑是东北地区内一类极具特色的居住建筑，与同时期其他居住建筑相比，更具灵活的适应性和文化多元性，承载着独特的文化内涵和丰富的时空结构。跨越一百多年历史直至今日，中东铁路住宅建筑的使用从未间断，记录了各时期完整的居住文化，有着独特的历史价值。

# Residences

The residence buildings of the CER were in the largest number, the widest distribution and most diverse types, which displays special characteristics from the view of planing design, plane and space structure, construction technique as well as artistic style of the buildings.

It could be divided into three types: single house, town house, and congregated dwelling house. The residence houses in different types were arranged in the residential areas by different combination models, such as determinants, perimetric pattern, mixed type, freestyle and so on. These three types of residence buildings had their own characteristics in terms of function and shape, which presented distinct and diverse artistic styles.

Single houses were mainly used by the officials of the CER, where some senior officials also made the house as reception and office. Town houses were mainly for the CER staff in the largest number, which were available for all cities and towns regardless of the station size and grade. According to the number of households, town house could be divided into two units, three units, four units and multiple units. The congregated dwelling house was generally used as worker's residences of the CER, which were divided into middle corridor type dwelling house and unit type dwelling house according to different plane layouts. According to different functions, all residence buildings in plane layout included bed room, living room, kitchen etc. The single house had large size in area, with much complicated function space, such as reception room, study, meeting room and servant room, each part of which was linked by hall, stairs and corridors etc. The use area of town house was smaller than that of the ordinary single house, whose plane layout was much simple and regular. The plane layout of the middle corridor type dwelling house was in the shape of "日" or "口", whose room units were often linked by a side corridor or inside corridor. Buildings were usually two or more floors, with open spaces of each floor as kitchens and bathrooms. The unit type dwelling house was a multi-storey building, with stairs between the upper and lower floors. There were 2—4 unit residences for each storey. The standardized design was widely used in residence construction of the CER, especially in development of town house, which was embodied in two aspects, plane standardization and component standardization. The standardized design of the residence buildings could make the modular production and construction with industrial characteristics possible, and accelerated the efficiency of building construction. Due to provide a uniform nature by standardized design, the residence buildings of the CER line became a special cultural symbol at that time.

Compared with other buildings, the warm and cold proof measures were adopted in design and construction of the CER residence buildings, which were mainly reflected in three aspects, site selection of residential area and style control of unit house, enclosing structure and construction methods, using heating facilities such as fireplace and hot wall. Comprehensive application of these insulation measures was a necessary condition for ensuring the construction and use of residence buildings of the CER in large number, which was also an important part of the regional architectural culture.

Residence buildings of the CER were a distinctive type in northeast of China. Compared with other residence buildings in the same period, it showed much flexible adaptability and cultural diversity, because of loading an unique cultural connotations and rich space time structure. Over a hundred years, many residence buildings of the CER have been used until now, which is a records of total residential culture of each period, with unique historical value.

哈尔滨铁路职工住宅历史照片 Historical photo of residence for staff of CER in Harbin

哈尔滨铁路职工住宅外廊历史照片 Historical photo of veranda of residence for Staff of CER in Harbin

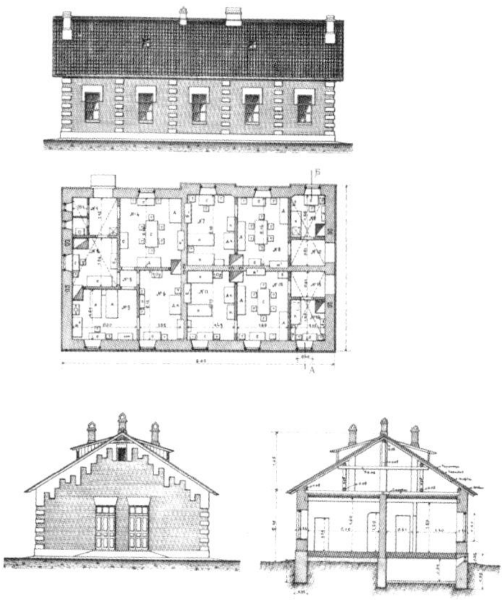

三户住宅设计图 1
Drawings of residence with 3 households1

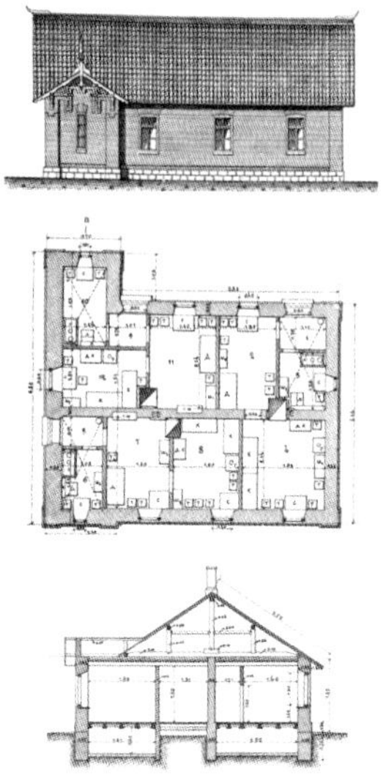

三户住宅设计图 2
Drawings of residence with 3 households 2

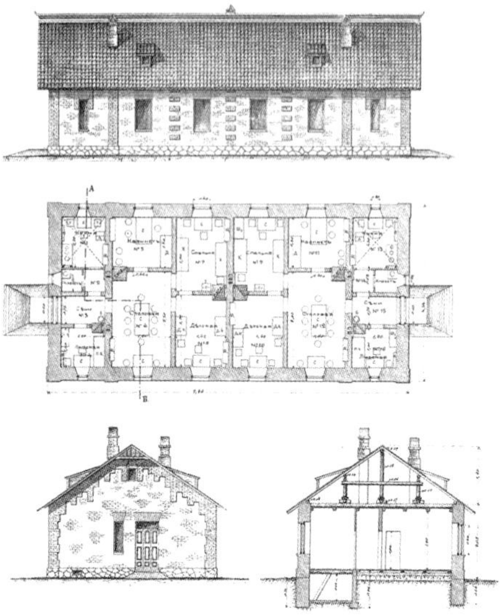

两户住宅设计图
Drawings of residence with 2 households

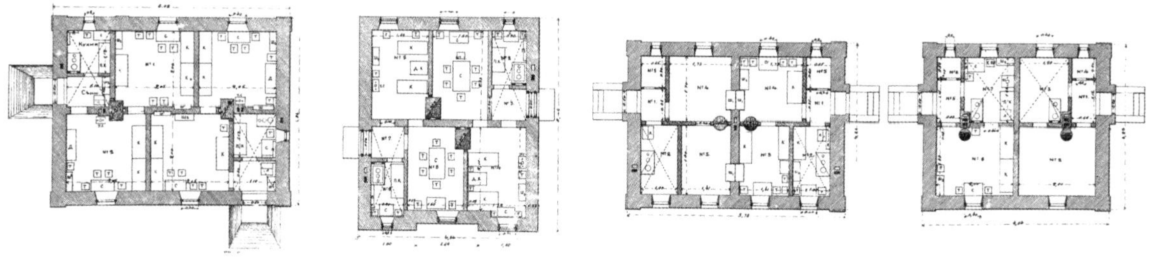

不同形式的联户式住宅平面设计图
Planning map of different types of town houses

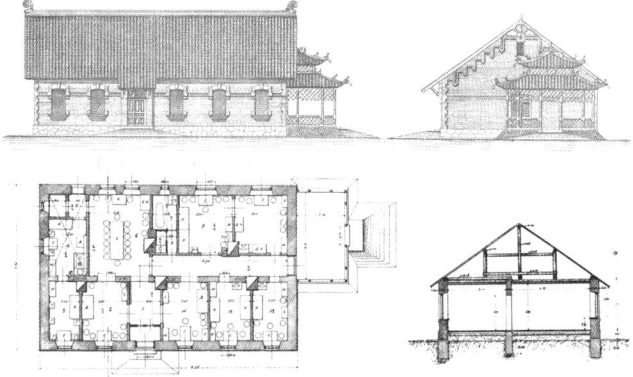

官邸设计图
Drawings of residence for junior officers

不同类型的普通官邸设计图
Drawings of different types of ordinary residences for junior officers

# ARCHITECTURAL CULTURAL HERITAGE OF CHINESE EASTERN RAILWAY

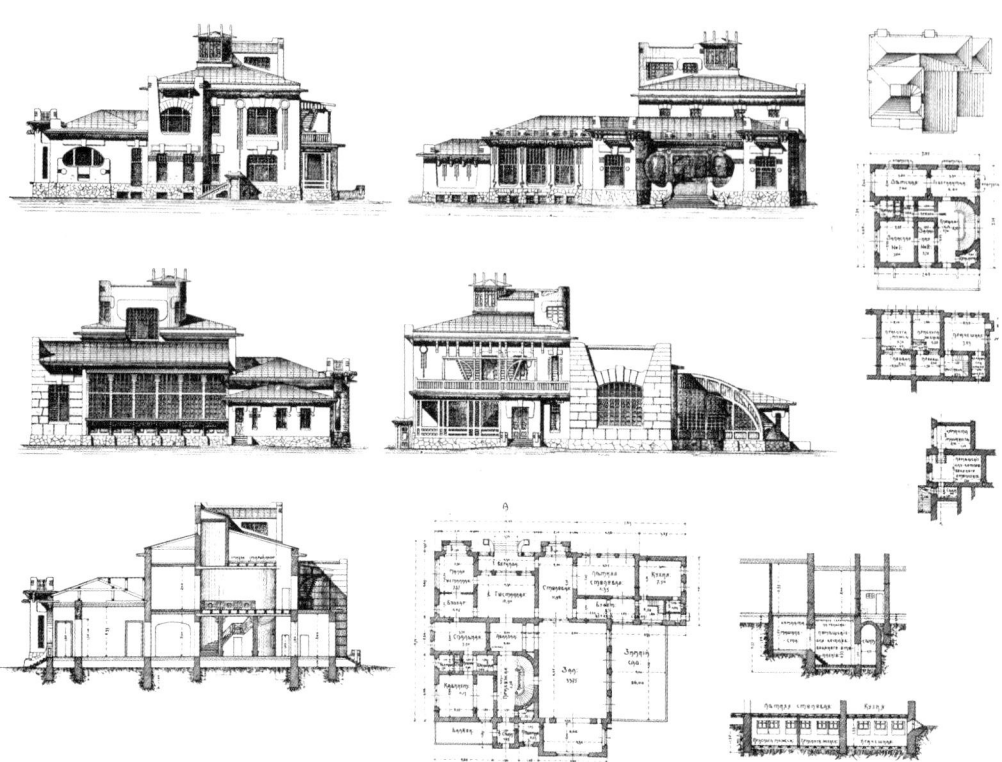

中东铁路官员住宅设计图 Drawings of residence for senior officer of CER

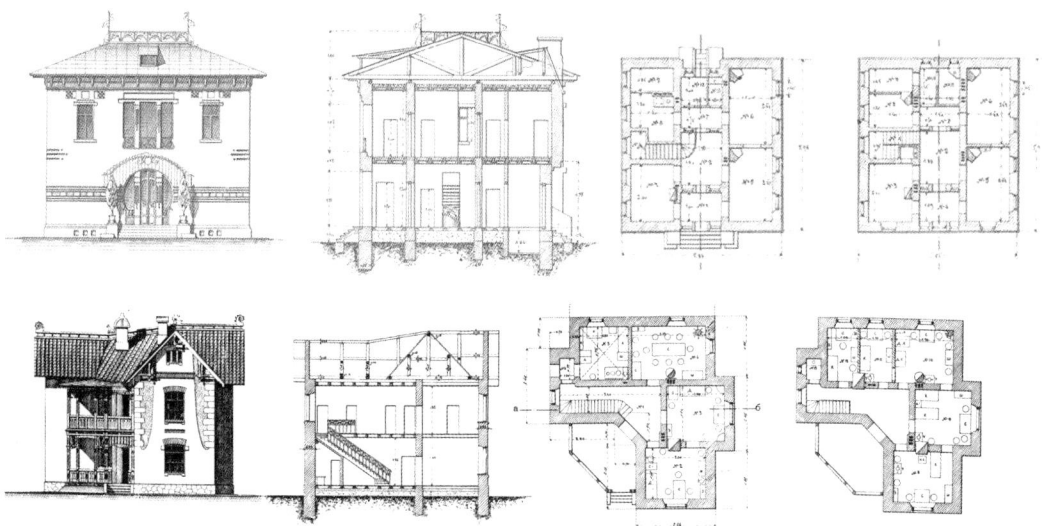

不同形式官邸设计图（30—60 平方沙绳）1 Drawings of different residence for officers (30—60 sagers) 1

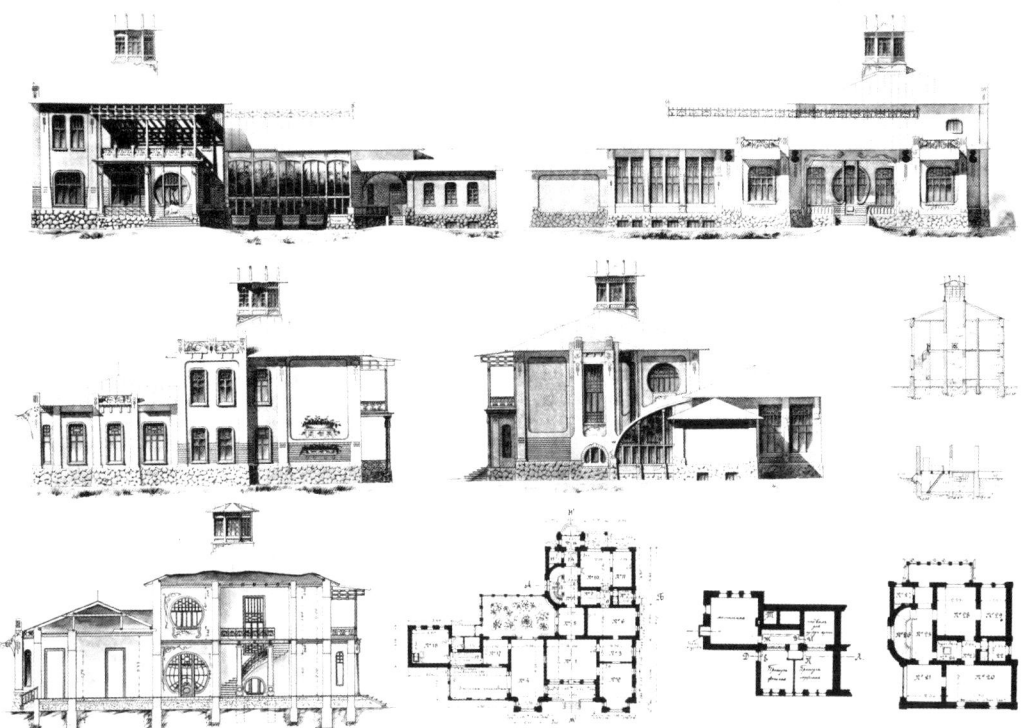

中东铁路军事指挥官住宅设计图 Drawings of residence for senior military officer of CER

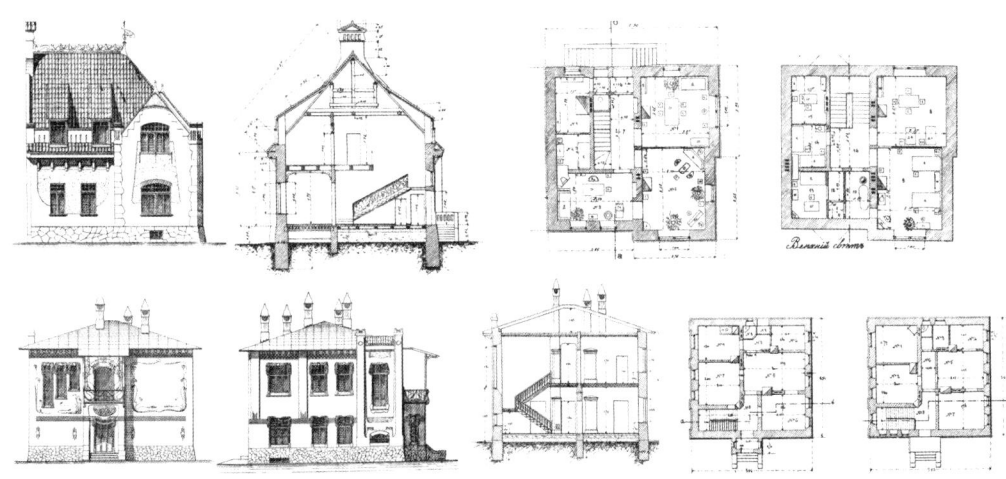

不同形式官邸设计图（30—60平方沙绳）2 Drawings of different residence for officers (30—60 sagers) 2

16 居住建筑 | 341

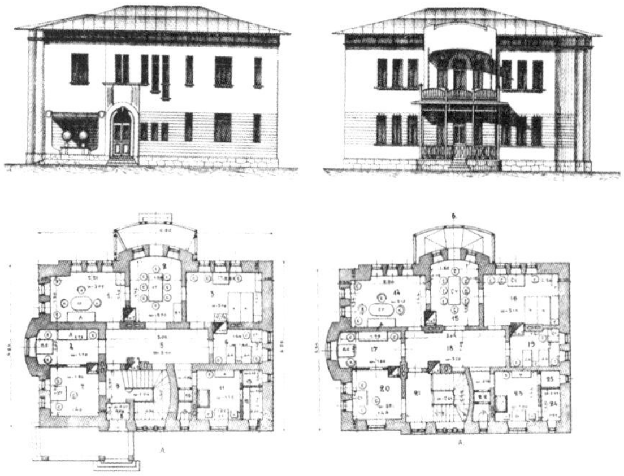

# ARCHITECTURAL CULTURAL HERITAGE OF CHINESE EASTERN RAILWAY

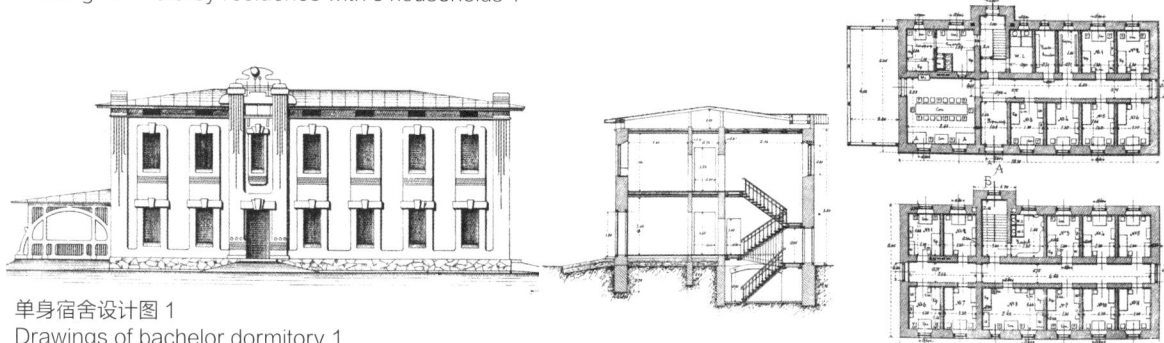

两户的二层住宅设计图 1
Drawings of 2-storey residence with 2 households 1

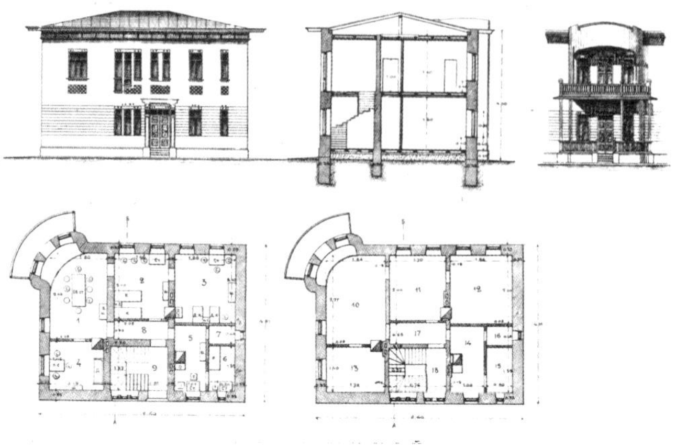

两户的二层住宅设计图 2
Drawings of 2-storey residence with 2 households 2

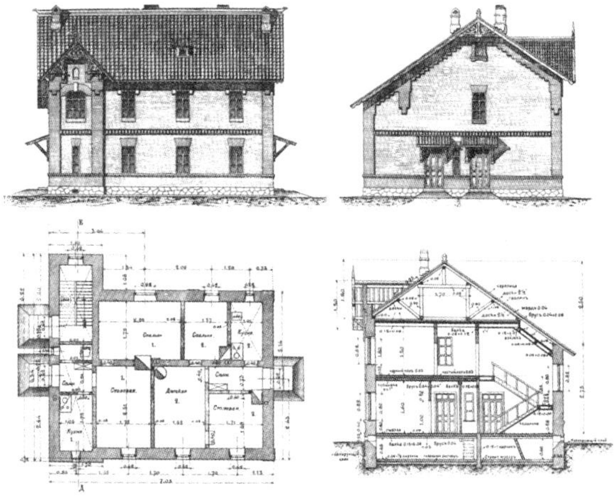

三户二层住宅设计图 1
Drawings of 2-storey residence with 3 households 1

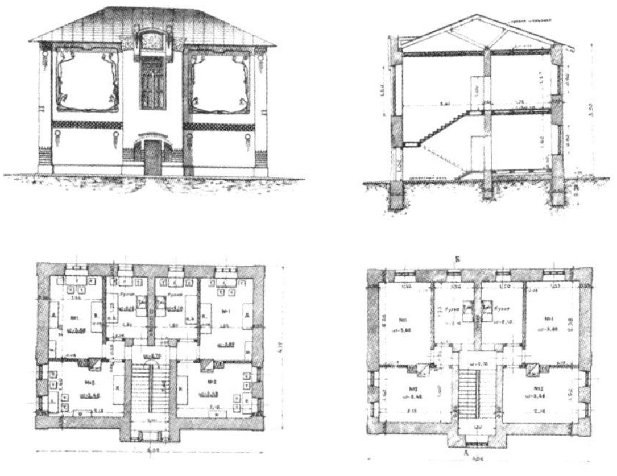

三户二层住宅设计图 2
Drawings of 2-storey residence with 3 households 2

单身宿舍设计图 1
Drawings of bachelor dormitory 1

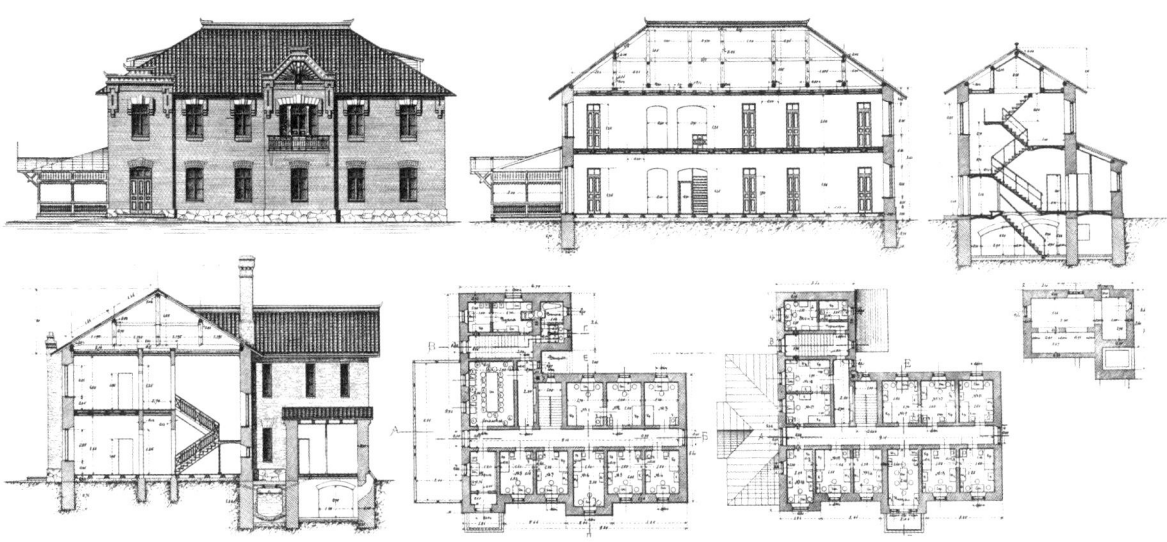

单身宿舍设计图 2 Drawings of bachelor dormitory 2

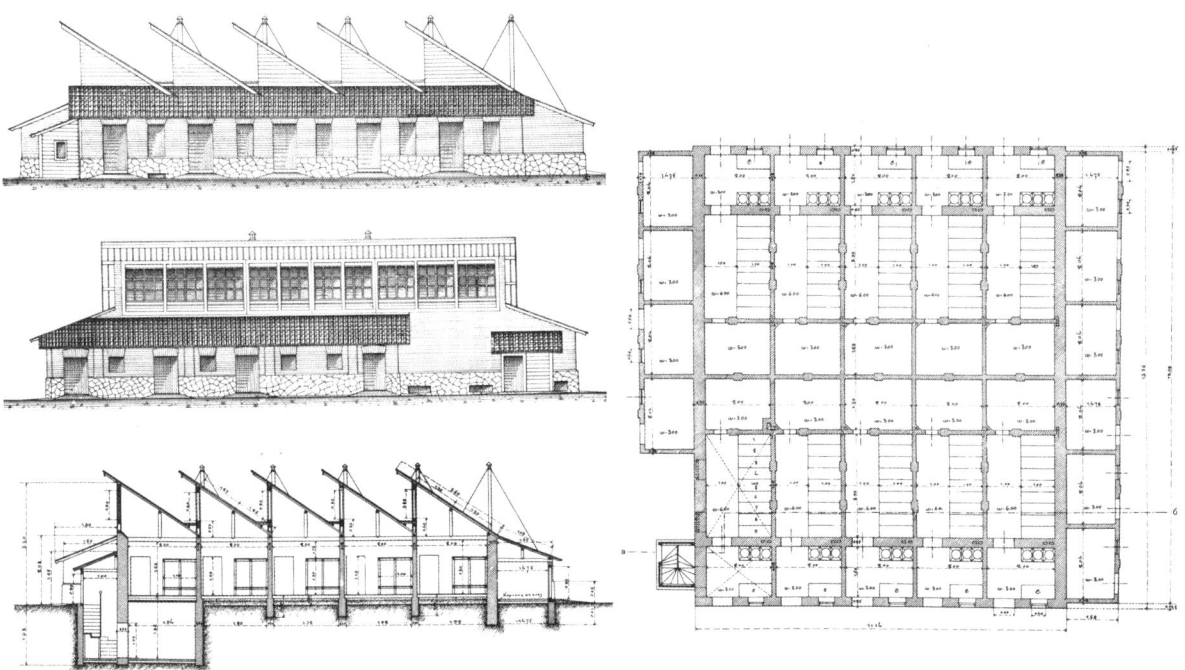

中国工人简易宿舍设计图 Drawings of simple dormitory for Chinese workers

16 居住建筑 | 343

# ARCHITECTURAL CULTURAL HERITAGE OF CHINESE EASTERN RAILWAY

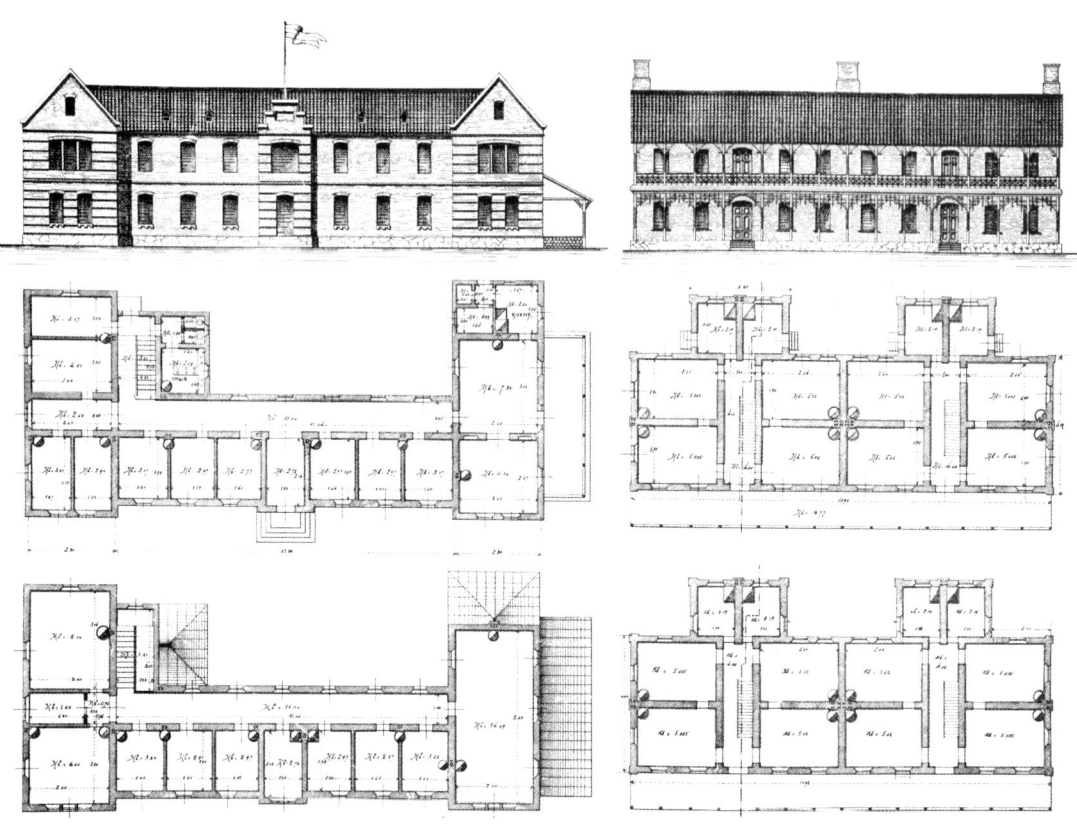

大连铁路服务人员住宅设计图 1
Drawings of residence for staff of railway in Dalian 1

大连铁路服务人员住宅设计图 2
Drawings of residence for staff of railway in Dalian 2

大连铁路服务人员住宅设计图 3
Drawings of residence for staff of railway in Dalian 3

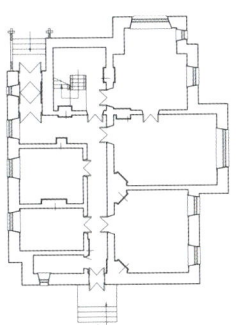

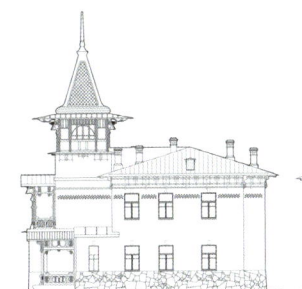

哈尔滨公司街中东铁路官员住宅历史照片、现状及测绘图
Historical photo, current condition and drawings of residence for senior officer of CER in Gongsi street, Harbin

哈尔滨中山路中东铁路官员住宅历史照片及现状
Historical photo and current condition of residence for senior officer of CER on Zhongshan rood, Harbin

16 居住建筑 | 345

# ARCHITECTURAL CULTURAL HERITAGE OF CHINESE EASTERN RAILWAY

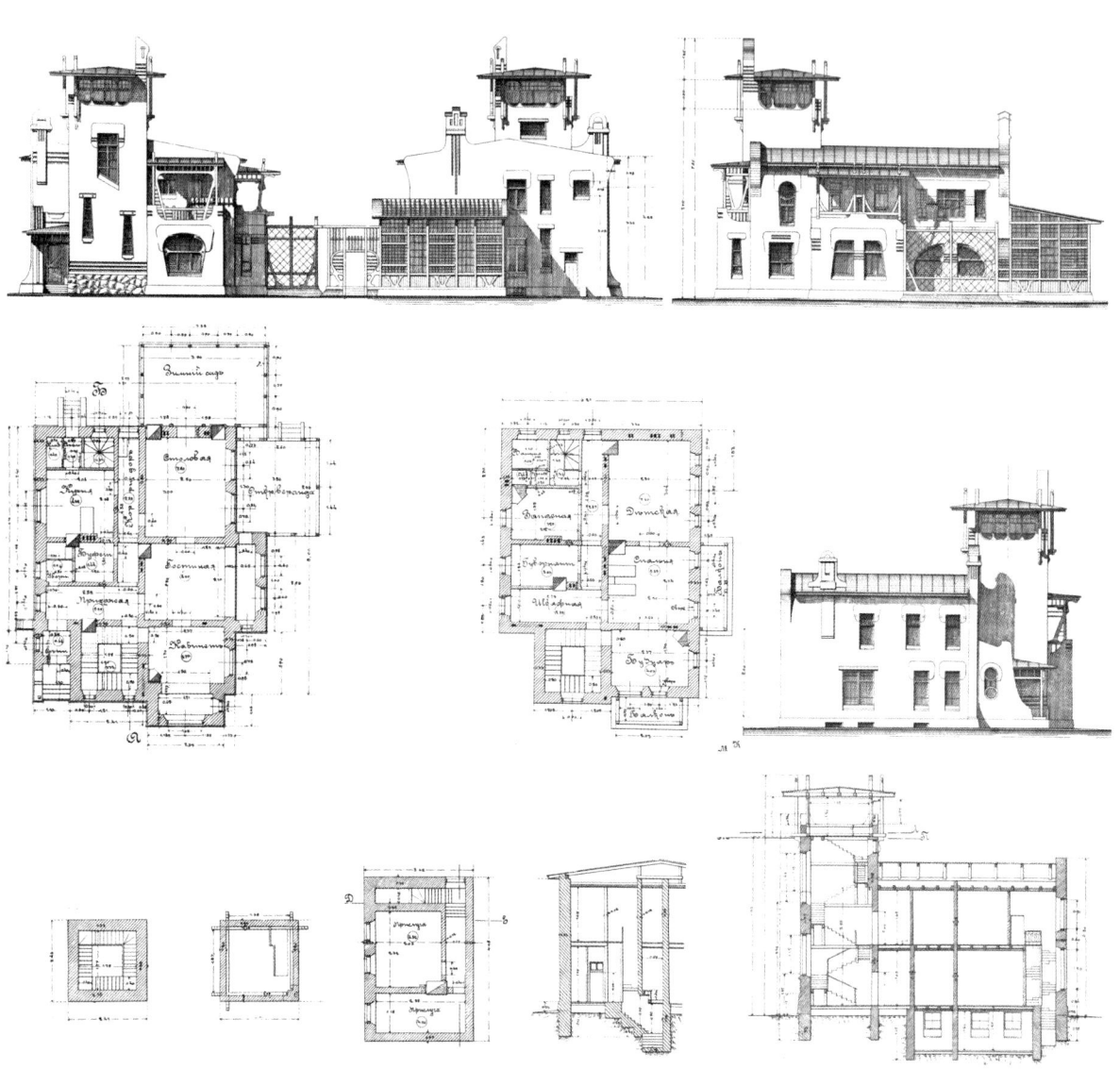

官员住宅设计图 Drawings of residence for senior officer

哈尔滨联发街中东铁路官员住宅 Residence for senior officer of CER in Lianfa street, Harbin

哈尔滨中山路 9 号中东铁路高级官员住宅历史照片
Residence for senior officer at No. 9, Zhongshan Rood, Harbin

旅顺工程师住宅历史照片
Historical photo of residence for engineer in Lüshun

中东铁路高级住宅
Residence for senior staff in Harbin

大连工人宿舍历史照片
Historical photo of dormitory in Dalian

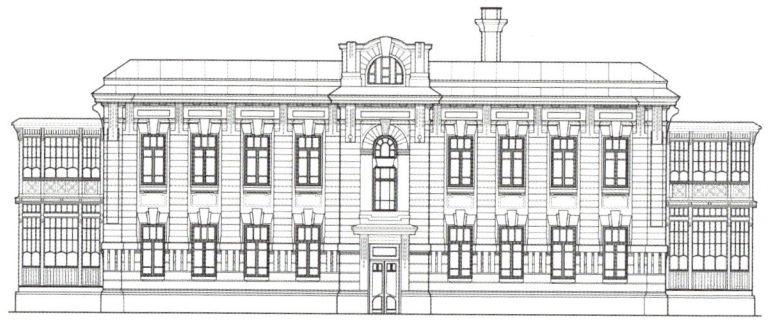
中东铁路高级住宅测绘图
Drawings of residence for senior staff in Harbin

大连老技术工人住宅历史照片
Historical photo of residence for skilled workers in Dalian

大连工人宿舍历史照片
Historical photos of dormitory for workers in Dalian

绥芬河铁路职工宿舍
Dormitory for railway staff in Suifenhe

16 居住建筑 | 349

ARCHITECTURAL CULTURAL HERITAGE OF CHINESE EASTERN RAILWAY

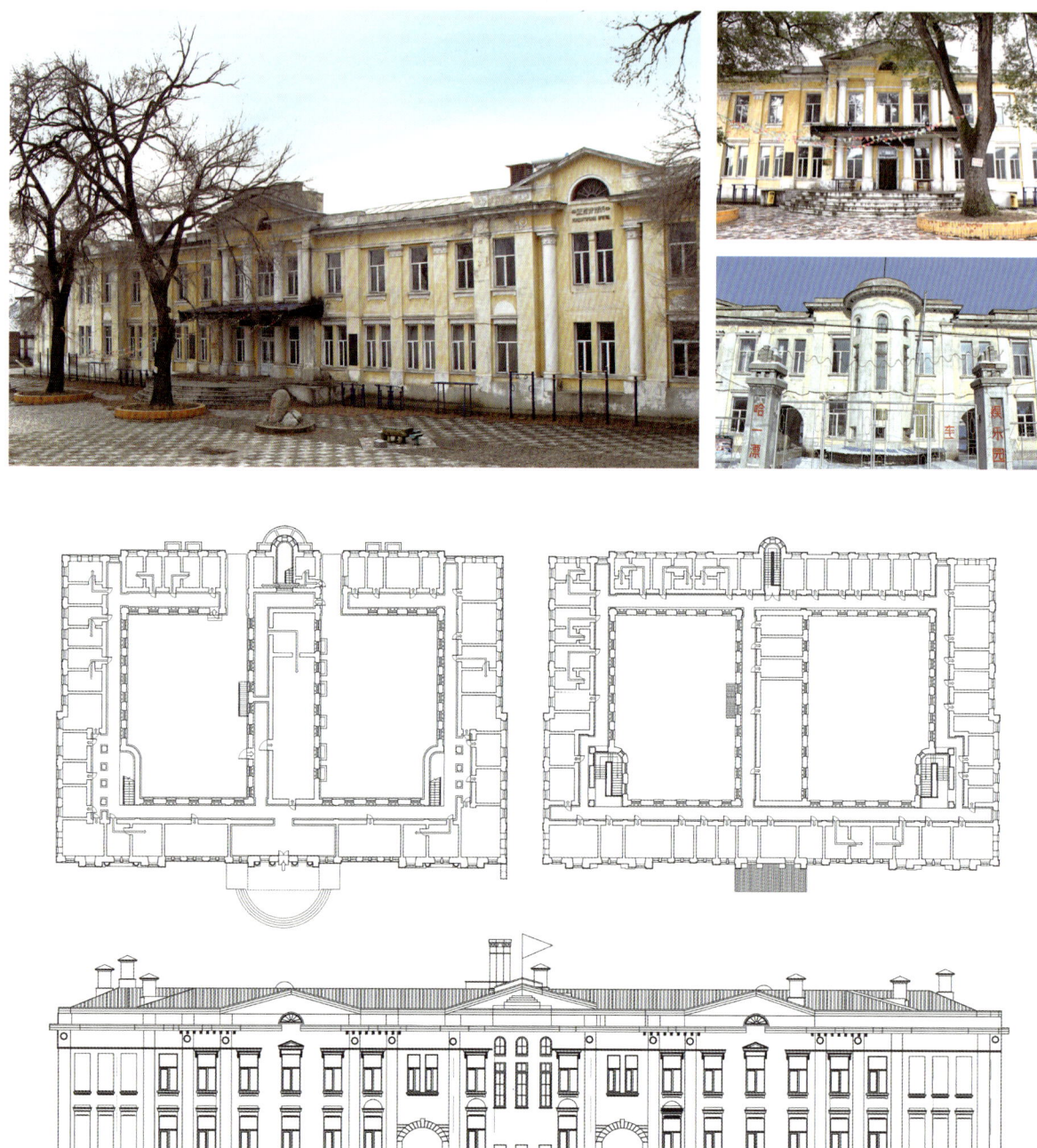

一面坡乘务员公寓现状及测绘图
Current condition and drawings of apartment for railway crew in Yimianpo

横道河子工程师住宅现状及测绘图
Current condition and drawings of residence for engineers in Hengdaohezi

# ARCHITECTURAL CULTURAL HERITAGE OF CHINESE EASTERN RAILWAY

绥芬河单身宿舍历史照片
Historical photo of bachelor dormitory in Suifenhe

海拉尔两层住宅历史照片
Historical photo of 2-storey residence in Hailaer

昂昂溪铁路职工宿舍
Dormitory for railway staff in Ang'angxi

扎兰屯铁路职工宿舍
Dormitory for railway staff in Zhalantun

一面坡铁路职工宿舍
Dormitory for railway staff in Yimianpo

横道河子铁路职工宿舍
Dormitory for railway staff in Hengdaohezi

海拉尔单身宿舍历史照片
Historical photo of bachelor dormitory in Hailaer

哈尔滨单身宿舍历史照片
Historical photo of bachelor dormitory in Harbin

满洲里铁路职工宿舍 1
Dormitory for railway staff in Manzhouli 1

满洲里铁路职工宿舍 2
Dormitory for railway staff in Manzhouli 2

满洲里铁路职工宿舍 3
Dormitory for railway staff in Manzhouli 3

满洲里铁路职工宿舍 4
Dormitory for railway staff in Manzhouli 4

16 居住建筑

# ARCHITECTURAL CULTURAL HERITAGE OF CHINESE EASTERN RAILWAY

绥芬河独户住宅历史照片 1
Historical photo of single house in Suifenhe 1

绥芬河独户住宅历史照片 2
Historical photo of single house in Suifenhe 2

绥芬河独户住宅历史照片 3
Historical photo of single house in Suifenhe 3

绥芬河独户住宅历史照片 4
Historical photo of single house in Suifenhe 4

绥芬河独户住宅历史照片 5
Historical photo of single house in Suifenhe 5

绥芬河独户住宅历史照片 6
Historical photo of single house in Suifenhe 6

扎兰屯独户住宅历史照片
Historical photo of single house in Zhalantun

穆棱独户住宅历史照片
Historical photo of single house in Muling

绥芬河住宅历史照片（两户）1
Historical photo of residence in Suifenhe (2 houseolds) 1

乌奴耳住宅历史照片（两户）
Historical photo of residence in Wunuer (2 houseolds)

绥芬河住宅历史照片（两户）2
Historical photo of residence in Suifenhe (2 houseolds) 2

大连住宅历史照片（两户）
Historical photo of residence in Dalian (2 houseolds)

绥芬河住宅历史照片（四户）1
Historical photo of residence in Suifenhe (4 houseolds) 1

绥芬河住宅历史照片（四户）2
Historical photo of residence in Suifenhe (4 houseolds) 2

大连住宅历史照片（六户）
Historical photo of residence in Dalian (6 houseolds)

16 居住建筑 | 355

# ARCHITECTURAL CULTURAL HERITAGE OF CHINESE EASTERN RAILWAY

横道河子联户式住宅现状及测绘图 Current condition and drawings of town house in Hengdaohezi

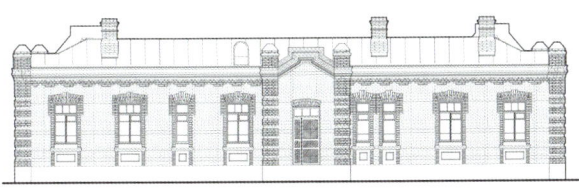
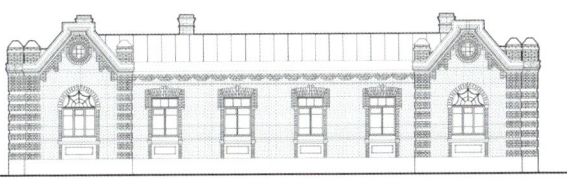

横道河子住宅现状及测绘图 1 Current condition and drawings of residence in Hengdaohezi 1

16 居住建筑 | 357

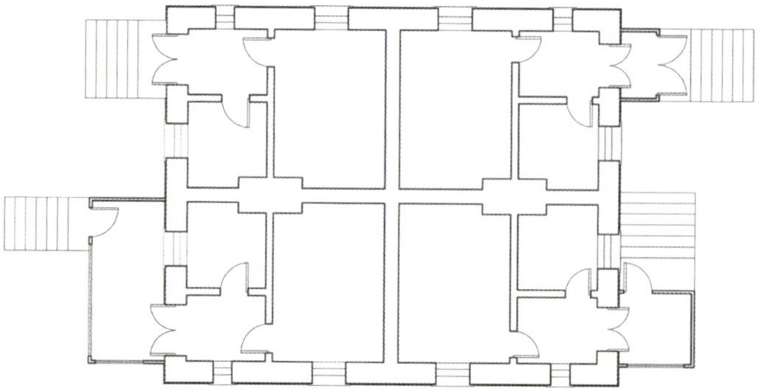

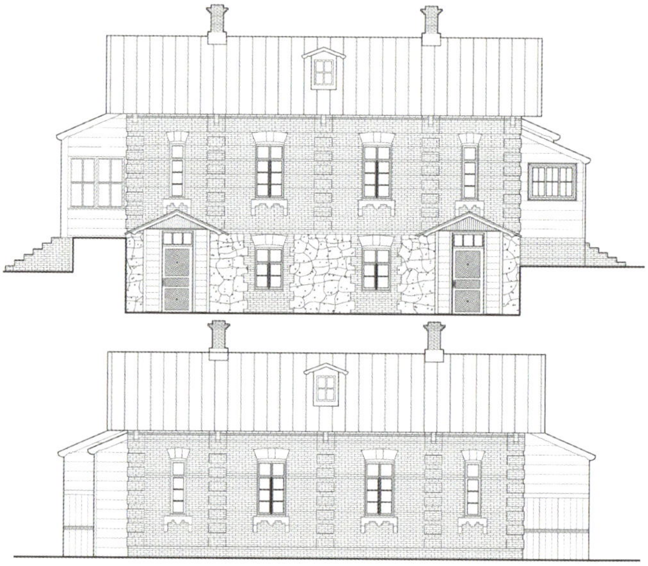

# ARCHITECTURAL CULTURAL HERITAGE OF CHINESE EASTERN RAILWAY

横道河子住宅现状及测绘图 2 Current condition and drawings of residence in Hengdaohezi 2

横道河子住宅现状及测绘图 3 Current condition and drawings of residence in Hengdaohezi 3

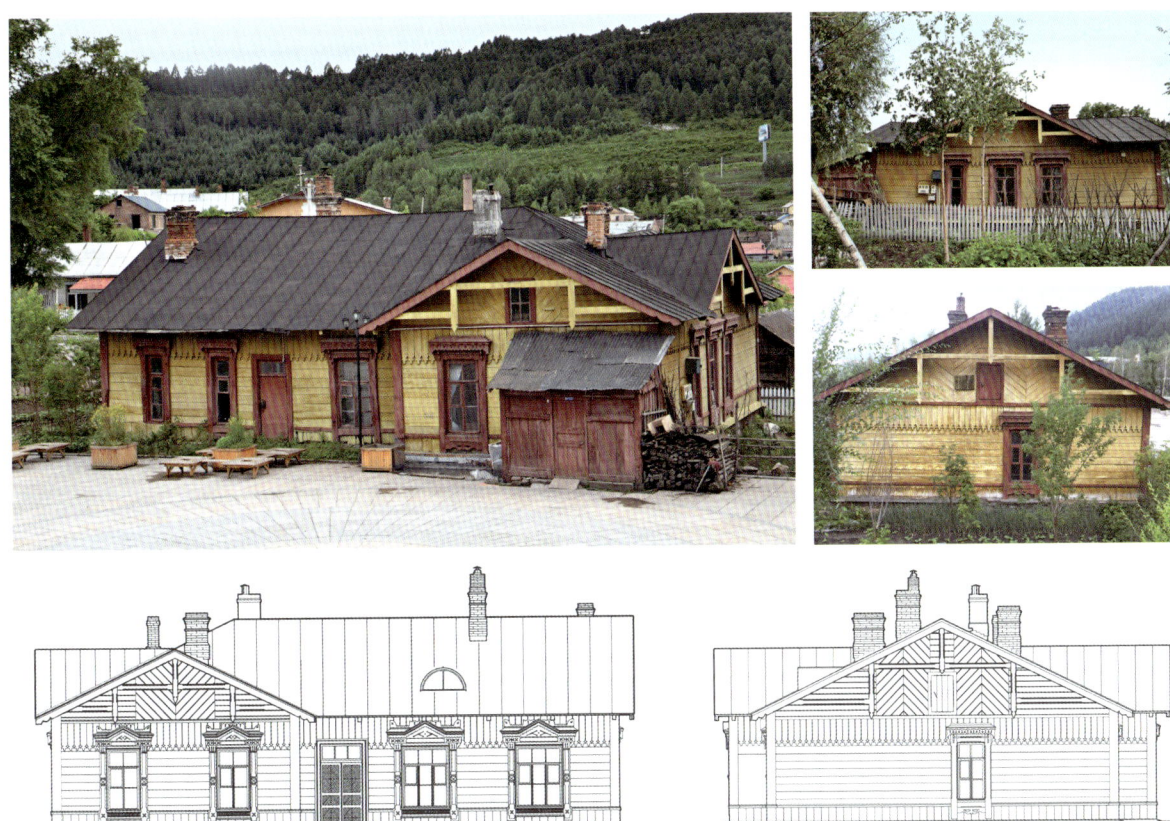

横道河子住宅现状及测绘图 4 Current condition and drawings of residence in Hengdaohezi 4

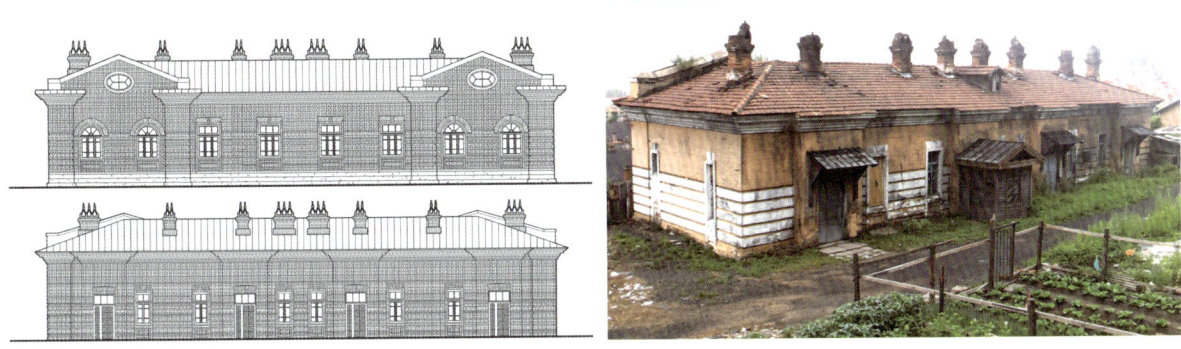

横道河子联户住宅现状及测绘图 Current condition and drawings of town house in Hengdaohezi

16 居住建筑 | 359

横道河子木住宅现状及测绘图 1 Current condition and drawings of wooden residence in Hengdaohezi 1

横道河子木住宅现状及测绘图 2 Current condition and drawings of wooden residence in Hengdaohezi 2

数量众多的横道河子砖石住宅 Masonry residences in Hengdaohezi

不同形式的穆棱住宅 Different types of residence in Muling

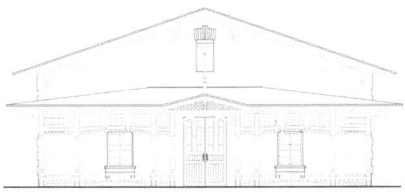
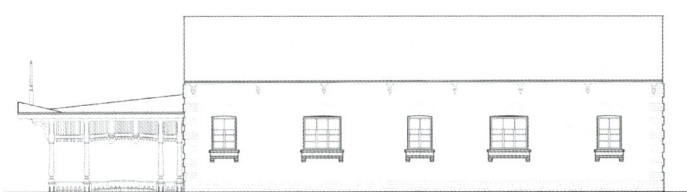

扎兰屯带外廊的住宅现状及测绘图 Current condition and drawings of residence with veranda in Zhalantun

扎兰屯带外廊的住宅 Residence with veranda in Zhalantun

扎兰屯砖石住宅 Masonry residence in Zhalantun

# ARCHITECTURAL CULTURAL HERITAGE OF CHINESE EASTERN RAILWAY

绥芬河不同形式的住宅 Different types of residence in Suifenhe

安达不同形式的住宅 Different types of residence in Anda

伊列克得联户式住宅
Town house in Yiliekede

平山住宅
Residence in Pingshan

石头河子集合住宅1
Congregated house in Shitouhezi 1

石头河子集合住宅2
Congregated house in Shitouhezi 2

下城子住宅
Residence in Xiachengzi

昂昂溪住宅 Residence in Ang'angxi

昂昂溪不同形式的住宅 Different types of residence in Ang'angxi

扎赉诺尔不同形式的住宅 Different types of residence in Zhalainuoer

庙台子住宅 Residence in Miaotaizi

马桥河住宅 Residence in Maqiaohe

# ARCHITECTURAL CULTURAL HERITAGE OF CHINESE EASTERN RAILWAY

满洲里砖石住宅 Masonry residence in Manzhouli

满洲里不同形式的石住宅 Different types of stone residence in Manzhouli

满洲里木住宅 Wooden residence in Manzhouli

满洲里不同形式的木住宅 Different types of wooden residence in Manzhouli

16 居住建筑 | 369

# ARCHITECTURAL CULTURAL HERITAGE OF CHINESE EASTERN RAILWAY

博克图砖住宅 1 Masonry residence in Boketu 1

博克图不同形式的砖石住宅 Different types of masonry residence in Boketu

博克图砖住宅 2 Masonry residence in Boketu 2

博克图不同形式的木住宅 Different types of wooden residence in Boketu

16 居住建筑 | 371

# ARCHITECTURAL CULTURAL HERITAGE OF CHINESE EASTERN RAILWAY

一面坡住宅  Residence in Yimianpo

一面坡不同形式的住宅1 Different types of residence in Yimianpo 1

一面坡不同形式的住宅 2 Different types of residence in Yimianpo 2

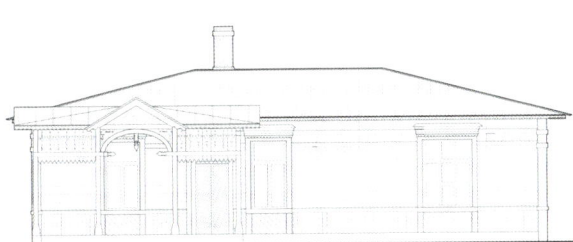

一面坡住宅现状及测绘图 1
Current condition and drawings of residence in Yimianpo 1

一面坡住宅现状及测绘图 2
Current condition and drawings of residence in Yimianpo 2

# ARCHITECTURAL CULTURAL HERITAGE OF CHINESE EASTERN RAILWAY

赫尔洪德住宅
Residence in Heerhongde

玉泉住宅
Residence in Yuquan

小岭住宅
Residence in Xiaoling

代马沟住宅 1
Residence in Daimagou 1

代马沟住宅 2
Residence in Daimagou 2

舍利屯住宅
Residence in Shelitun

新南沟住宅 1
Residence in Xinnangou 1

新南沟住宅 2
Residence in Xinnangou 2

新南沟住宅 3
Residence in Xinnangou 3

尚家住宅
Residence in Shangjia

宋站住宅 1
Residence in Songzhan

宋站住宅 2
Residence in Songzhan

富拉尔基住宅 1
Residence in Fulaerji 1

富拉尔基住宅 2
Residence in Fulaerji 2

富拉尔基住宅 3
Residence in Fulaerji 3

肇东住宅 1
Residence in Zhaodong 1

肇东住宅 2
Residence in Zhaodong 2

肇东住宅 3
Residence in Zhaodong 3

双城住宅 1
Residence in Shuangcheng 1

双城住宅 2
Residence in Shuangcheng 2

双城住宅 3
Residence in Shuangcheng 3

哈拉苏住宅
Residence in Halasu

德惠住宅 1
Residence in Dehui 1

德惠住宅 2
Residence in Dehui 2

# ARCHITECTURAL CULTURAL HERITAGE OF CHINESE EASTERN RAILWAY

不同形式的住宅门斗  Different types of entrances of residence

不同形式的住宅窗户 Different types of windows of residence

# 17 道桥设施

中东铁路全长 2 489.2 千米，途经平原、丘陵、山地、江河、湿地等多种地理环境，地形变化复杂，高程变化急剧，因此开凿涵隧、架设桥梁成为必不可少的工程内容，各种工程设施如涵洞、桥梁、隧道的形态和工艺堪称中东铁路的一大特色，代表了中东铁路建设工程的最高技术成就。

## 17.1 桥梁类型与特点

中东铁路沿线桥梁包括石拱桥、钢桁架桥、钢筋混凝土桥。石拱桥多为连续拱券结构，形式优美流畅，通过组合不同的跨度和高度的桥孔，满足不同条件下的建设需求，其桥孔跨度有 5 俄丈、6 俄丈、10 俄丈、12 俄丈（1 俄丈 =2.134 米）等多种规格，数量从单孔到多孔。位于穆棱站的穆棱河铁路大桥跨度为 6 俄丈 ×10 孔，是中东铁路跨度最长的石拱桥。钢桁架桥技术更先进，可以实现石拱桥达不到的跨度。按照钢桁架在桥梁中的位置，可以分为上承式钢桁架桥（多在中东铁路南部支线使用）和下承式钢桁架桥；按照钢桁架的形式，可分为华伦式桁架桥、普拉特桁架桥和豪氏桁架桥等。多种桁架形式和位置相互组合，形成了丰富的桥梁形式。钢桁架桥桥孔跨度有 10 俄丈、15 俄丈和 35 俄丈三种规格，以适应不同的桥梁跨度需求。中东铁路中一些重要的桥梁工程如伊敏河铁路大桥、嫩江大桥、松花江大桥、牡丹江大桥都采用了钢桁架桥梁形式。中东铁路钢桁架桥梁所用钢材产自比利时、波兰和俄国，钢材出厂时均为零部件，凝结了当时前沿的技术成果。除了石拱桥和钢桁架桥，中东铁路中还有钢筋混凝土桥，跨度一般不超过 3 俄丈，采用简单的铁网式配筋形式，多应用于中东铁路南部支线。另外还有一种位于铁路站点内、供铁路两侧居民通行的跨线天桥，这类桥梁较为轻盈，虽为日常生活用桥，但形态上铁路工业特征明显，典型实例如昂昂溪天桥。

## 17.2 隧道、涵洞及铁路展线

中东铁路沿线的隧道包括兴安岭隧道，绥芬河一号隧道、二号隧道、三号隧道，大观岭隧道，代马沟隧道等。由于施工速度和地形条件的限制，隧道质量参差不齐，既有完整衬砌的隧道，如绥芬河一号隧道，拱顶和两侧壁体均用石材完整衬砌；也有局部衬砌的隧道，如代马沟隧道，内部拱顶完整衬砌，两侧局部衬砌，部分石材暴露在隧道内部，空间凌乱。中东铁路的隧道除满足机车正常通行外，还可解决轨道转弯、提升高度的需求，如绥芬河二号隧道、磨刀石——代马沟隧道都是采用弧形隧道解决转弯问题。涵洞主要解决铁路两侧落差及可能形成的汇水、积水问题，一些尺寸较大和净空较高的涵洞还可供铁路两侧民众穿行之用。涵洞在中东铁路中有半圆形和椭圆形两种形态，跨度也比较标准，一般有 0.5 俄丈、0.75 俄丈、1.0 俄丈、1.5 俄丈、2.0 俄丈、2.5 俄丈、3.0 俄丈七种规格，对应的高度最低 1.02 俄丈，最高 2.75 俄丈。涵洞长度一般随铁路路基宽度而定，最小长度 10 俄丈（爱河站附近），最大长度 36.36 俄丈（兴安岭展线附近）。铁路展线是中东铁路中常见的工程设施，与隧道、涵洞结合设置，以供机车迂回上升、翻山爬坡之用，形态有 S 形、U 形、波浪形及螺旋形等。实例如位于中东铁路西线的兴安岭展线，其采用螺旋展线形式，全长 4 俄里（1 俄里 ≈ 1.066 8 千米），提升高度 24 俄丈，道路坡度 12‰。各种各样的展线解决了机车功率不足、建设隧道困难的问题，是难得的工程成就。

### 17.3 道桥设施的分布

从早期的中东铁路高程设计图来看，铁路高程自西向东变化明显。西部大兴安岭地区地势起伏，各站之间的海拔变化较大，中部松嫩平原地势较低，几乎处于同一海拔。而东部的长白山余脉地区则地势起伏急剧，各站之间海拔变化很大，因东、西地区地势的起伏变化而集中了大量的桥隧工程设施。道桥设施分布的位置以干线满洲里西侧 0 公里处为起点，南部支线以哈尔滨为起点，依距离标注（详见附录 1）。中东铁路全线桥梁、涵洞共计约 1 000 座，仅东部线就有 695 座，尤以石头河子到高岭子之间的张广才岭地区最密集，在 40.8 俄里长度的铁路内竟有桥梁、涵洞约 64 座，平均每 0.63 俄里就出现一座。东部线还有隧道 6 座，集中在山底到代马沟和绥芬河到边境之间。西部线桥梁、涵洞总计约 305 座，隧道 1 座。多数桥梁、涵洞集中分布在免渡河至哈拉苏之间，在 187.6 俄里的长度内共有桥梁、涵洞合计 144 座，平均每 1.3 俄里就出现一座。西部线的道桥设施创造了若干中东铁路之最，如位于哈尔滨的松花江铁路大桥全长 445 俄丈，是中东铁路最长的桥梁，位于兴安岭的隧道全长 1 442.85 俄丈（3 079 米），是中东铁路长度最长、施工最艰难的隧道。隧道东西两侧入口均设计成当时流行的新艺术风格，在中东铁路所有的工程设施中属于孤例，具有极高的艺术价值。铁路展线较多地出现在中东铁路东部线，如洗马展线、大观岭展线、太岭展线、细鳞河展线等。

## Bridges, Tunnels and Other Infrastructures

The CER ran across plain, hill, mountain, river, wetland and so on, passing many complex topographies and changeable elevations, which made excavating tunnel and erecting bridge to be essential engineering work. The style and technology of different engineering facilities were considered as a major feature of the CER, including culvert, bridge, tunnel and so on, which had represented the most excellent technological achievement in architectural heritage of the CER line.

Bridges along the CER included stone arch bridge, steel truss bridge and steel reinforced concrete bridge. Stone arch bridge often adopted the continuous arch structure that makes it possible to form beautiful and smooth style. The bridge with different arches combined different heights and widths was able to meet the needs of construction requirement in different conditions. The steel truss bridge was widely used in construction of the CER because of its advanced technology that makes the bridge span wider than that of stone arch bridge. According to the positions of steel truss in the bridge, steel truss bridge could be divided into top bear steel truss bridge (often used in the southern branch of the CER) and through type steel truss bridge. And according to the type of steel truss, steel truss bridge could also be divided into Warren truss bridge, Pratt truss bridge and Howe truss bridge. The incorporation of different steel truss types and positions let these kinds of bridge become much abundant. Some important bridges along the CER line were constructed in steel truss type , such as Yimin River Bridge, Nenjiang River Bridge, Songhua River Bridge and Mudanjiang River Bridge. The steel materials used in steel truss bridge of CER were produced in Belgium, Poland and Russia, including all component and parts. This was indeed the advanced technology in that time. Besides stone arch bridge and steel truss bridge, there was a steel reinforced concrete bridge with short span. Also, there was a bridge within the station for people crossing the railroad on both sides. These types of bridge in a typical railroad style were very useful for people's everyday life, such as Ang'angxi Overbridge.

Tunnels along the CER line mainly included xing'anling tunnel, Suifenhe No. 1 tunnel, Suifenhe No. 2 tunnel, Suifenhe No. 3 tunnel, Daguanling tunnel and Daimagou tunnel. The tunnels were used not only to meet locomotives passing through, but also to solve the problems like track turn and promoting the height, for instance, Suifenhe No. 2 tunnel and Modaoshi to Daimagou tunnel were both designed to be the arc tunnel to meet the track turn. Culvert was mainly built for solving the problems of the height difference on both sides of the railway and drainage of the formed accumulative water. Some large and high culverts could become a traffic pathway for residents who live both side of it. Extension line of the CER was a kind of common facility that makes tunnel combining with culvert together for trains to climb the mountain and go up circuitously. The form of extension line was multifarious, such as S-shape, U-shape, wavy shape and spiral shape, for example, xing'anling extension line in western branch of the CER in spiral shape. The different kinds of extension line were able to solve the problem in insufficient power of locomotives and construction difficulty of tunnel, becoming valuable engineering achievement.

From the early design drawing, the height of the CER line changed obviously from west to east. The distribution of bridges, tunnels and other infrastructures along the CER was marked by distance, and the starting point of which, on the main line, was located at the west side of Manzhouli, while that of the southern branch is in Harbin. The western part of the line was Daxing'anling area in fluctuated landform, whose altitude among different stations changed greatly. Songnen plain in middle part was much low and flat terrain with almost the same elevation level. Changbai mountain area in east part of the line was fluctuated largely in topography, whose altitude among different stations also changed very much. The height difference between east and west area leads to many bridges and tunnels to be built. There were nearly 1,000 bridges and culverts along the CER, of which 695 bridges were located in the eastern branch, and 305 bridges were sited in the western branch including a tunnel. Extension line of the railway appeared almost in the west and east branches, but mainly in east branch, such as Xima extension line, Daguanling extension line, Tailing extension line, Xilinhe extension line and so on.

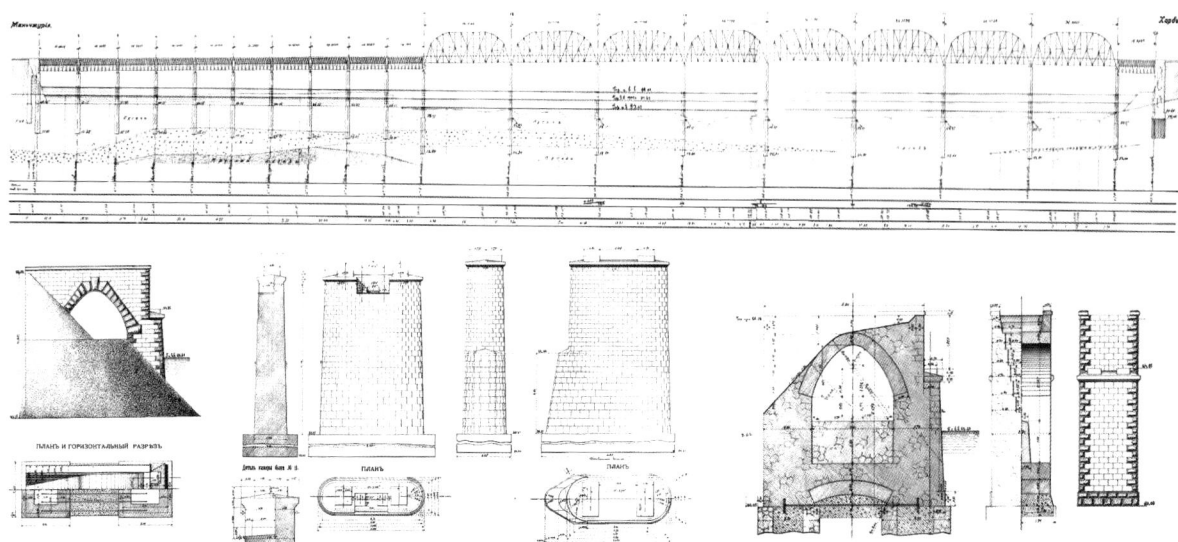

第一松花江大桥设计图 Drawings of the No.1 Songhua River Bridge

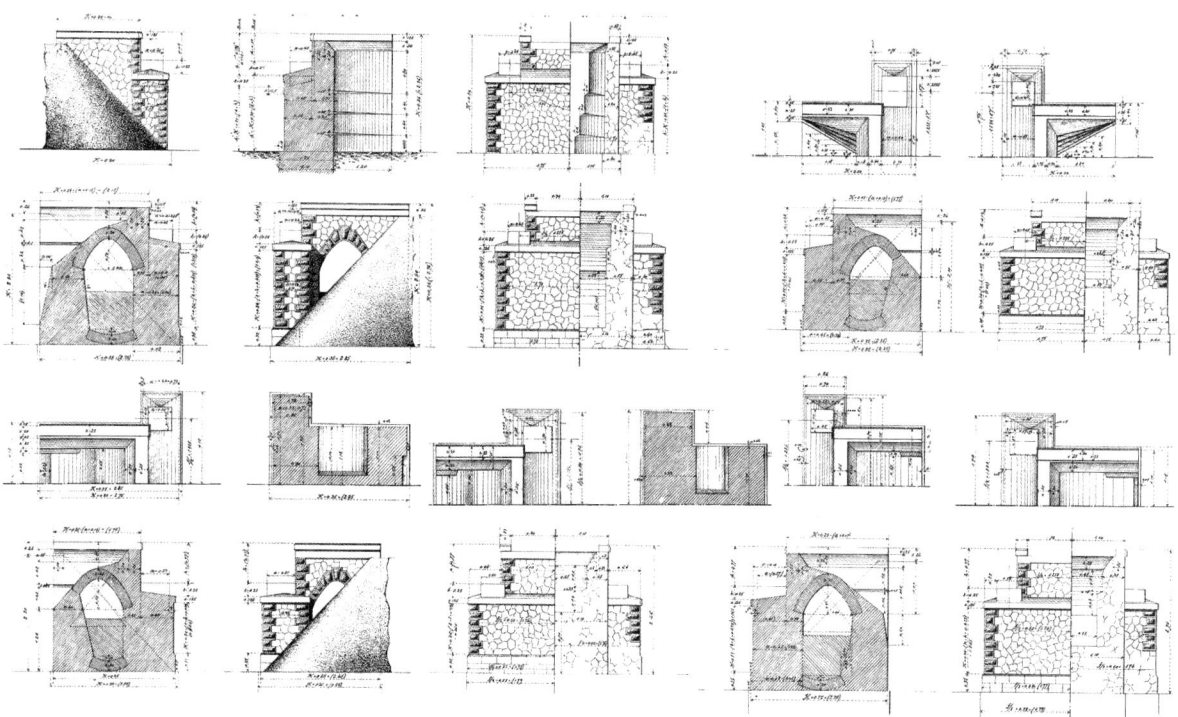

桥墩设计图 Drawings of piers

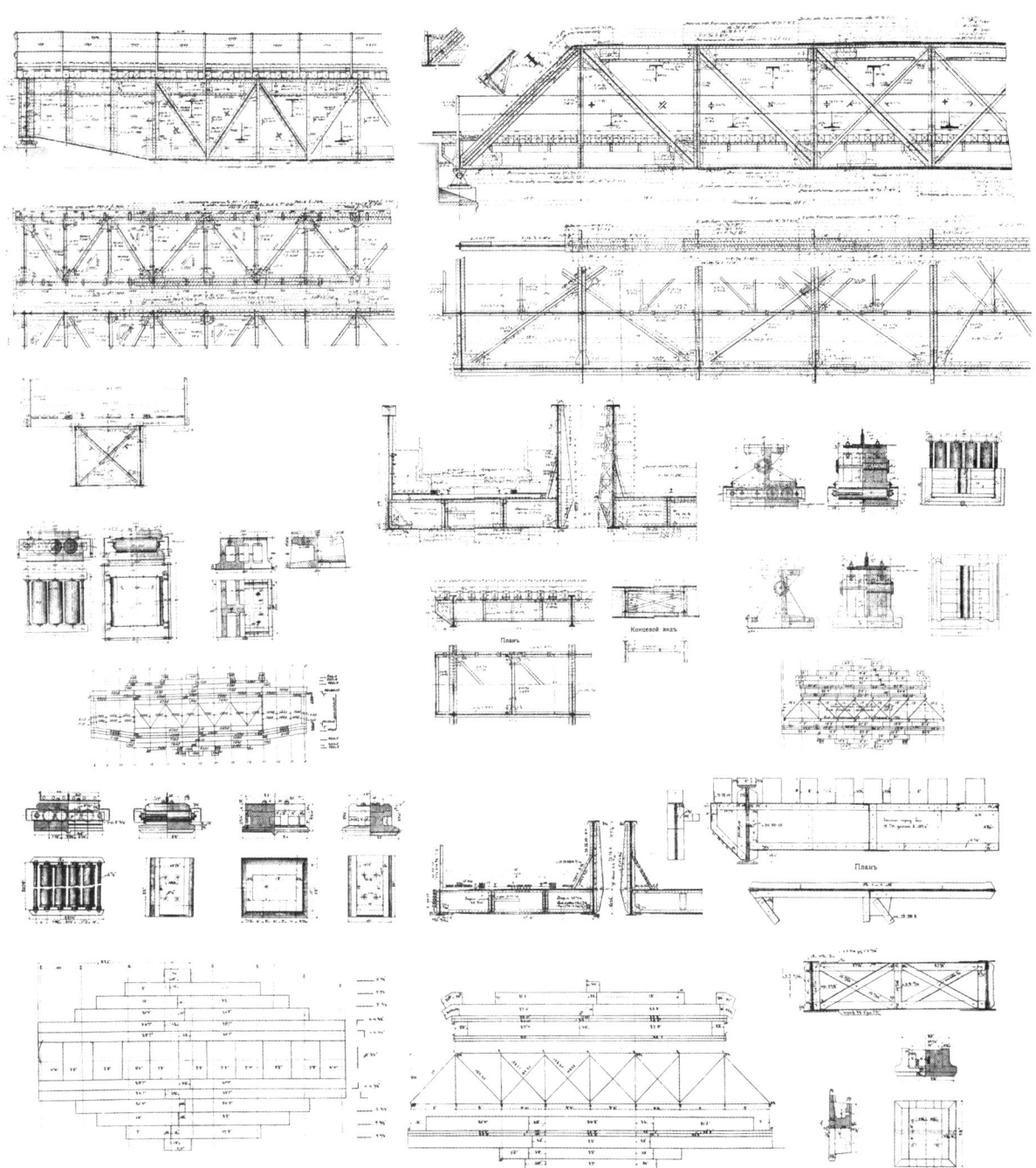

桥梁上部不同跨度的梁架设计图 Drawings of beams in different spans on the upper part of bridges

第一松花江大桥施工历史照片
Historical photos of construction process of the No. 1 Songhua River Bridge

第一松花江大桥历史照片
Historical photo of the No. 1 Songhua River Bridge

牡丹江大桥历史照片
Historical photo of bridge spans the Mudan River

嫩江大桥历史照片
Historical photos of bridge spans the Nen River

# ARCHITECTURAL CULTURAL HERITAGE OF CHINESE EASTERN RAILWAY

第二松花江大桥历史照片
Historical photo of the No. 2 Songhua River Bridge

东线 1 231 俄里 牡丹江 跨度 195 俄丈 历史照片
Historical photo of bridge spans the Mudan River (east line 1,231 verst, 195 sagenes)

南线 728 俄里 沙河 跨度 180 俄丈 历史照片
Historical photo of bridge spans the Sha River (south line 728 verst, 180 sagenes)

南线 292 俄里 东辽河 跨度 135 俄丈 历史照片
Historical photo of bridge spans the East Liao River (south line 292 verst, 135 sagenes)

南线 728 俄里沙河 跨度 180 俄丈 历史照片
Historical photo of bridge spans the Sha River (south line 728 verst, 180 sagenes)

南线 439 俄里 柴河 跨度 135 俄丈 历史照片
Historical photo of bridge spans the Chai River (south line 439 verst, 135 sagenes)

南线 599 俄里 太子河 跨度 50 俄丈 历史照片
Historical photo of bridge spans the Taizi River
(south line 599 verst, 50 sagenes)

东线 1 052 俄里 蚂蜒河 跨度 40 俄丈 历史照片
Historical photo of bridge spans the Mayan River
(south line 1,052 verst, 40 sagenes)

南线 486 俄里 蒲河 跨度 20 俄丈 历史照片
Historical photo of bridge spans the Pu River
(south line 486 verst, 20 sagenes)

苇沙河铁路桥历史照片
Historical photo of railway bridge spans the Weisha River

南线 694 俄里 下洼子 跨度 20 俄丈 历史照片
Historical photo of bridge in Xiawazi (south line 694 verst, 20 sagenes)

南线 742 俄里 跨度 10 俄丈 历史照片
Historical photo of bridge on south line 742 verst (10 sagenes)

# ARCHITECTURAL CULTURAL HERITAGE OF CHINESE EASTERN RAILWAY

南线 816 俄里 跨度 10 俄丈 历史照片
Historical photo of bridge on south line 816 verst (10 sagenes)

南线 877 俄里 桥孔跨度 2.5 俄丈 历史照片
Historical photo of bridge on south line 877 verst (2.5 sagenes)

南线 104 俄里 跨度 6 俄丈 历史照片
Historical photo of bridge on south line 104 verst (6 sagenes)

西线 517 俄里 跨度 4 俄丈 历史照片
Historical photo of bridge on west line 517 verst (4 sagenes)

南线 833 俄里 路堤高度 5.32 俄丈 历史照片
Historical photo of bridge on south line 833 verst (5.32 sagenes)

东线 1 291 俄里 跨度 10 俄丈 历史照片
Historical photo of bridge on east line 1,291 verst (10 sagenes)

南线 129 俄里 跨度 2 俄丈 历史照片
Historical photo of bridge on south line 129 verst (2 sagenes)

西线 19 俄里 跨度 3 俄丈 历史照片
Historical photo of bridge on west line 19 verst (3 sagenes)

南线 834 俄里 桥孔跨度 2.5 俄丈 历史照片
Historical photo of bridge on south line 834 verst (2.5 sagenes)

南线 834 俄里 桥孔跨度 1 俄丈 临时过梁跨度 2.5 俄丈 历史照片
Historical photo of bridge on south line  834 verst (1 sagene)

第一松花江大桥 The No.1 Songhua River Bridge

细鳞河桥 Bridge spans the Xilin River　　　　西岭口桥墩 Piers in Xilingkou

第二松花江大桥 The No. 2 Songhua River Bridge

富拉尔基江桥遗址 Ruins of bridge in Fulaerji

迎水寺桥 Bridge in Yingshuisi

# ARCHITECTURAL CULTURAL HERITAGE OF CHINESE EASTERN RAILWAY

满洲里站跨线天桥历史照片 Historical photo of overpass in Manzhouli station

公主岭站跨线天桥 Overpass in Gongzhuling station

昂昂溪站跨线天桥 Overpass in Ang'angxi station

# ARCHITECTURAL CULTURAL HERITAGE OF CHINESE EASTERN RAILWAY

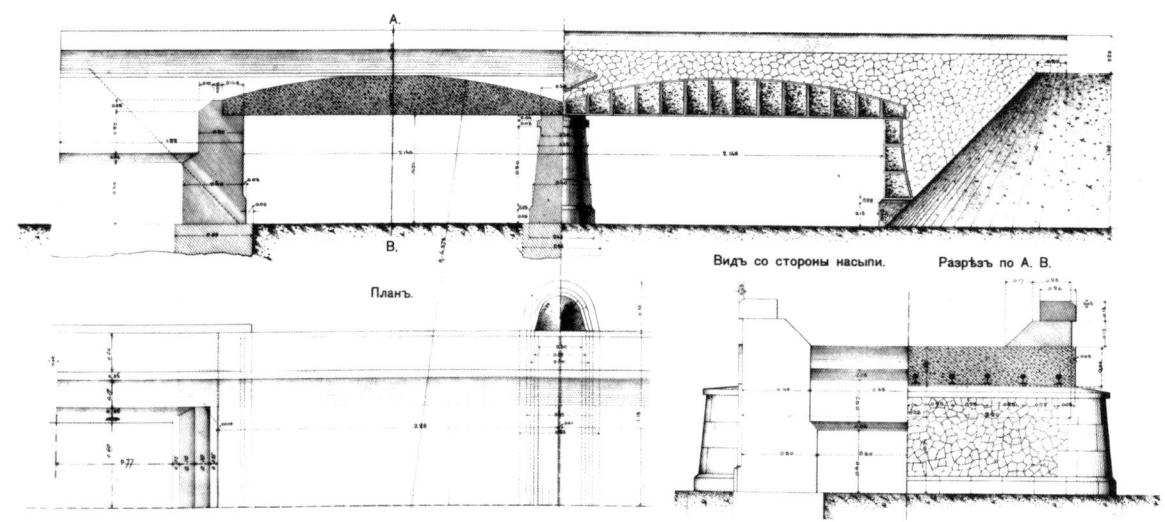

钢筋混凝土桥设计图 Drawings of steel reinforced concrete bridge

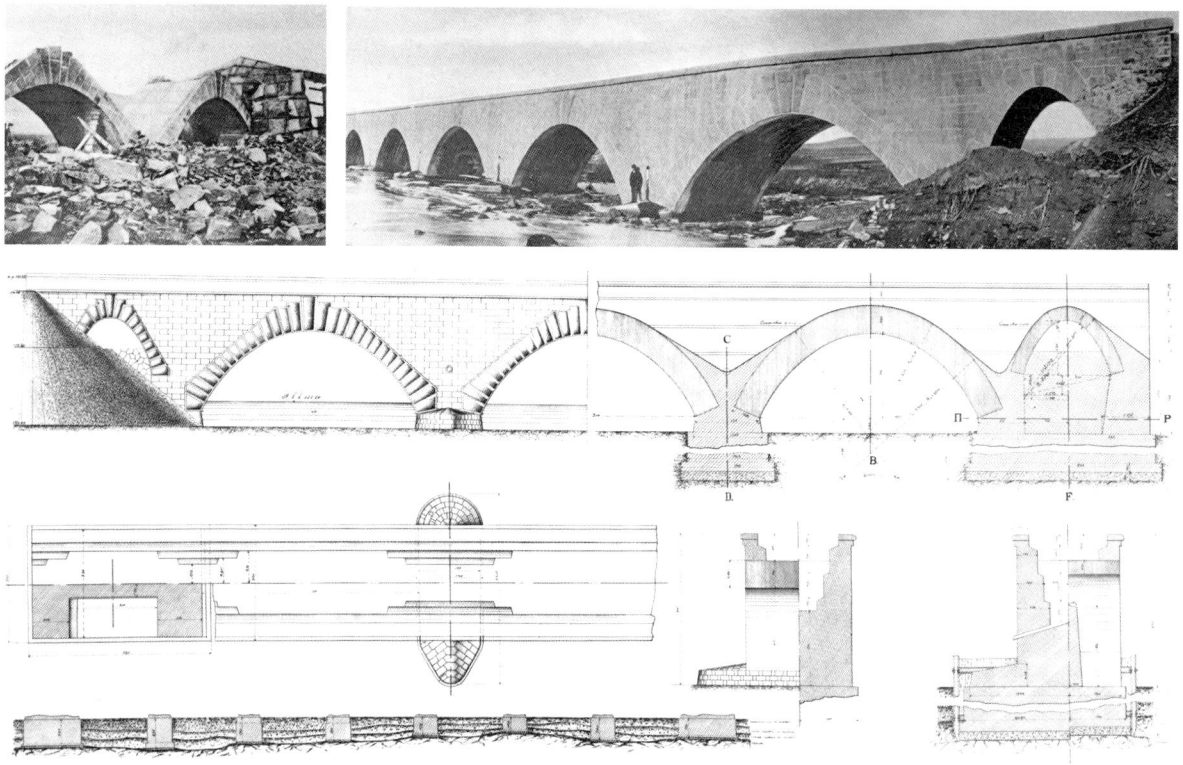

马桥河石桥历史照片及设计图 Historical photos and drawings of stone arch bridge spans Maqiaohe

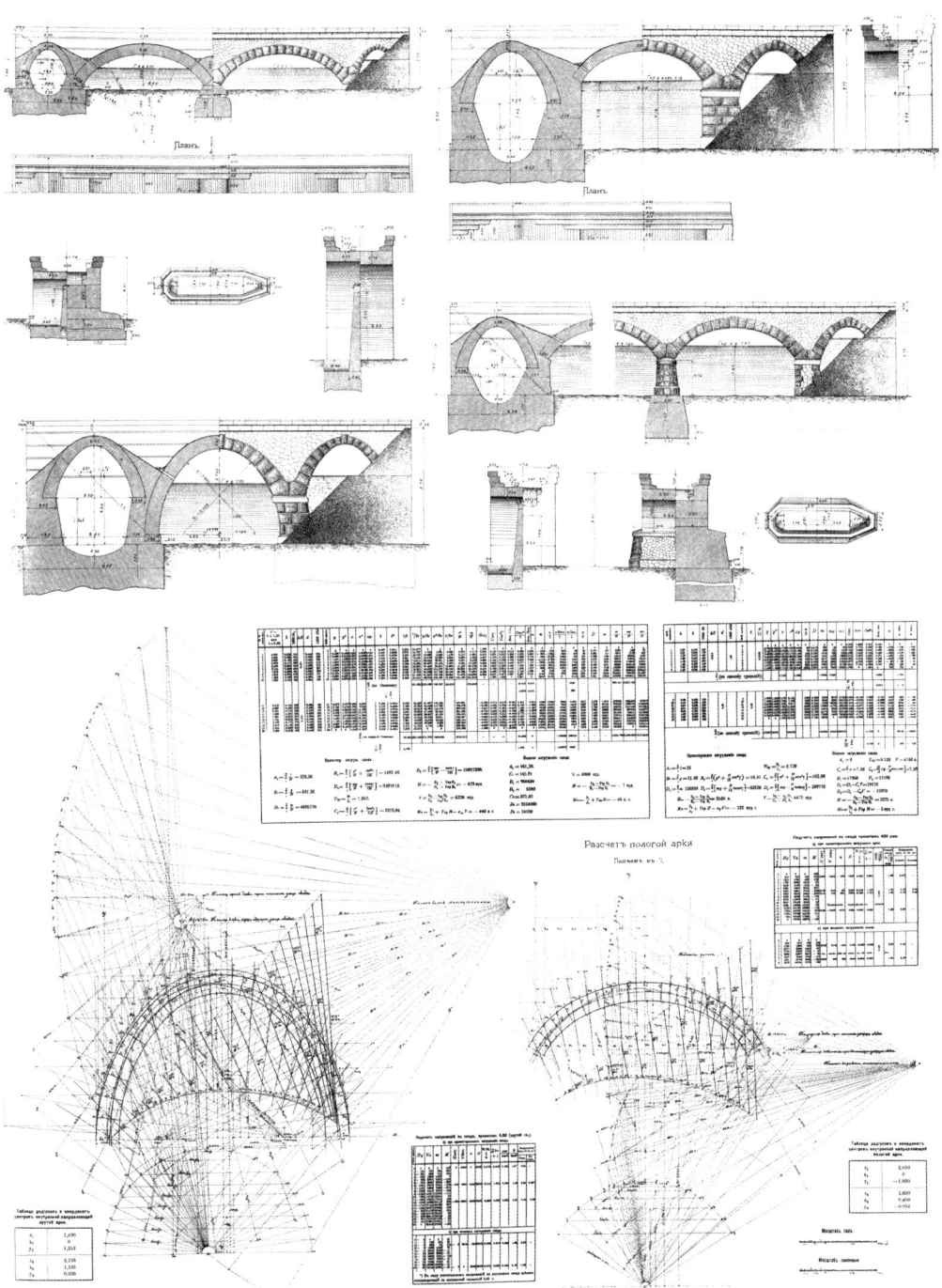

石桥设计标准图 Standardized drawings of stone arch bridge

# ARCHITECTURAL CULTURAL HERITAGE OF CHINESE EASTERN RAILWAY

东线 1 298 俄里 穆棱河历史照片
Historical photos of bridge spans the Muling River on east line 1,298 verst

南线 826 俄里 龙河历史照片
Historical photo of bridge spans the Long River on south line 826 verst

东线 1 378 俄里 小绥芬河历史照片
Historical photos of bridge spans the small Suifen River on east line 1,378 verst

东线 1 315 俄里 腰岭子河历史照片
Historical photo of bridge spans the Yaolingzi River on east line 1,315 verst

东线 1 387 俄里 八道河子历史照片
Historical photo of bridge in Badaohezi on east line 1,387 verst

# ARCHITECTURAL CULTURAL HERITAGE OF CHINESE EASTERN RAILWAY

穆棱大桥
Bridge in Muling

大观岭两座石桥遗址
Ruins of two stone bridges in Daguanling

高岭子石桥
Bridge in Gaolingzi

治山大桥
Bridge in Zhishan

高岭子石桥遗址
Ruins of stone bridge in Gaolingzi

太岭与细鳞河间大桥
Bridge between Tailing and Xilinhe

山底大桥
Bridge in Shandi

河西与绥阳之间石桥
Stone bridge between Hexi and Suiyang

一面坡蚂蜒河大桥
Bridge spans the Mayan River in Yimianpo

绥芬河石桥
Stone bridge in Suifenhe

太岭与细鳞河间石桥
Stone bridge between Tailing and Xilinhe

免渡河大桥
Bridge in Mianduhe

卧牛河与三道桥间石桥
Bridge between Woniuhe and Sandaoqiao

兴安岭隧道展线全景历史照片 Historical photo of panorama of tunnel through Hinggan Mountain

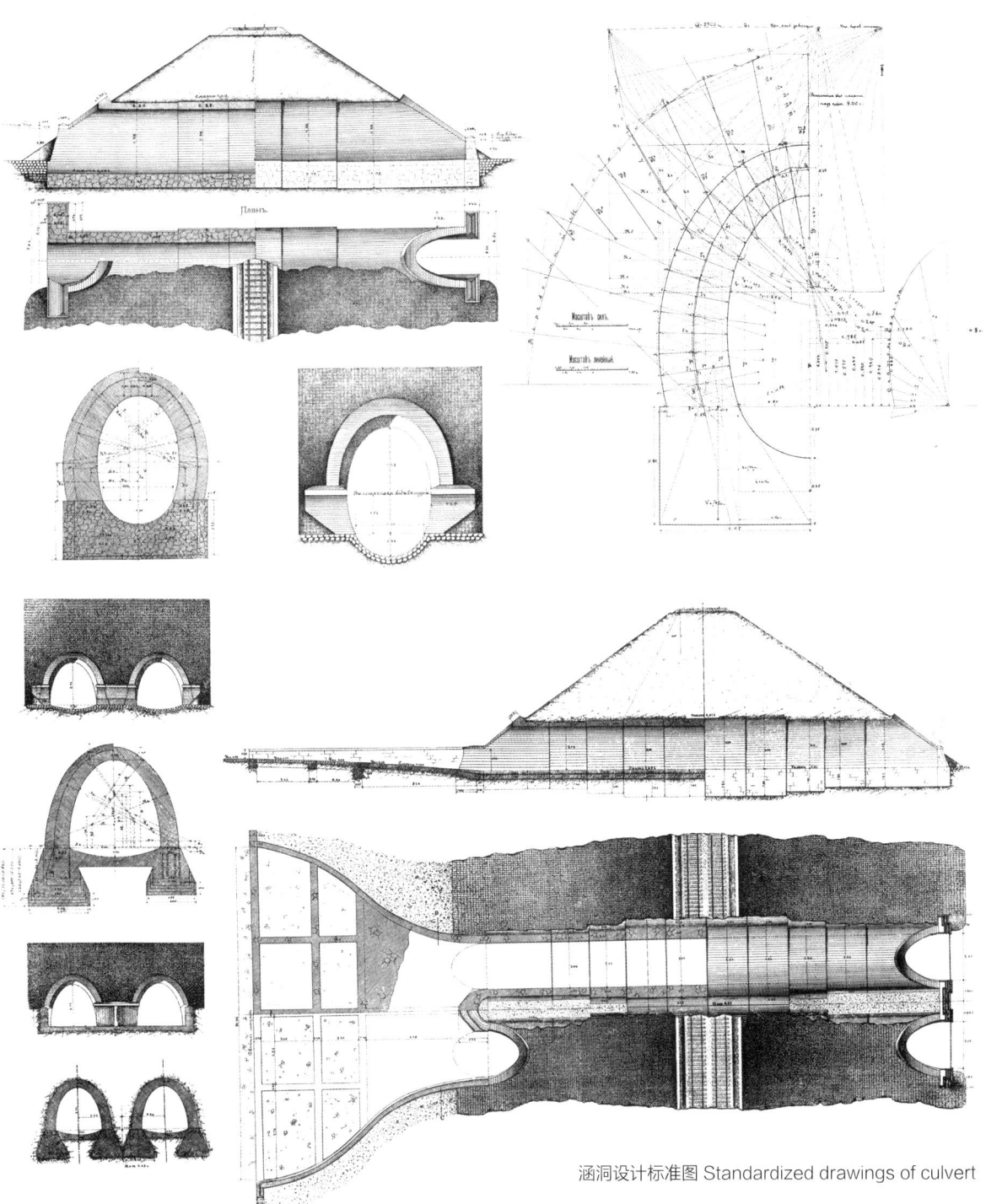

涵洞设计标准图 Standardized drawings of culvert

17 道桥设施

西线 518 俄里 涵洞历史照片
Historical photo of culvert on west line 518 verst

东线 341 俄里 涵洞历史照片
Historical photo of culvert on east line 341 verst

南线 891 俄里 涵洞历史照片
Historical photo of culvert on south line 891 verst

南线 846 俄里 涵洞历史照片
Historical photo of culvert on south line 846 verst

南线 843 俄里 涵洞历史照片
Historical photo of culvert on south line 843 verst

东线 1 350 俄里 涵洞历史照片
Historical photo of culvert on east line 1,350 verst

西线 373 俄里 兴安岭涵洞历史照片
Historical photos of culvert through Hinggan Mountain on west line 373 verst

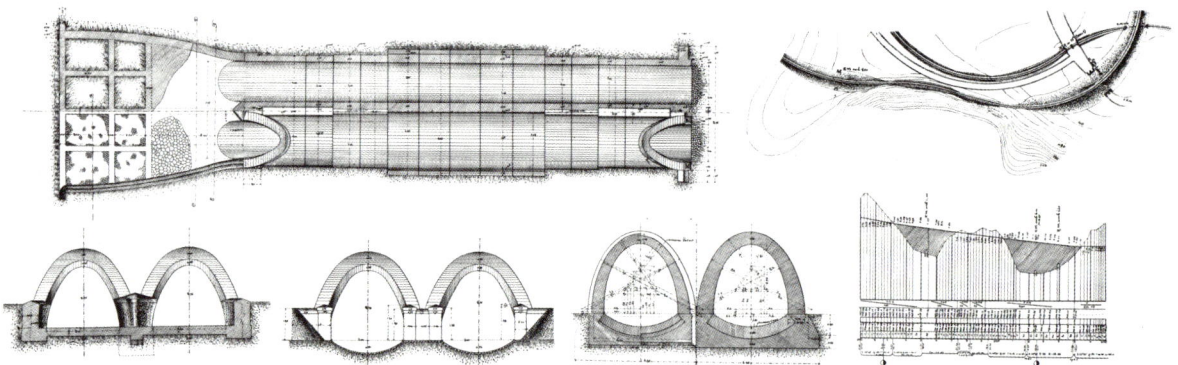

涵洞施工图 Construction drawing of culvert

绥阳涵洞 1 Culvert in Suiyang 1

绥阳涵洞 2 Culvert in Suiyang 2

新南沟双涵洞 Culverts in Xinnangou

新南沟涵洞 Culvert in Xinnangou

紫沟涵洞 Culvert in Zigou　　博克图涵洞 1 Culvert in Boketu 1　　博克图涵洞 2 Culvert in Boketu 2

沙力涵洞 2 Culvert in Shali 2

沙力涵洞 1 Culvert in Shali 1　　沙力涵洞 3 Culvert in Shali 3

沙力涵洞 4 Culvert in Shali 4　　沙力涵洞 5 Culvert in Shali 5

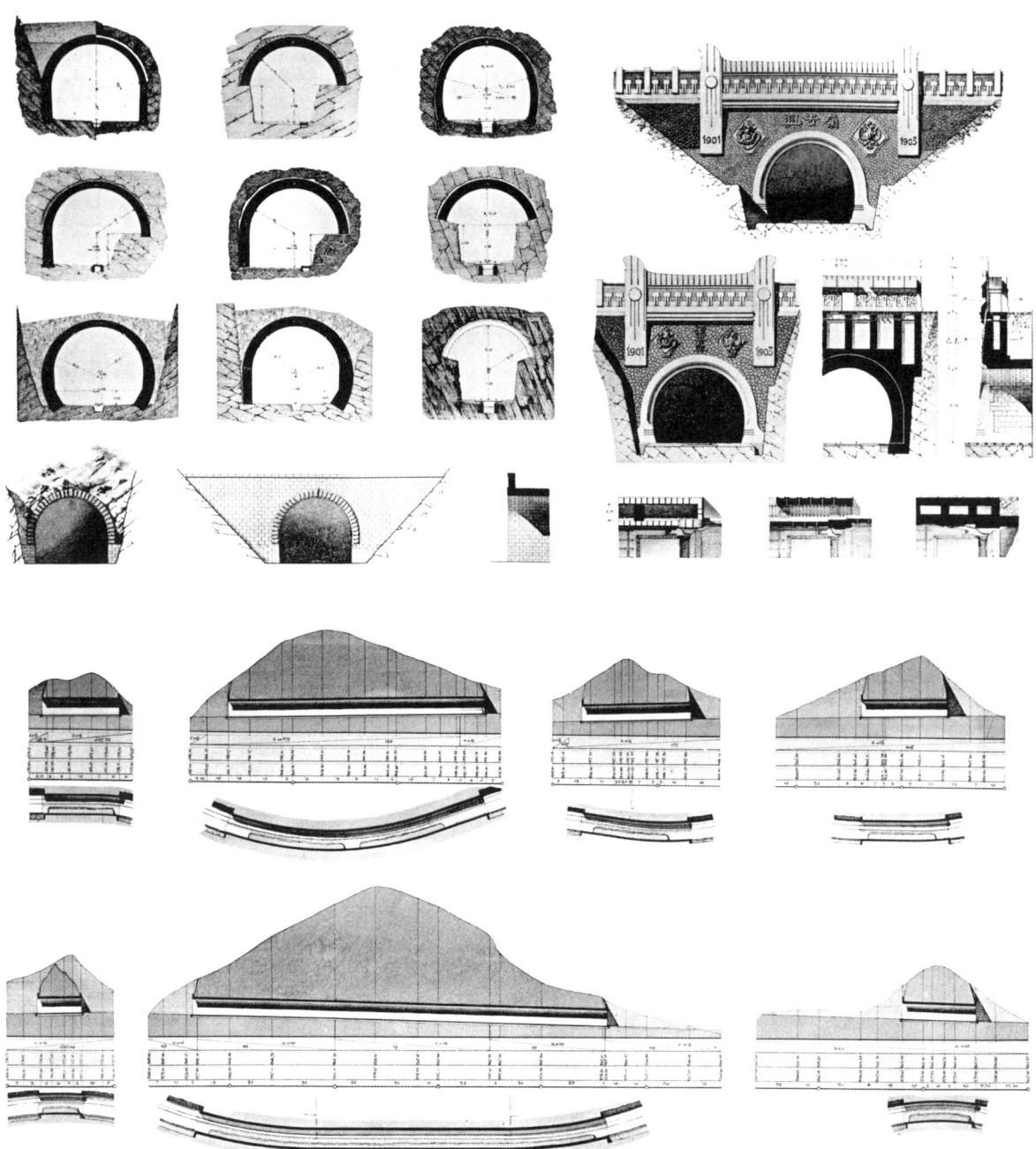

西部线 兴安岭隧道设计图 Drawings of tunnel through Hinggan Mountain on west line

兴安岭隧道历史照片
Historical photo of tunnel through Hinggan Mountain

兴安岭隧道施工历史照片
Historical photos of construction process of tunnel through Hinggan Mountain

# ARCHITECTURAL CULTURAL HERITAGE OF CHINESE EASTERN RAILWAY

东线 1 415 俄里 长度 36 俄丈 东入口历史照片
Historical photo of east entrance of tunnel on east line 1,415 verst (36 sagenes)

东线 1 414 俄里 长度 20 俄丈 历史照片
Historical photo of tunnel on east line 1,414 verst (20 sagenes)

东线 1 412 俄里 长度 120.85 俄丈 东入口历史照片
Historical photo of east entrance of tunnel on east line 1,412 verst (120.85 sagenes)

东线 1 410 俄里 长度 51.50 俄丈 西入口历史照片
Historical photo of west entrance of tunnel on east line 1,410 verst (51.5 sagenes)

兴安岭隧道
Tunnel through Hinggan Mountain

# 18 铁路机车

　　铁路机车可以分为两个部分,即牵引机车与运载车厢。中东铁路时期的牵引机车多为比利时、英国、俄国制造的欧式蒸汽机车,车架为板式,燃烧室以铜板铸造,牵引力约为 6 000 至 14 000 千克。中东铁路修建时期俄国已经有成熟的机车设计与制造水平,中东铁路哈尔滨总工厂即是"集蒸汽机车、客车、货车维修、加工"为一体的综合性工厂,满足不同需求的牵引机车也有相应的设计图纸记录保存。根据功能类型不同,运载车厢可分为多种,包括客运硬座车、客运卧铺车、公务车、行李车厢、生活物资厢、邮政车厢、医务车厢、卫生车厢、餐车车厢、冷藏车厢、供水车厢、囚车车厢、一般矿车以及平板运矿车等,几乎能够满足当时沿线地区一切生活和生产需求。另外,还有高等豪华的专车与花车,车上设有卧室、起居室、客厅以及独立的餐厅等,各项设施一应俱全。作为介于建筑空间和机械设施之间的特殊空间装置,车厢的设计和建造技术同样面对空间和流线问题,因此每类车厢均有标准化的图纸,对功能和形式进行了细致入微的设计。与牵引机车相比,运载车厢设计与建造的技术性不强,空间自由,在艺术性上有更大的发挥余地,等级较高的车厢室内装饰与软装均十分考究,大量采用当时流行的新艺术风格装饰元素。中东铁路上运行的蒸汽机车在设计和制造上充分体现了当时最先进的技术水平和最前卫的艺术潮流,可谓近代工业技术与艺术的完美统一。

## Traction Locomotives

　　The traction locomotive of Chinese Eastern Railway were mostly the steam locomotive in European style that is made in Belguim, England and Russia, whose locomotive tractive effort was from 6,000 kg to 14,000 kg, with flat frame and combustion chamber in copper casting. Russian engineers had had mature technology in locomotive design and manufacturing technique during the construction of Chinese Eastern Railway. According to the functional requirement, train carriage was divided into different types, including passenger hard seat, passenger sleeper, official, luggage, living material, post service, medical treatment, sanitary vehicle, restaurant, cold storage, water supply, prison van and flat mineral vehicle and so on. In addition, there are high-class luxury and festooned carriage, including bed room, living room, wash room and independent dining room etc. Since the decorative element of Art-nouveau style being the most popular in Europe at that time had been widely used in train carriage of Chinese Eastern Railway, the interior decoration and furniture was very sophisticated that displays characteristic of that period.

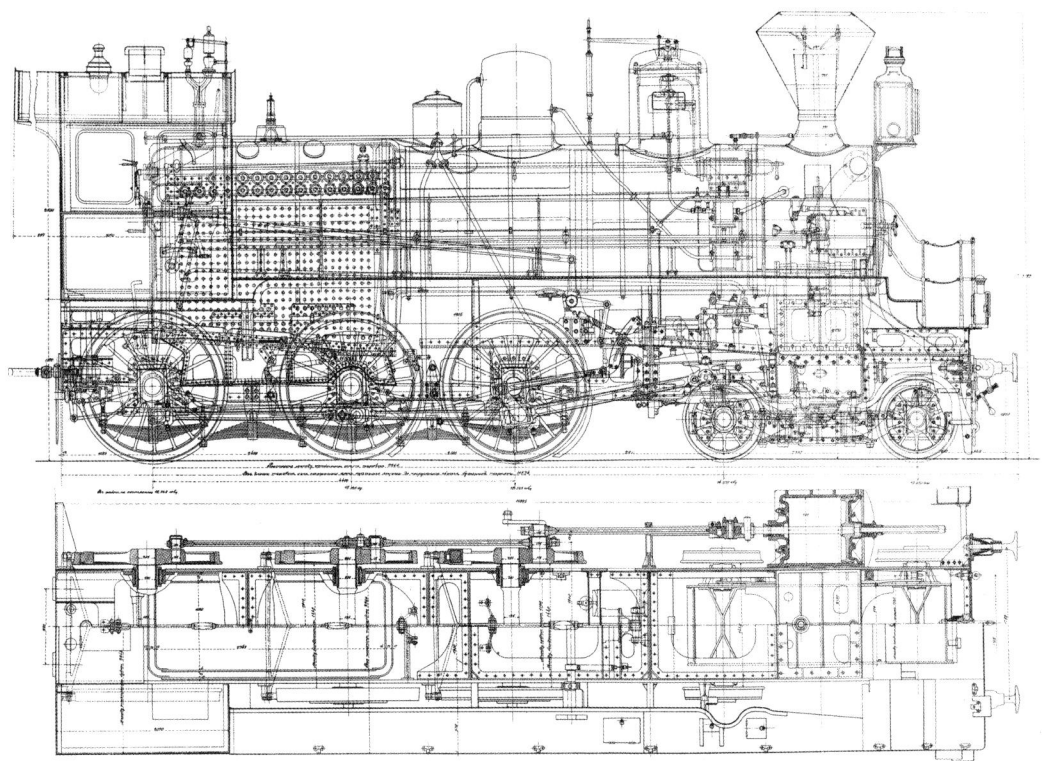

机车设计图 Drawings of traction locomotive

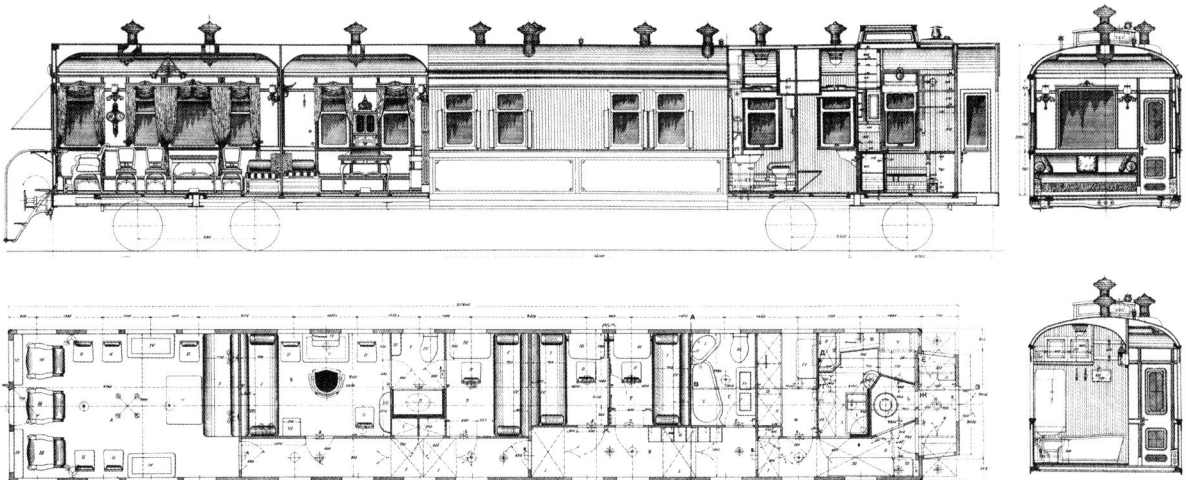

公务车厢设计图 Drawings of official carriage

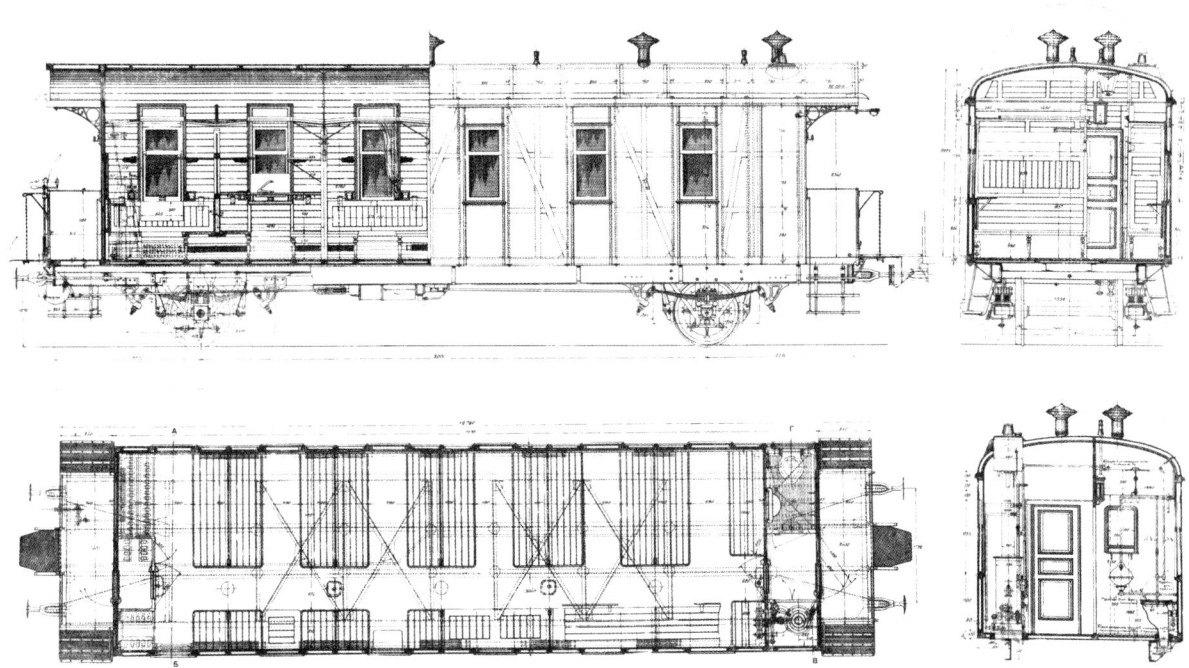

医务车厢设计图 Drawings of medical carriage

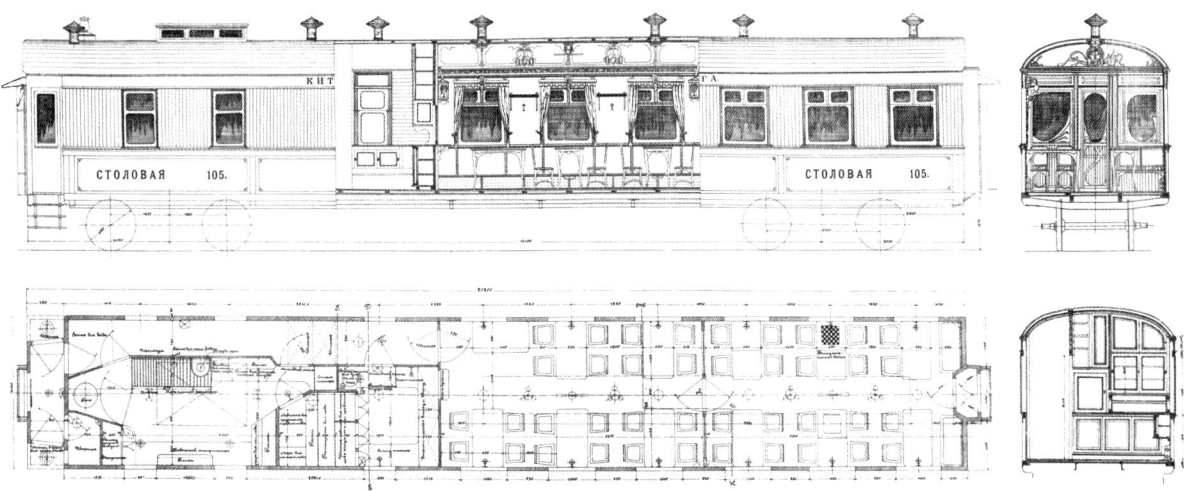

餐车车厢设计图 Drawings of restaurant carriage

# ARCHITECTURAL CULTURAL HERITAGE OF CHINESE EASTERN RAILWAY

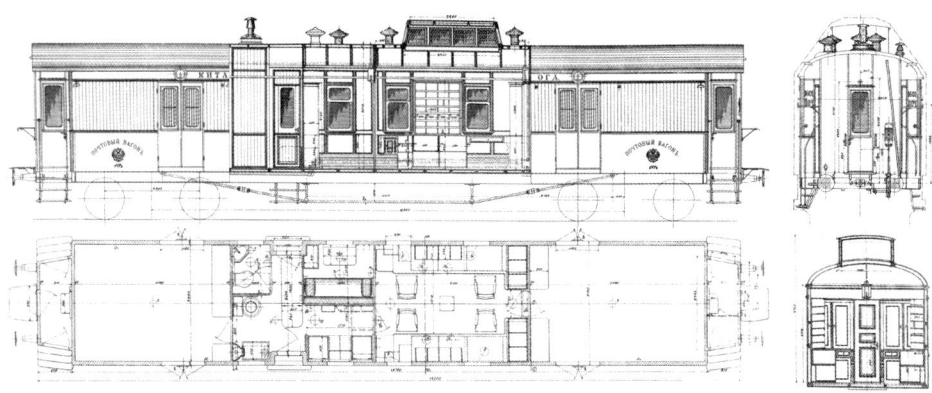

邮车车厢设计图 Drawings of post service carriage

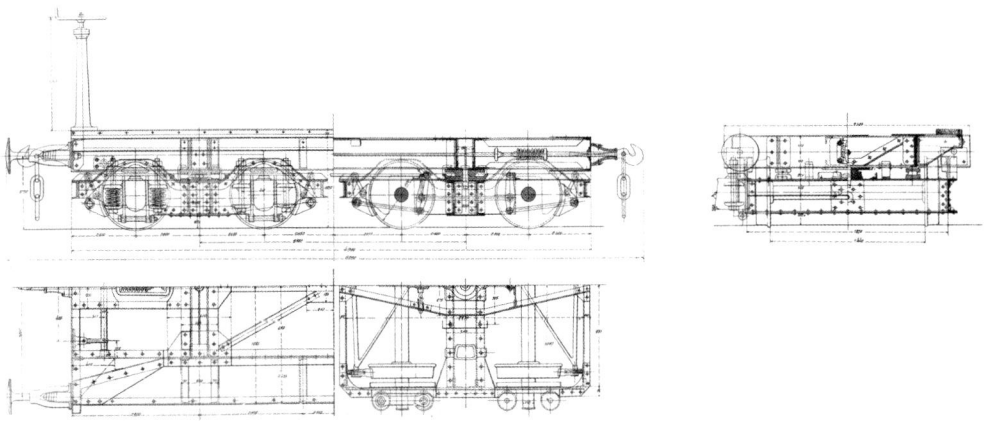

轨道车设计图 Drawings of railcar

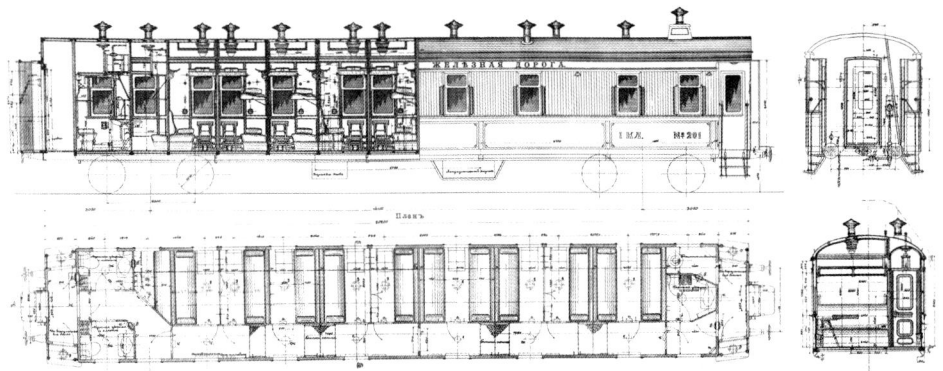

客车车厢设计图 Drawings of passenger carriage

宝德威式机车 Baodewei locomotive

货车机车 Truck locomotive

高等级车厢 Carriages in high-class

急行车之花车 Float

水箱车 Carriage for water supply

三等车厢 Carriage in 3rd class

车厢内客厅 Drawing room in the carriage

车厢内餐车1 Dinning room in the carriage 1

车厢内起居室 Living room in the carriage

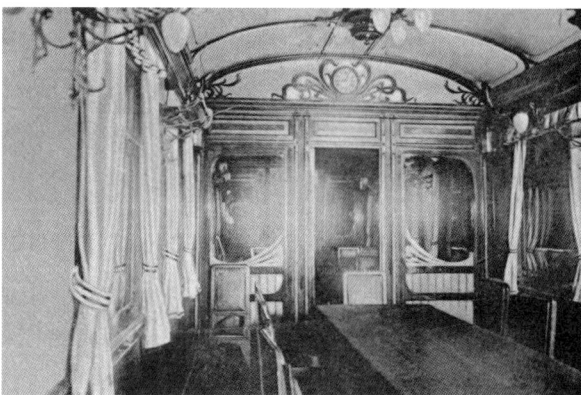
车厢内餐车2 Dinning room in the carriage 2

车厢内餐厅3 Dinning room in the carriage 3

车厢内餐车 4 Dinning room in the carriage 4

一等客车 Carriage in 1st-class

车厢内高等餐厅 High-class dinning room in the carriage

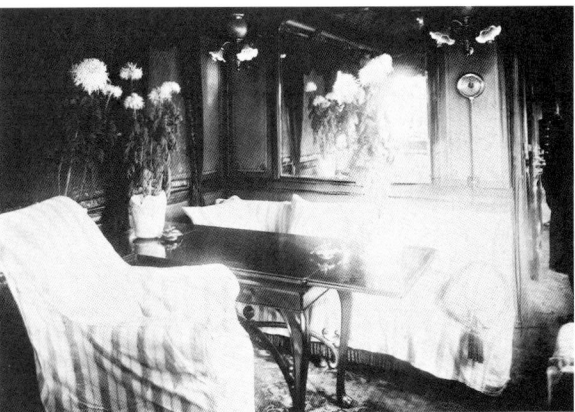

包车客厅 Drawing room of chartered van

# 附录 1 车站、会让站分布简图
## Appendix 1 A Diagram of Stations and Passing Loops of the CER

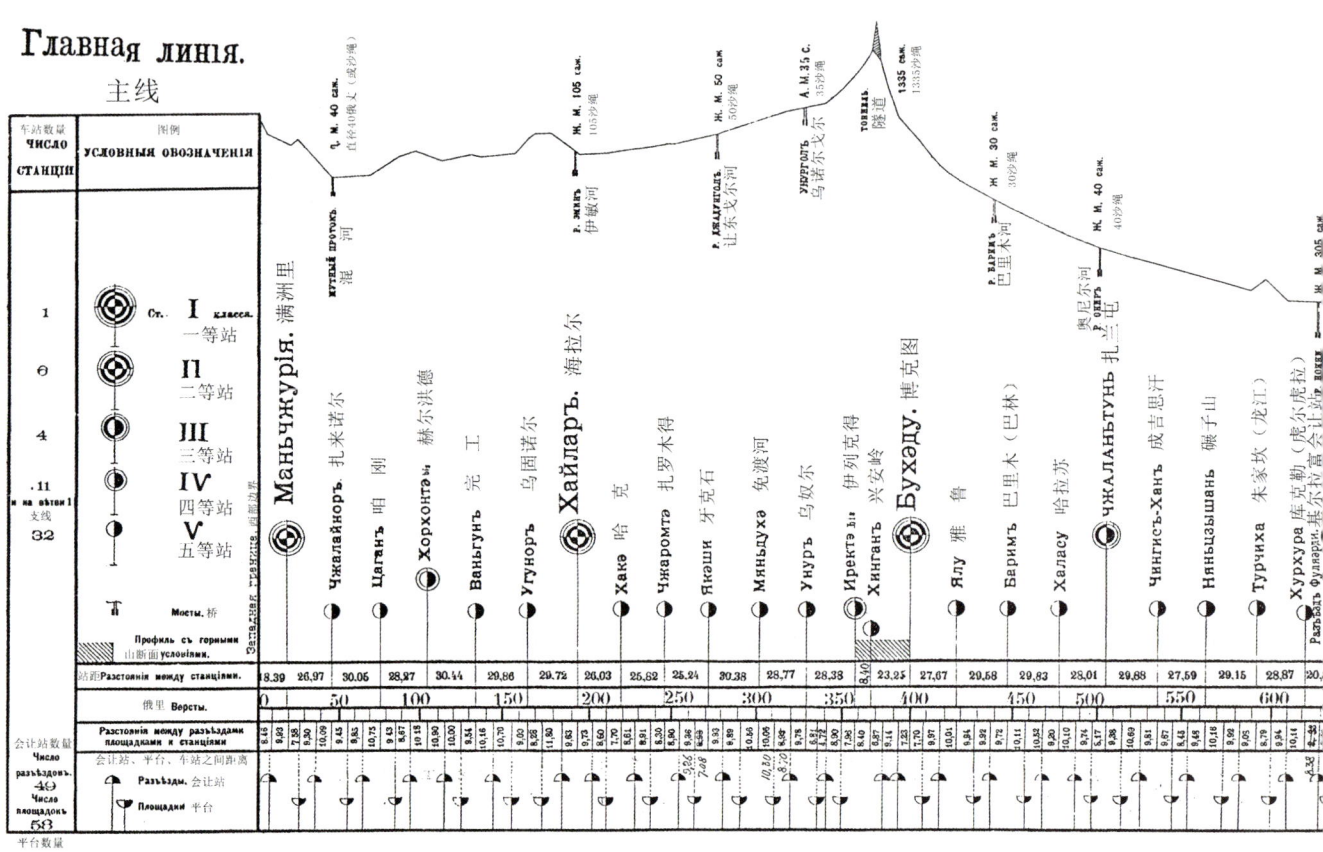

主线 The Main Line

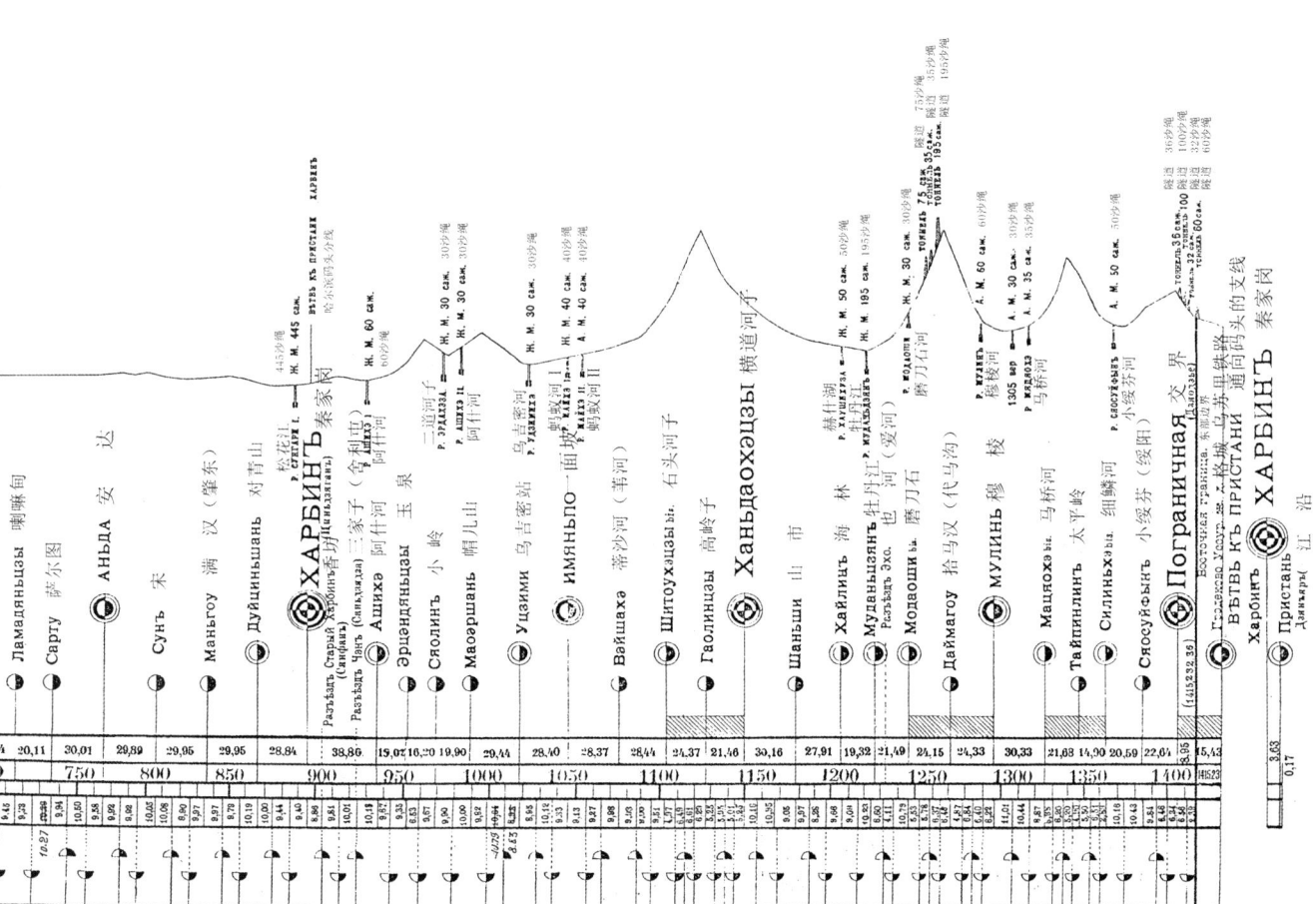

附录1 车站、会让站分布简图

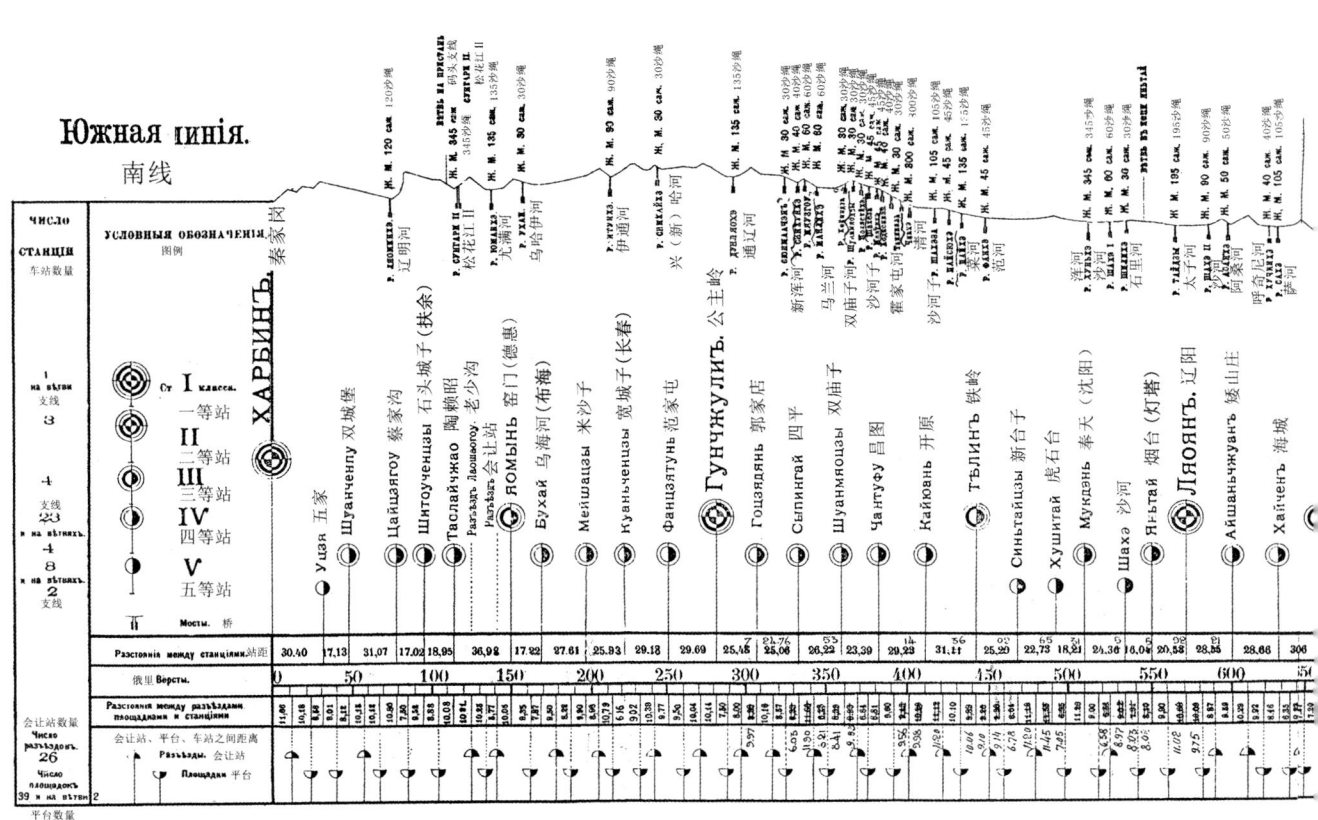

南部支线  The Southern Branch

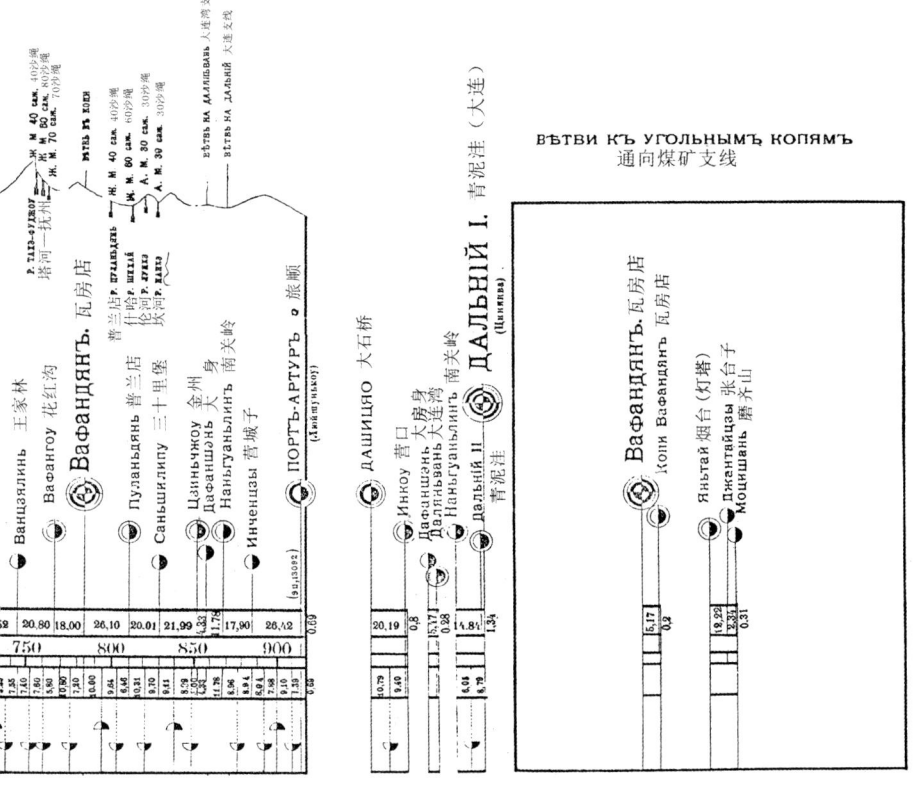

1沙绳（俄丈）＝2.134米

1俄里＝1.06公里

1903年4月印制
总工程师办公室技术部印刷出版

## 附录 2　铁路供水站点分布图
## Appendix 2　A Diagram of Water Supply Stations of the CER

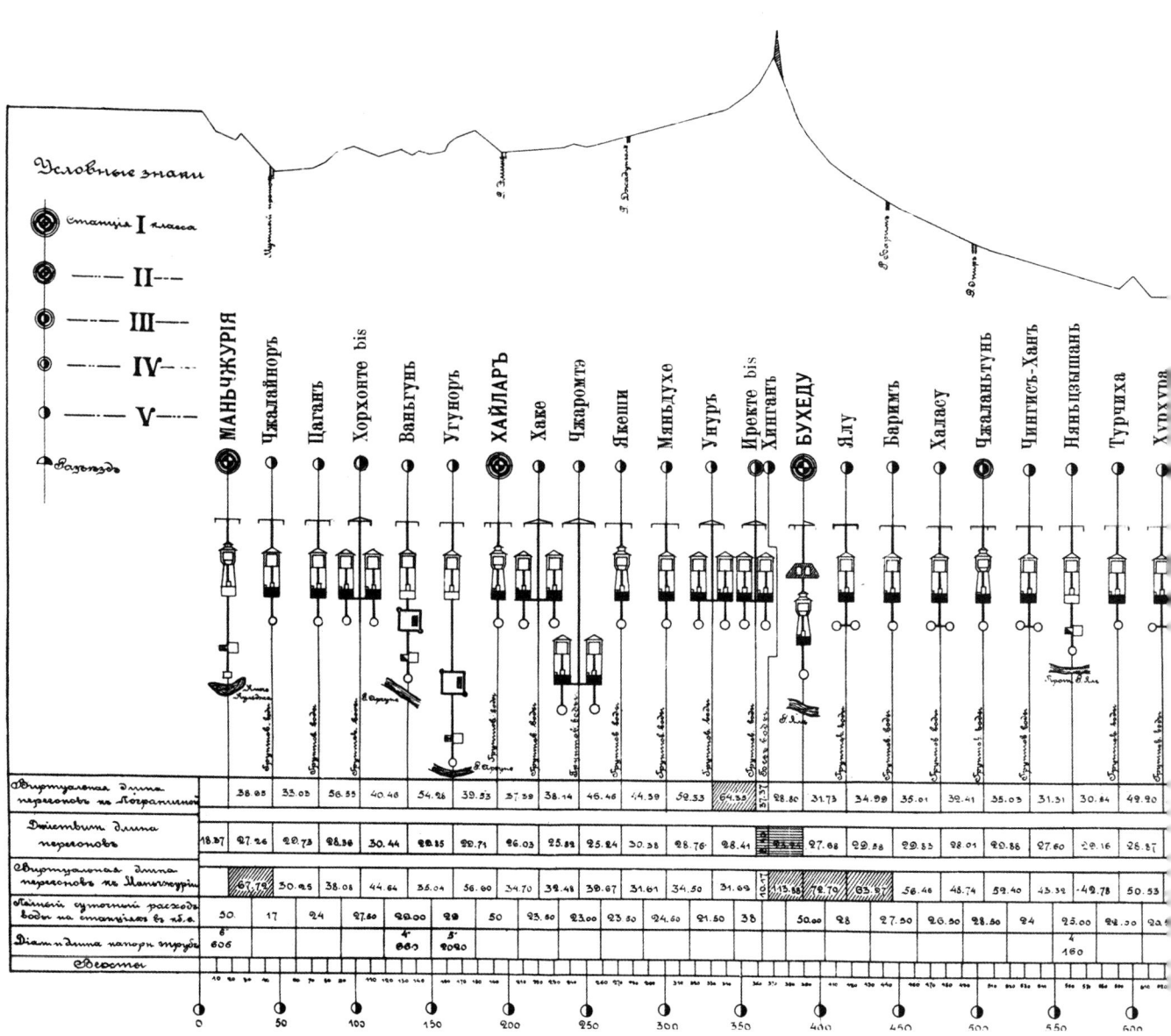

主线　The Main Line

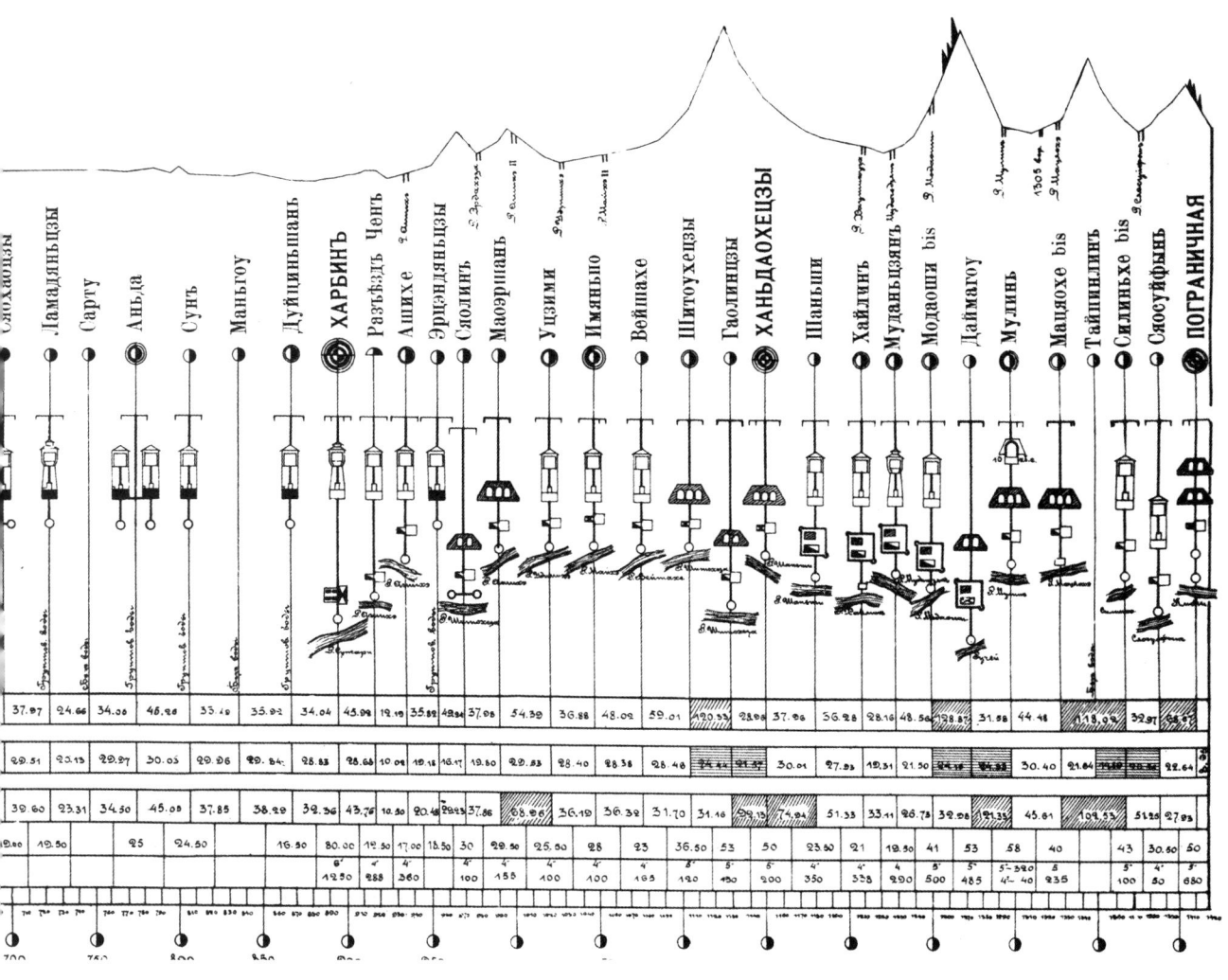

附录2 铁路供水站点分布图

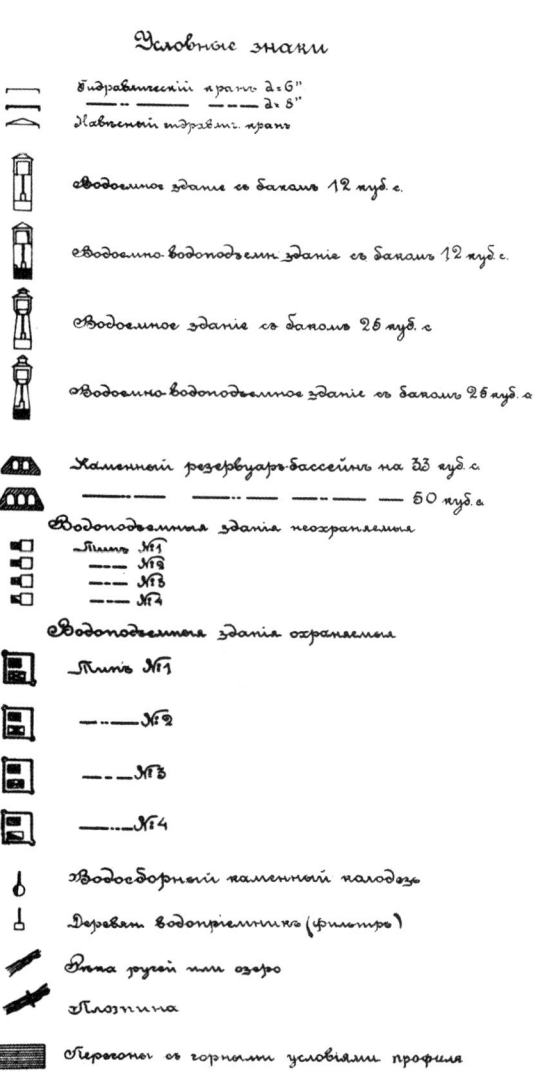
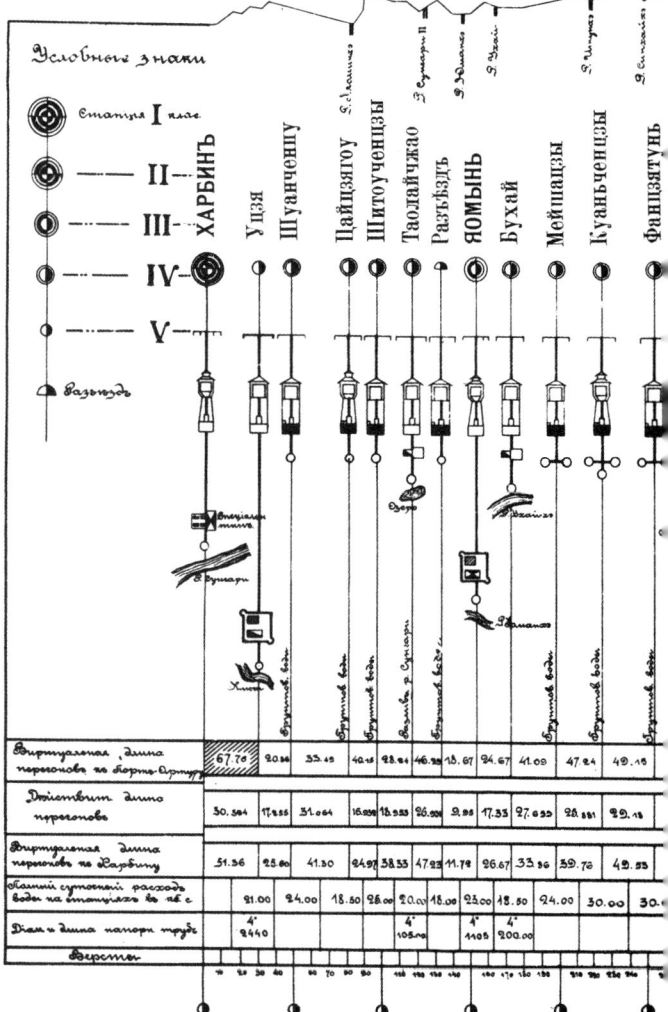

南部支线 The Southern Branch

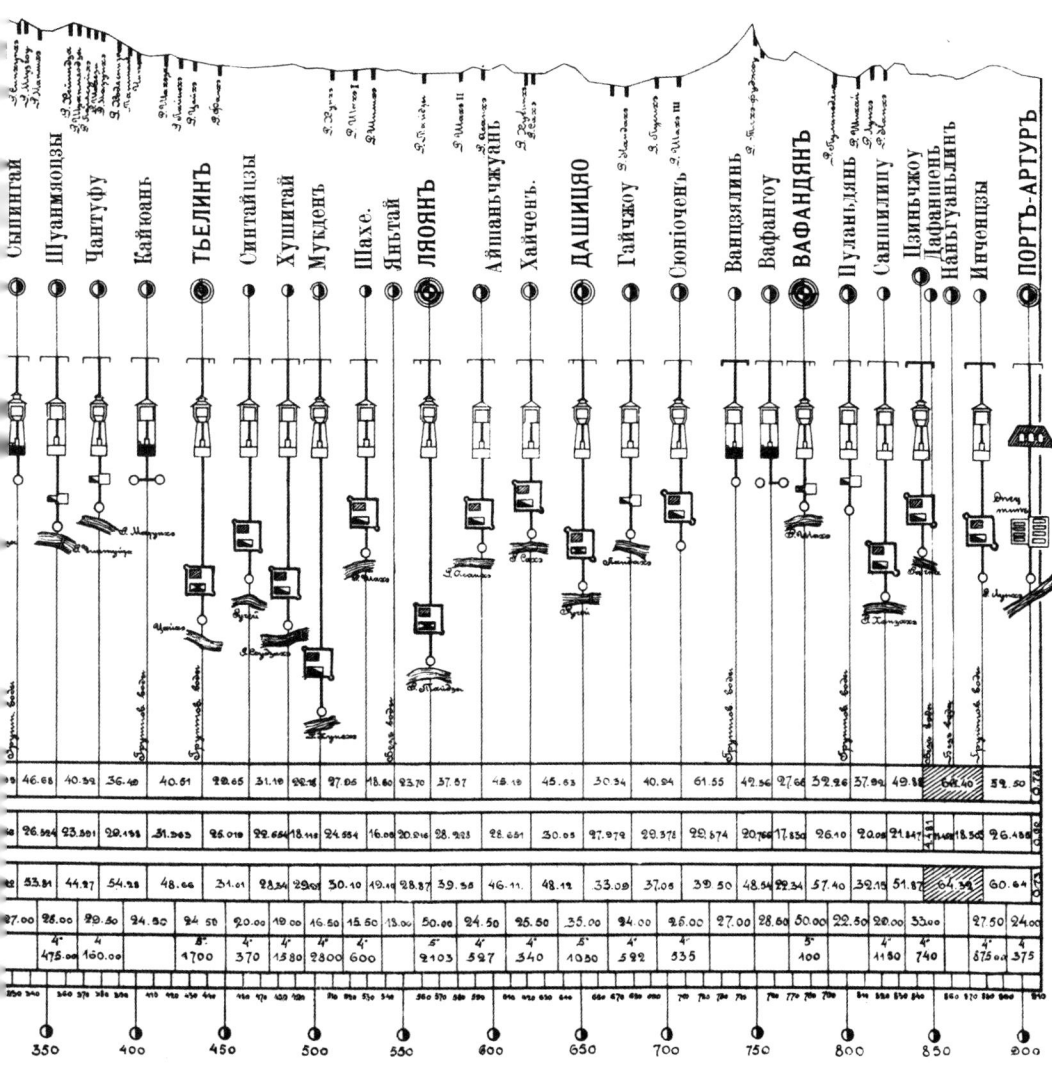

附录 2 铁路供水站点分布图

# 参考文献
References

[1] 陈秋杰. 西伯利亚大铁路修建及其影响研究(1917年前)[D]. 长春:东北师范大学, 2011.

[2] 李济棠. 中俄密约和中东铁路的修筑[M]. 哈尔滨:黑龙江人民出版社, 1989.

[3] 刘大平,李国友. 文化线路视野下的中东铁路建筑文化解读[M]. 哈尔滨:哈尔滨工业大学出版社,2018.

[4] 郑长椿. 中东铁路历史编年[M]. 哈尔滨: 黑龙江人民出版社, 1987.

[5] 刘松茯. 哈尔滨城市建筑的现代转型与模式探析[M]. 北京:中国建筑工业出版社, 2003.

[6] 王向远. 日本对中国的文化侵略:学者、文化人的侵华战争[M]. 北京:解放军文艺出版社, 2005.

[7] 王淑杰,张勇枝. 满洲之最的"中东铁路哈尔滨总工厂"[J]. 中国地名, 2005（2）: 53-58.

[8] 图尔莫夫.百年前邮政明信片上的中国[M]. 张艳玲,译. 哈尔滨:哈尔滨工业大学出版社, 2006.

[9] 旅顺博物馆."满铁"旧影：旅顺博物馆藏"满铁"老照片[M].北京: 中国人民大学出版社, 2007.

[10] 武国庆.建筑艺术长廊——中东铁路老建筑寻踪[M].哈尔滨:黑龙江人民出版社, 2008.

[11] 程维荣.近代东北铁路附属地[M].上海:上海社会科学院出版社, 2008.

[12] 王铁樵. 百年满洲里——纪念满洲里诞生110周年(1901—2011)[M].海拉尔:内蒙古文化出版社, 2011.

[13] 哈尔滨铁路局志编审委员会.哈尔滨铁路局志(1896—1994)[M]北京:中国铁道出版社, 1996.

[14] 哈尔滨建筑艺术馆.哈尔滨旧影大观[M].哈尔滨:黑龙江人民出版社, 2005.

# 图片来源
## Picture Credits

前环衬历史照片，74页左上历史照片，83页左中历史照片，90页右中照片，93页下设计图，95页下历史照片，96页右下照片，100页下设计图，115页上历史照片，140页照片，203页右下历史照片，267页历史照片，268页设计图及历史照片，269页左中、右中历史照片，270页上历史照片，272页右上历史照片，275页左上历史照片，276页右下历史照片，277页右中历史照片，313页下设计图，原载于《建筑艺术长廊——中东铁路老建筑寻踪》（武国庆.黑龙江人民出版社，2008年）

54页历史照片，58页左下历史照片，63页右下历史照片，92页上历史照片，203页左下历史照片，213页历史照片，227页上历史照片，284页上历史照片，301页历史照片，302页历史照片及设计图，303页历史照片，304页左下、右下历史照片，P322页右下历史照片，原载于《百年前邮政明信片上的中国》（图尔莫夫.哈尔滨工业大学出版社，2006年）

59页设计图，60～61页设计图，62页设计图，65页设计图，68页上设计图，70页设计图，71页左页设计图，81页设计图，86页设计图，108页设计图，109页设计图，118页设计图，121页设计图，123页上设计图，124页历史照片，128页设计图，137页设计图，158～161页设计图，169页上设计图，171页设计图，173页设计图，174页上设计图，176页上设计图，177页中设计图及历史照片，181页设计图，182页设计图，194页设计图，195页设计图，196页上设计图，197页设计图及历史照片，198页设计图，199页设计图，202页设计图，232页左设计图，249页上设计图，250页右设计图，251页上设计图，252页上设计图，284页下设计图，286页设计图，288页设计图，289页上设计图，304页上设计图，310页设计图，317页设计图及历史照片，318页设计图，319页设计图，338～344页设计图，346页设计图，382页设计图，383页设计图，394页设计图及历史照片，395页设计图，401页设计图，404页上设计图，406页设计图，412～414页设计图，附录2，原载于《Альбом сооружений и типовых чертежей Китайской Восточной железной дороги（1897—1903）》

63页右上照片，193页历史照片，216页历史照片，218页历史照片，234页历史照片，273页左下历史照片，289页左中历史照片，290页下历史照片，298页历史照片，308页右下历史照片，332页历史照片，325页历史照片，392页上历史照片，原载于《百年满洲里——纪念满洲里诞生110周年（1901—2011）》（王铁樵. 内蒙古文化出版社，2011年）

64页上历史照片，68页下历史照片，72页历史照片，75页左上，76页左下历史照片，77页上历史照片，78页上历史照片，79页上历史照片，82页左上、右上历史照片，83页右中、左下历史照片，84左下历史照片，85页左历史照片，87页左历史照片，88页左上、左中历史照片，89页左历史照片，91左中历史照片，95页下历史照片，97页上历史照片，101页上历史照片，110页历史照片，114页上历史照片，116页历史照片，117页左中、右中、右下历史照片，138页下历史照片，139页上历史照片，162页上历史照片，163页历史照片，165页上、左中、右中历史照片，248页历史照片，321页上历史照片，322页左上历史照片，385页历史照片，386页左上历史照片，387页右中历史照片，407页上历史照片，410页历史照片，原载于《Альбом видов китайской восточной жел. дор.》

69页上历史照片，80页左上历史照片，311页下历史照片，原载于《满铁附属地经营沿革全史》

69页左下、右下历史照片，74页右上历史照片，75页右上历史照片，76页右上历史照片，82页左中历史照片，83页左上、右上、右下历史照片，84页上历史照片，88页左下历史照片，117页左下历史照片，119页历史照片，122页右下历史照片，123页左下、右下历史照片，129页历史照片，138页上历史照片，146页历史照片，164页历史照片，165页左下、右下历史照片，169页左下、右下历史照片，170页右中历史照片，174页左中、右中历史照片，176页左中、右中历史照片，183页右上历史照片，184页上历史照片，196页左下、右下历史照片，200页历史照片，201页历史照片，249页左下、右下历史照片，251页下历史照片，252页下历史照片，253页历史照片，256页下历史照片，273页左上、右上历史照片，280页历史照片，287页下历史照片，289页右中、左下、右下历史照片，321页左下、右下历史照片，322页右上历史照片，328页上历史照片，336页历史照片，337页历史照片，348页右上、右中历史照片，349页历史照片，352页左上、右上历史照片，353页左上、右上，354页历史照片，355页历史照片，384页历史照片，386页除左上以外历史照片，387页除右中以外历史照片，388页历史照片，389页历史照片，396页历史照片，397页历史照片，402页历史照片，403页历史照片，407页左中、右中、左下、右下历史照片，408页历史照片，409页左上、右上历史照片，415页左上、右上、左中、右下照片，416页右上、右中照片，后环衬历史照片，原载于《Альбом сооружения

Китайско-восточной железной дороги（1897—1903）》

71页右下历史照片，82页左下、右下历史照片，91页左下历史照片，117页上历史照片，139页下历史照片，244页历史照片，291页历史照片，原载于《"满铁"旧影——旅顺博物馆藏"满铁"老照片》（旅顺博物馆编. 中国人民大学出版社，2007年）

154页历史照片，162页左中、右中历史照片，262页历史照片，P266页历史照片，272页除右上以外历史照片，273页左中、右中、右下历史照片，276页除右下以外历史照片，277页除右中以外历史照片，378页历史照片，400页历史照片，415页右中、左下照片，416页左上、左下、右下照片，417页照片，原载于 Views of the Chinese Eastern Railway [case], 1903—1919

345页左下历史照片，348页左上历史照片，原载于《哈尔滨旧影大观》（哈尔滨建筑艺术馆编. 黑龙江人民出版社，2005年）

58页上历史照片，66页历史照片，71页右上历史照片，80页右上历史照片，80页中历史照片，230页上历史照片，314页历史照片，320页历史照片，326页上历史照片，345页左上历史照片，来源不详

94页历史照片翻拍自双城火车站展板
231页上图翻拍自旅顺鸡冠山暗堡展板
附录1图由武国庆先生提供

其余照片、图纸均为作者自摄、自绘

# 后 记

　　自2010年开始接触中东铁路建筑文化遗产起，至今已九年有余的时间。随着时间的延伸，我们对这份遗产的价值有了越来越多的认识，也投入了更多的情感在其中。但同时也越发感到这份具有文化线路属性的建筑文化遗产仍有着诸多值得我们继续不断去深入挖掘的地方，要做和可以做的事情还很多。这期间，我们先后完成了国家自然科学基金资助项目和中俄政府间科技合作项目；撰写了四部相关的学术著作，发表了多篇相关的学术研究论文；并培养了十余名硕士与博士研究生。本书所包含的内容是以往课题研究工作的延续，具有以下几个特点：

　　1.为了更好地完成课题的研究工作，多年来我们对中东铁路建筑遗产进行了比较全面的调研，在这个过程中对其功能类型的丰富和多样有了深刻的理解。从公共建筑到工业建筑，从站区建筑到居住建筑；大到中东铁路管理局的办公楼、高等级站舍与机车库，小到铁路沿线的浴室与公厕，本书所介绍的这些功能复杂的建筑遗产类型，真实地再现了中东铁路沿线的历史生活场景，这也是最容易揭示其建筑文化遗产多样性的视角。

　　2.一般来说，对于建筑史的研究，除了进行大量现场实际案例的田野调查之外，不但要掌握大量丰富的历史文献，更应该注重历史图片和设计图纸档案等文献的搜集，以及对典型建筑遗产的测绘。由于中东铁路最初是由沙俄主持设计与建造的，后又被日本人占有，其间虽经过岁月的流逝而有所改变，但在这些建筑遗产的形态特征上仍可以看到历史留下的历史印迹。本书汇集了较多能直观展示中东铁路建筑文化遗产形态特征的文献资料，包括早期的设计图纸与现存遗产的测绘图，以及大量的历史与现状图片，并做了必要的解读。这些文献可以让读者更为直观、清晰地把握这份遗产的基本形态特征，同时也有助于揭示其复杂性。

　　3.近些年来，中东铁路建筑遗产的研究已经逐渐引起诸多国内外相关学者的广泛关注，尤其是俄罗斯建筑历史学的研究学者更为关心这一课题研究的进展。国外很多东北亚地区近代史研究、铁路发展史以及铁路工业遗产研究的学者，也都对此表现出极大的兴趣。为了更好地进行国际化的交流，本书选择了中英两种文字，希望有助于对中东铁路建筑文化遗产研究国际化趋势的推进。

　　最后，对在本书撰写与编辑过程中付出极大心血的各位表示感谢，何璐茜、王岩、王秋玉三位女士热心帮助进行了英文翻译；多名硕博研究生参与了部分文字的初稿撰写与文字修改；大部分现存建筑图片由博士研究生司道光拍摄。此外，李国友老师从俄罗斯搜集来的图文资料成为本书非常重要的内容，使本书的学术价值得以提升。总之，正是诸位的齐心合作，才使这本书的出版成为可能。

刘大平<br>2019.8.30

# Postscript

It has been more than nine years from getting in touch with the CER architectural heritage in 2010. As time going on, we have more and more clearly understood the value of these heritages, and also put into great emotion in it. Meanwhile, there are still a lot of things of the heritage with cultural route nature deserving us to dig deep gradually. In the meantime, we have finished the National Natural Science Funds and the Project of Scientific and Technological Cooperation between China and Russia Government, written four related academic monographs, as well as published multiple relevant research papers and trained more than 10 master and PHD students. The content of this book is an extension of previous research, with the following characteristics:

1. In order to better finish the research project, much comprehensive investigation of the CER heritage have been carried out for years, in which the richness and diversity of its functional types have been better understood from public buildings to industry buildings and from station buildings to residential buildings, from the large buildings as office building of the CER administration, high grade station house and locomotive shed to the small buildings as bath room and toilet. These architectural types with complicated functions vividly portray the historical living scene along the line, which become a visual angle to reveal the diversity of the architectural cultural heritage.

2. Generally speaking, the architectural historical study is much special, except a large number of actual on-site cases and field surveys, which not only emphasizes to obtain some necessary text materials, but also needs to collect a large number of files, historical photos and design drawings, as well as to map the typical architectural heritage. Since the CER line was originally designed and constructed by Tsarist Russia, and then occupied and managed by Japanese for a long time, the historical print of the CER architectural heritage in construction pattern still can be seen. In this book, a large number of document information are collected and interpreted, including early design drawing and existed heritage mapping map, as well as massive historical and present photos. It will be helpful for us to directly grasp the basic form feature of the heritage, and to display its complexity.

3. In recent years, the study on the CER architectural heritage has been paid widely attention by many researchers at home and abroad, especially the researchers in Russian architectural history and the experts who are interested in the modern history of the northeast Asia, as well as the railway development history and railway industry heritage. In order to meet the needs of international exchange, this book is written in both of Chinese and English, which will be helpful for driving on an international study of the CER architectural heritage.

Finally, we are extremely grateful to all person making a lot of hard work in the process of the book editing, in which doctoral student He Luxi, Ms. Wang Yan and Ms. Wang Qiuyu are responsible for the English translation and revision, doctoral student Si Daoguang takes a lot of photographs of the existed buildings, some master and doctoral students also participate in the first draft writing and modifying. Besides, Mr. Li Guoyou gathered a number of graphic and textual materials from Russia, which became an important source information to promote academic value of the book. In a word, it is our heart-to-heart cooperation to achieve its publication.

LIU Daping<br>
30th August, 2019

## 图书在版编目(CIP)数据

中东铁路建筑文化遗产 / 刘大平，卞秉利，李琦著.
—哈尔滨：哈尔滨工业大学出版社，2020.1
（地域建筑文化遗产及城市与建筑可持续发展研究丛书）
ISBN 978-7-5603-8520-4

Ⅰ. ①中… Ⅱ. ①刘… ②卞…③李… Ⅲ. ①铁路沿线—古建筑—文化遗产—研究—东北地区 Ⅳ.
①K928.713

中国版本图书馆CIP数据核字(2019)第207035号

| | |
|---|---|
| 策划编辑 | 杨　桦 |
| 责任编辑 | 陈　洁　那兰兰　王晓丹　佟　馨 |
| 装帧设计 | 卞秉利 |
| 出版发行 | 哈尔滨工业大学出版社 |
| 社　　址 | 哈尔滨市南岗区复华四道街10号　邮编150006 |
| 传　　真 | 0451-86414749 |
| 网　　址 | http://hitpress.hit.edu.cn |
| 印　　刷 | 哈尔滨市石桥印务有限公司 |
| 开　　本 | 889mm×1194mm　1/16　印张27.5　插页4　字数500千字 |
| 版　　次 | 2020年1月第1版　2020年1月第1次印刷 |
| 书　　号 | ISBN 978-7-5603-8520-4 |
| 定　　价 | 268.00元 |

(如因印装质量问题影响阅读，我社负责调换)